CHAPTER 1
PRIMITIVE Boyfriend

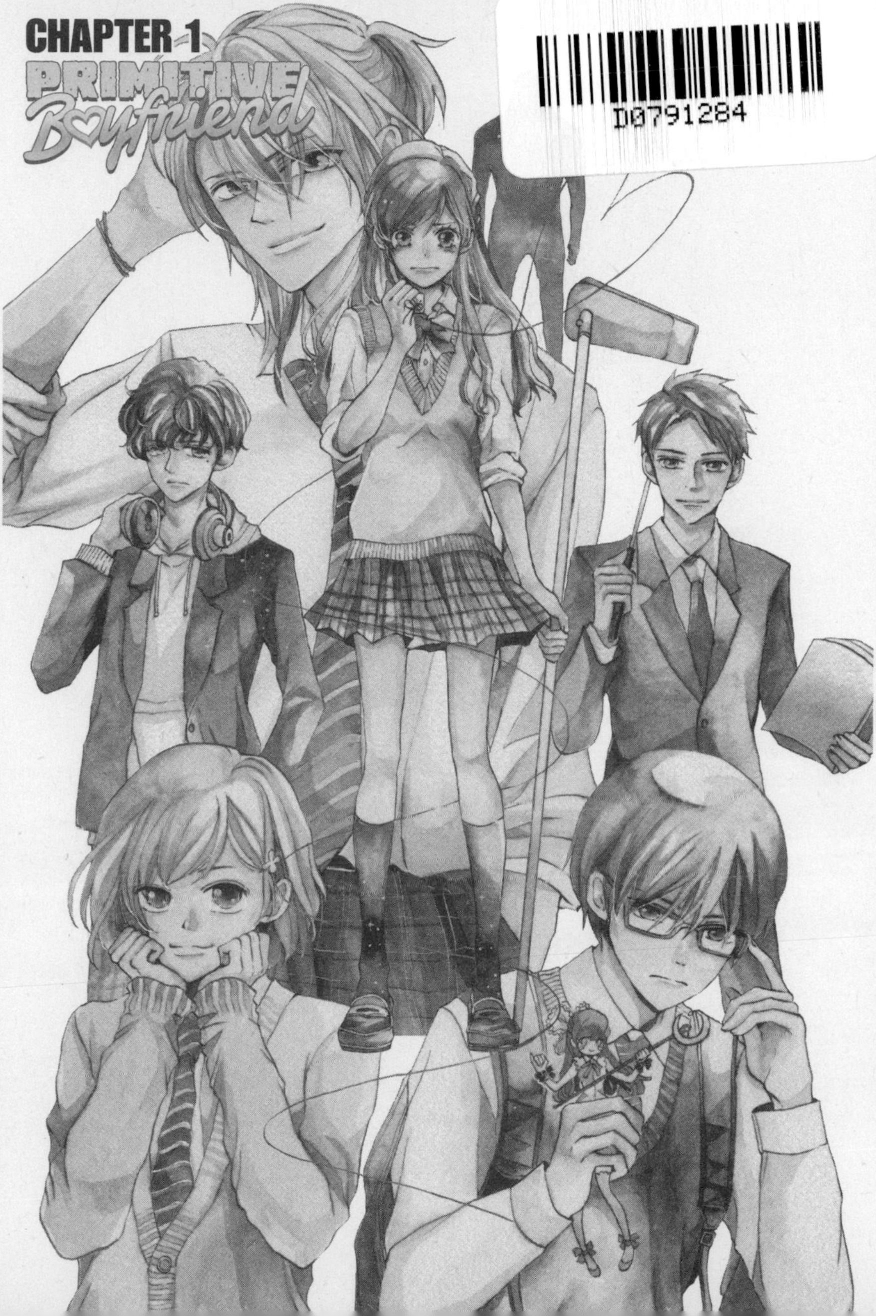

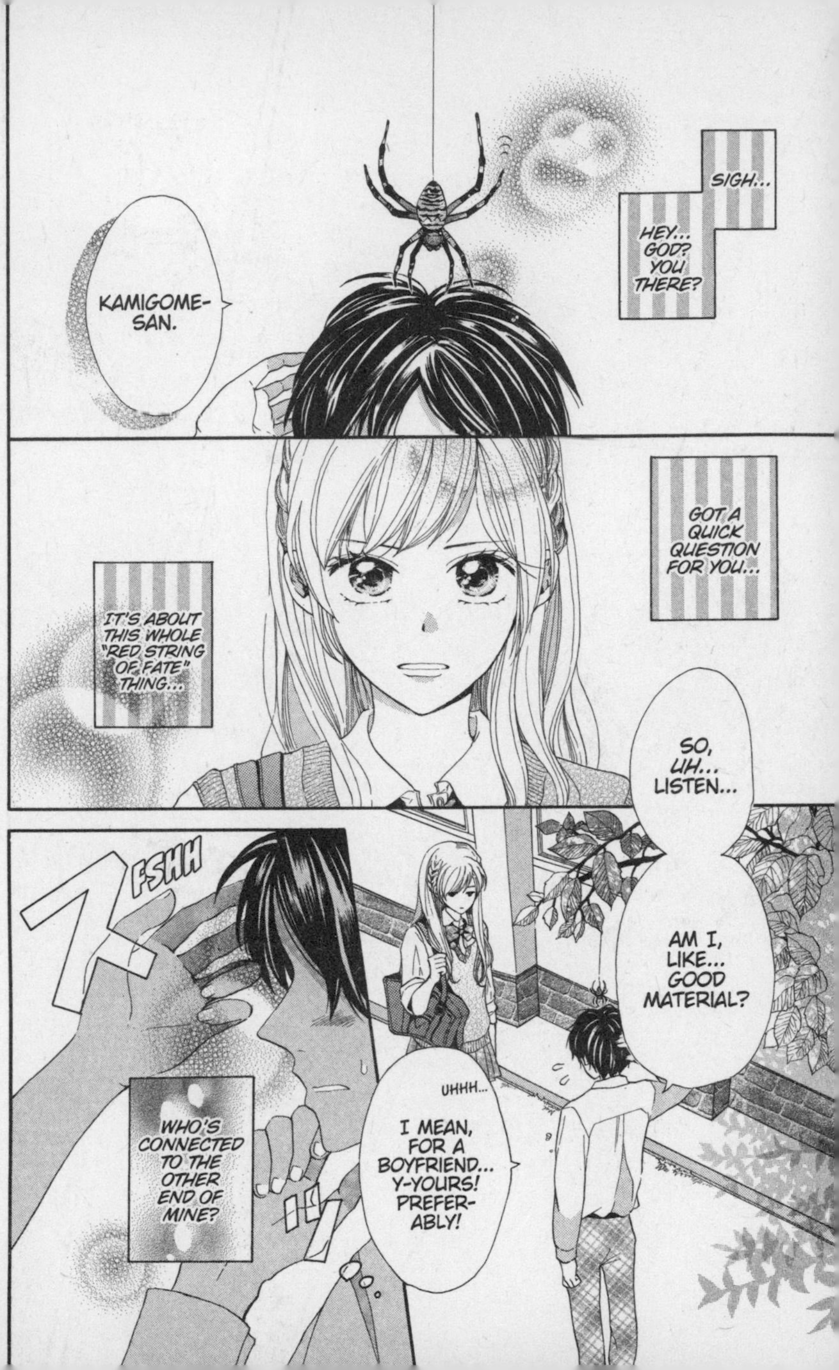
SIGH...
HEY... GOD? YOU THERE?
KAMIGOME-SAN.
GOT A QUICK QUESTION FOR YOU...
IT'S ABOUT THIS WHOLE "RED STRING OF FATE" THING...
SO, UH... LISTEN...
AM I, LIKE... GOOD MATERIAL?
UHHH...
I MEAN, FOR A BOYFRIEND... Y-YOURS! PREFER-ABLY!
FSHH
WHO'S CONNECTED TO THE OTHER END OF MINE?

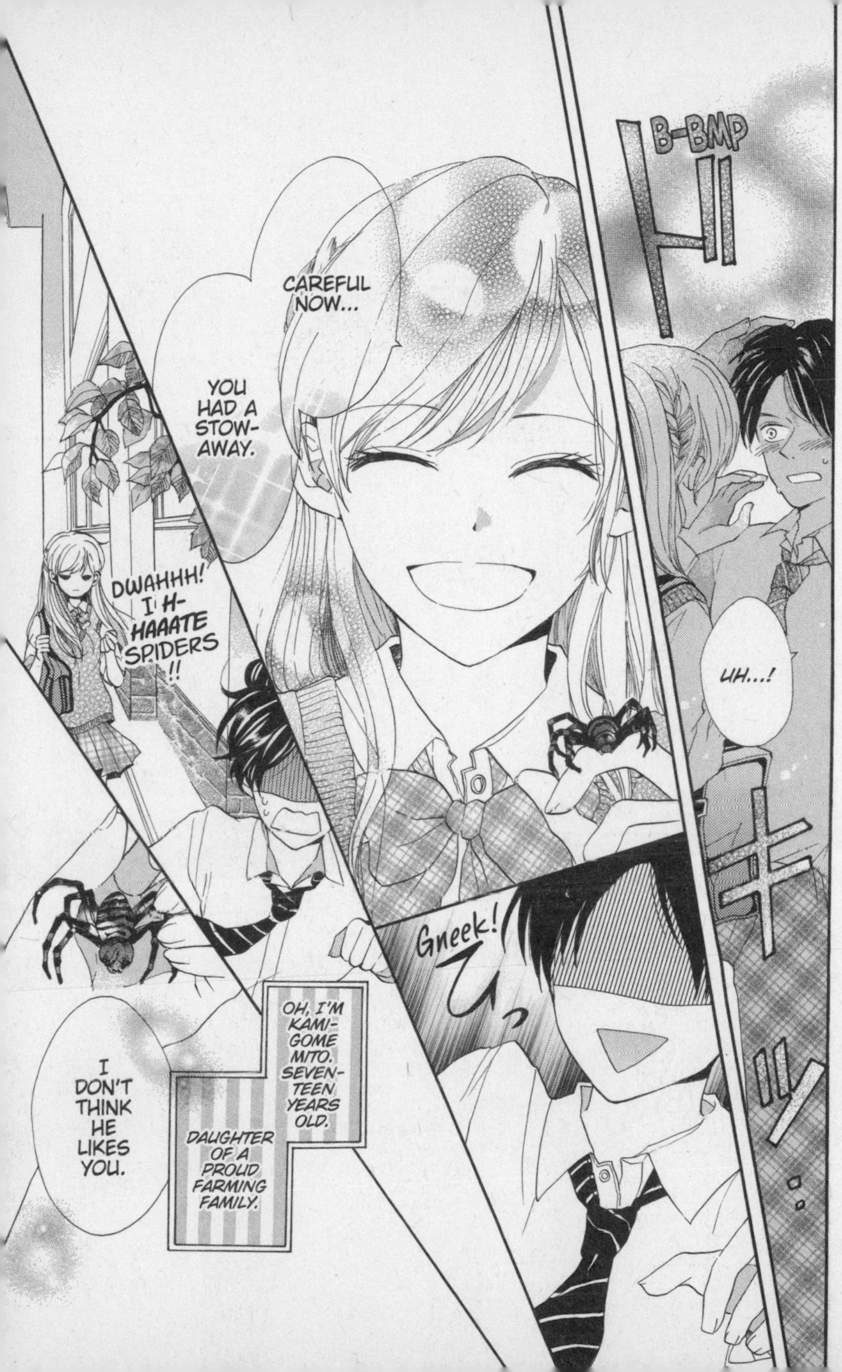
B-BMP
UH...!
CAREFUL NOW...
YOU HAD A STOWAWAY.
Gneek!
DWAHHH! I H-HAAATE SPIDERS!!
OH, I'M KAMIGOME MITO. SEVENTEEN YEARS OLD.
DAUGHTER OF A PROUD FARMING FAMILY.
I DON'T THINK HE LIKES YOU.

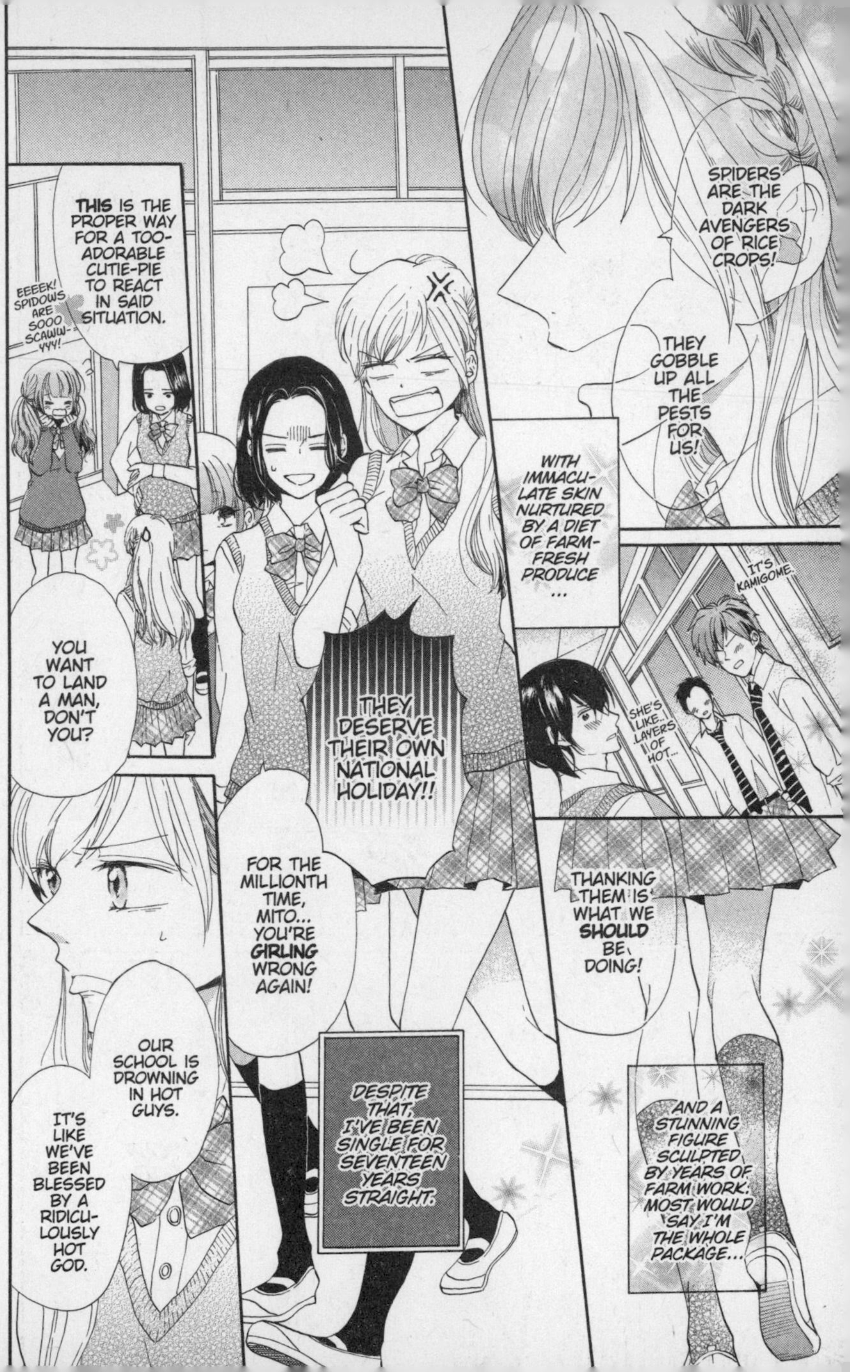
SPIDERS ARE THE DARK AVENGERS OF RICE CROPS!
THEY GOBBLE UP ALL THE PESTS FOR US!
THEY DESERVE THEIR OWN NATIONAL HOLIDAY!!
WITH IMMACULATE SKIN NURTURED BY A DIET OF FARM-FRESH PRODUCE...
IT'S KAMIGOME.
SHE'S LIKE... LAYERS OF HOT...
THANKING THEM IS WHAT WE **SHOULD** BE DOING!
FOR THE MILLIONTH TIME, MITO... YOU'RE **GIRLING** WRONG AGAIN!
THIS IS THE PROPER WAY FOR A TOO-ADORABLE CUTIE-PIE TO REACT IN SAID SITUATION.
EEEEK! SPIDOWS ARE SOOO SCAWWYYY!
YOU WANT TO LAND A MAN, DON'T YOU?
AND A STUNNING FIGURE SCULPTED BY YEARS OF FARM WORK. MOST WOULD SAY I'M THE WHOLE PACKAGE...
DESPITE THAT, I'VE BEEN SINGLE FOR SEVENTEEN YEARS STRAIGHT.
OUR SCHOOL IS DROWNING IN HOT GUYS.
IT'S LIKE WE'VE BEEN BLESSED BY A RIDICULOUSLY HOT GOD.

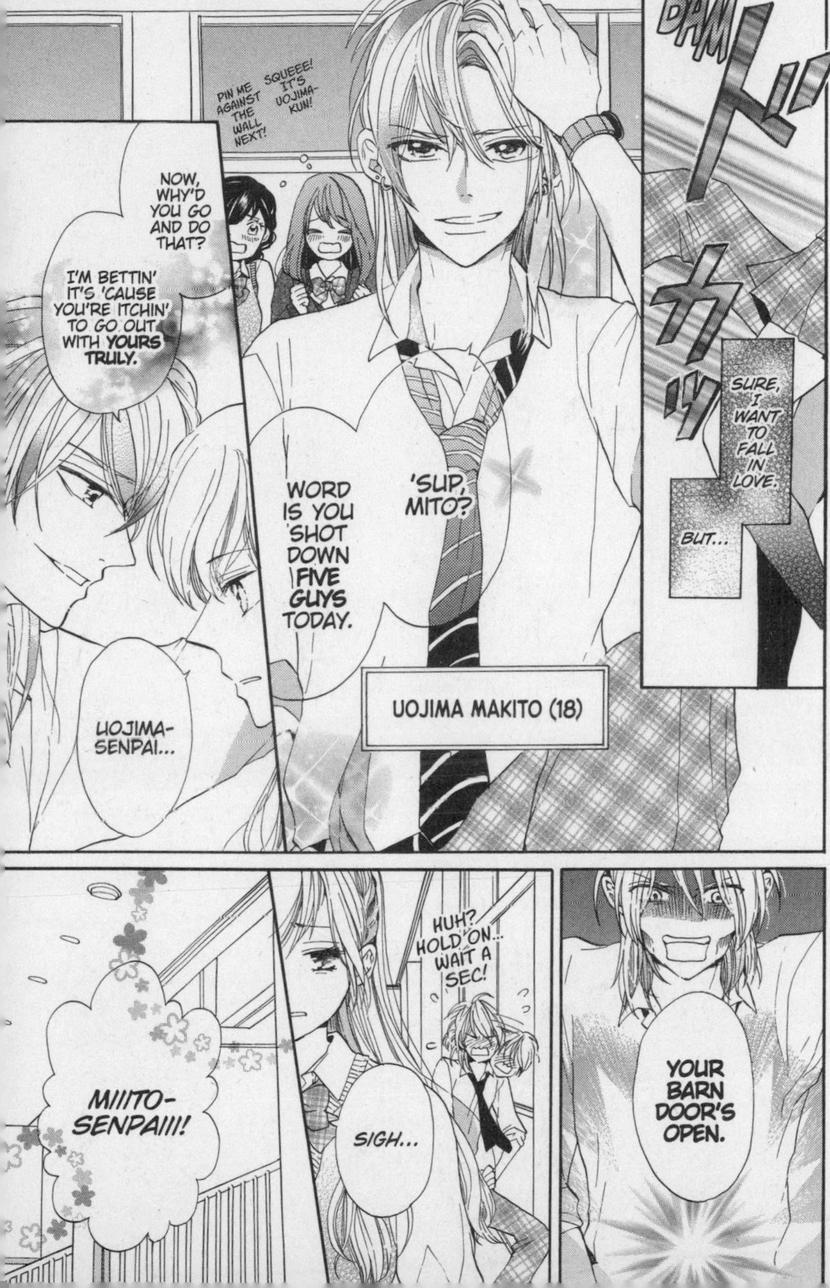
BAM
SURE, I WANT TO FALL IN LOVE.
BUT...
SQUEEE! IT'S UOJIMA-KUN!
PIN ME AGAINST THE WALL NEXT!
'SUP, MITO?
WORD IS YOU SHOT DOWN FIVE GUYS TODAY.
NOW, WHY'D YOU GO AND DO THAT?
I'M BETTIN' IT'S 'CAUSE YOU'RE ITCHIN' TO GO OUT WITH YOURS TRULY.
UOJIMA MAKITO (18)
UOJIMA-SENPAI...
YOUR BARN DOOR'S OPEN.
HUH? HOLD ON... WAIT A SEC!
SIGH...
MIIITO-SENPAIII!

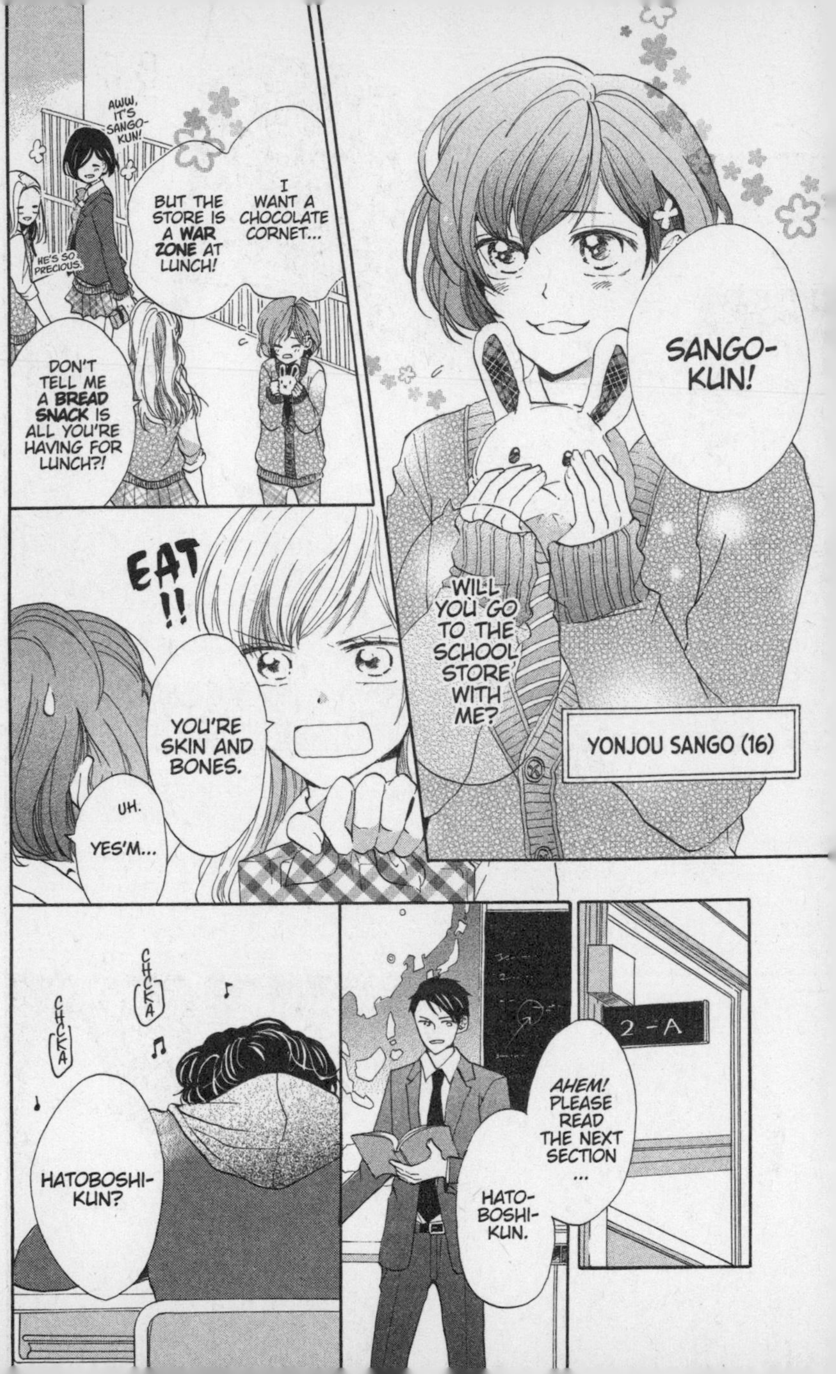
SANGO-KUN!
WILL YOU GO TO THE SCHOOL STORE WITH ME?
YONJOU SANGO (16)
I WANT A CHOCOLATE CORNET...
BUT THE STORE IS A WAR ZONE AT LUNCH!
AWW, IT'S SANGO-KUN!
HE'S SO PRECIOUS.
DON'T TELL ME A BREAD SNACK IS ALL YOU'RE HAVING FOR LUNCH?!
EAT!!
YOU'RE SKIN AND BONES.
UH.
YES'M...
2-A
AHEM! PLEASE READ THE NEXT SECTION...
HATOBOSHI-KUN.
CHCKA
CHCKA
HATOBOSHI-KUN?

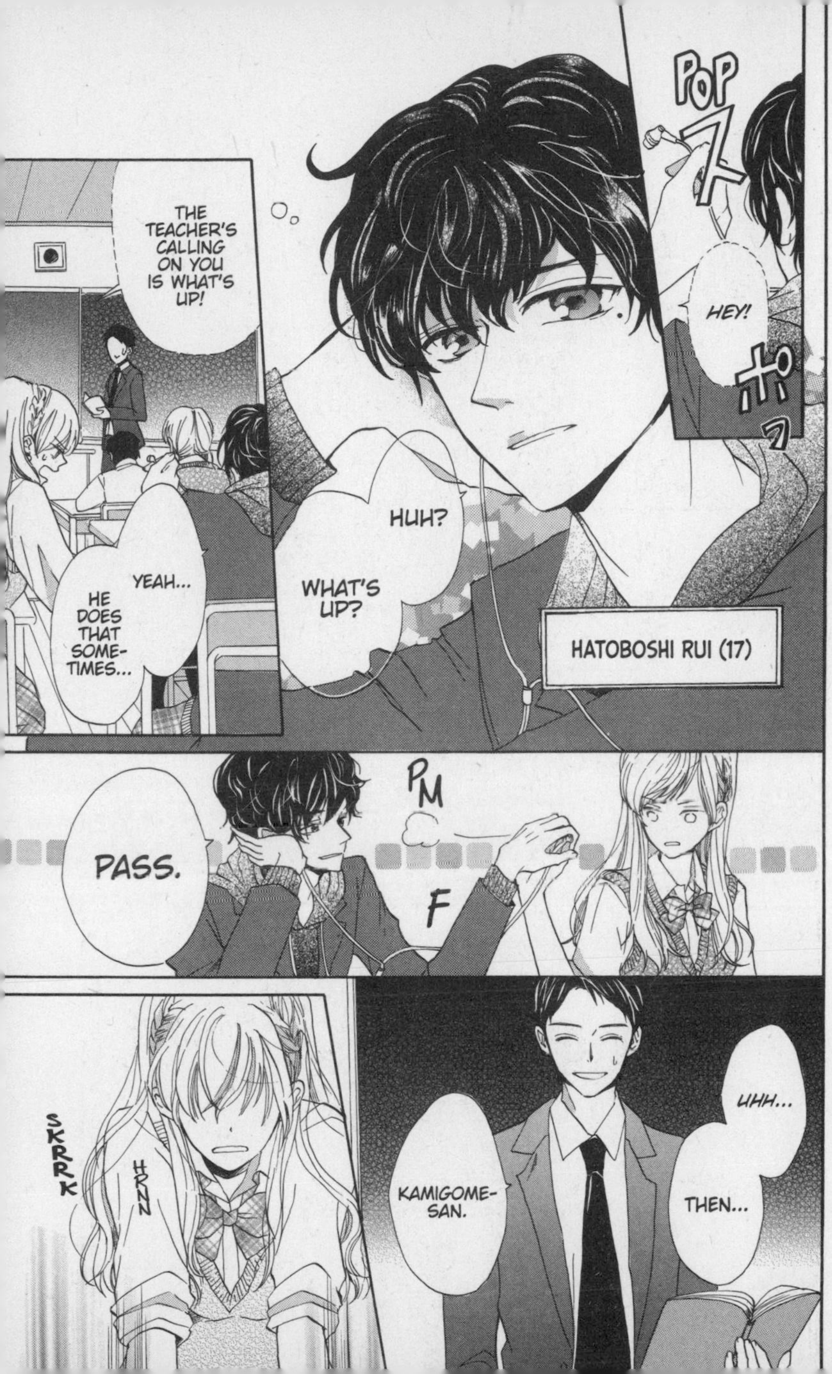
POP
HEY!
HUH?
WHAT'S UP?
HATOBOSHI RUI (17)
THE TEACHER'S CALLING ON YOU IS WHAT'S UP!
YEAH...
HE DOES THAT SOME-TIMES...
PM
F
PASS.
UHH...
THEN...
KAMIGOME-SAN.
SKRRK
HRNN

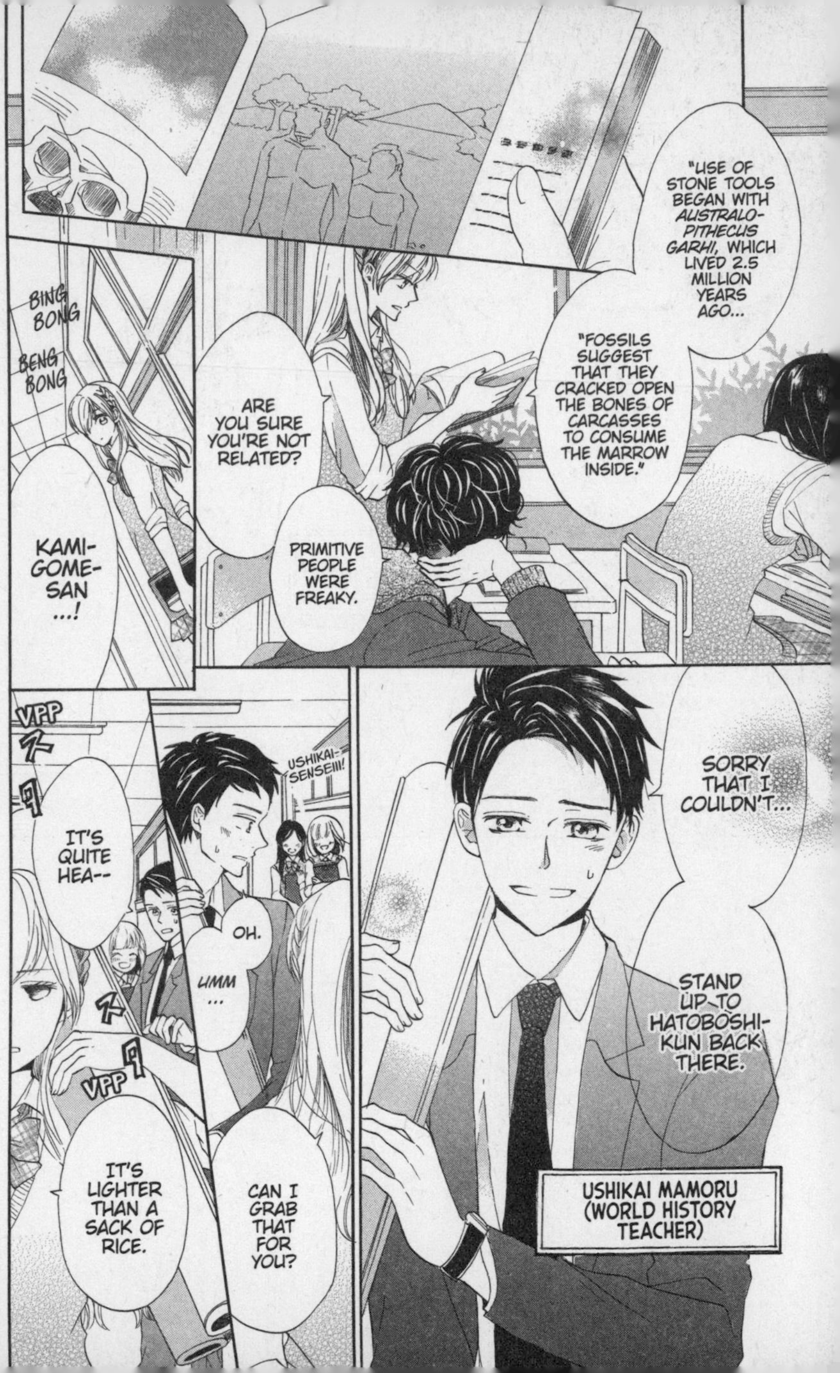

"USE OF STONE TOOLS BEGAN WITH *AUSTRALOPITHECUS GARHI*, WHICH LIVED 2.5 MILLION YEARS AGO...
"FOSSILS SUGGEST THAT THEY CRACKED OPEN THE BONES OF CARCASSES TO CONSUME THE MARROW INSIDE."
ARE YOU SURE YOU'RE NOT RELATED?
PRIMITIVE PEOPLE WERE FREAKY.
BING BONG
BENG BONG
KAMI-GOME-SAN ...!
SORRY THAT I COULDN'T...
STAND UP TO HATOBOSHI-KUN BACK THERE.
USHIKAI MAMORU (WORLD HISTORY TEACHER)
USHIKAI-SENSEIII!
VPP
IT'S QUITE HEA--
OH.
UMM ...
VPP
CAN I GRAB THAT FOR YOU?
IT'S LIGHTER THAN A SACK OF RICE.

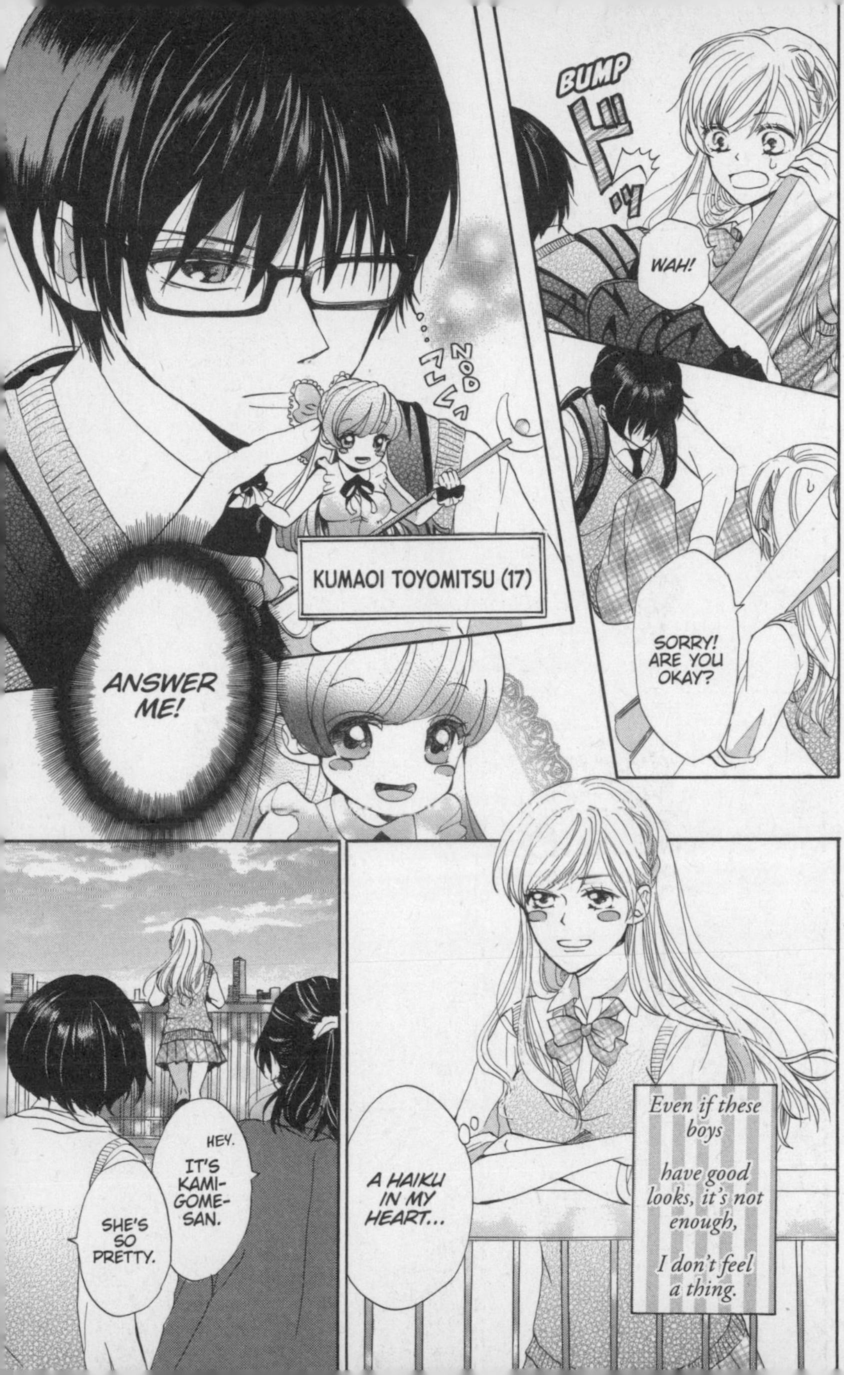
BUMP
WAH!
SORRY! ARE YOU OKAY?
NOD
KUMAOI TOYOMITSU (17)
ANSWER ME!
A HAIKU IN MY HEART...
Even if these boys have good looks, it's not enough, I don't feel a thing.
HEY. IT'S KAMI-GOME-SAN.
SHE'S SO PRETTY.

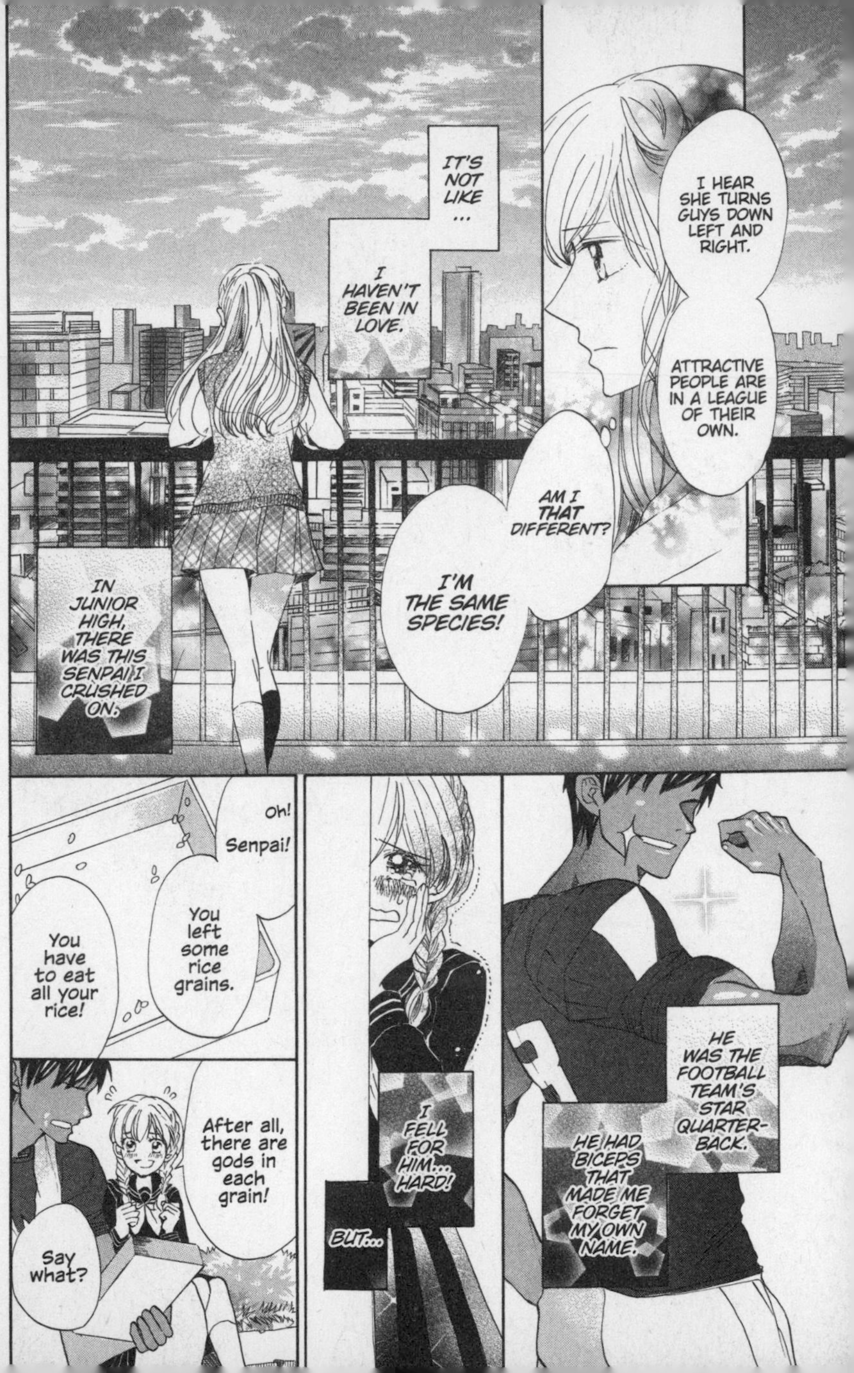
I HEAR SHE TURNS GUYS DOWN LEFT AND RIGHT.
ATTRACTIVE PEOPLE ARE IN A LEAGUE OF THEIR OWN.
IT'S NOT LIKE...
I HAVEN'T BEEN IN LOVE.
AM I THAT DIFFERENT?
I'M THE SAME SPECIES!
IN JUNIOR HIGH, THERE WAS THIS SENPAI I CRUSHED ON.
HE WAS THE FOOTBALL TEAM'S STAR QUARTER-BACK.
HE HAD BICEPS THAT MADE ME FORGET MY OWN NAME.
I FELL FOR HIM... HARD!
BUT...
Oh!
Senpai!
You left some rice grains.
You have to eat all your rice!
After all, there are gods in each grain!
Say what?

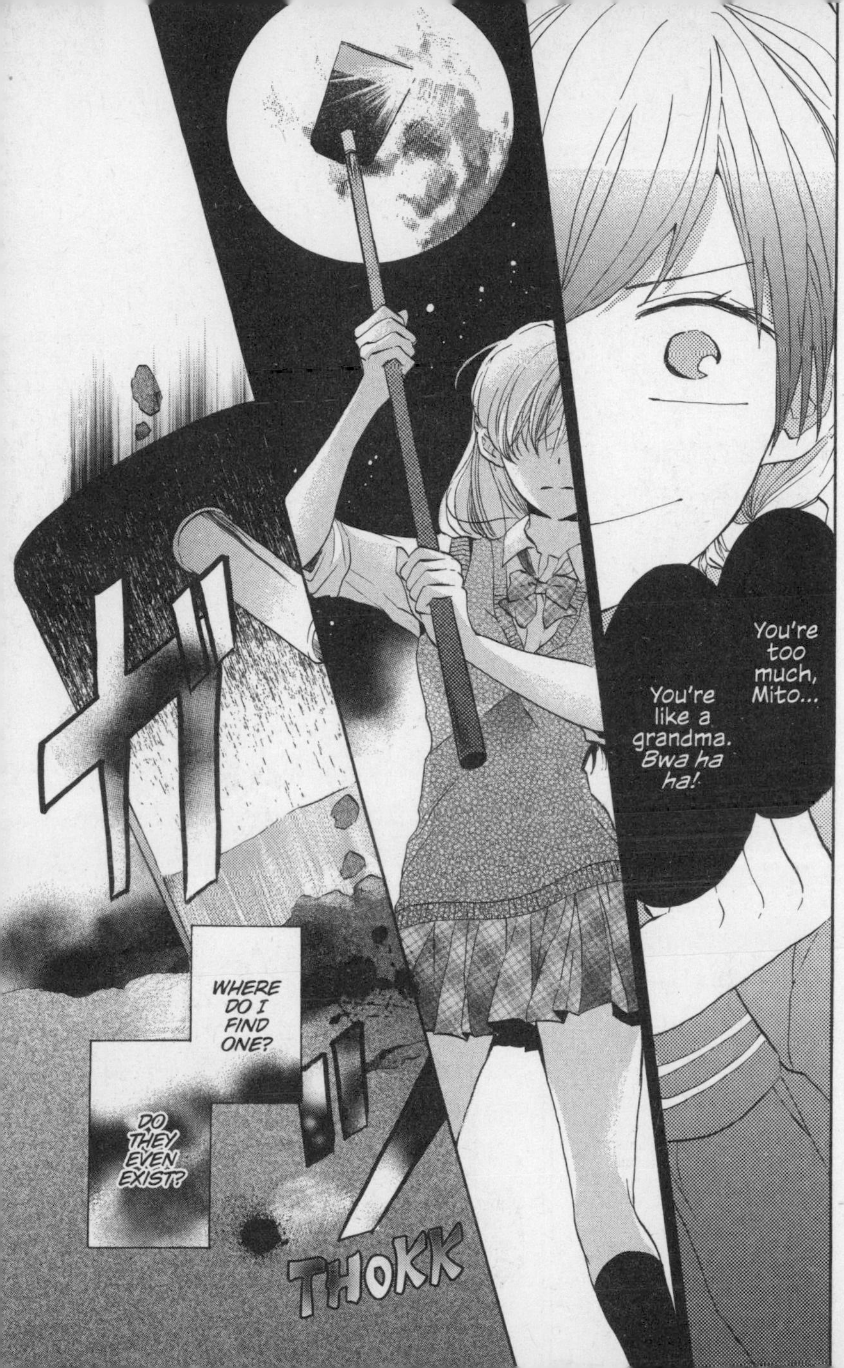
You're too much, Mito...
You're like a grandma. Bwa ha ha!
WHERE DO I FIND ONE?
DO THEY EVEN EXIST?
THOKK

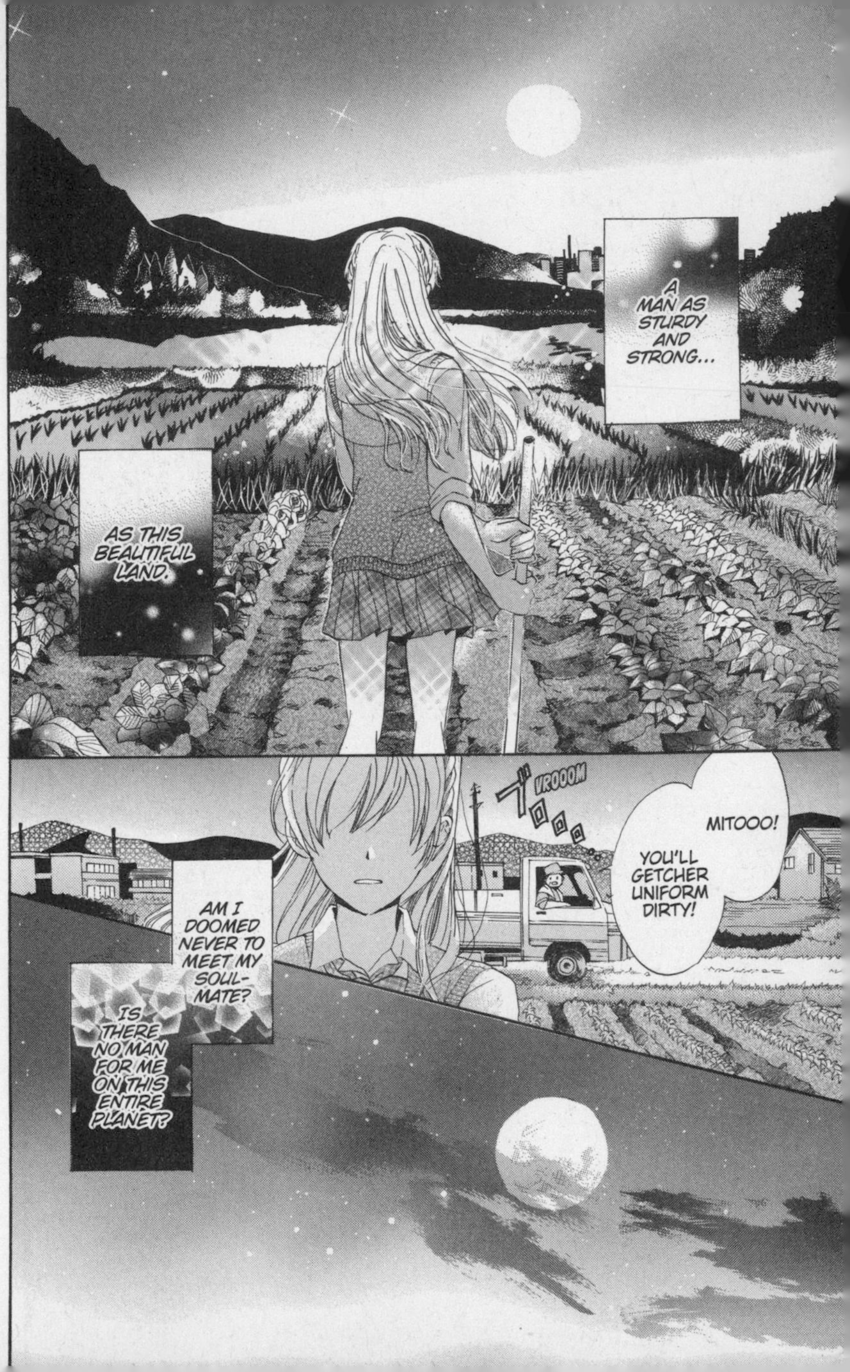
A MAN AS STURDY AND STRONG...
AS THIS BEAUTIFUL LAND.
VROOOM
MITOOO!
YOU'LL GETCHER UNIFORM DIRTY!
AM I DOOMED NEVER TO MEET MY SOUL-MATE?
IS THERE NO MAN FOR ME ON THIS ENTIRE PLANET?

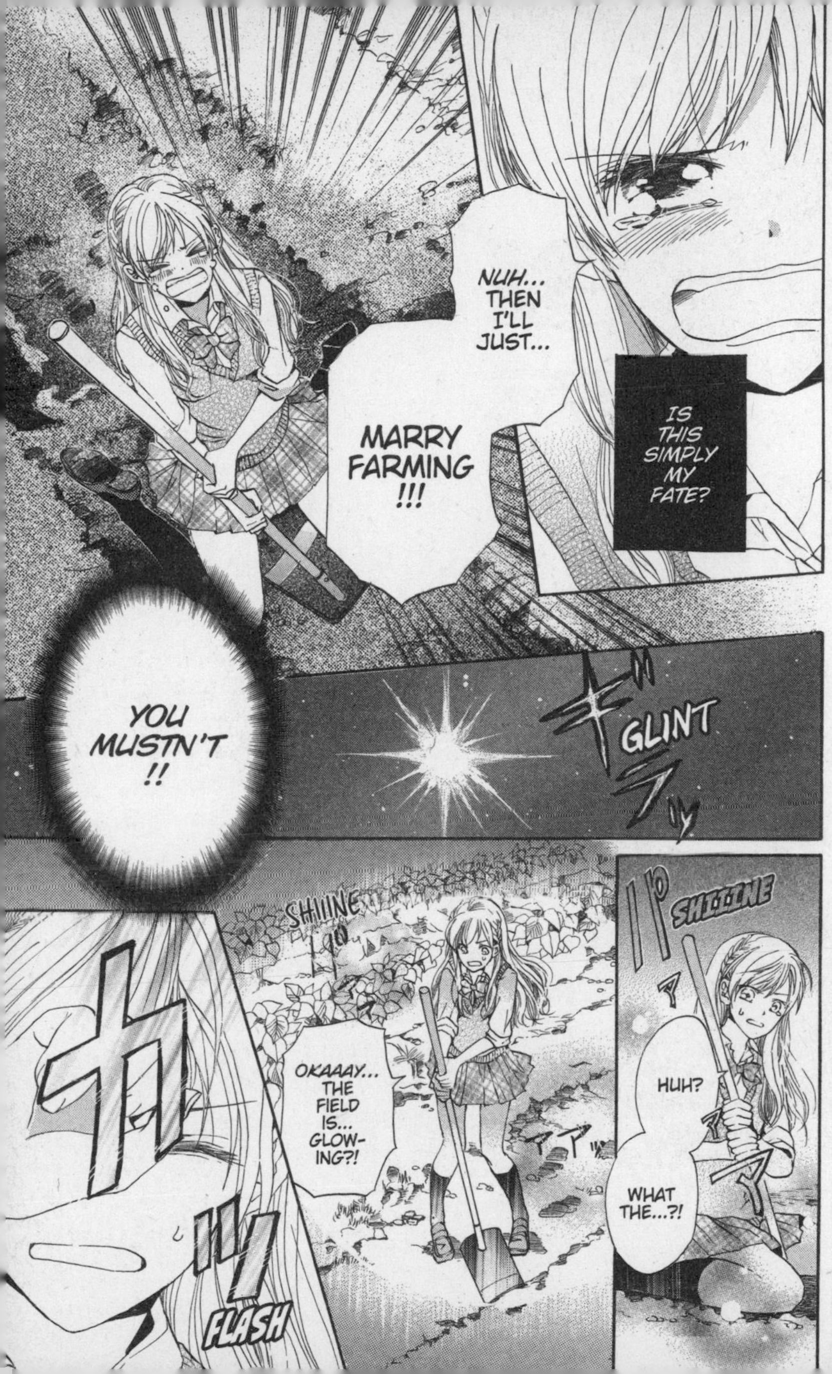
IS THIS SIMPLY MY FATE?
NUH... THEN I'LL JUST...
MARRY FARMING !!!
GLINT
YOU MUSTN'T !!
SHIIINE
HUH?
WHAT THE...?!
SHIIINE
OKAAAY... THE FIELD IS... GLOW-ING?!
FLASH

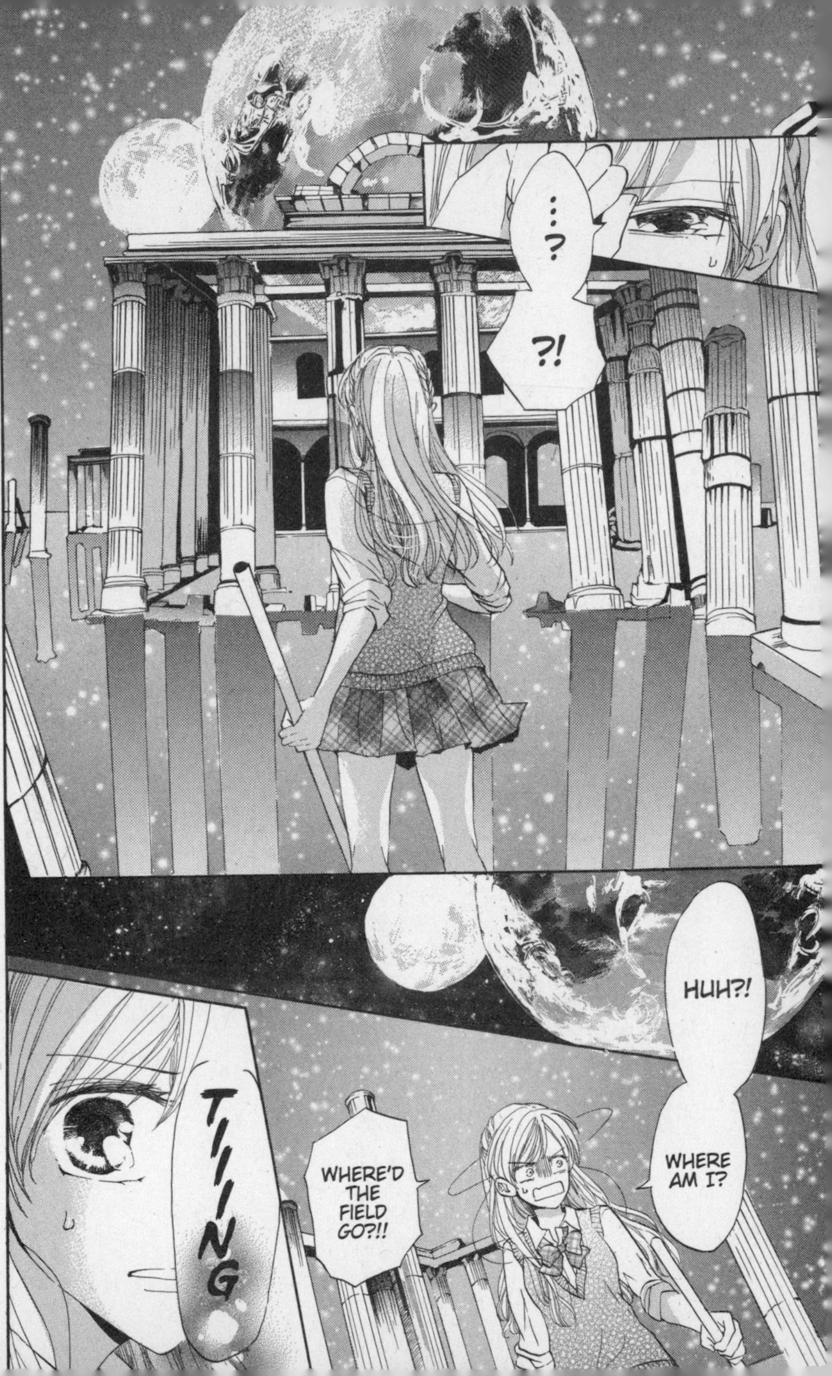
...?
?!
HUH?!
WHERE AM I?
WHERE'D THE FIELD GO?!!
TIIING

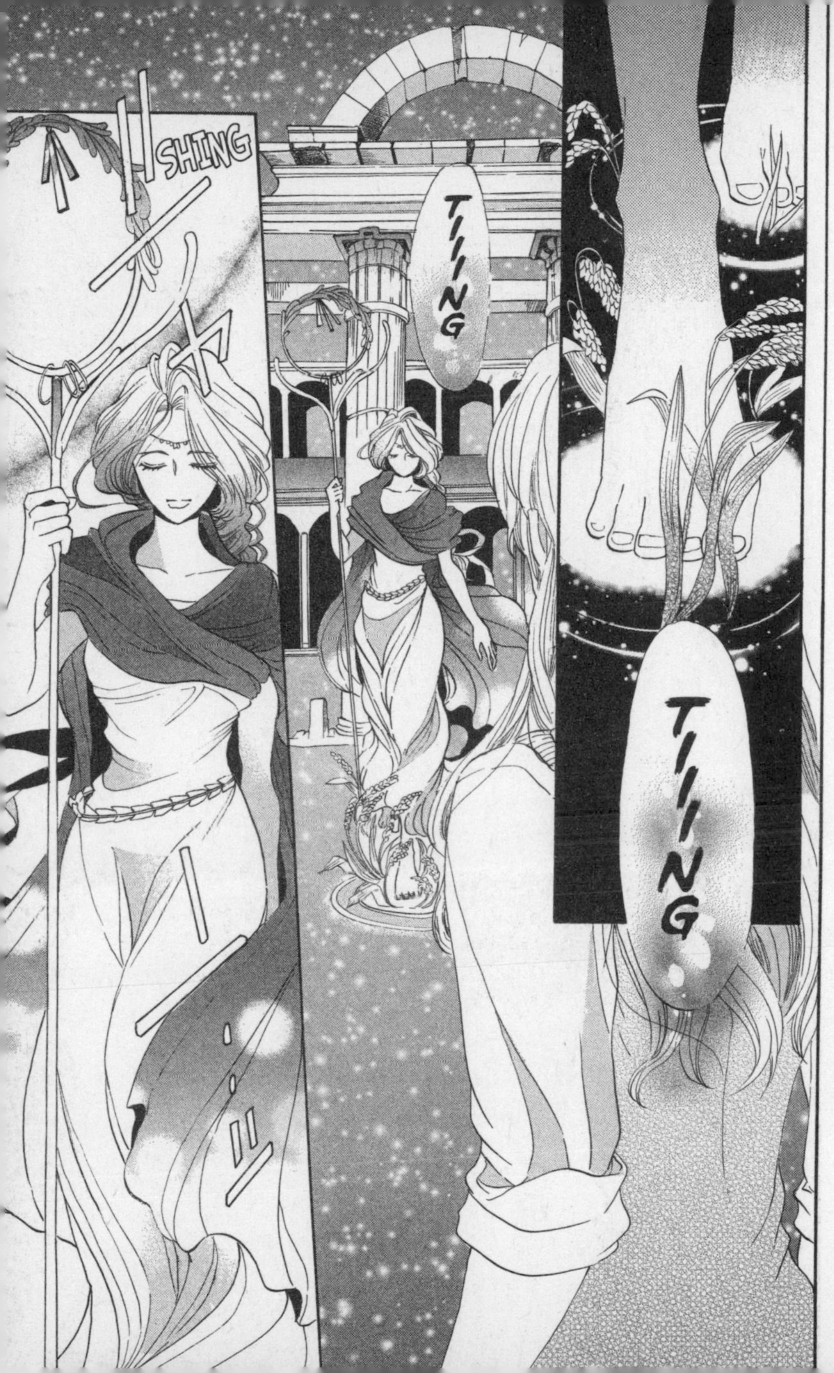
TIIING
TIIING
SHING

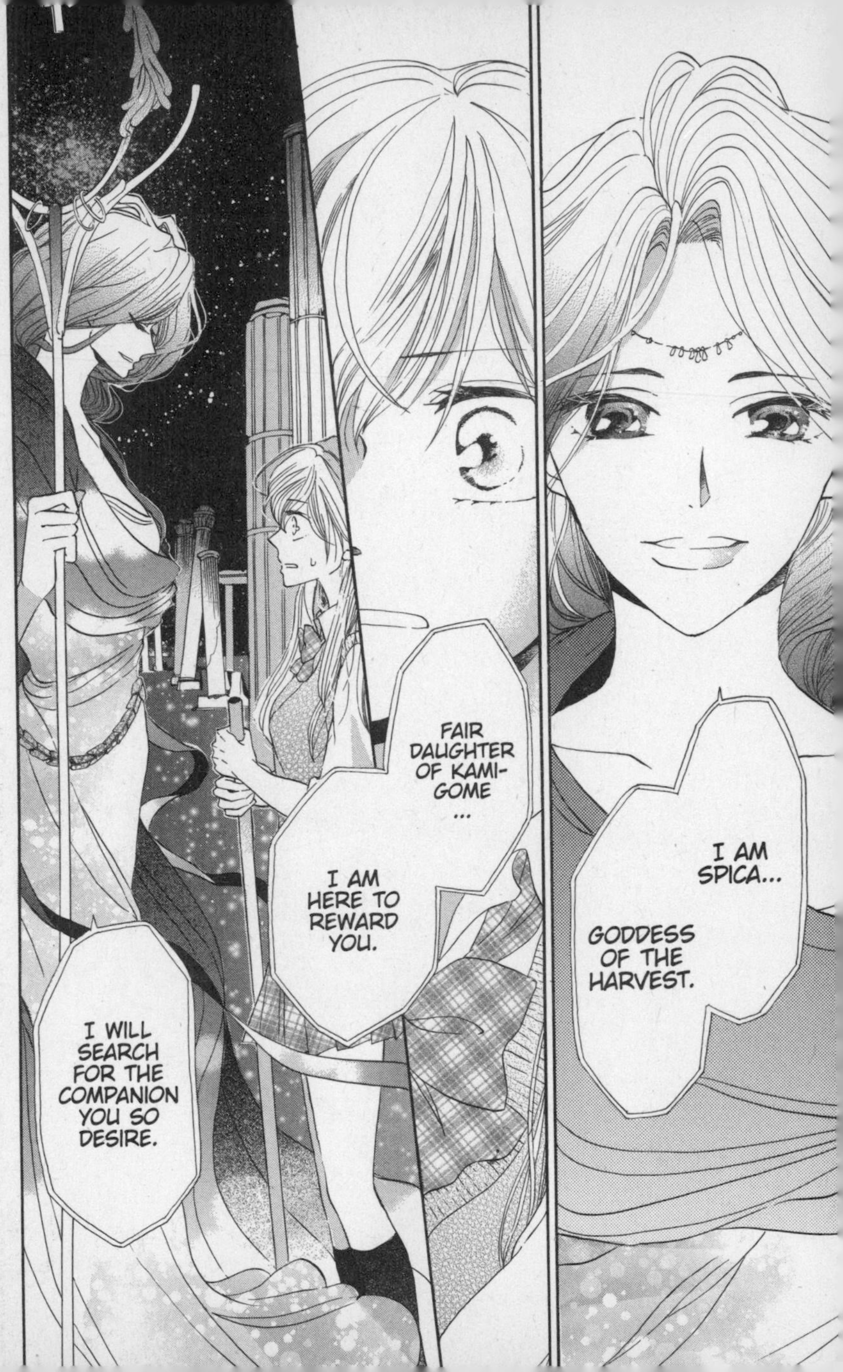
I AM SPICA...
GODDESS OF THE HARVEST.
FAIR DAUGHTER OF KAMI-GOME ...
I AM HERE TO REWARD YOU.
I WILL SEARCH FOR THE COMPANION YOU SO DESIRE.

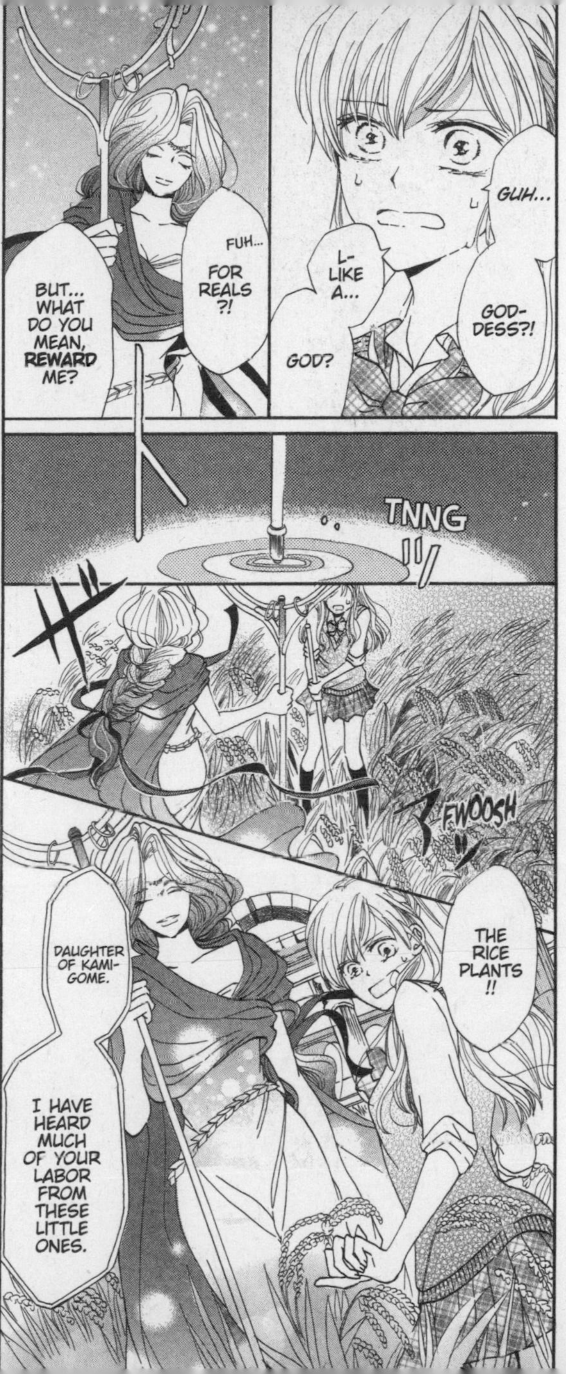
GUH...
L-LIKE A...
GOD-DESS?!
GOD?
FUH... FOR REALS?!
BUT... WHAT DO YOU MEAN, REWARD ME?
TNNG
FWOOSH
THE RICE PLANTS!!
DAUGHTER OF KAMI-GOME.
I HAVE HEARD MUCH OF YOUR LABOR FROM THESE LITTLE ONES.

1

NICE TO MEET YOU. I'M YOSHINEKO KITAFUKU.

THANKS **SO** MUCH FOR PICKING UP THIS BOOK, *PRIMITIVE BOYFRIEND, VOLUME 1!*

I HOPE YOU'LL ENJOY THIS HEART-POUNDING ADVENTURE ALONG WITH OUR DASHING HEROINE, MITO.

HERE'S ME FEELING 360 DEGREES OF GRATITUDE... SO MUCH THAT I'M PROSTRATING MYSELF IN OUTER SPACE!!

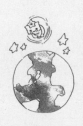

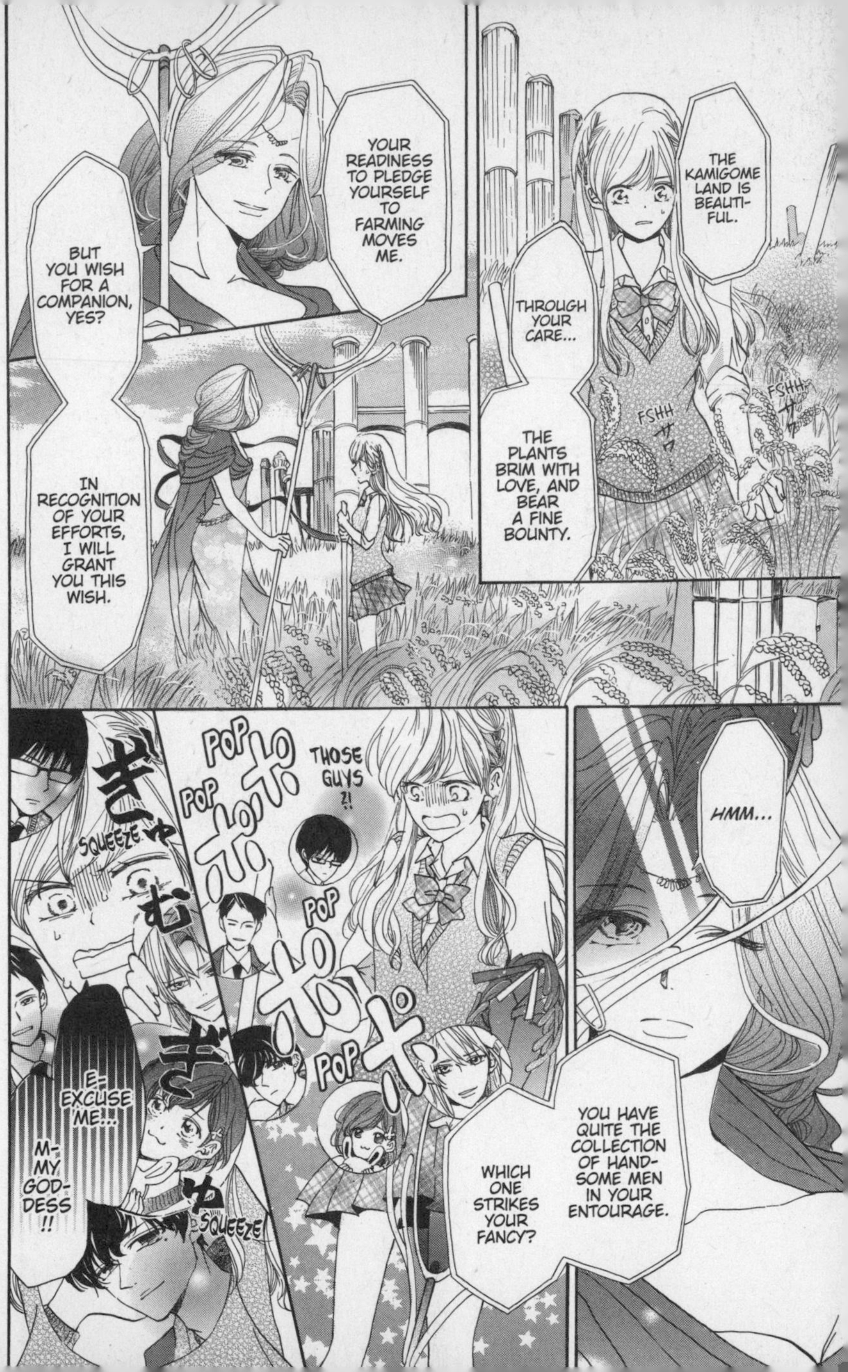
THE KAMIGOME LAND IS BEAUTIFUL.
THROUGH YOUR CARE...
FSHH
FSHH
THE PLANTS BRIM WITH LOVE, AND BEAR A FINE BOUNTY.
YOUR READINESS TO PLEDGE YOURSELF TO FARMING MOVES ME.
BUT YOU WISH FOR A COMPANION, YES?
IN RECOGNITION OF YOUR EFFORTS, I WILL GRANT YOU THIS WISH.
HMM...
YOU HAVE QUITE THE COLLECTION OF HANDSOME MEN IN YOUR ENTOURAGE.
WHICH ONE STRIKES YOUR FANCY?
THOSE GUYS?!
POP
POP
POP
POP
SQUEEZE
E-EXCUSE ME...
M-MY GODDESS!!
SQUEEZE

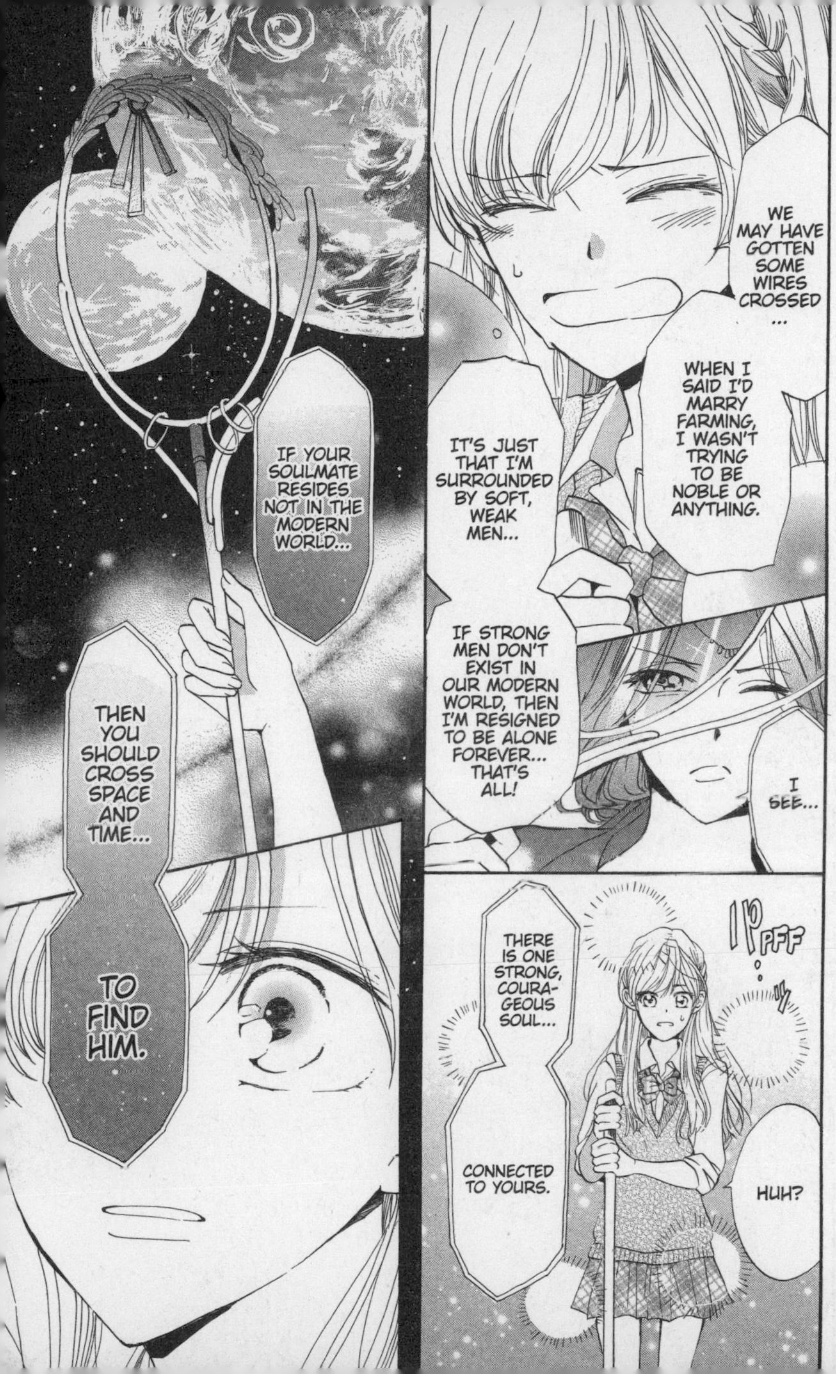
WE MAY HAVE GOTTEN SOME WIRES CROSSED...
WHEN I SAID I'D MARRY FARMING, I WASN'T TRYING TO BE NOBLE OR ANYTHING.
IT'S JUST THAT I'M SURROUNDED BY SOFT, WEAK MEN...
IF STRONG MEN DON'T EXIST IN OUR MODERN WORLD, THEN I'M RESIGNED TO BE ALONE FOREVER... THAT'S ALL!
I SEE...
PFFF
THERE IS ONE STRONG, COURA-GEOUS SOUL...
HUH?
CONNECTED TO YOURS.
IF YOUR SOULMATE RESIDES NOT IN THE MODERN WORLD...
THEN YOU SHOULD CROSS SPACE AND TIME...
TO FIND HIM.

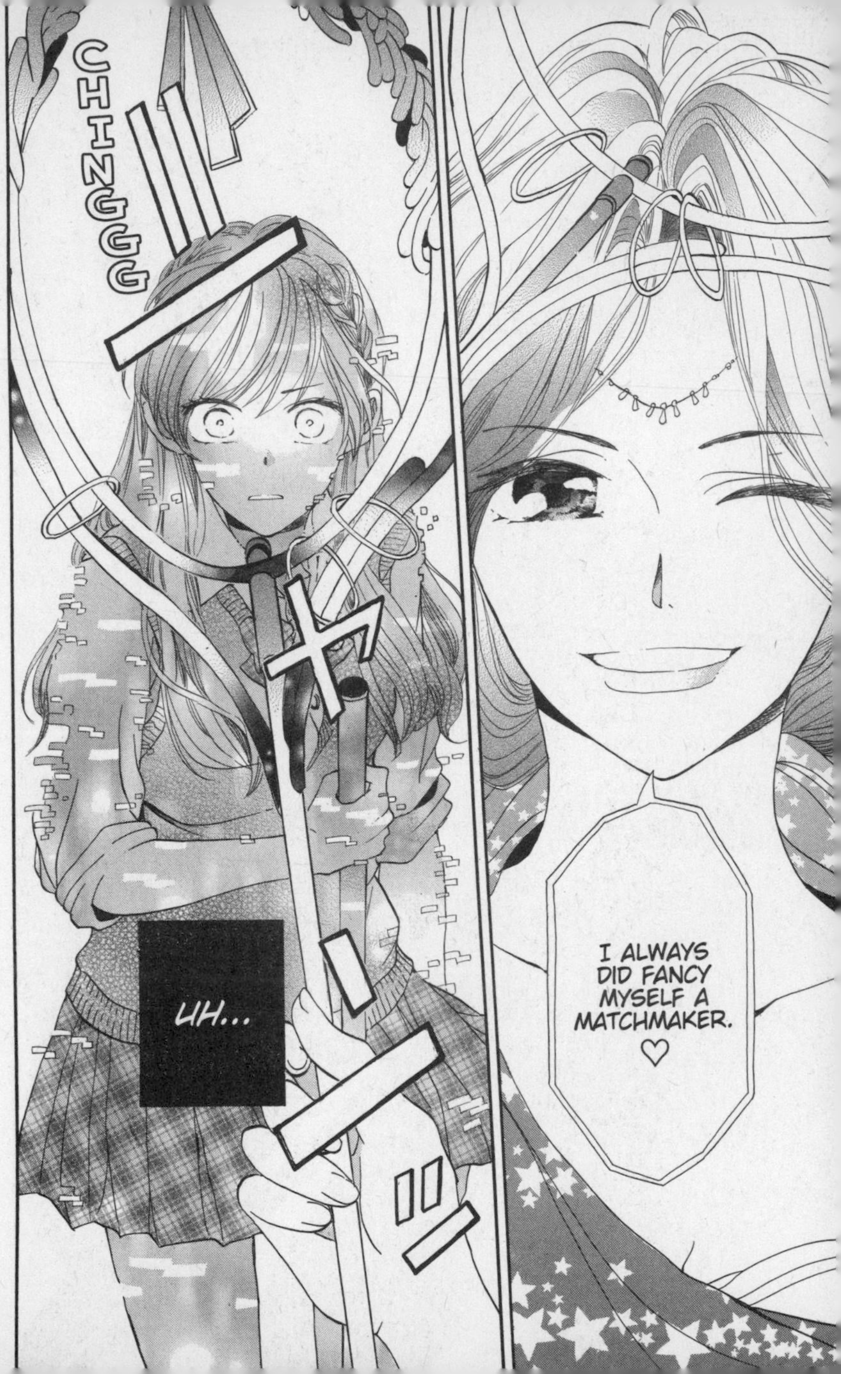
I ALWAYS DID FANCY MYSELF A MATCHMAKER. ♡
CHINGGG
UH...

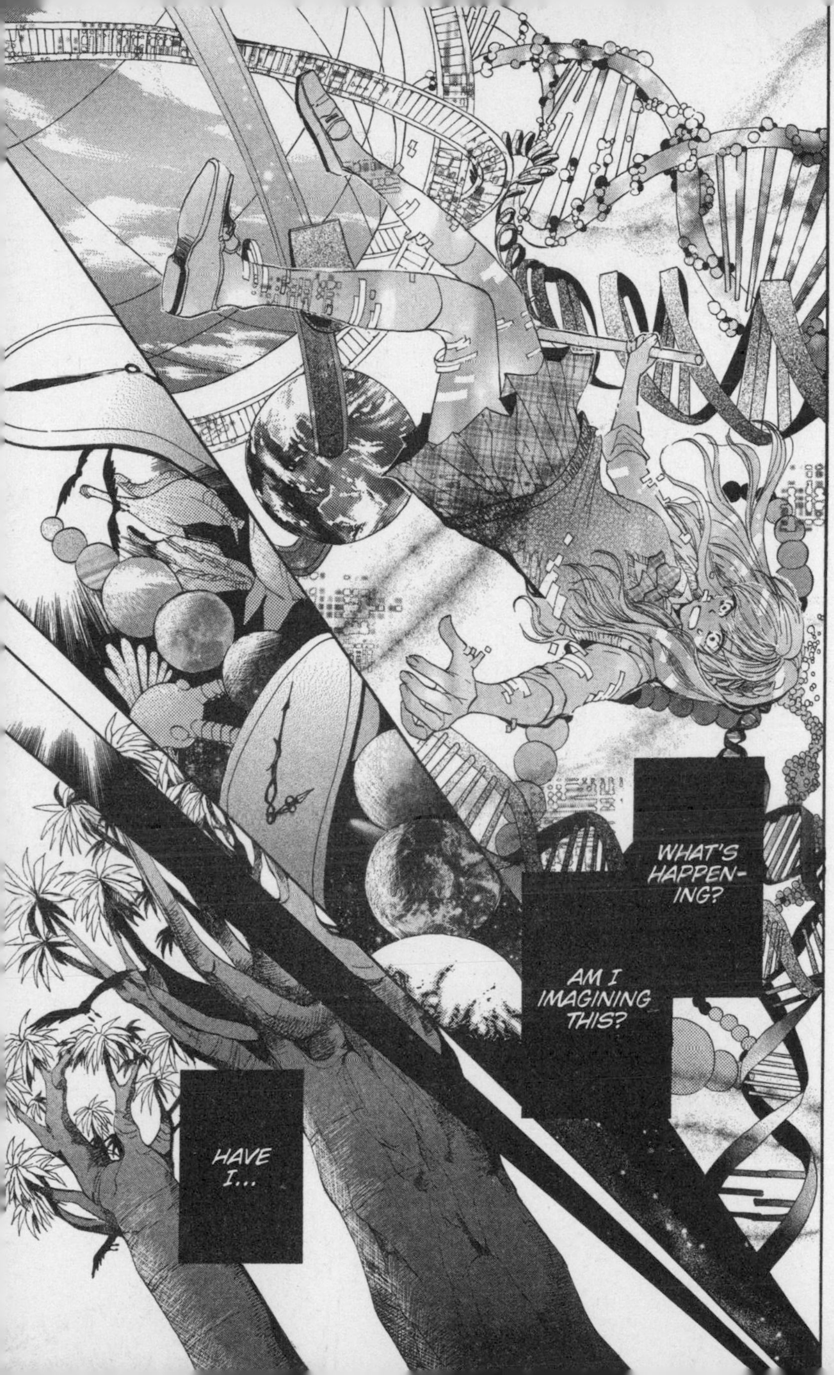
WHAT'S HAPPEN-ING?
AM I IMAGINING THIS?
HAVE I...

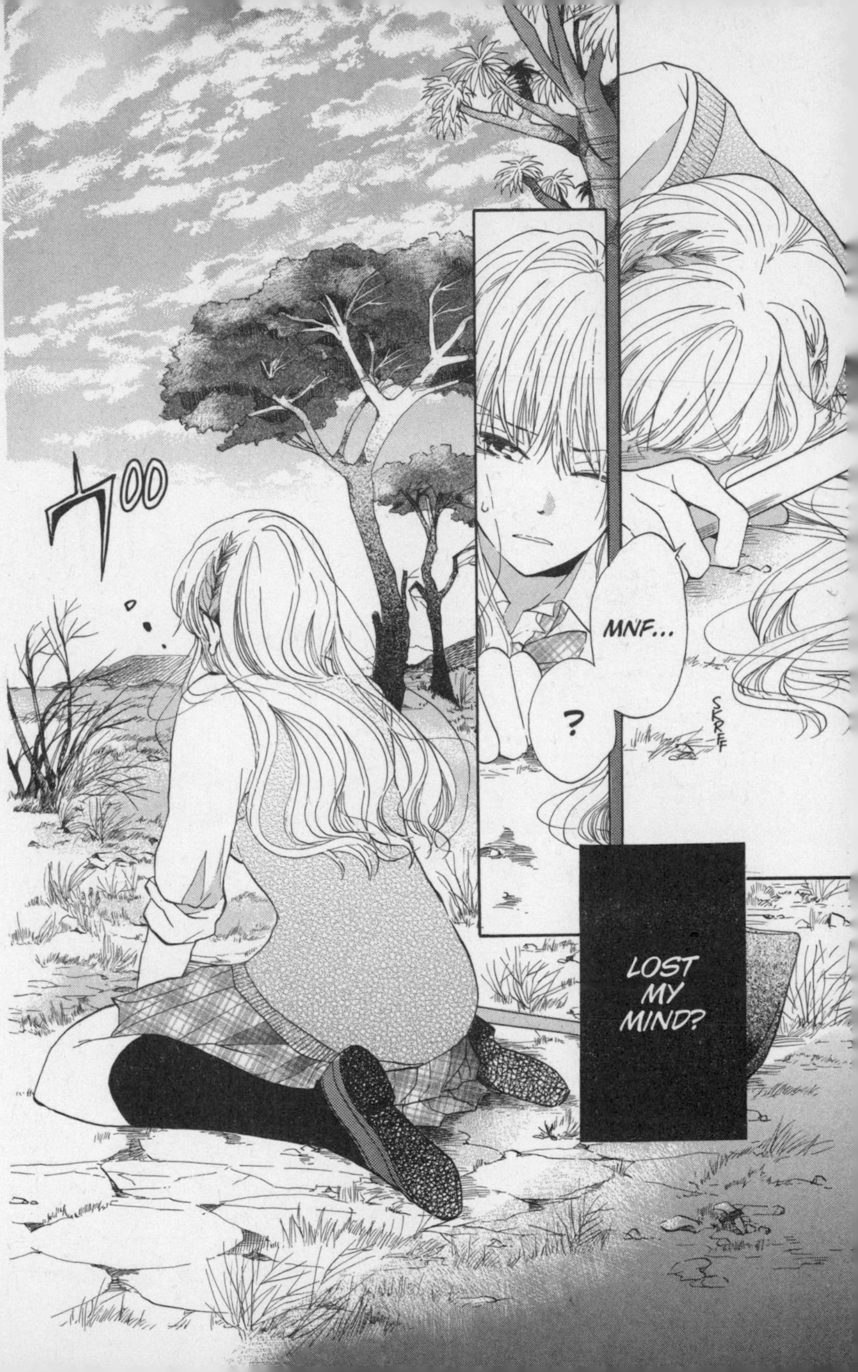
MNF...
?
SKREF
LOST MY MIND?

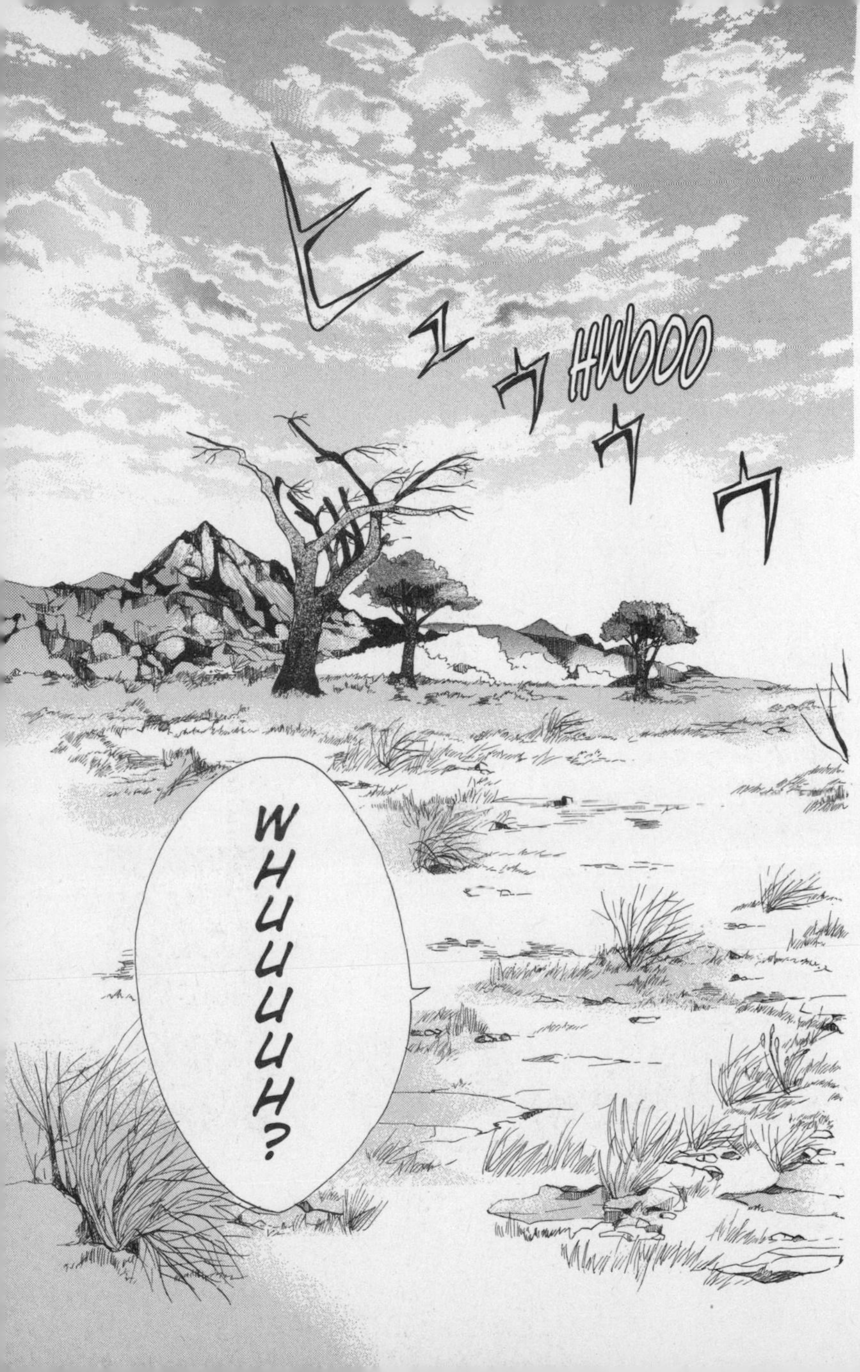
ヒュウウウ
HWOOO
WHUUUUH?

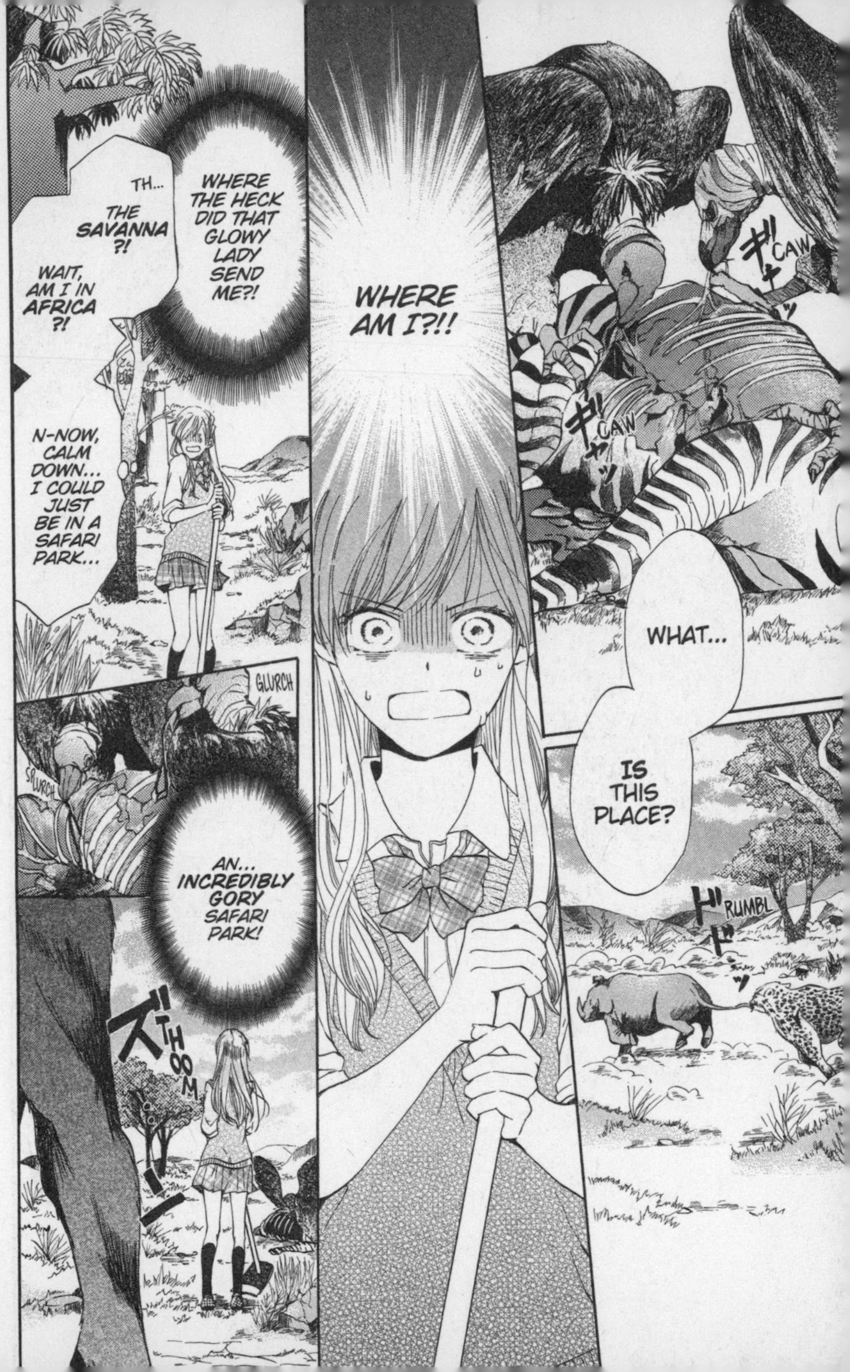
CAW
CAW
WHAT...
IS THIS PLACE?
RUMBL
WHERE AM I?!!
WHERE THE HECK DID THAT GLOWY LADY SEND ME?!
TH...
THE SAVANNA?!
WAIT, AM I IN AFRICA?!
N-NOW, CALM DOWN... I COULD JUST BE IN A SAFARI PARK...
GLURCH
SLURCH
AN... INCREDIBLY GORY SAFARI PARK!
THOOM

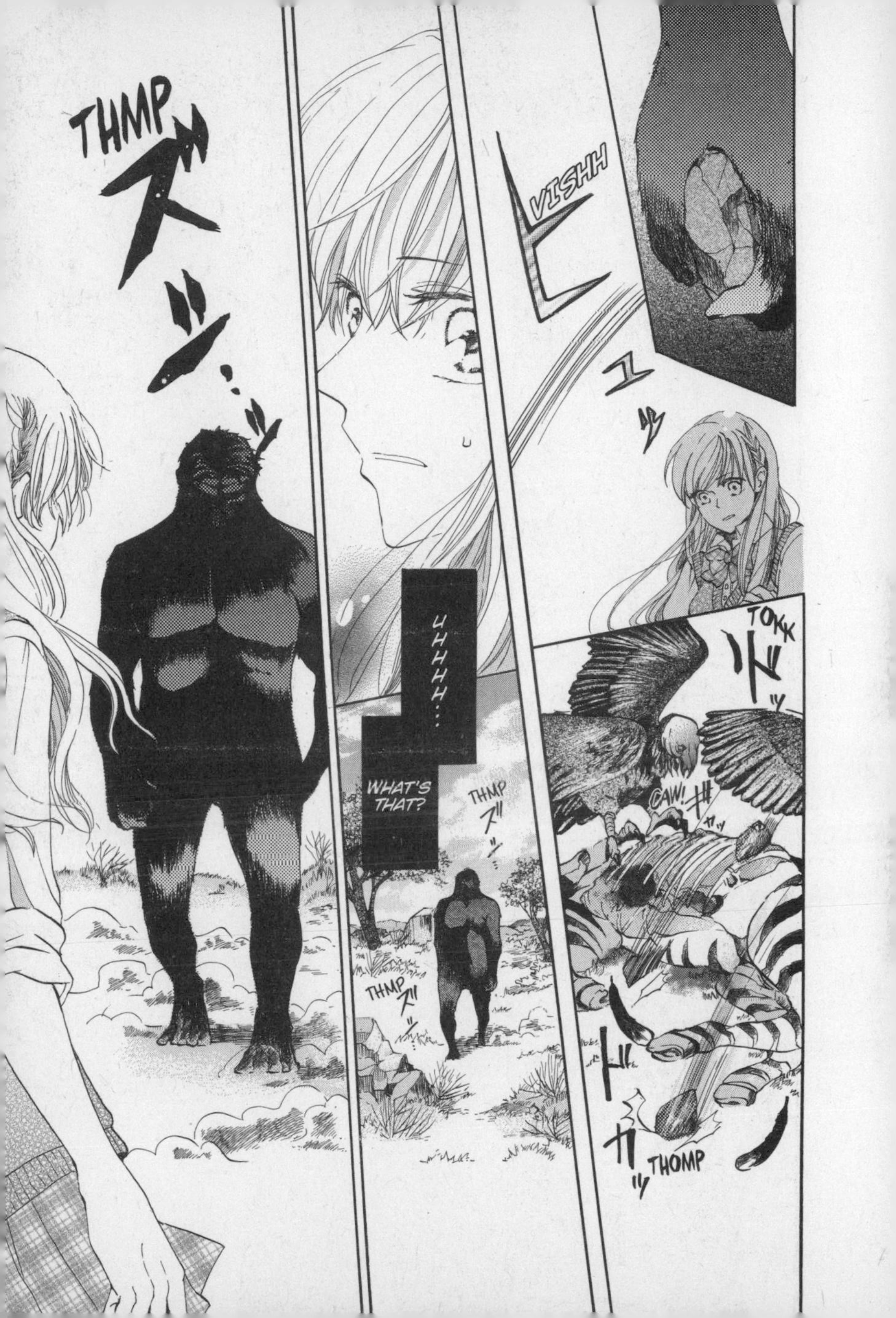
VISHH
TOKK
CAW!
THOMP
UHHHH...
WHAT'S THAT?
THMP
THMP
THMP

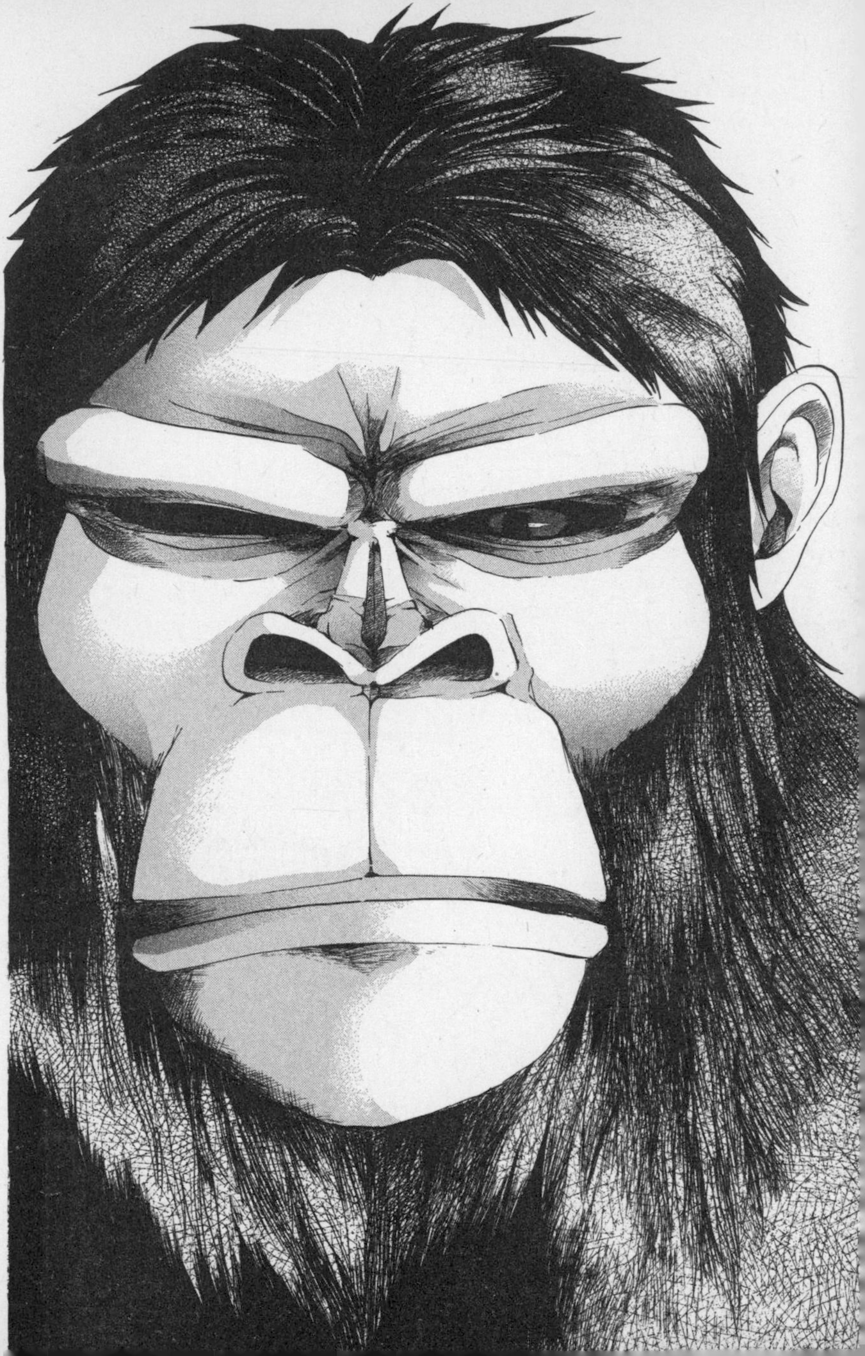

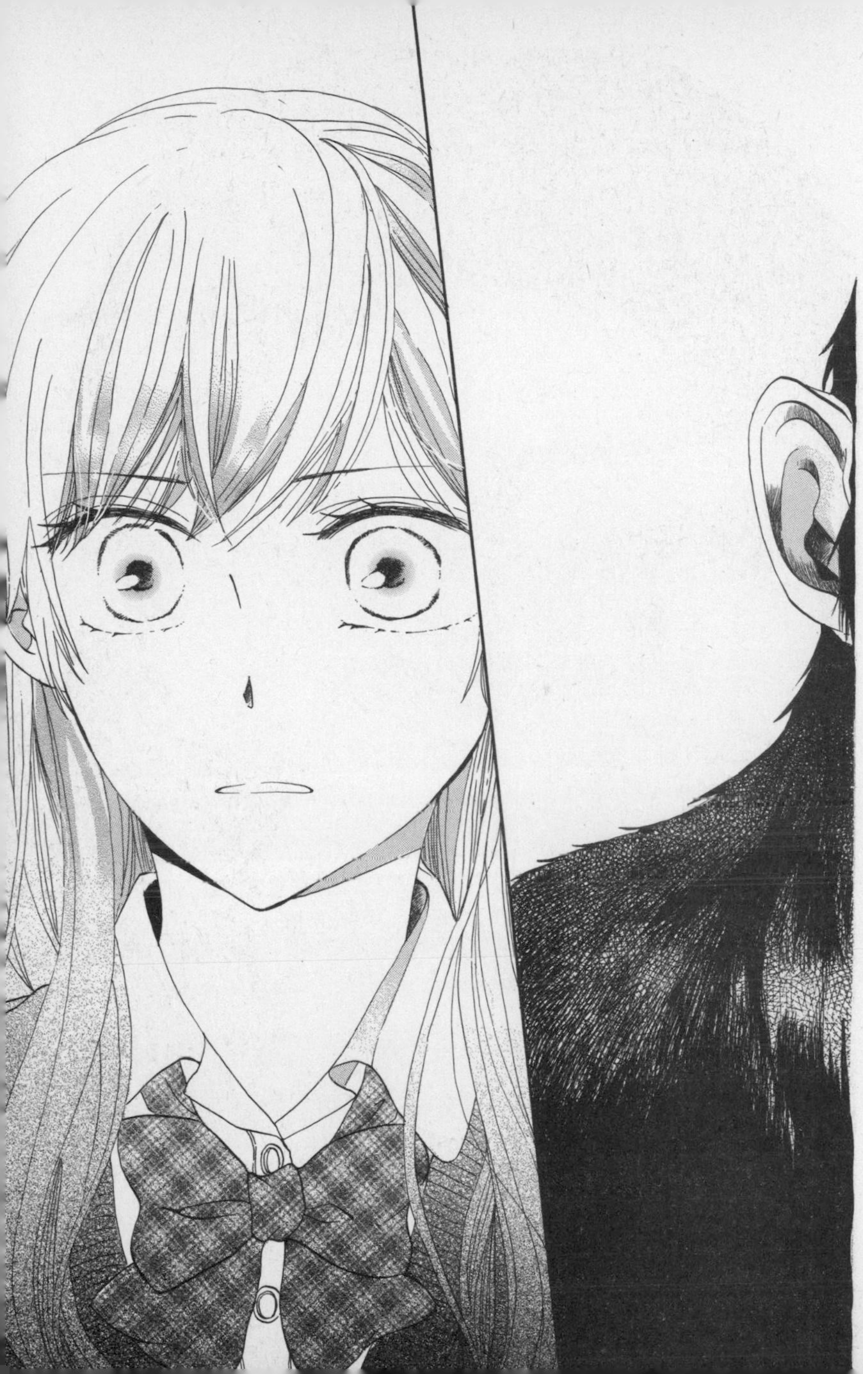

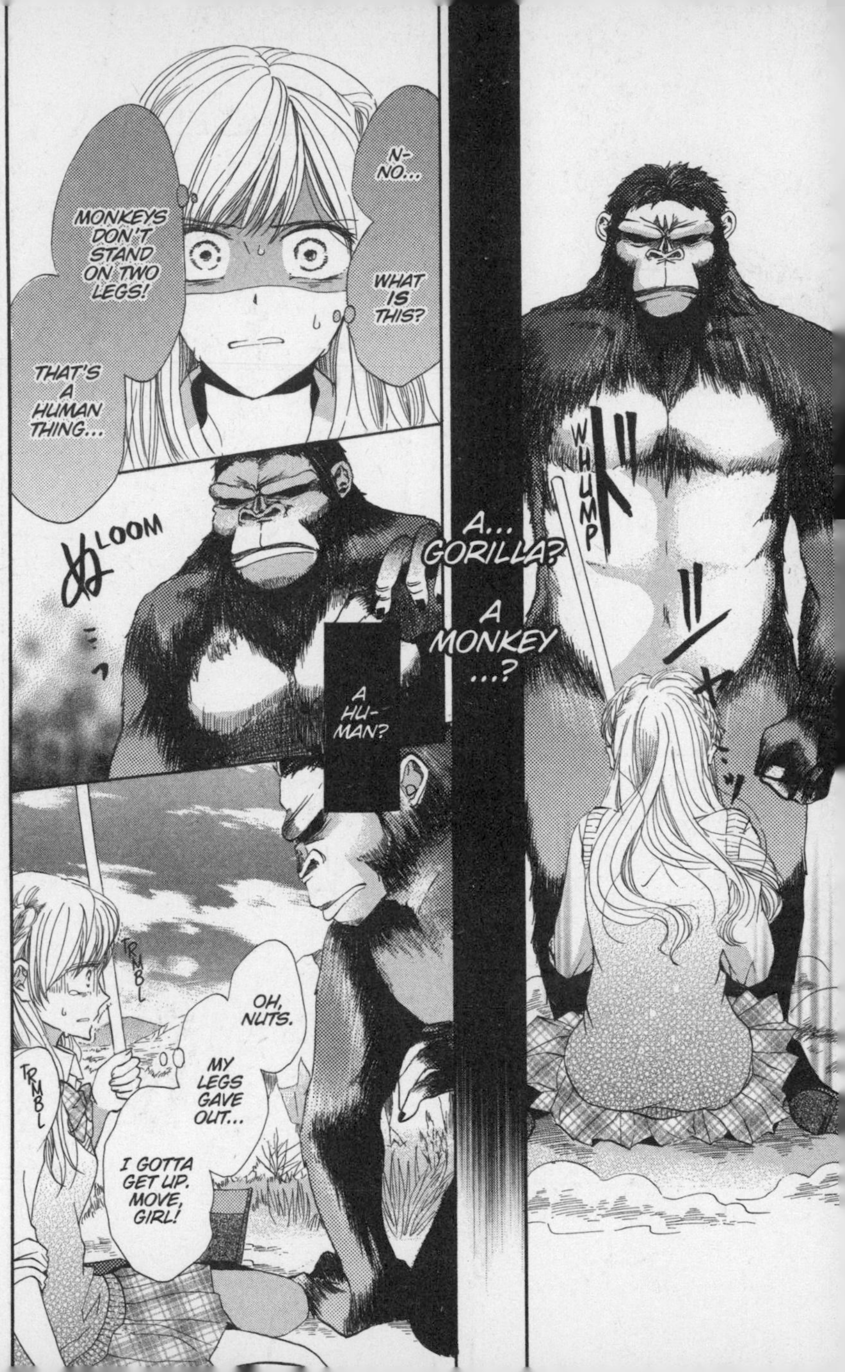
WHUMP
A... GORILLA?
A MONKEY ...?
N-NO...
WHAT IS THIS?
MONKEYS DON'T STAND ON TWO LEGS!
THAT'S A HUMAN THING...
LOOM
A HUMAN?
OH, NUTS.
MY LEGS GAVE OUT...
I GOTTA GET UP. MOVE, GIRL!
TRMBL
TRMBL

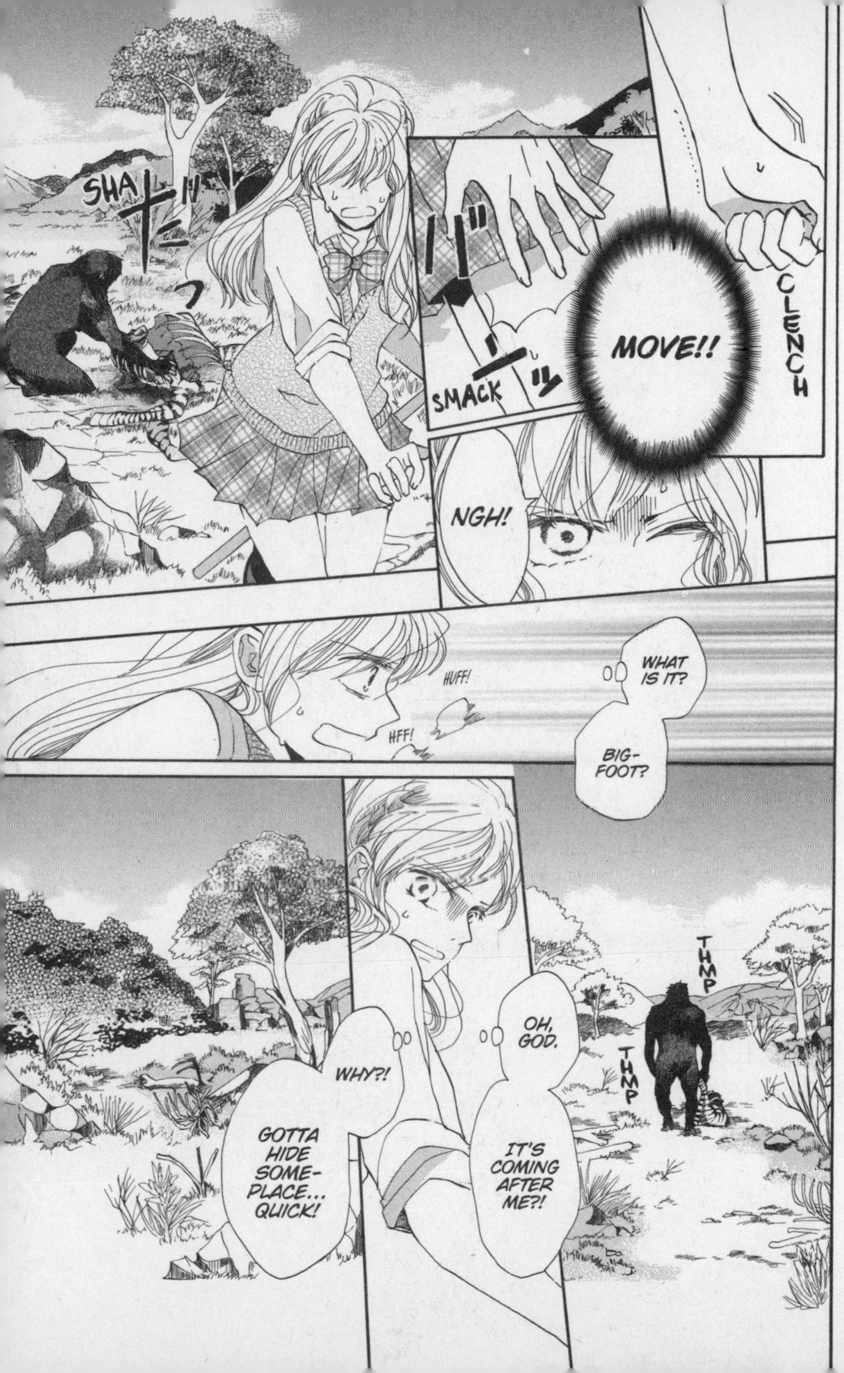
CLENCH
MOVE!!
SMACK
NGH!
SHA
WHAT IS IT?
BIG-FOOT?
HUFF!
HFF!
THMP
THMP
OH, GOD.
IT'S COMING AFTER ME?!
WHY?!
GOTTA HIDE SOME-PLACE... QUICK!

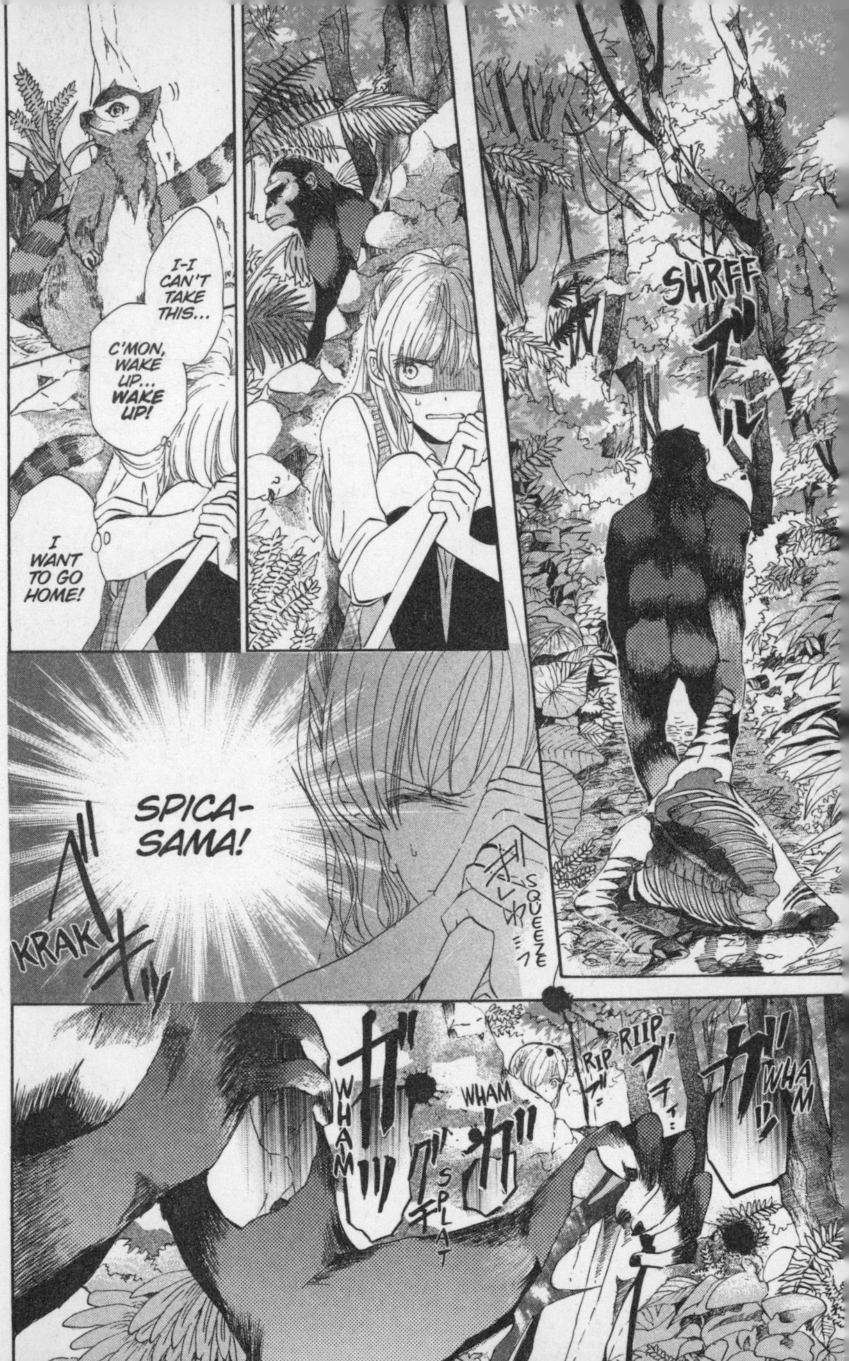
SHRFF
I-I CAN'T TAKE THIS...
C'MON, WAKE UP... WAKE UP!
I WANT TO GO HOME!
SQUEEZE
SPICA-SAMA!
KRAK
WHAM
RIIP
RIP
WHAM
SPLAT
WHAM

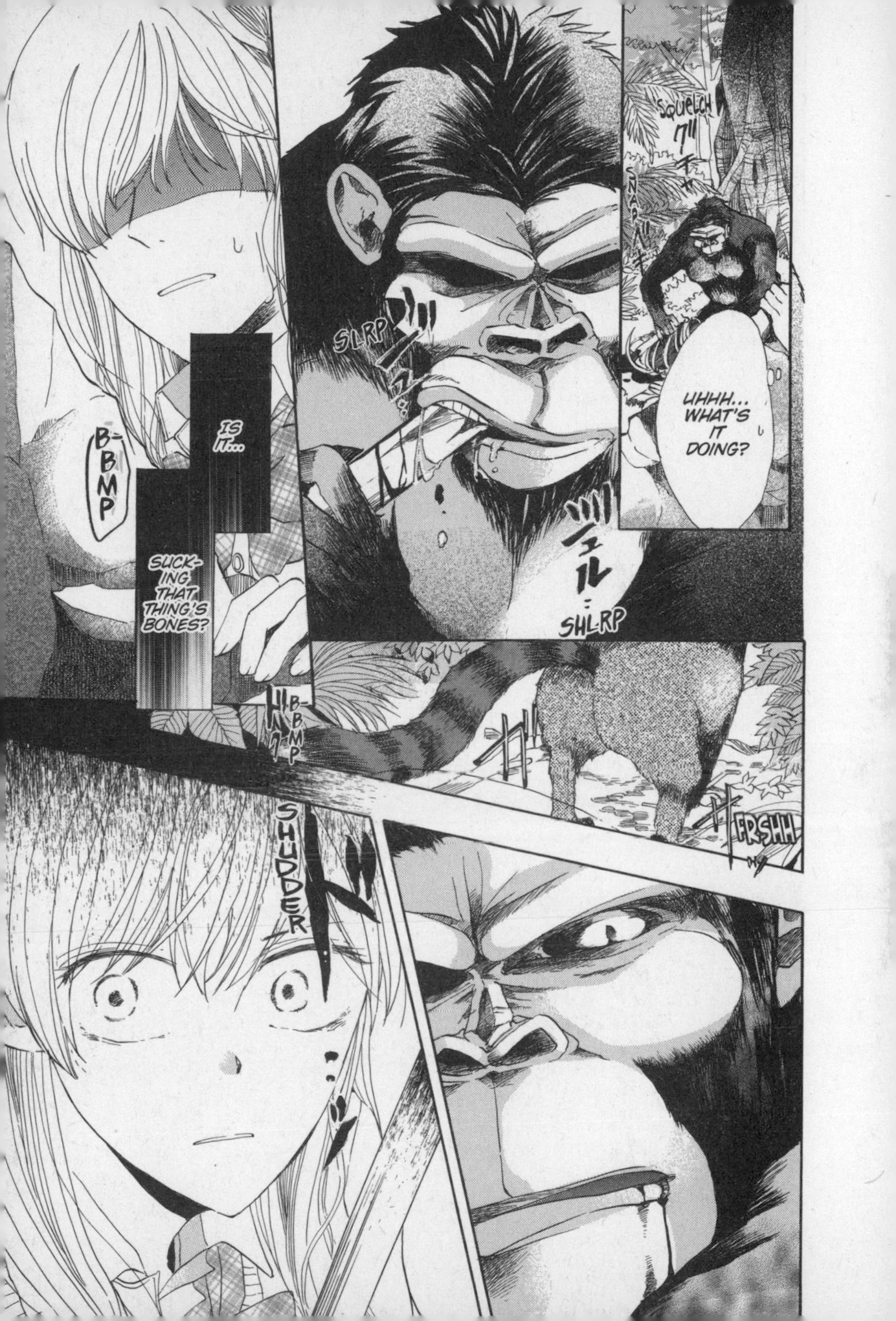
SQUELCH
SNAP
UHHH... WHAT'S IT DOING?
SLRP
SHLRP
IS IT...
SUCKING-ING THAT THING'S BONES?
B-BMP
FRSHH
B-BMP
SHUDDER

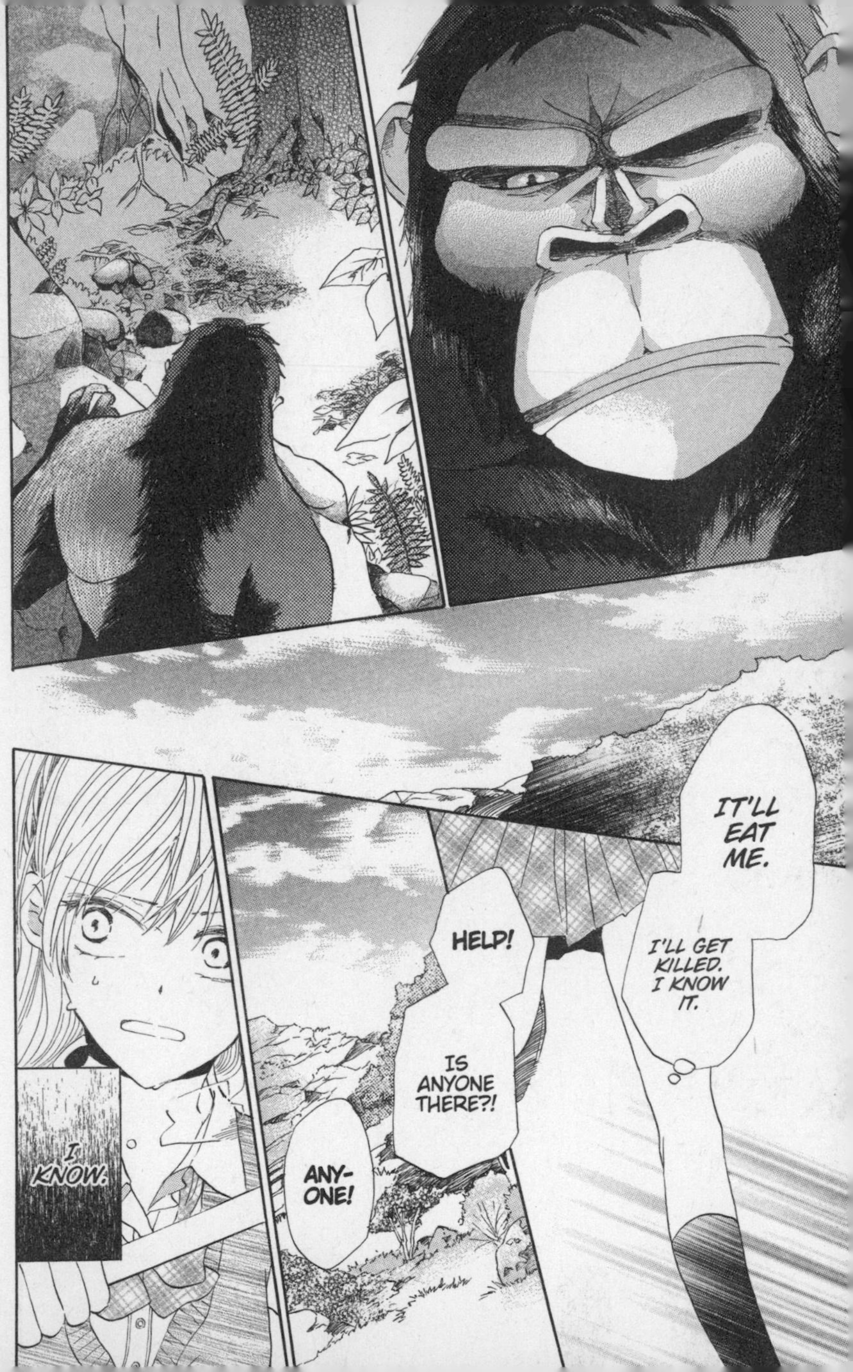
IT'LL EAT ME.
I'LL GET KILLED. I KNOW IT.
HELP!
IS ANYONE THERE?!
ANY-ONE!
I KNOW.

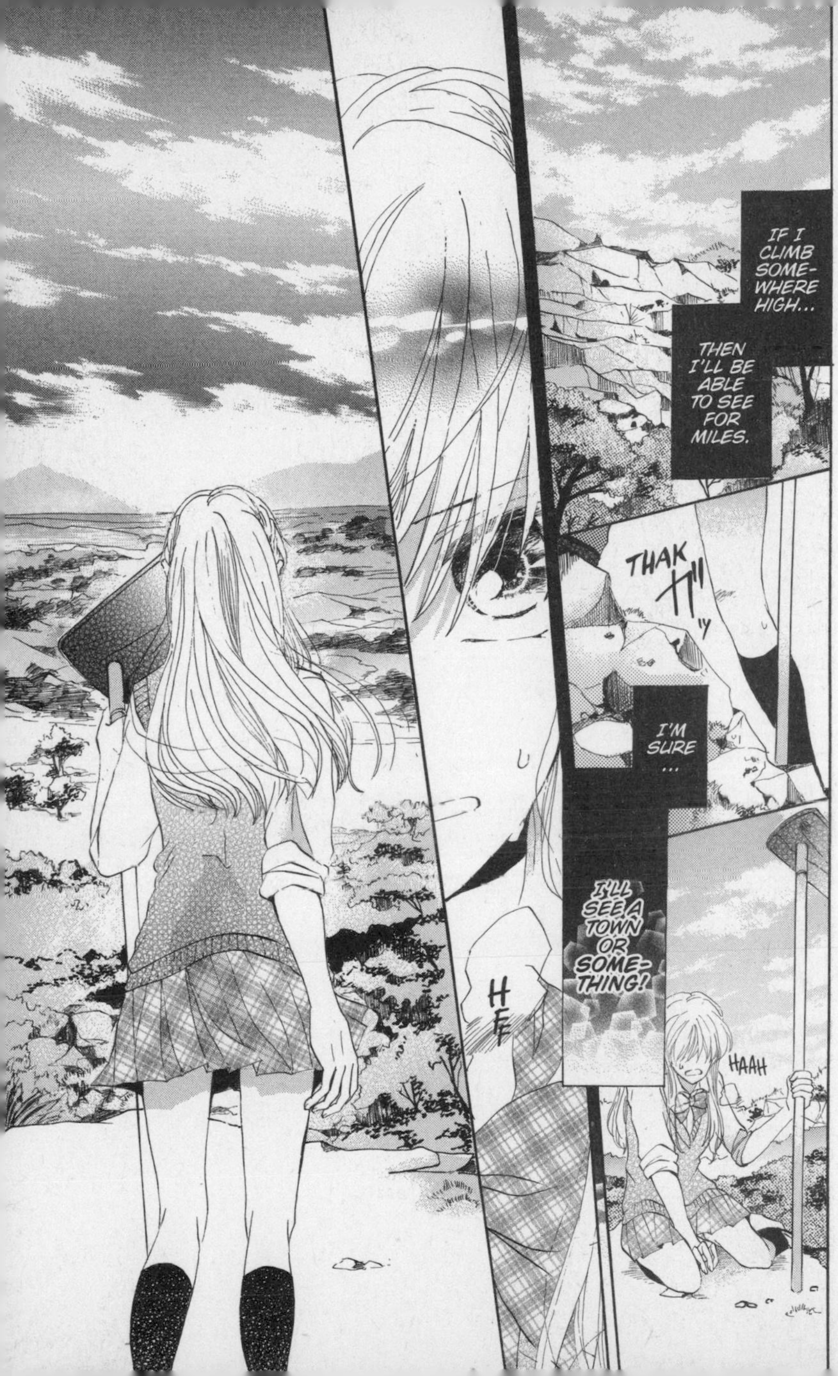
IF I CLIMB SOME-WHERE HIGH...
THEN I'LL BE ABLE TO SEE FOR MILES.
THAK
I'M SURE ...
I'LL SEE A TOWN OR SOME-THING!
HAAH
HFF

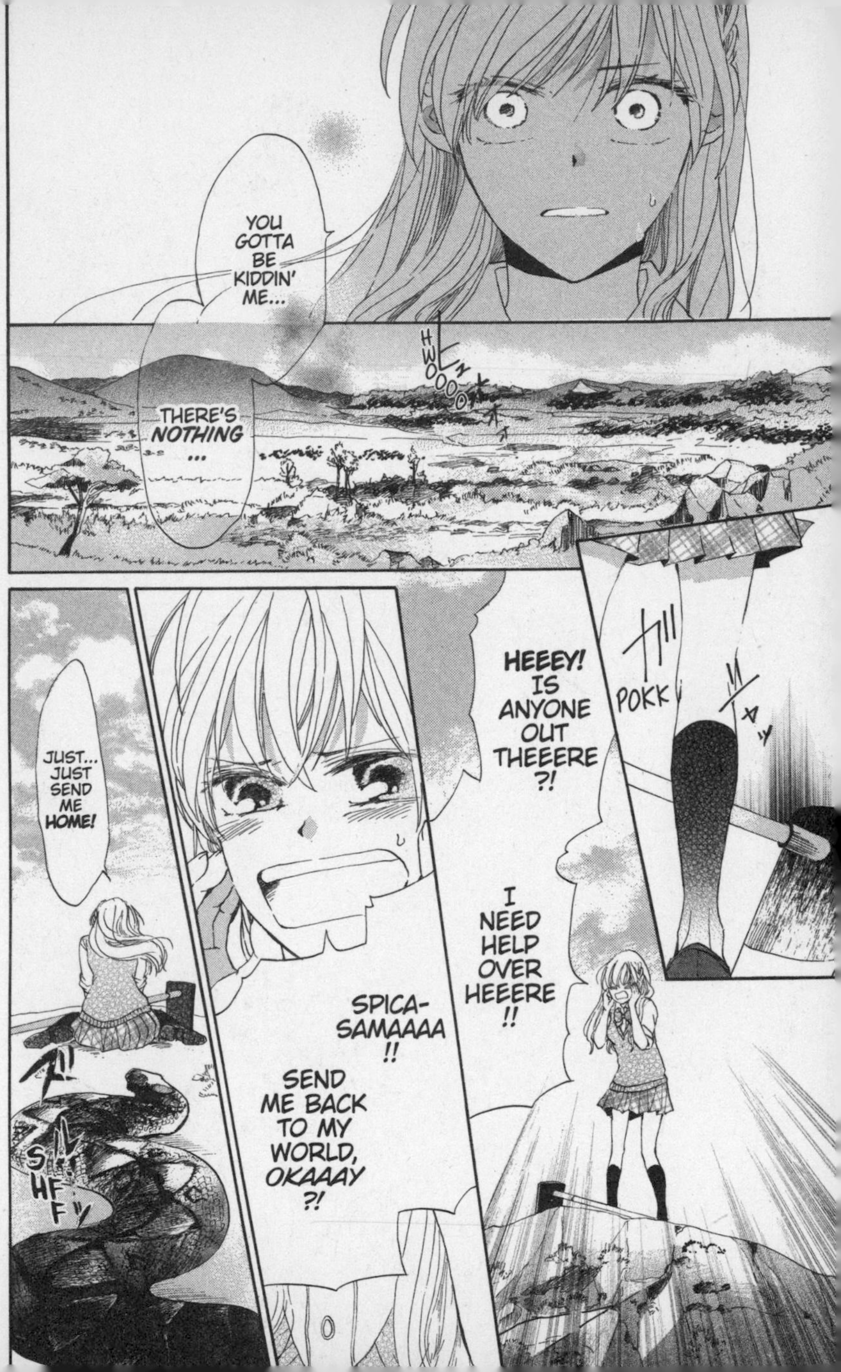
YOU GOTTA BE KIDDIN' ME...
HWOOOO
THERE'S *NOTHING* ...
POKK
HEEEY! IS ANYONE OUT THEEERE ?!
I NEED HELP OVER HEEERE !!
SPICA-SAMAAAA !!
SEND ME BACK TO MY WORLD, *OKAAAY* ?!
JUST... JUST SEND ME **HOME!**
SHF

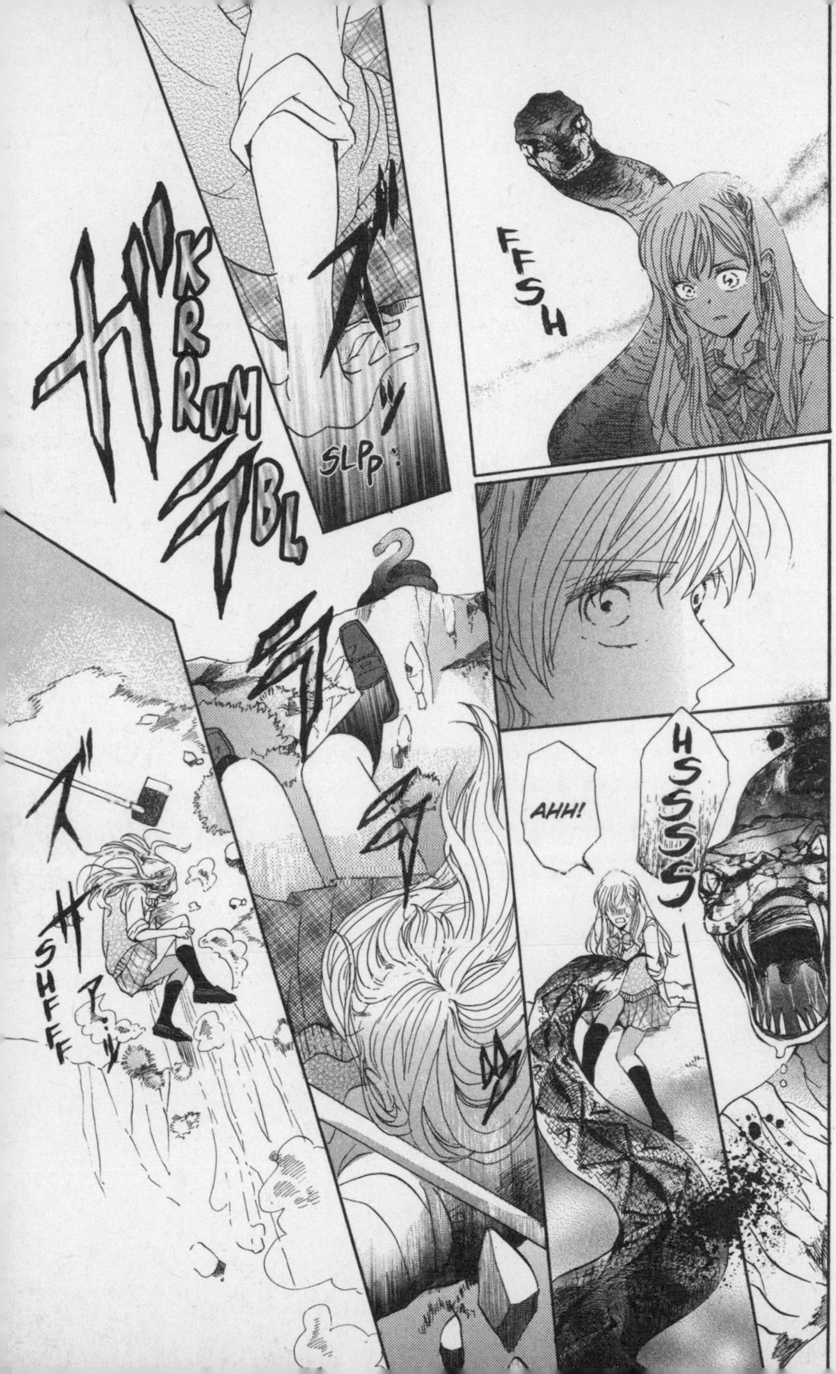
FFSH
SLPP
KRRUMBL
AHH!
HSSSS
SHFFF

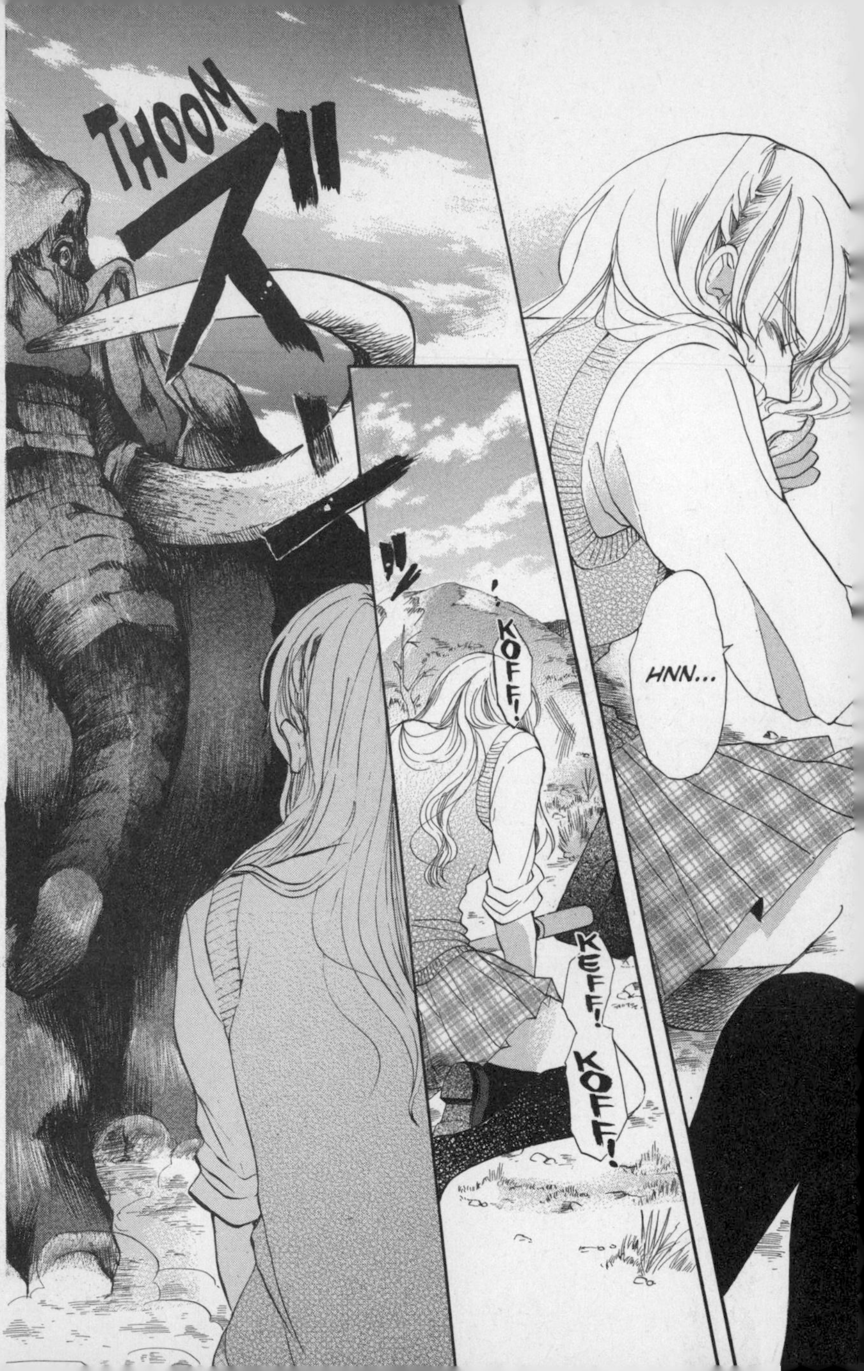
HNN...
KOFF!
KEFF! KOFF!
THOOM

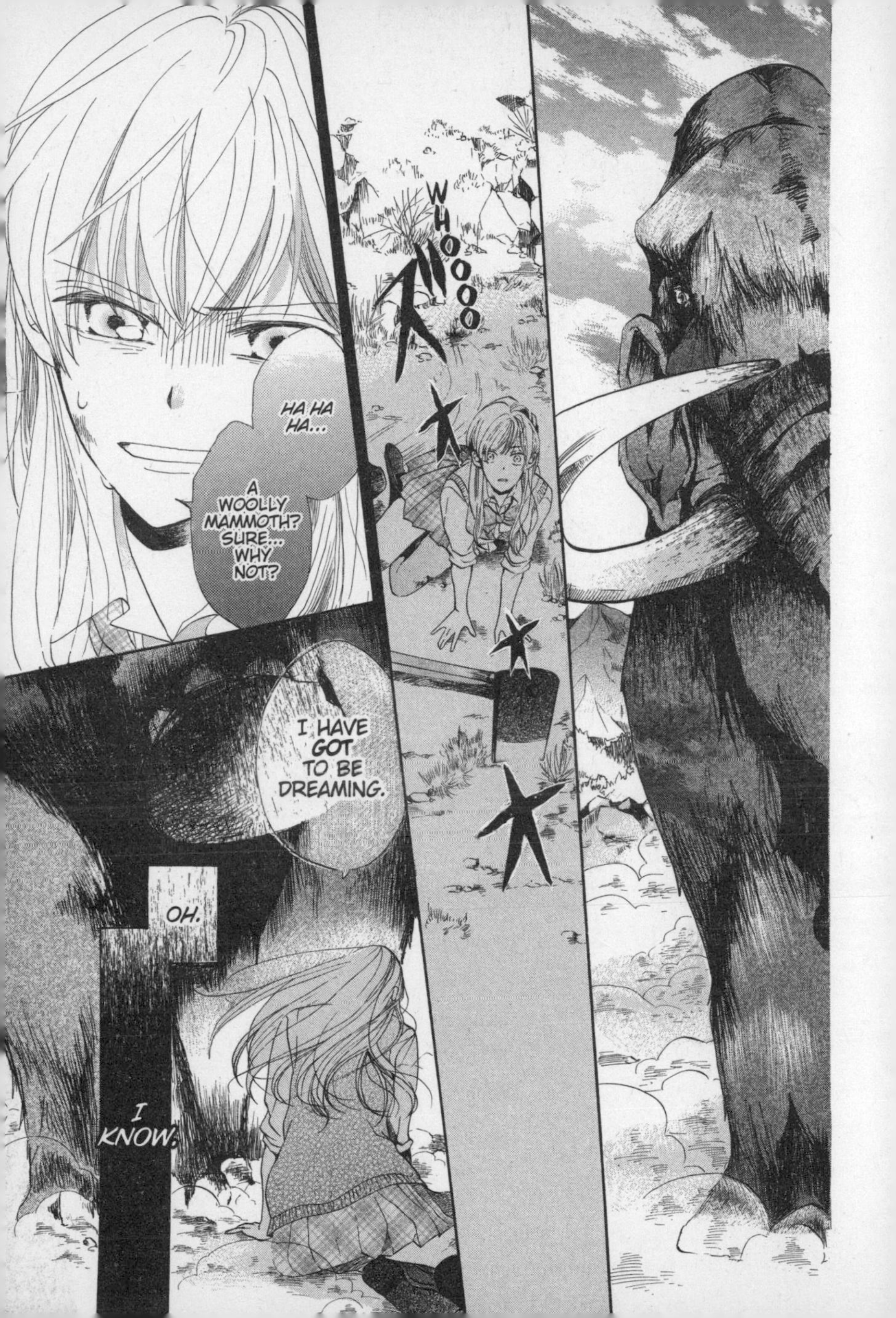
WHOOOOO
HA HA HA...
A WOOLLY MAMMOTH? SURE... WHY NOT?
I HAVE GOT TO BE DREAMING.
OH.
I KNOW.

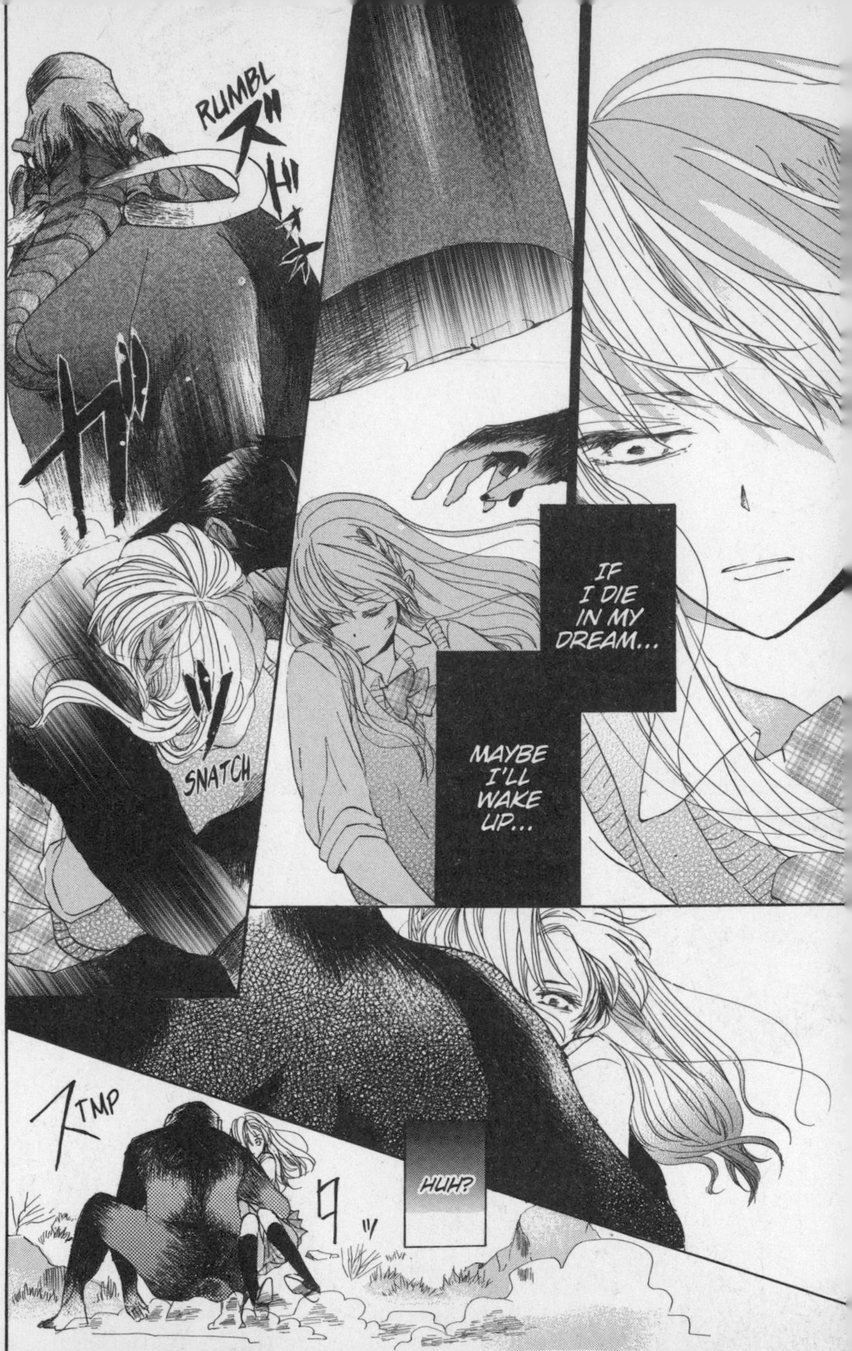
IF I DIE IN MY DREAM...
MAYBE I'LL WAKE UP...
RUMBL
SNATCH
HUH?
TMP

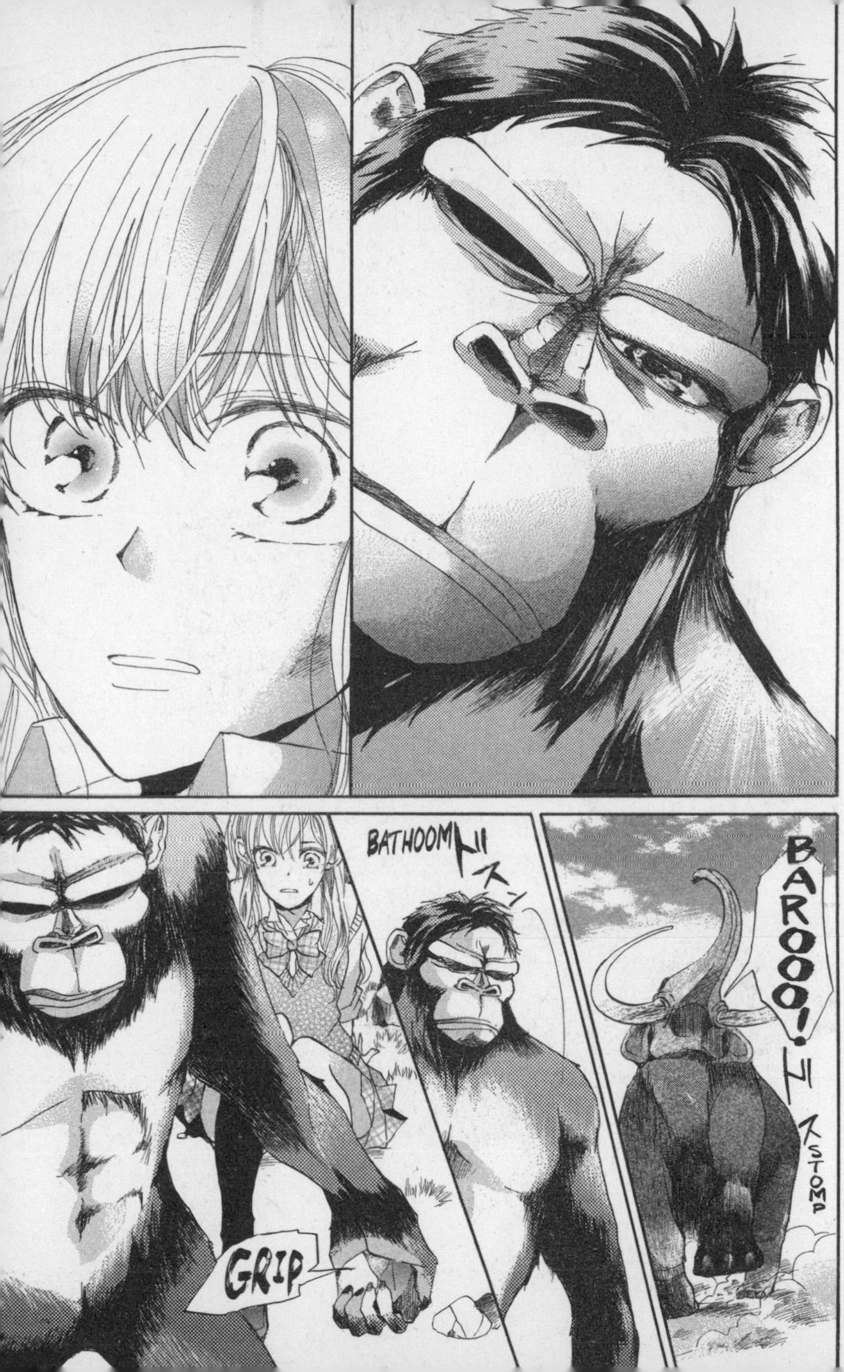
BAROOOO!
STOMP
BATHOOM
GRIP

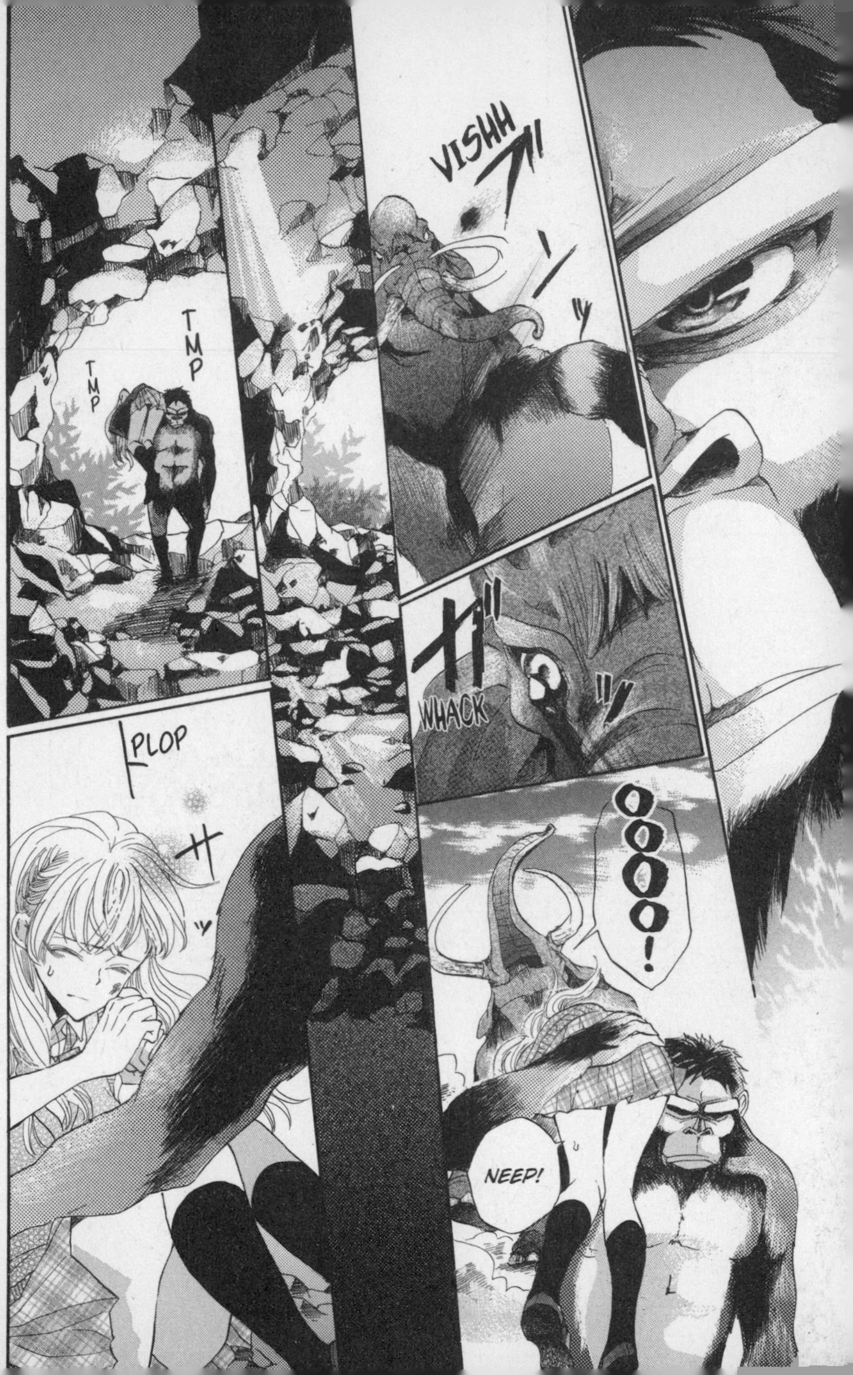
VISHH
WHACK
OOOO!
NEEP!
TMP
TMP
PLOP

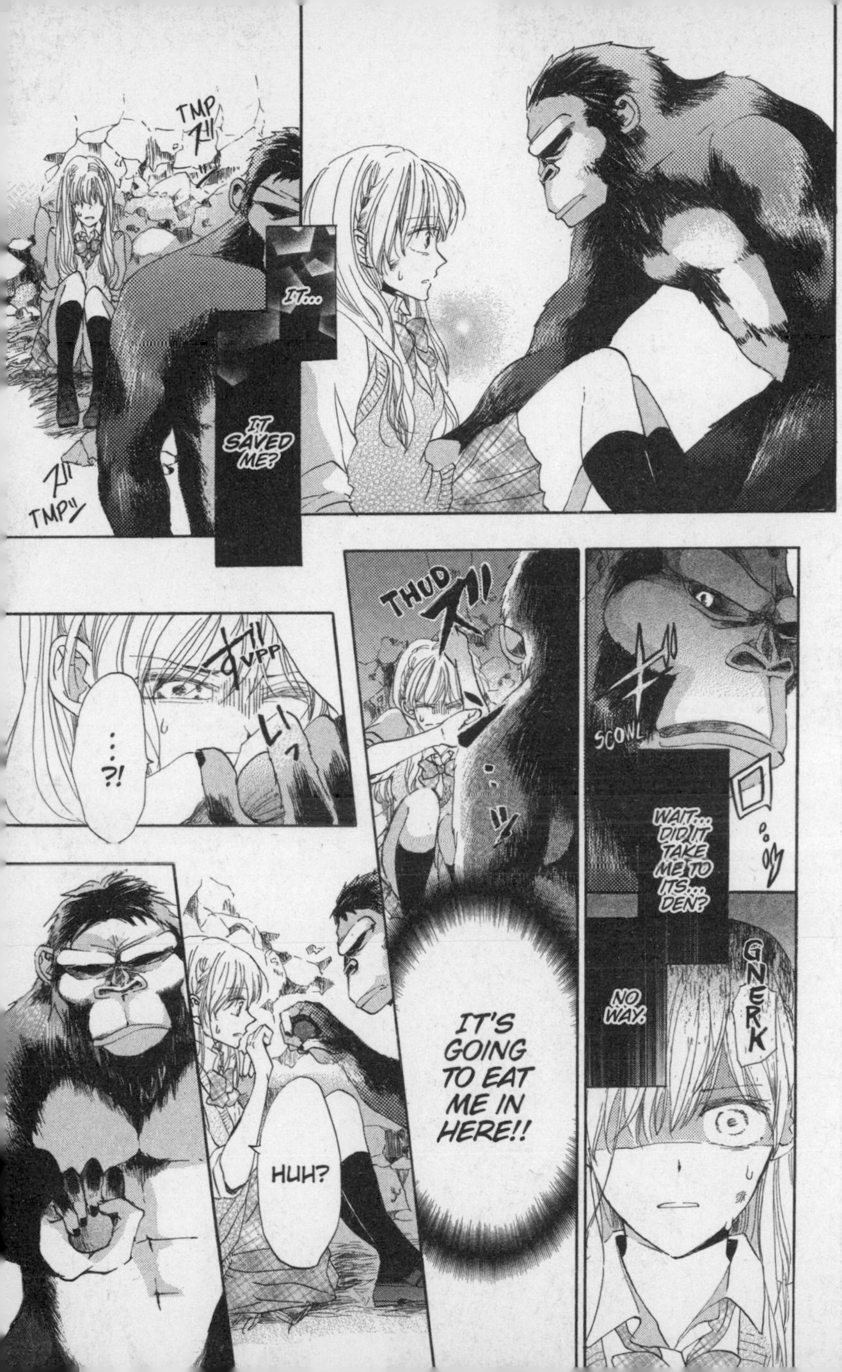
IT...
IT SAVED ME?
TMP
TMP
SCOWL
WAIT... DID IT TAKE ME TO ITS... DEN?
GNERK
NO WAY.
THUD
IT'S GOING TO EAT ME IN HERE!!
VPP
...?!
HUH?

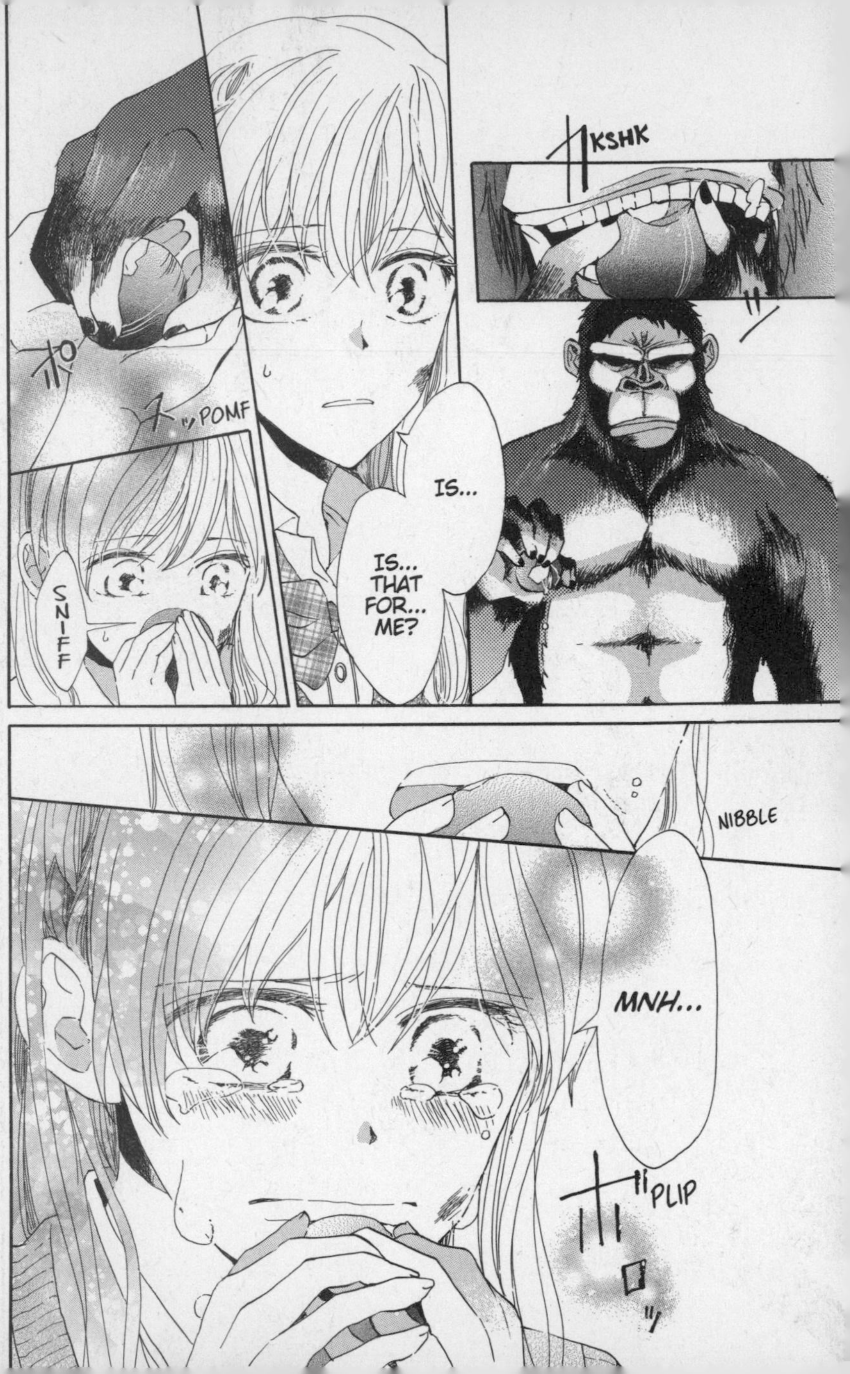
KSHK
IS...
IS... THAT FOR... ME?
POMF
SNIFF
NIBBLE
MNH...
PLIP

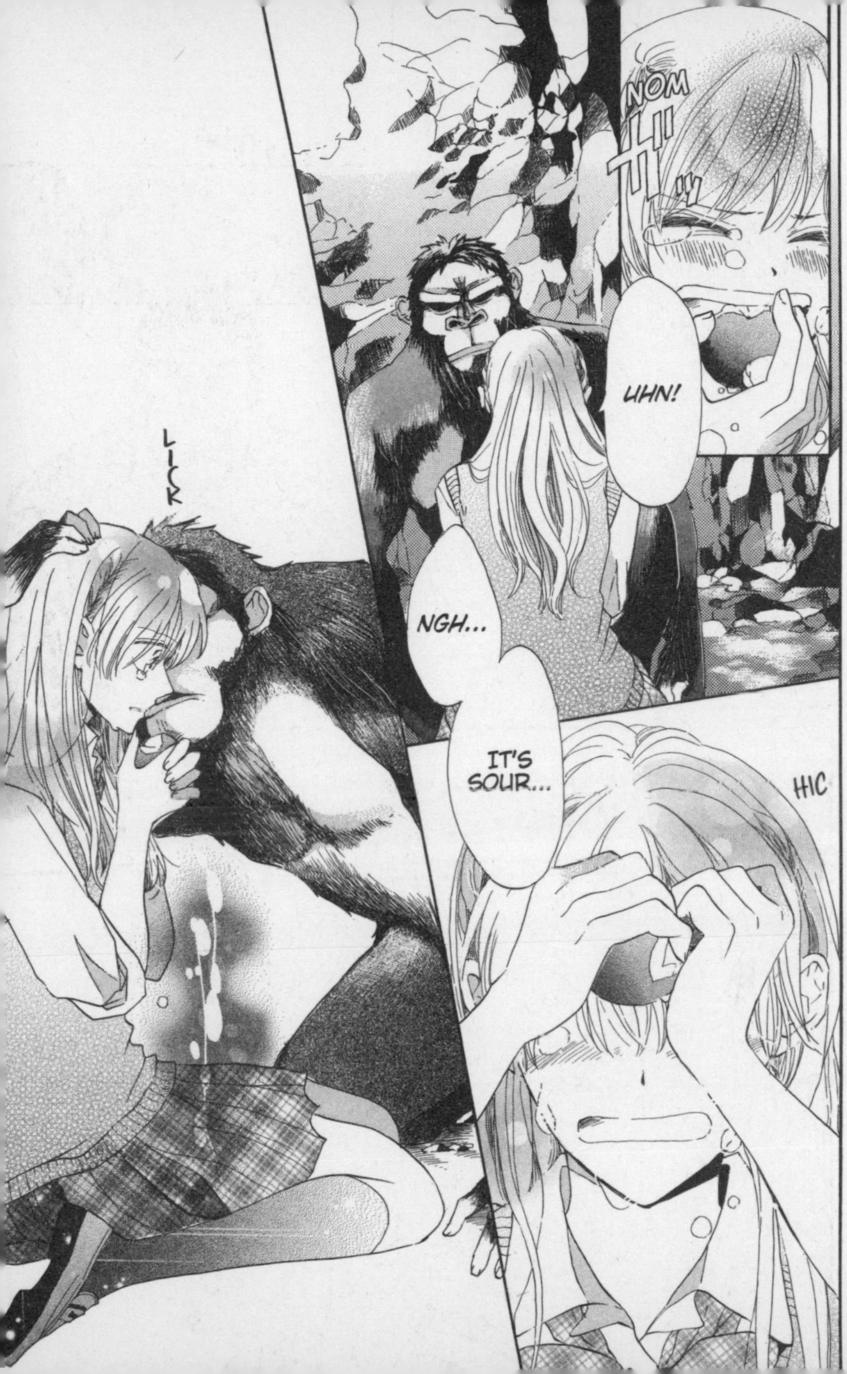
NOM
UHN!
NGH...
IT'S SOUR...
HIC
LICK

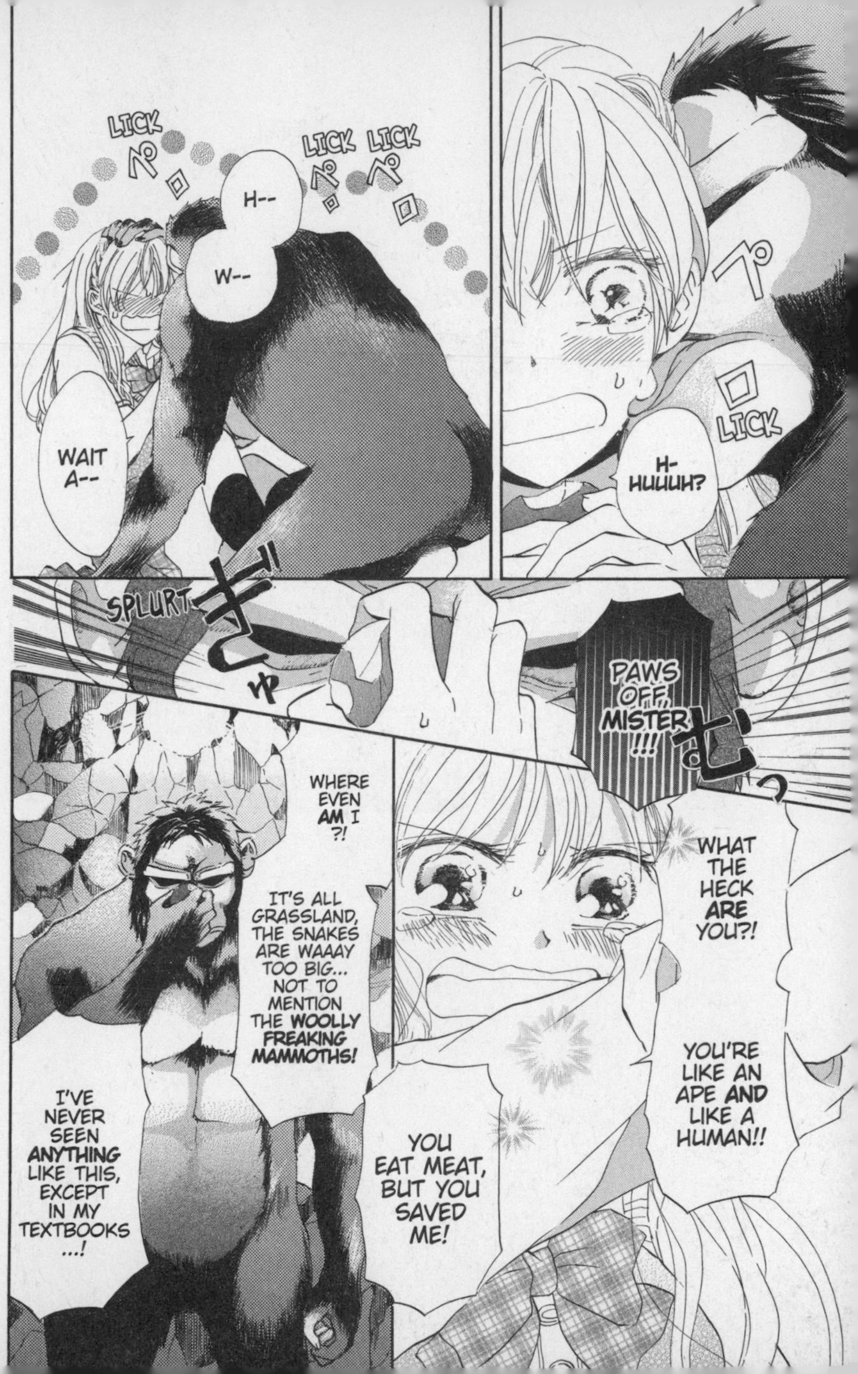
ペロ
LICK
H-HUUUH?
LICK
ペロ
LICK LICK
ペロペロ
H--
W--
WAIT A--
SPLURT
ぎゅ
PAWS OFF, MISTER!!!
むっ
WHAT THE HECK ARE YOU?!
YOU'RE LIKE AN APE AND LIKE A HUMAN!!
YOU EAT MEAT, BUT YOU SAVED ME!
WHERE EVEN AM I ?!
IT'S ALL GRASSLAND, THE SNAKES ARE WAAAY TOO BIG... NOT TO MENTION THE WOOLLY FREAKING MAMMOTHS!
I'VE NEVER SEEN ANYTHING LIKE THIS, EXCEPT IN MY TEXTBOOKS ...!

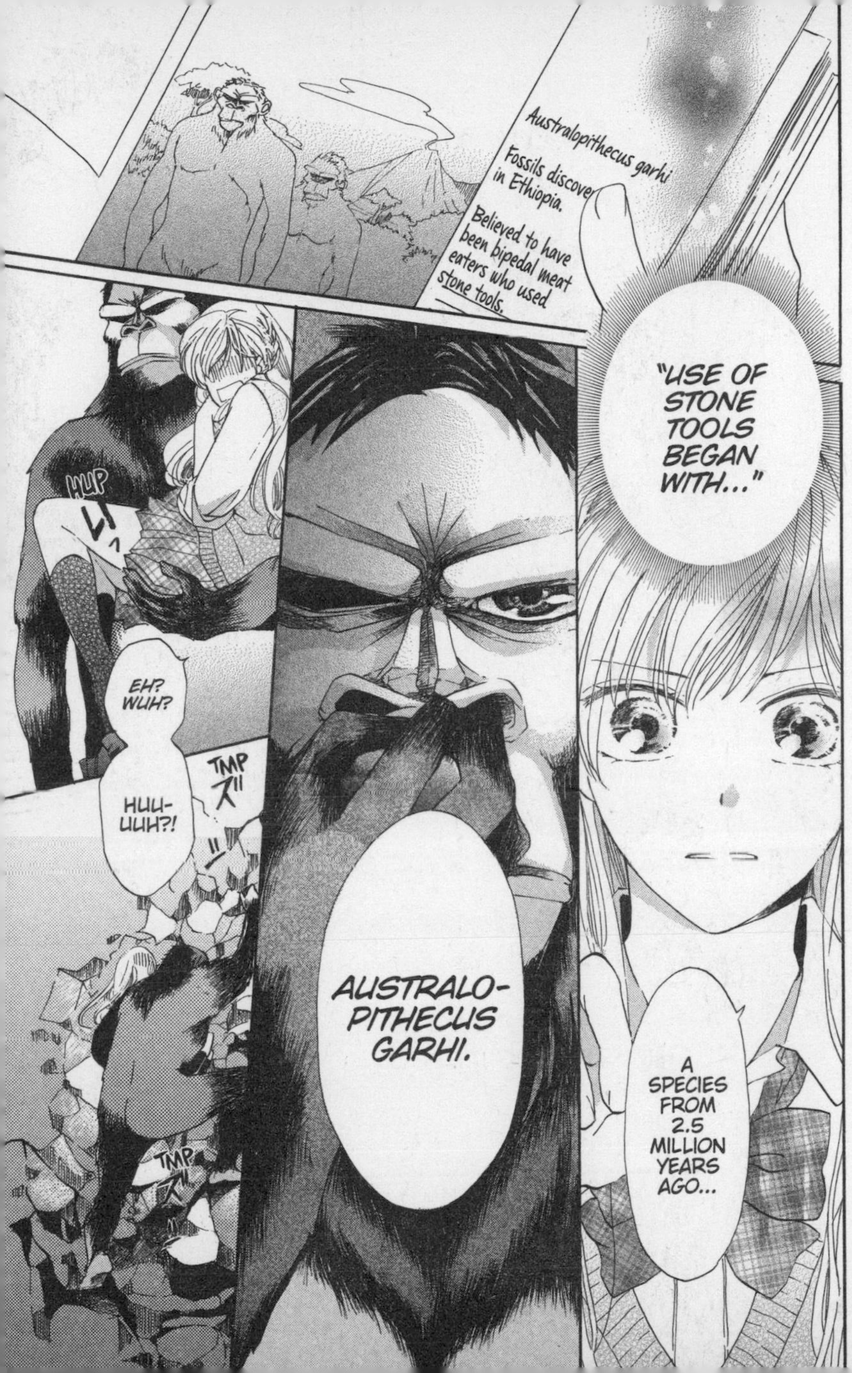
Australopithecus garhi
Fossils discove in Ethiopia.
Believed to have been bipedal meat eaters who used stone tools.
"USE OF STONE TOOLS BEGAN WITH..."
A SPECIES FROM 2.5 MILLION YEARS AGO...
AUSTRALO-PITHECUS GARHI.
HUP
EH? WUH?
TMP
HUU-UUH?!
TMP

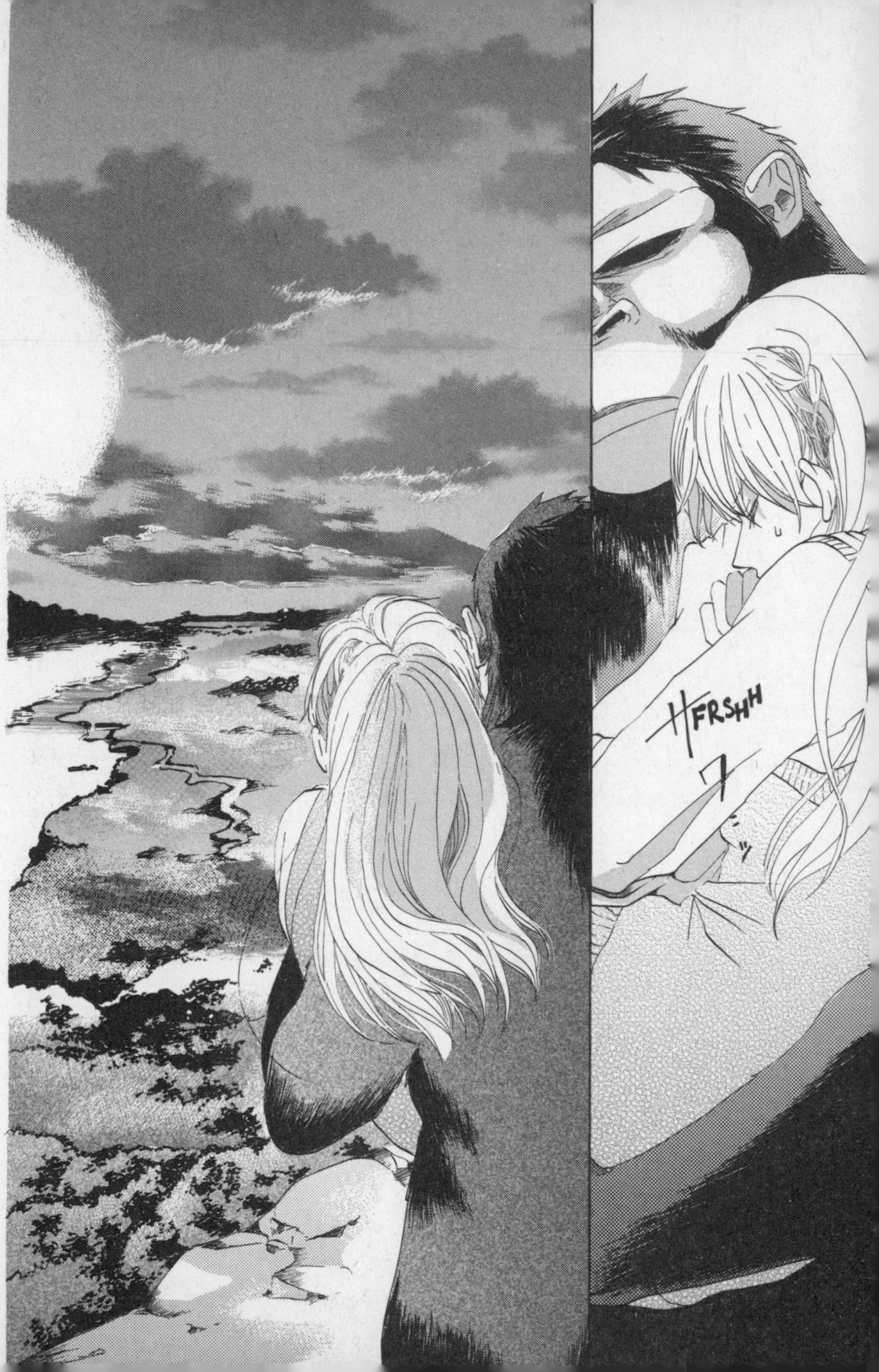
HFRSHH

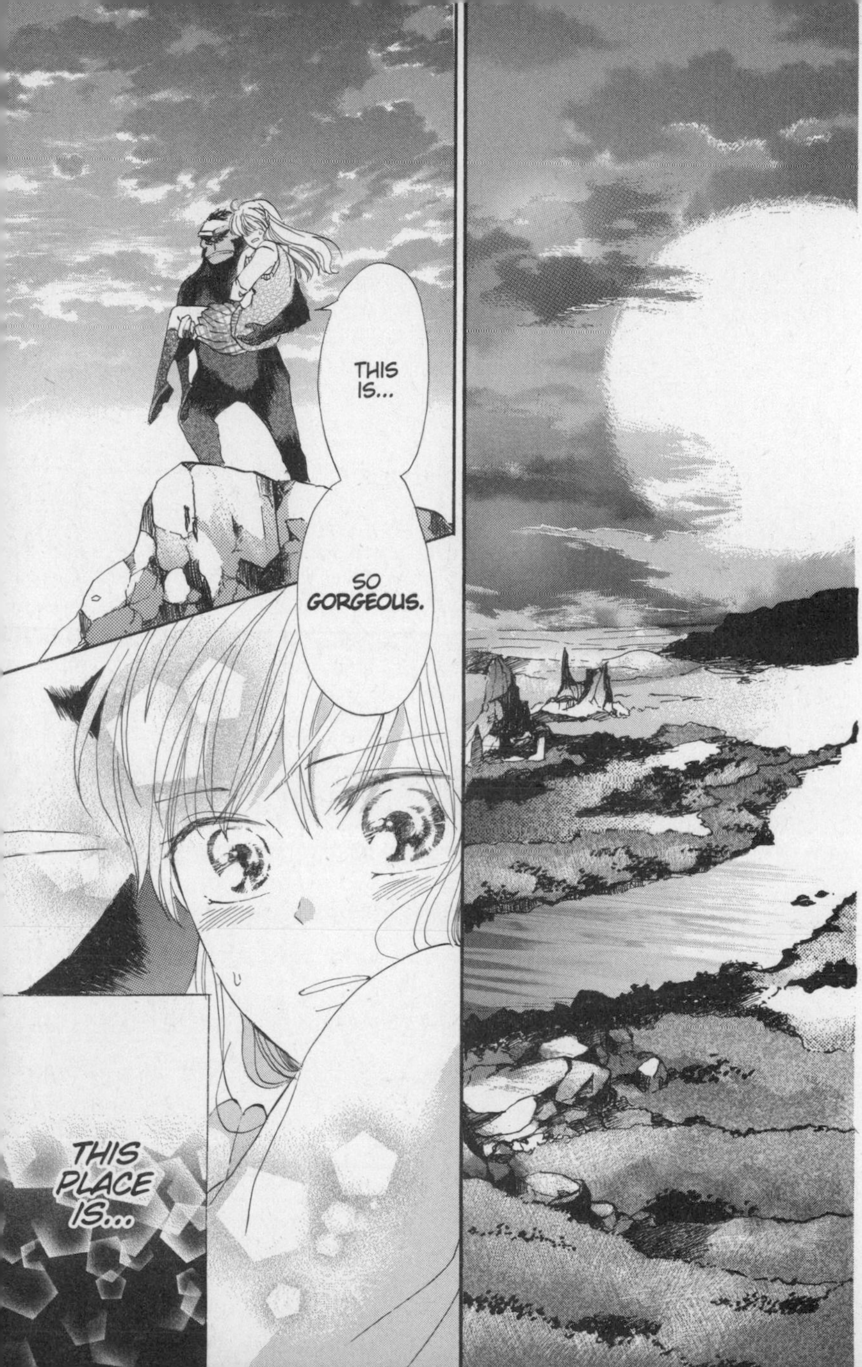
THIS IS...
SO GORGEOUS.
THIS PLACE IS...

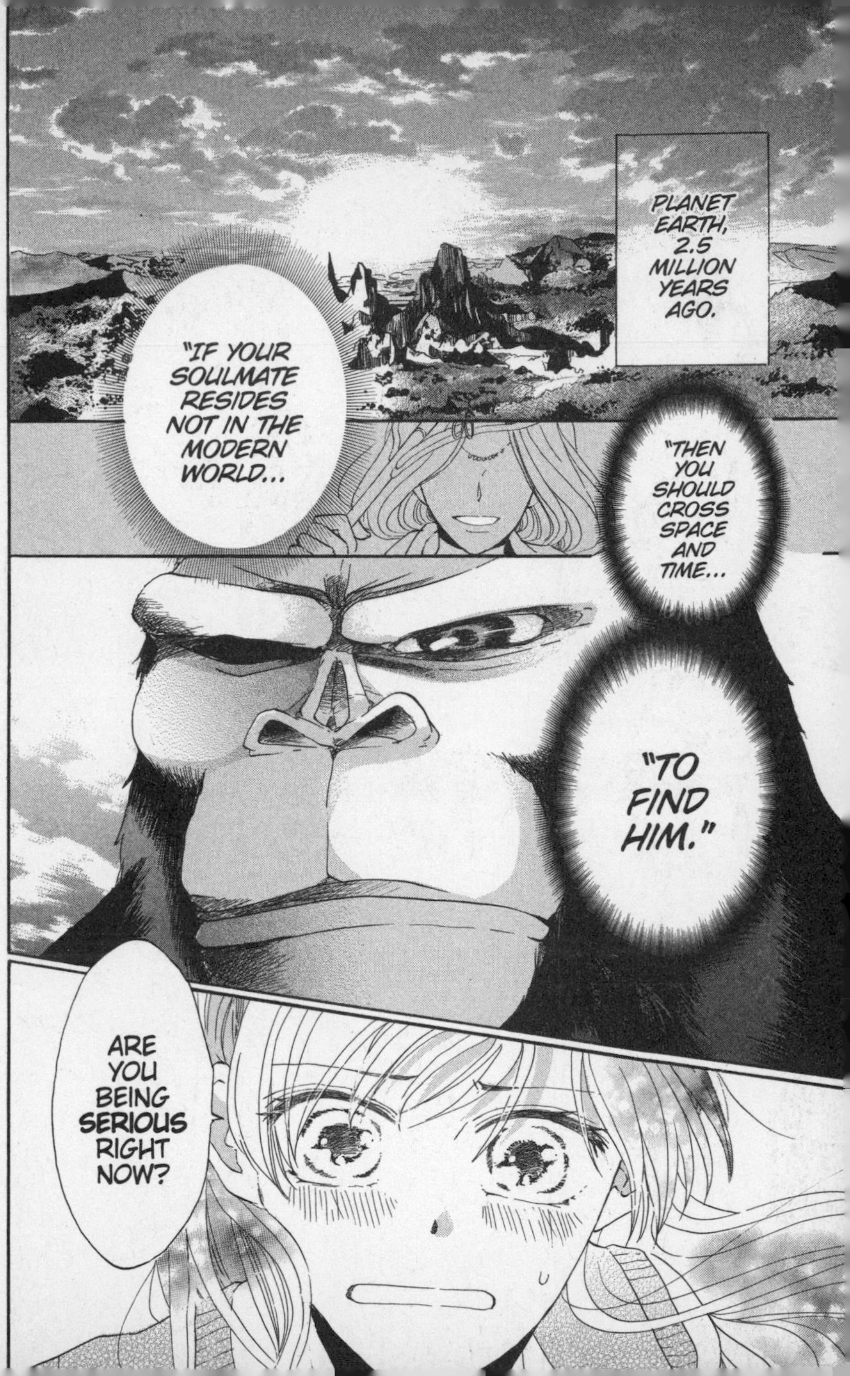
PLANET EARTH, 2.5 MILLION YEARS AGO.
"IF YOUR SOULMATE RESIDES NOT IN THE MODERN WORLD...
"THEN YOU SHOULD CROSS SPACE AND TIME...
"TO FIND HIM."
ARE YOU BEING SERIOUS RIGHT NOW?

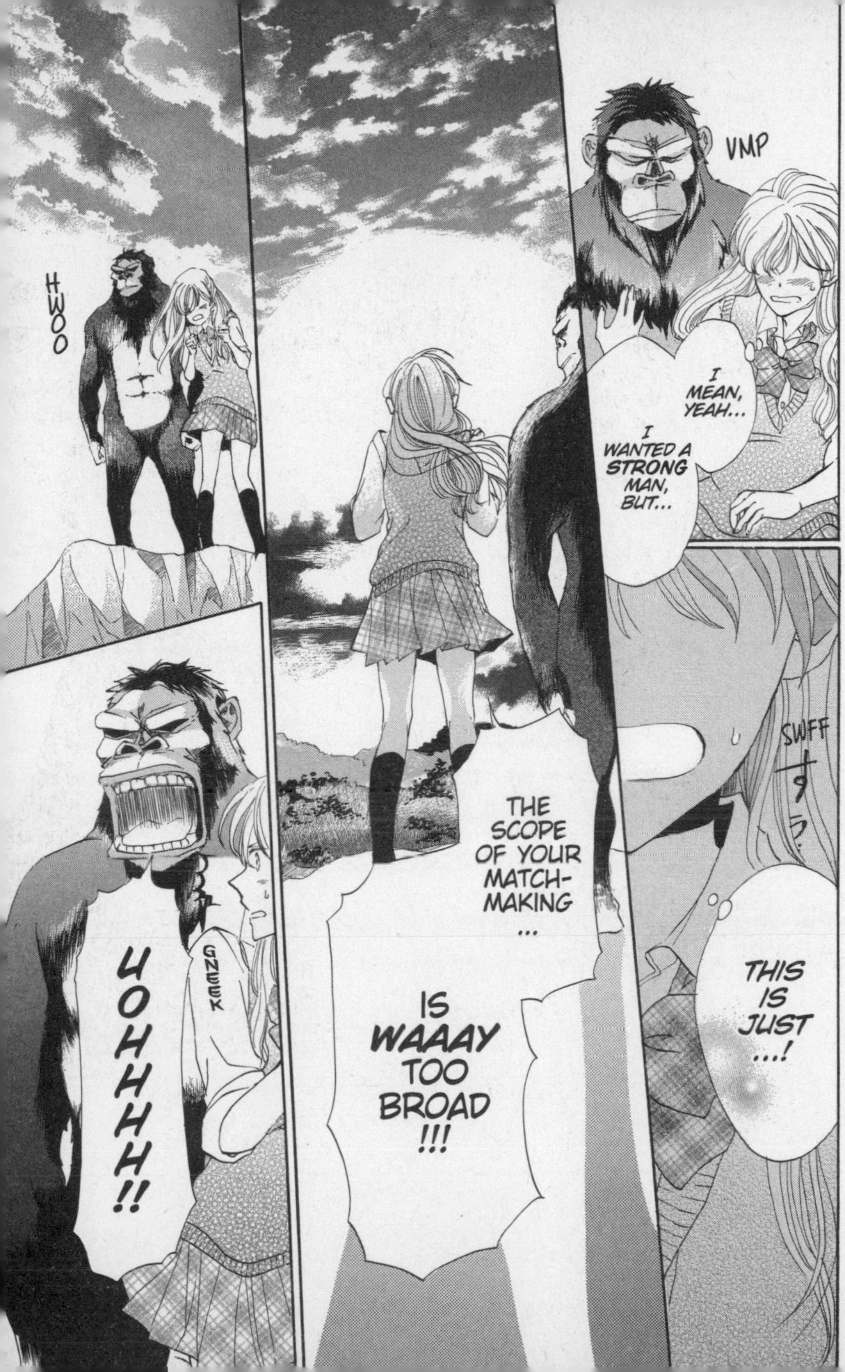
VMP
I MEAN, YEAH...
I WANTED A STRONG MAN, BUT...
SWFF
THIS IS JUST ...!
THE SCOPE OF YOUR MATCH-MAKING ...
IS WAAAY TOO BROAD!!!
HWOO
UOHHHHH!!
GNEEK

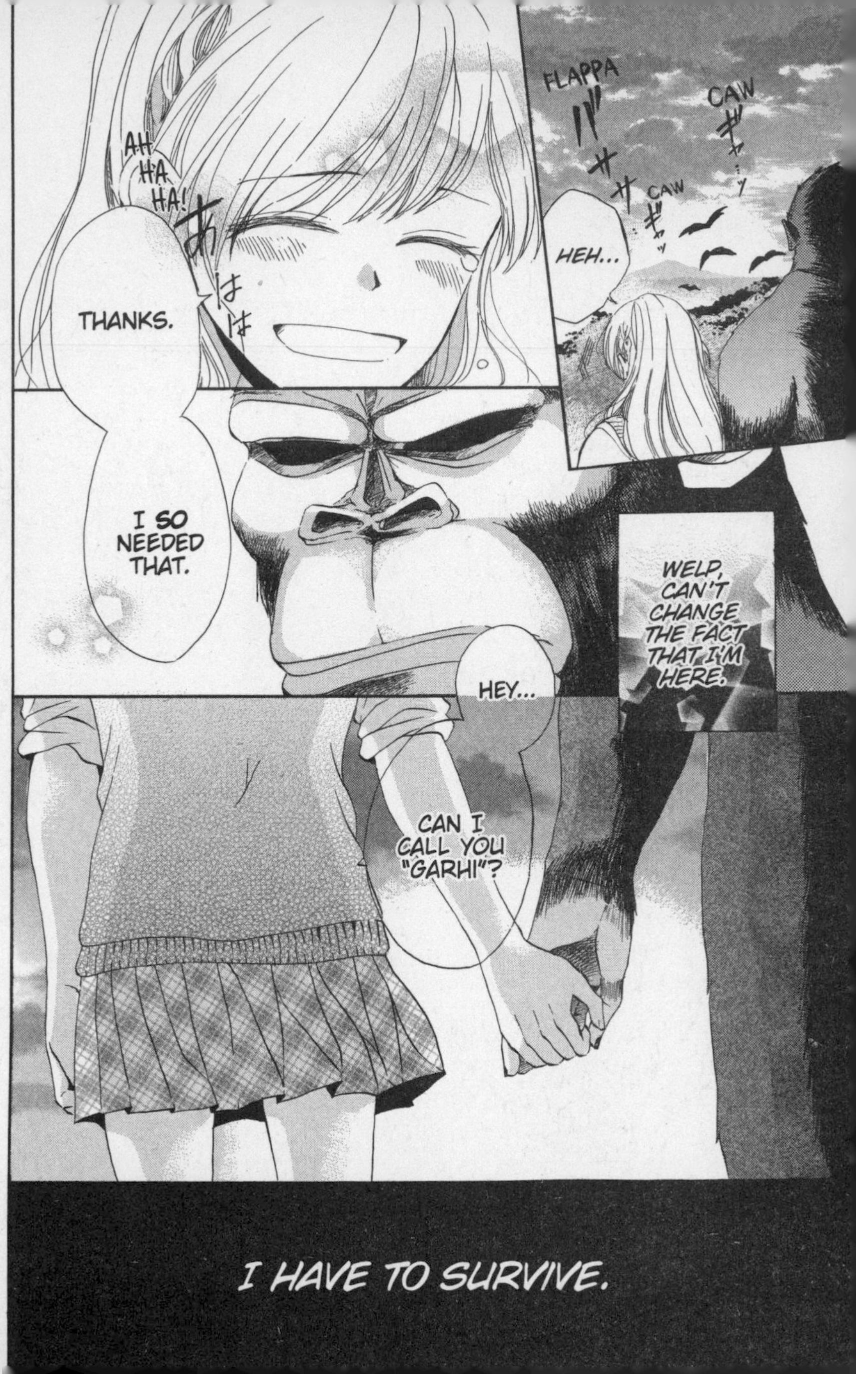
FLAPPA
CAW
CAW
HEH...
AH HA HA!
THANKS.
I SO NEEDED THAT.
WELP, CAN'T CHANGE THE FACT THAT I'M HERE.
HEY...
CAN I CALL YOU "GARHI"?
I HAVE TO SURVIVE.

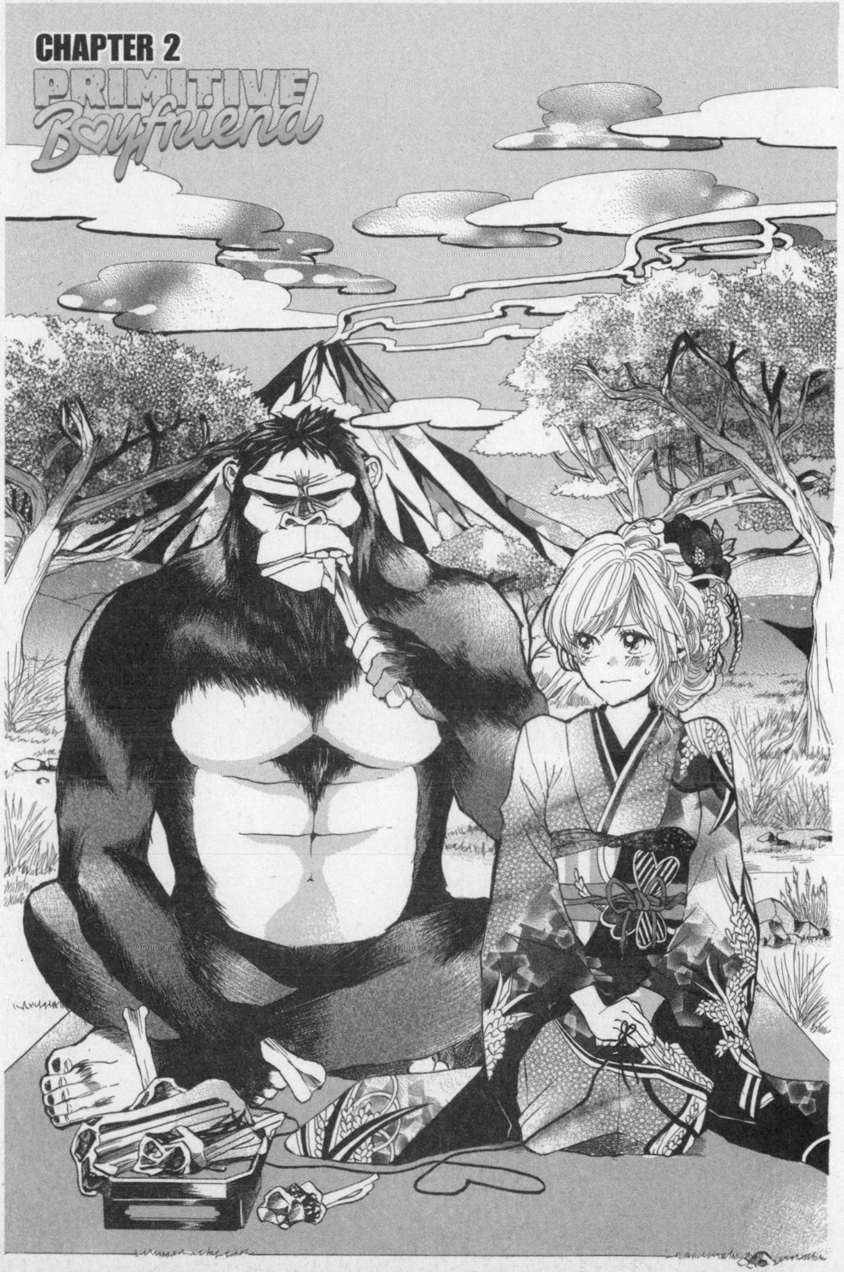
CHAPTER 2
PRIMITIVE
Boyfriend

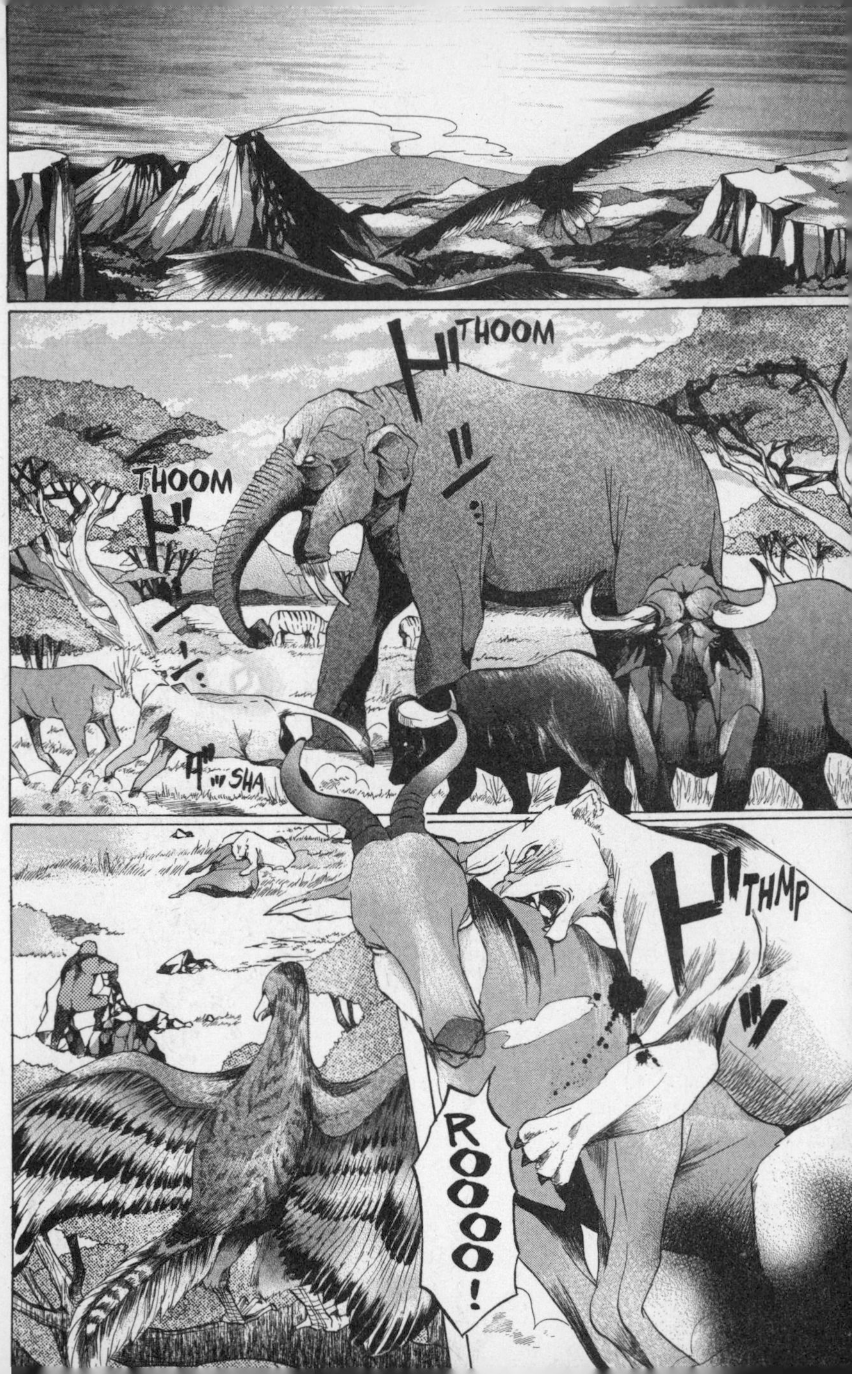
THOOM
THOOM
SHA
THMP
ROOOO!

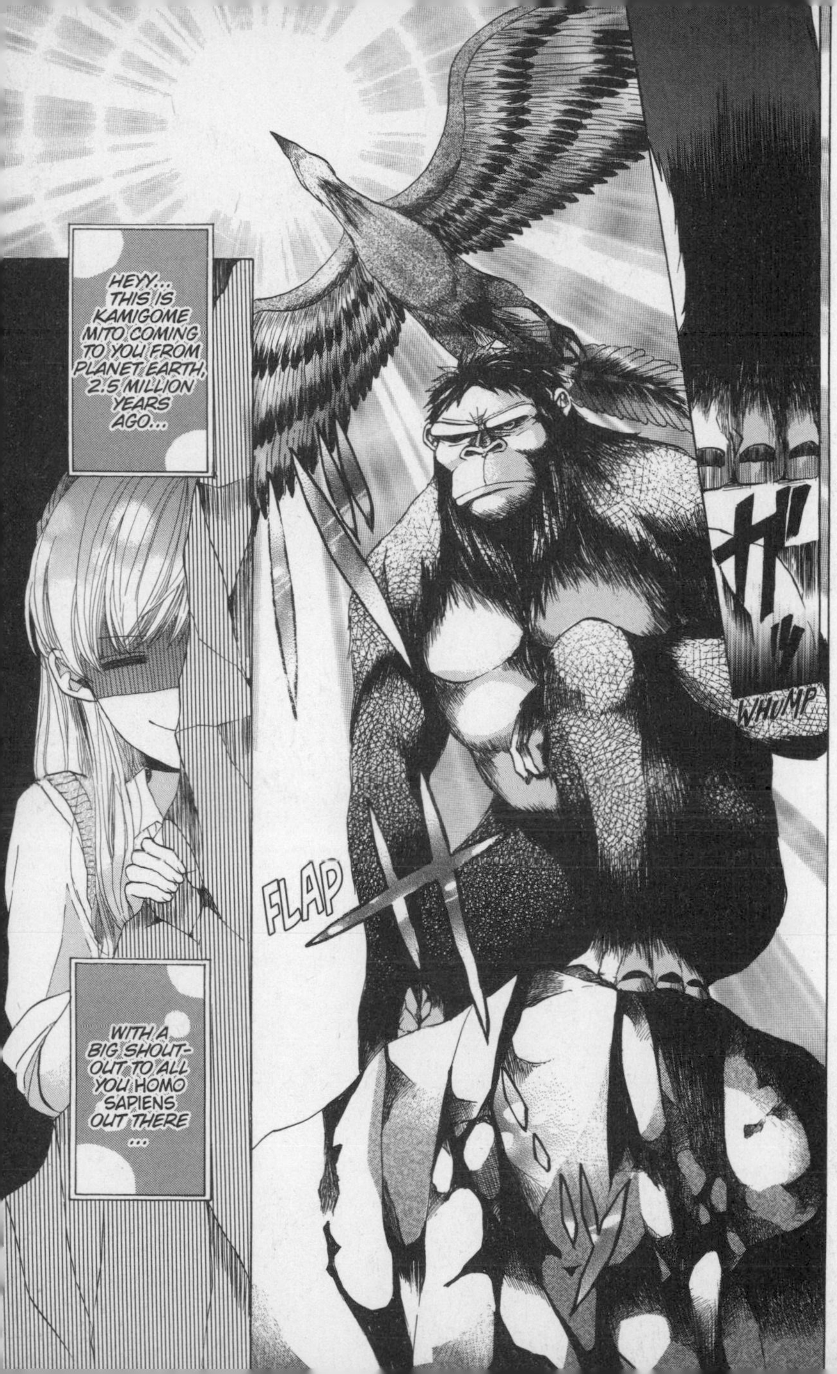
HEYY... THIS IS KAMIGOME MITO COMING TO YOU FROM PLANET EARTH, 2.5 MILLION YEARS AGO...
ザッ
WHUMP
FLAP
WITH A BIG SHOUT-OUT TO ALL YOU HOMO SAPIENS OUT THERE ...

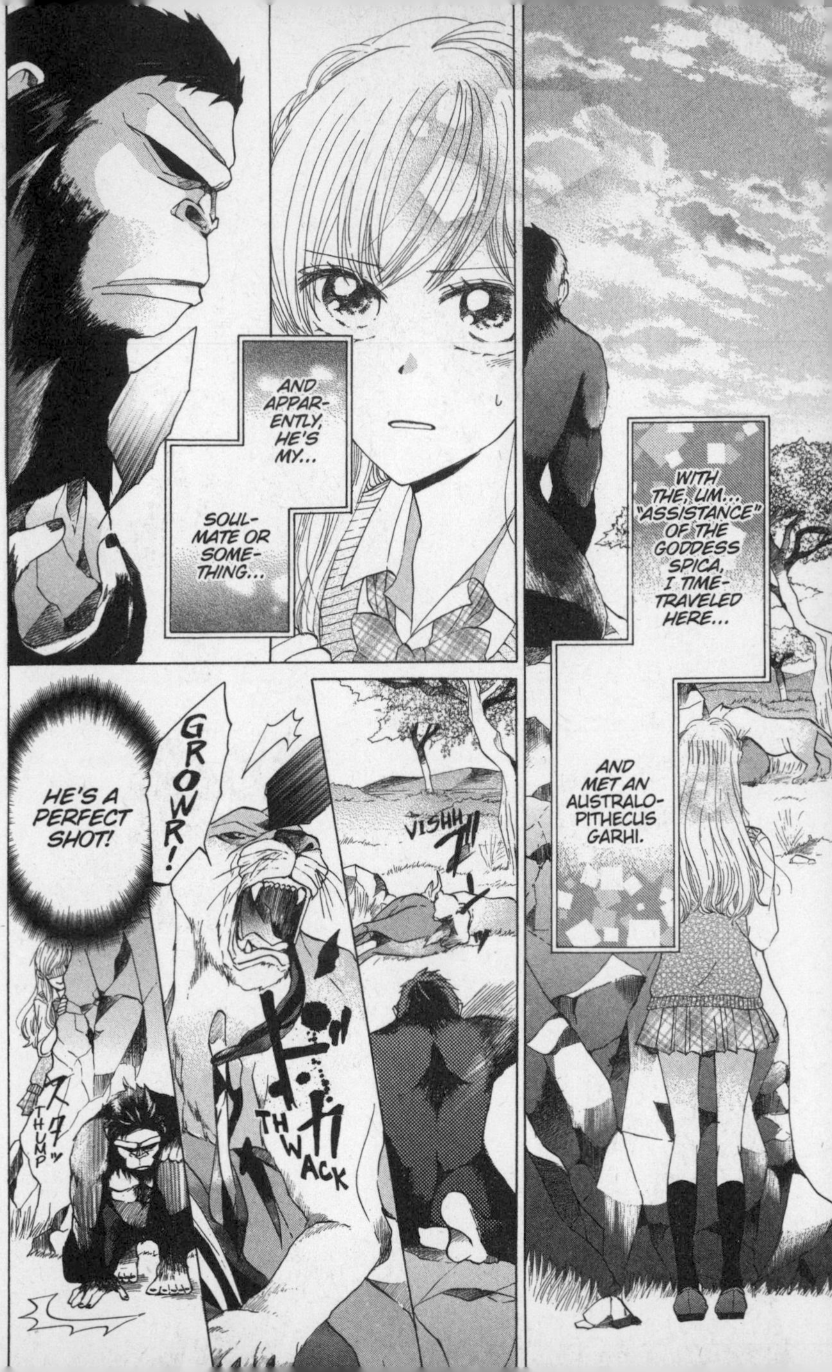
WITH THE, UM... "ASSISTANCE" OF THE GODDESS SPICA, I TIME-TRAVELED HERE...
AND MET AN AUSTRALOPITHECUS GARHI.
AND APPARENTLY, HE'S MY...
SOULMATE OR SOMETHING...
GROWR!
VISHH
THWACK
HE'S A PERFECT SHOT!
THUMP

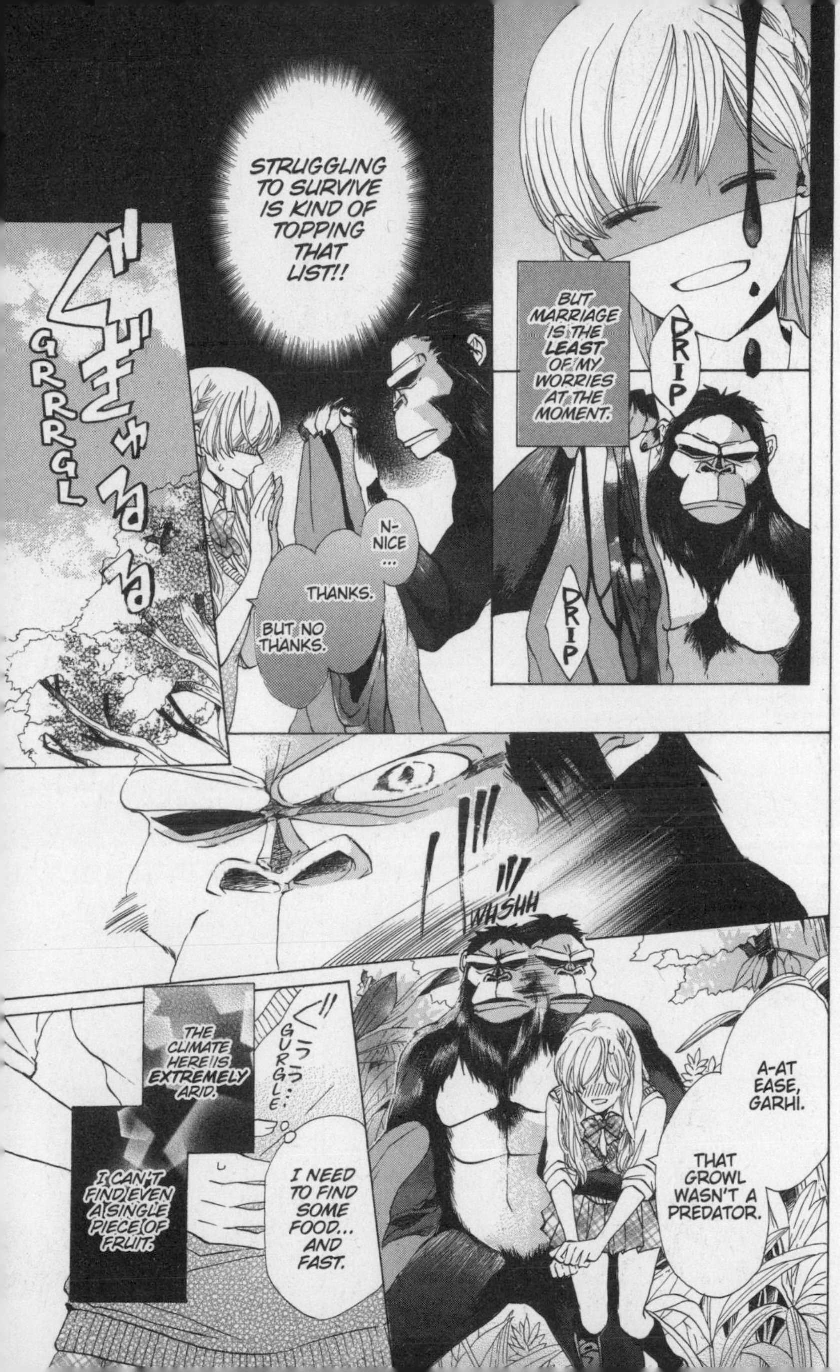
BUT MARRIAGE IS THE LEAST OF MY WORRIES AT THE MOMENT.
DRIP
DRIP
STRUGGLING TO SURVIVE IS KIND OF TOPPING THAT LIST!!
N-NICE...
THANKS.
BUT NO THANKS.
GRRRGL
WHSHH
A-AT EASE, GARHI.
THAT GROWL WASN'T A PREDATOR.
GURGLE...
I NEED TO FIND SOME FOOD... AND FAST.
THE CLIMATE HERE IS EXTREMELY ARID.
I CAN'T FIND EVEN A SINGLE PIECE OF FRUIT.

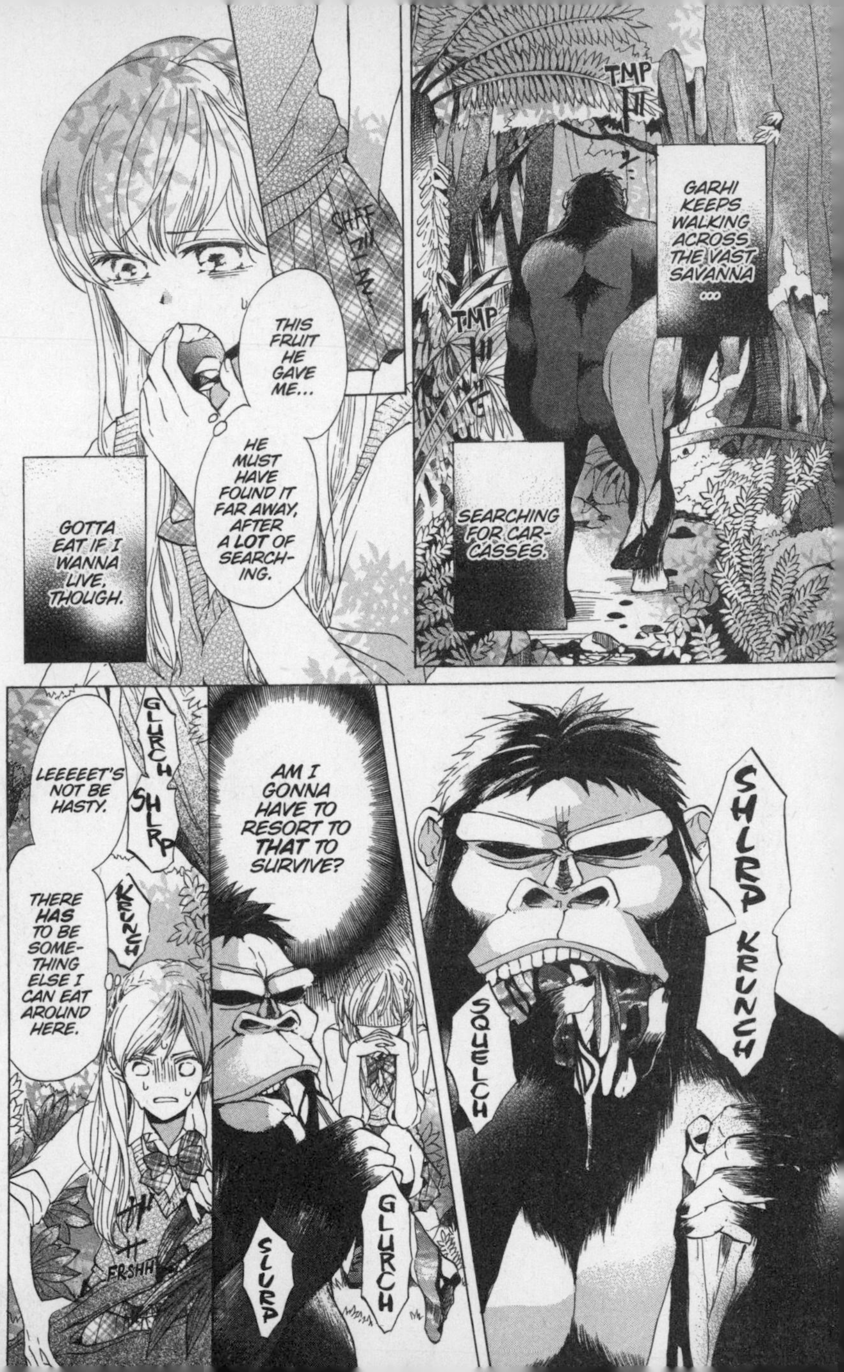
TMP
GARHI KEEPS WALKING ACROSS THE VAST SAVANNA...
TMP
SEARCHING FOR CAR-CASSES.
SHFF
THIS FRUIT HE GAVE ME...
HE MUST HAVE FOUND IT FAR AWAY, AFTER A LOT OF SEARCH-ING.
GOTTA EAT IF I WANNA LIVE, THOUGH.
SHLRP KRUNCH
SQUELCH
AM I GONNA HAVE TO RESORT TO THAT TO SURVIVE?
GLURCH
SLURP
LEEEEET'S NOT BE HASTY.
GLURCH
SHLRP
KRUNCH
THERE HAS TO BE SOME-THING ELSE I CAN EAT AROUND HERE.
FRSHH

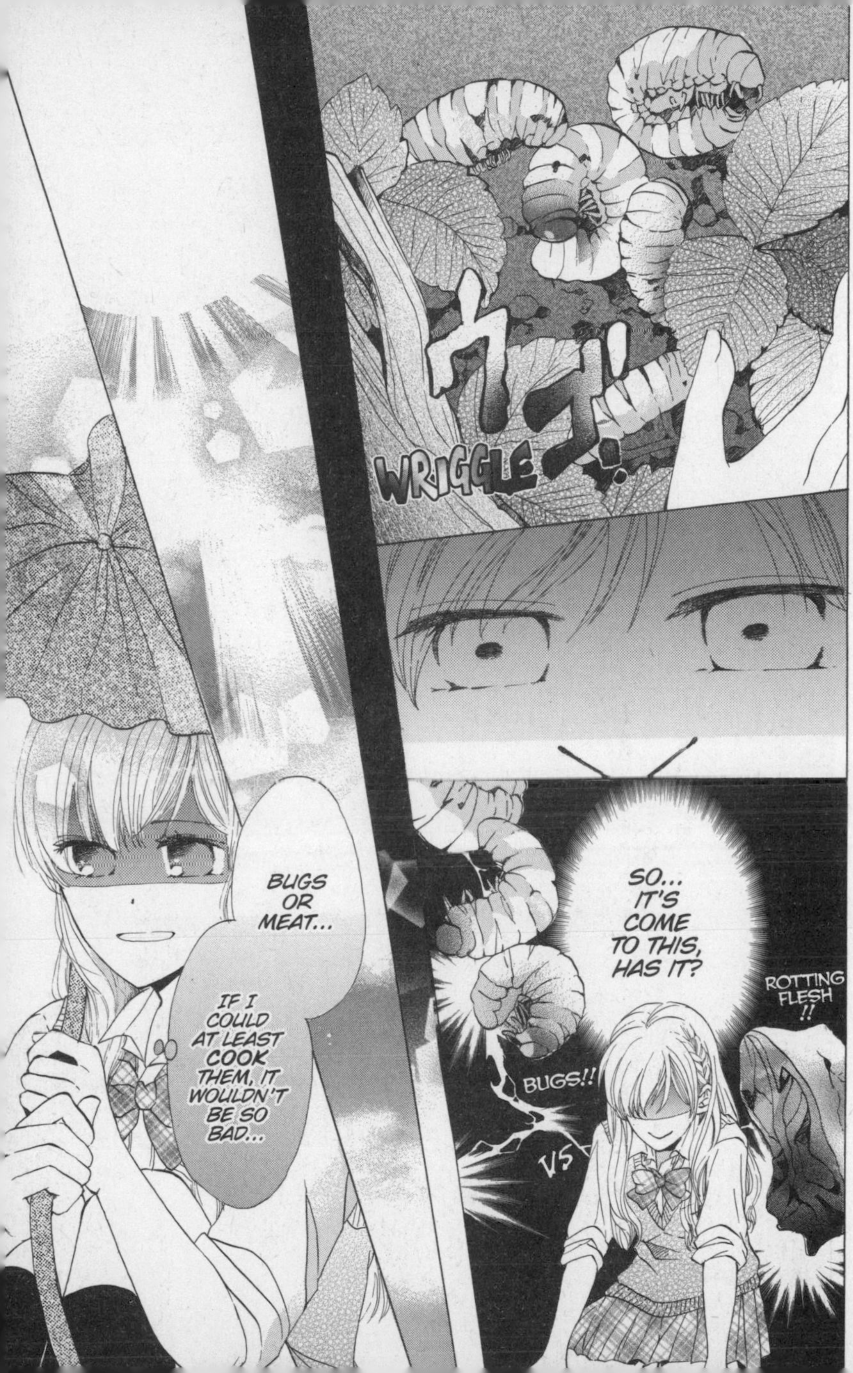
ウゾ
WRIGGLE
SO... IT'S COME TO THIS, HAS IT?
ROTTING FLESH!!
BUGS!!
VS
BUGS OR MEAT...
IF I COULD AT LEAST COOK THEM, IT WOULDN'T BE SO BAD...

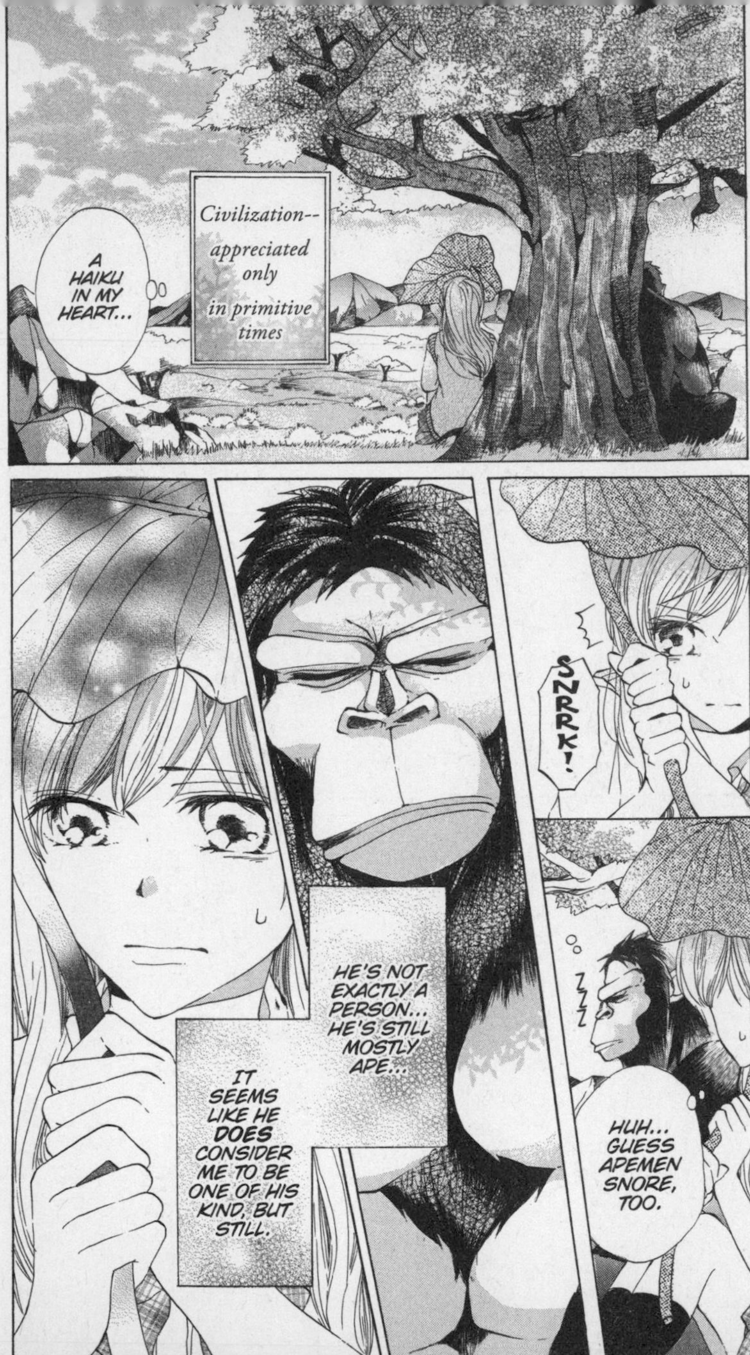
Civilization--
appreciated only in primitive times
A HAIKU IN MY HEART...
SNRRK!
ZZZ
HUH... GUESS APEMEN SNORE, TOO.
HE'S NOT EXACTLY A PERSON... HE'S STILL MOSTLY APE...
IT SEEMS LIKE HE DOES CONSIDER ME TO BE ONE OF HIS KIND, BUT STILL.

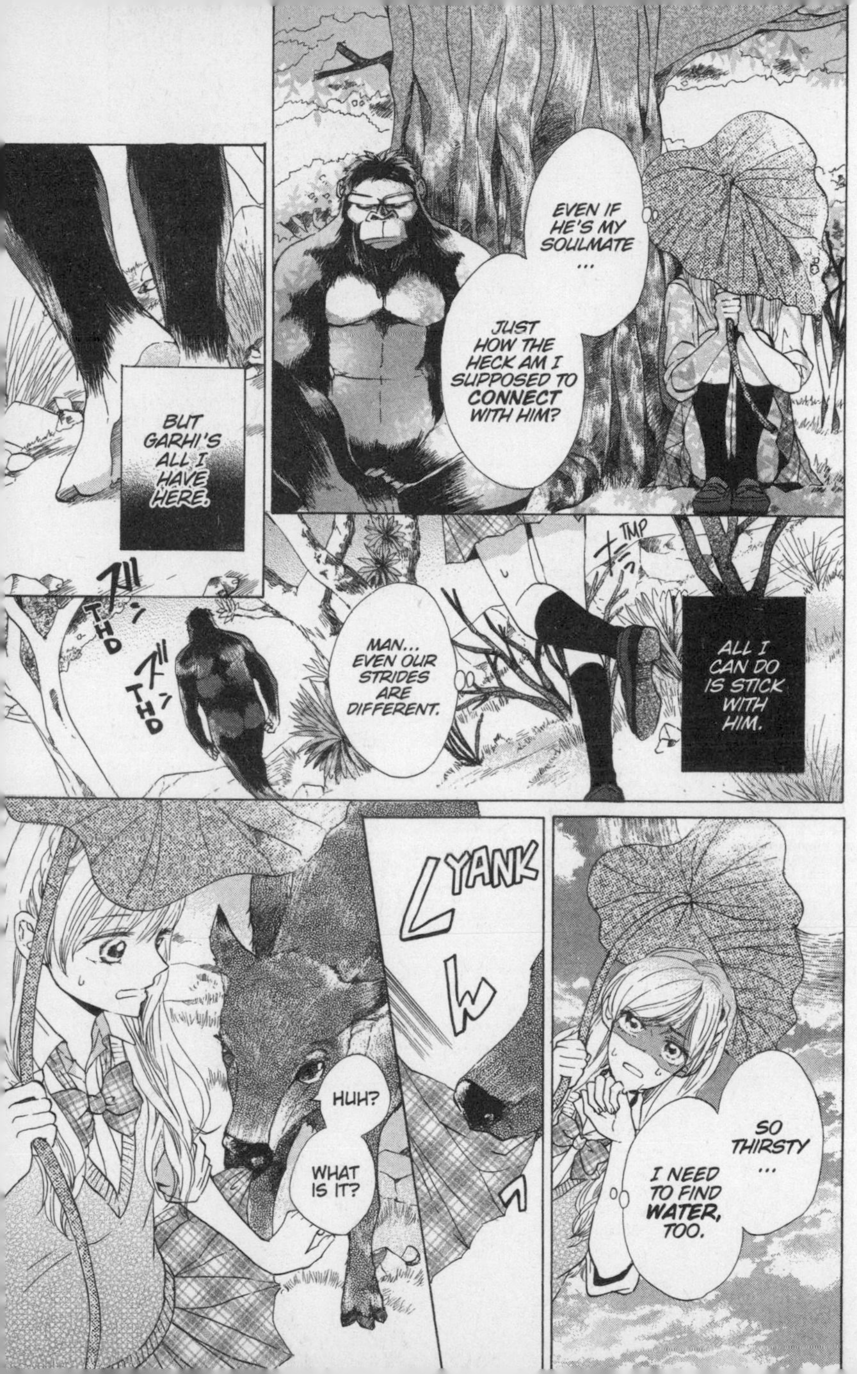

EVEN IF HE'S MY SOULMATE ...
JUST HOW THE HECK AM I SUPPOSED TO CONNECT WITH HIM?
BUT GARHI'S ALL I HAVE HERE.
TMP
ALL I CAN DO IS STICK WITH HIM.
MAN... EVEN OUR STRIDES ARE DIFFERENT.
THD
THD
SO THIRSTY ...
I NEED TO FIND WATER, TOO.
YANK
HUH?
WHAT IS IT?

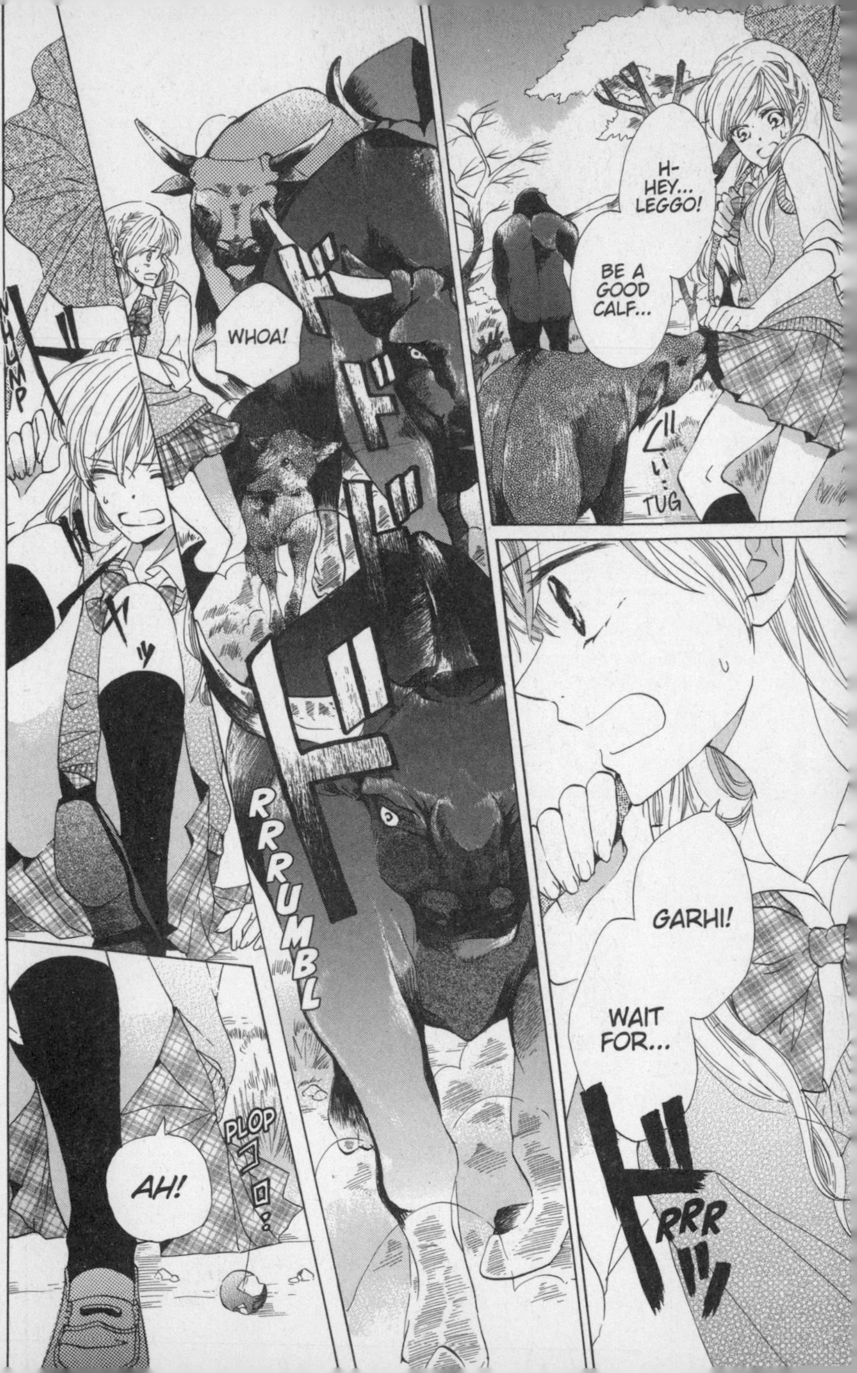
H-HEY... LEGGO!
BE A GOOD CALF...
TUG
WHOA!
RRRUMBL
WHUMP
GARHI!
WAIT FOR...
RRR
AH!
PLOP

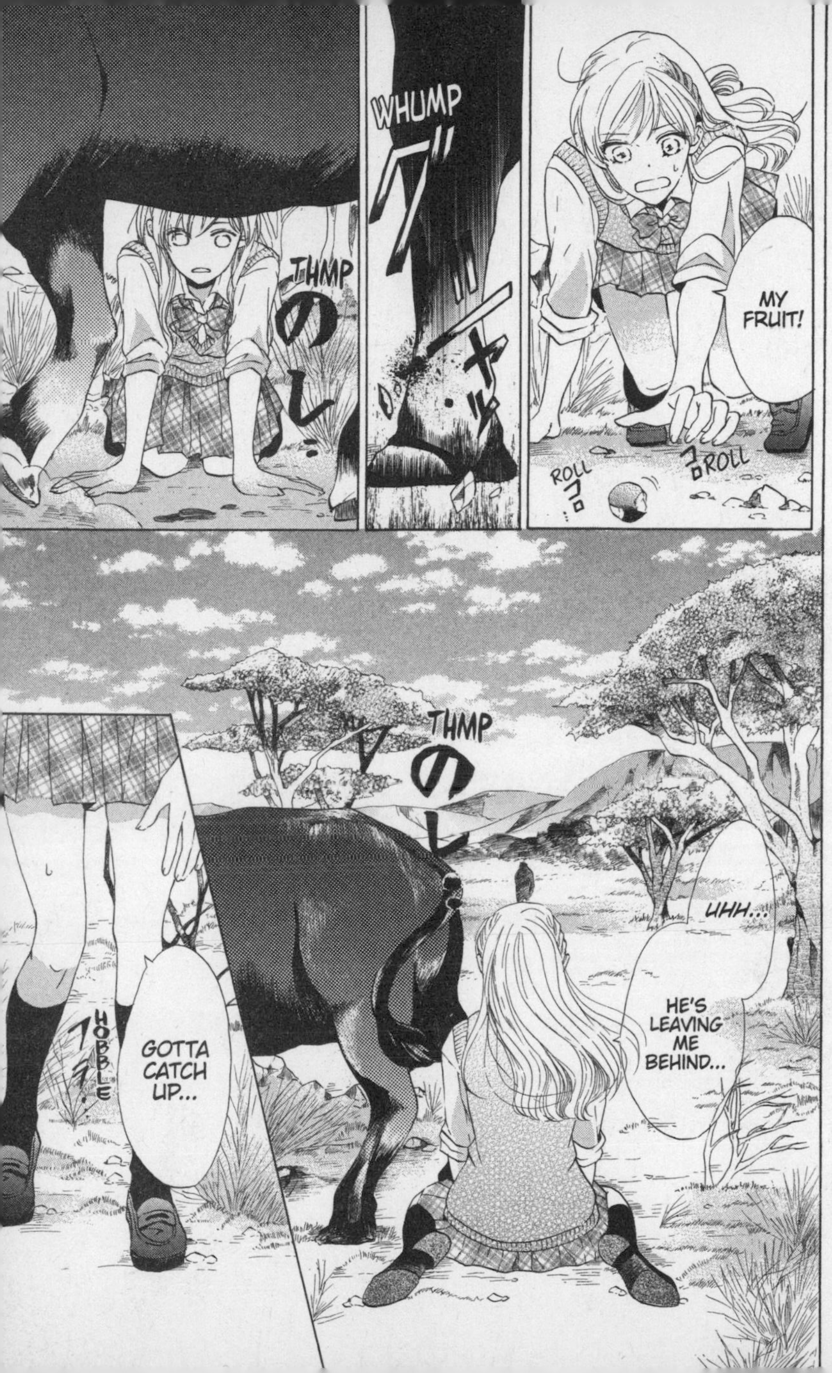
MY FRUIT!
ROLL
ROLL
WHUMP
THMP
のし
UHH...
HE'S LEAVING ME BEHIND...
THMP
のし
GOTTA CATCH UP...
HOBBLE

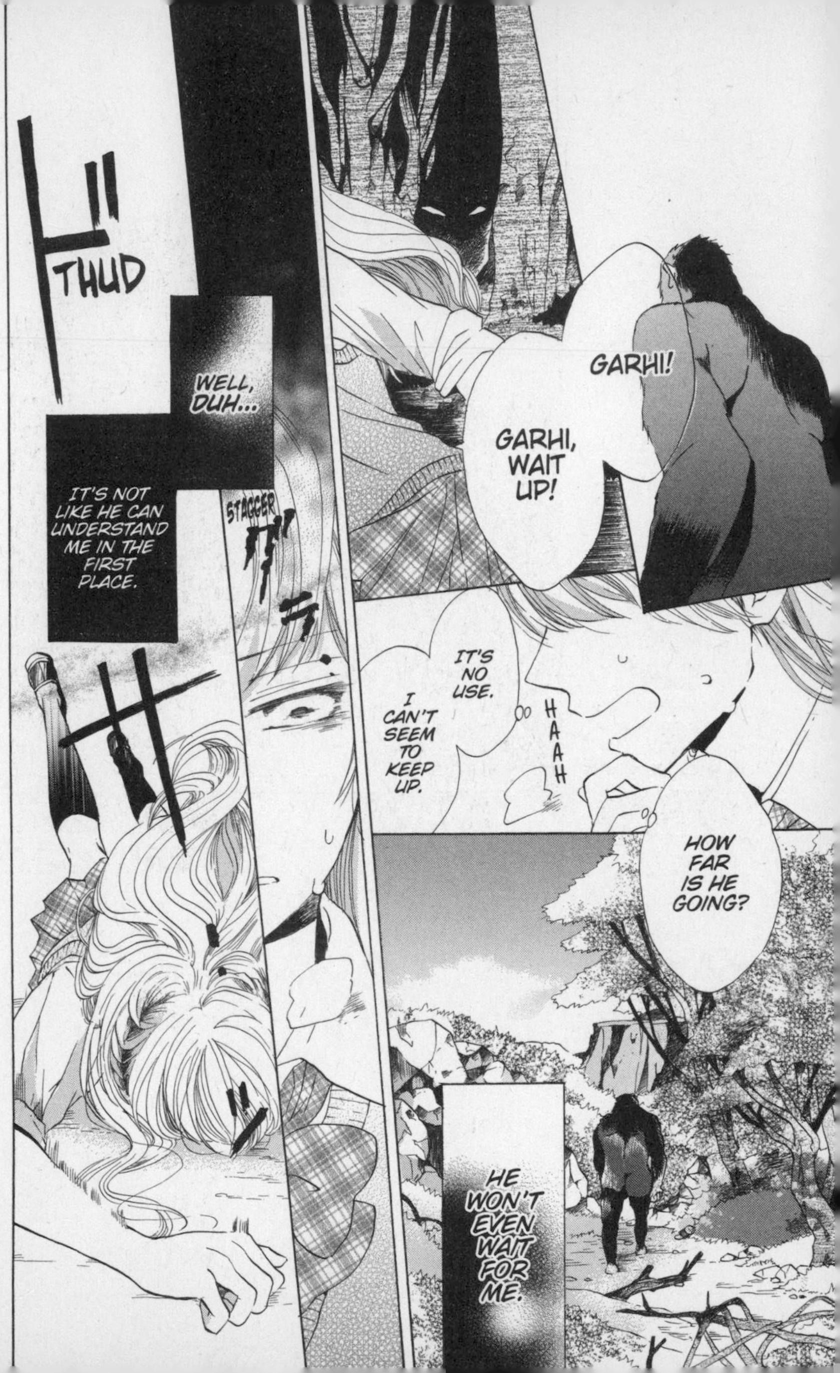
GARHI!
GARHI, WAIT UP!
IT'S NO USE.
HAAH
I CAN'T SEEM TO KEEP UP.
HOW FAR IS HE GOING?
HE WON'T EVEN WAIT FOR ME.
STAGGER
WELL, DUH...
IT'S NOT LIKE HE CAN UNDERSTAND ME IN THE FIRST PLACE.
THUD

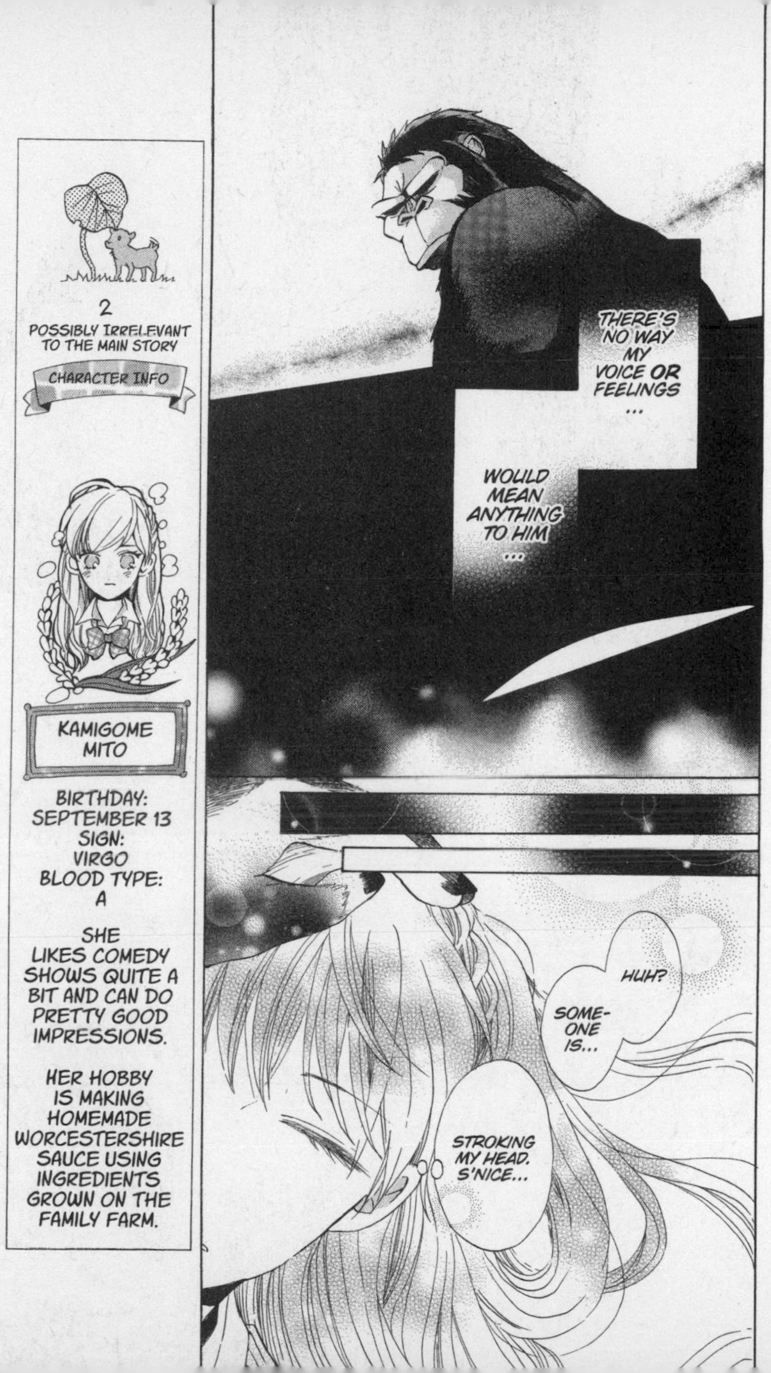
THERE'S NO WAY MY VOICE OR FEELINGS...
WOULD MEAN ANYTHING TO HIM...
HUH?
SOME-ONE IS...
STROKING MY HEAD. S'NICE...

2

POSSIBLY IRRELEVANT TO THE MAIN STORY

CHARACTER INFO

KAMIGOME MITO

BIRTHDAY: SEPTEMBER 13
SIGN: VIRGO
BLOOD TYPE: A

SHE LIKES COMEDY SHOWS QUITE A BIT AND CAN DO PRETTY GOOD IMPRESSIONS.

HER HOBBY IS MAKING HOMEMADE WORCESTERSHIRE SAUCE USING INGREDIENTS GROWN ON THE FAMILY FARM.

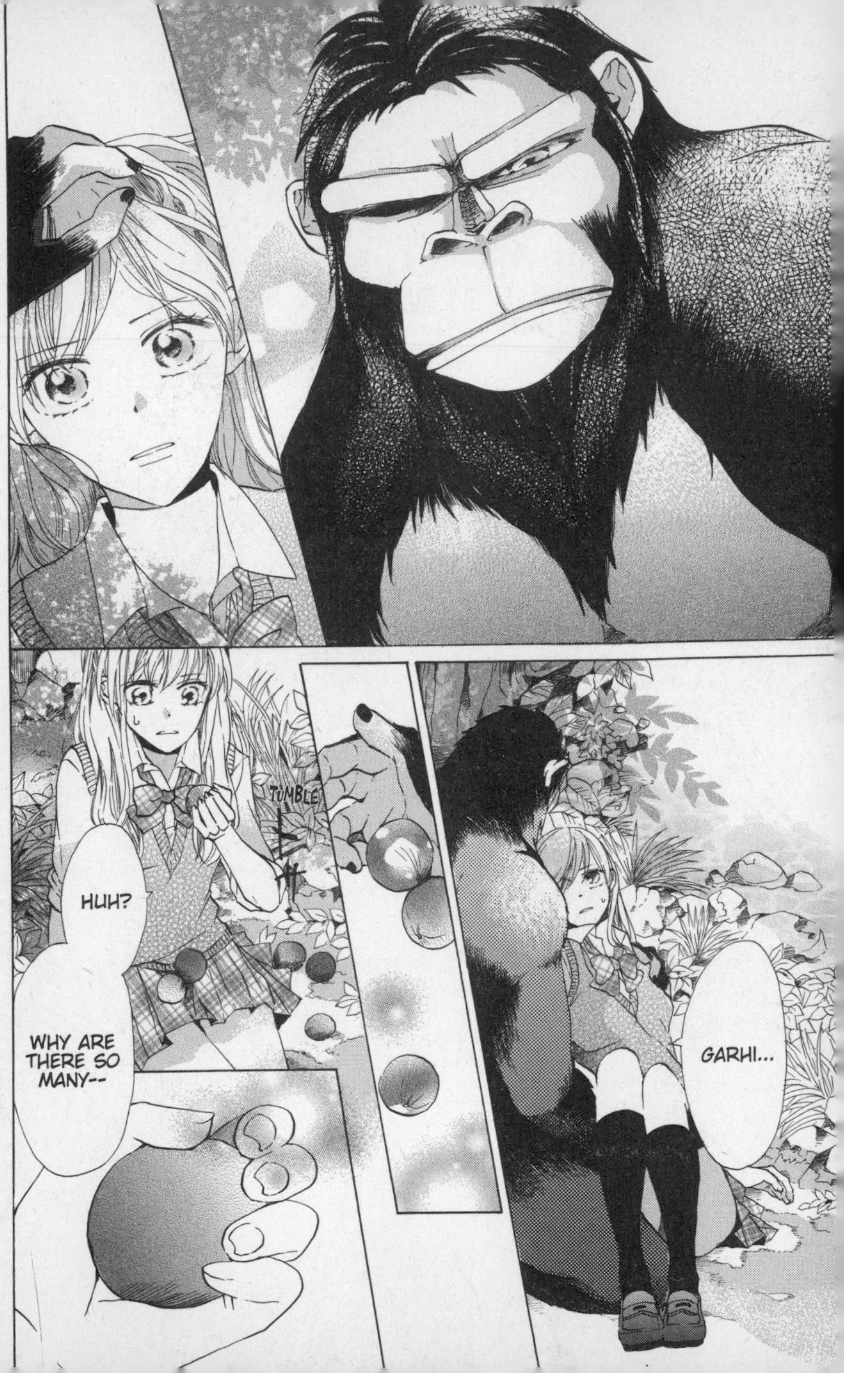
GARHI...
TUMBLE
HUH?
WHY ARE THERE SO MANY--

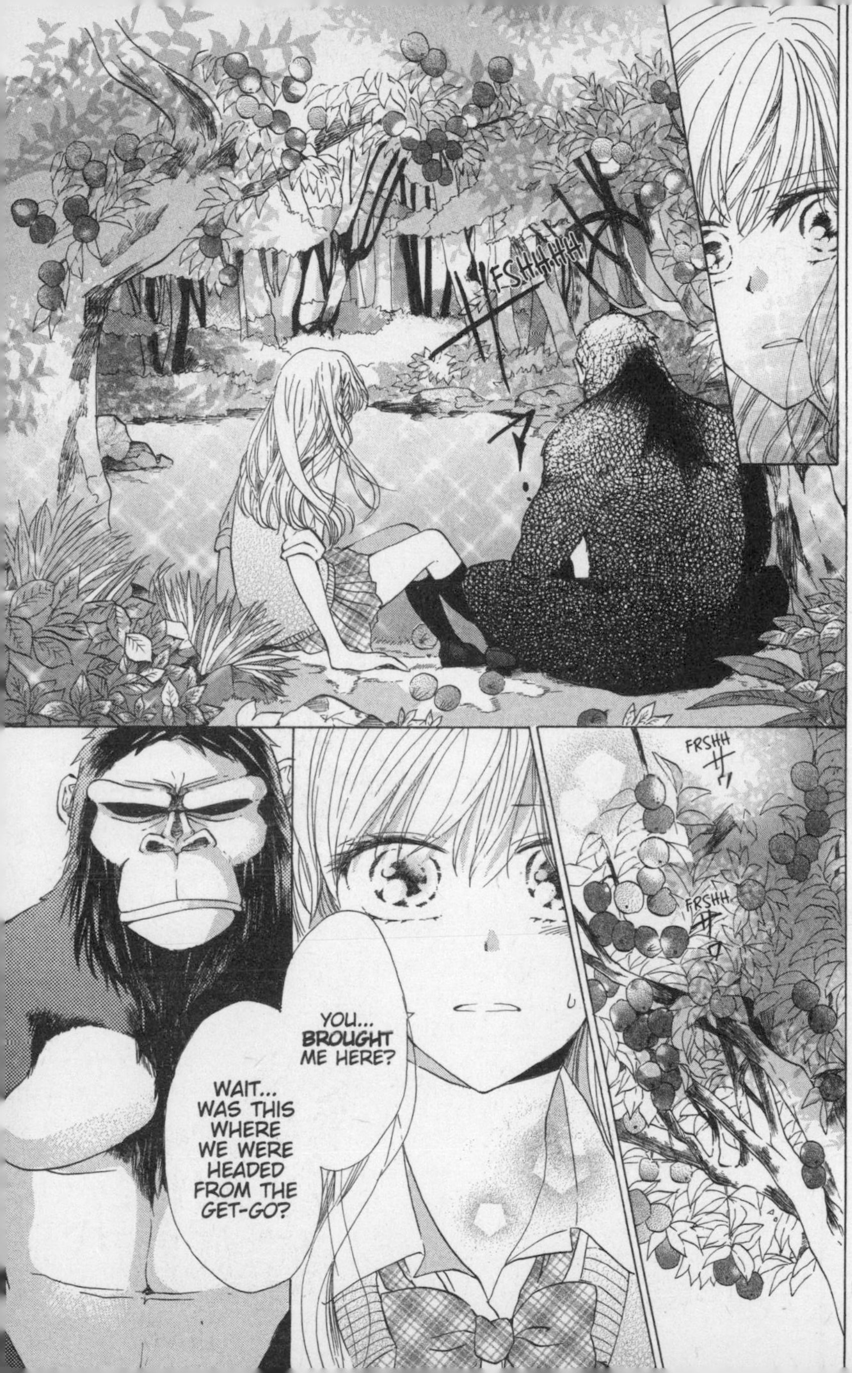
FSHHHHH
FRSHH
FRSHH
YOU... BROUGHT ME HERE?
WAIT... WAS THIS WHERE WE WERE HEADED FROM THE GET-GO?

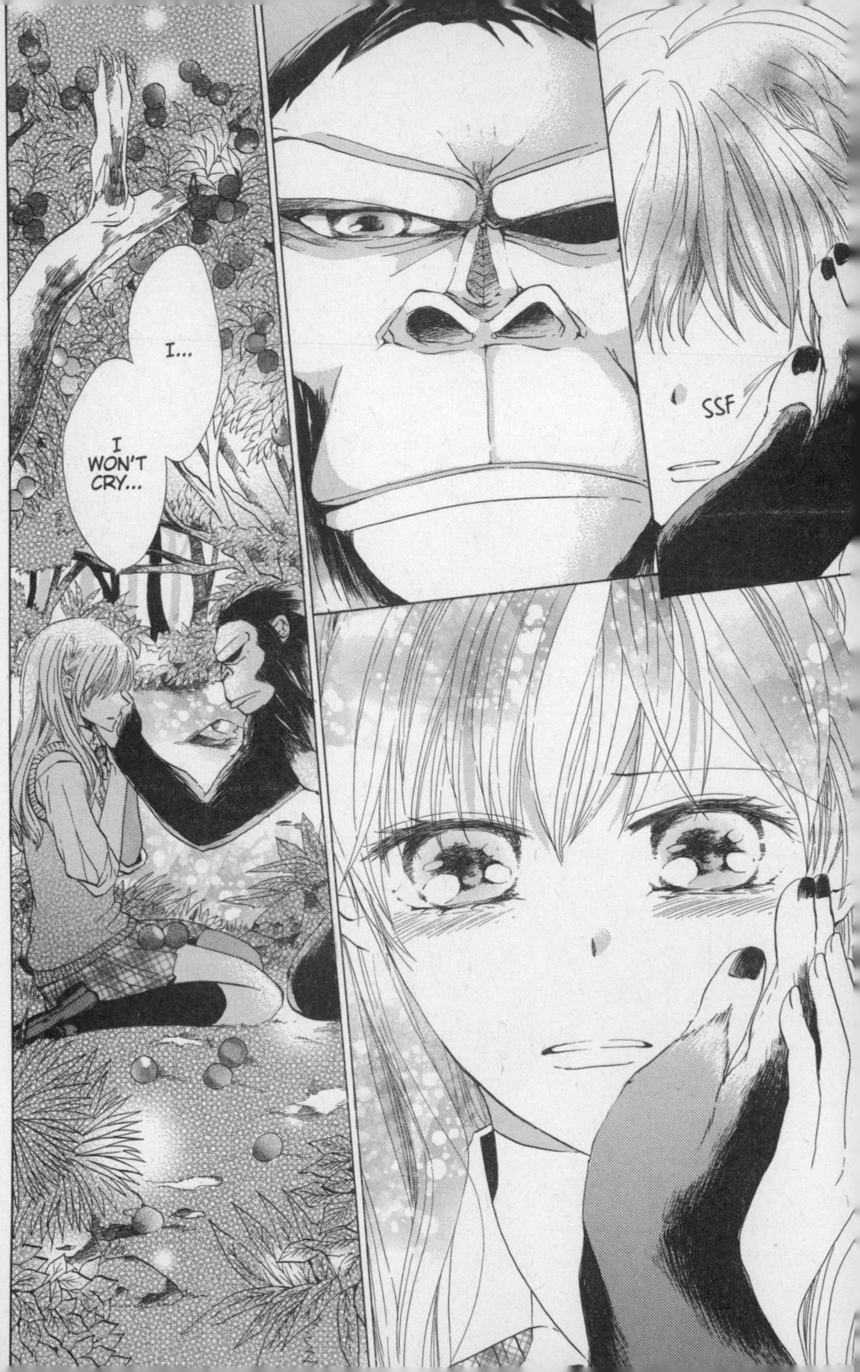
SSF
I...
I WON'T CRY...

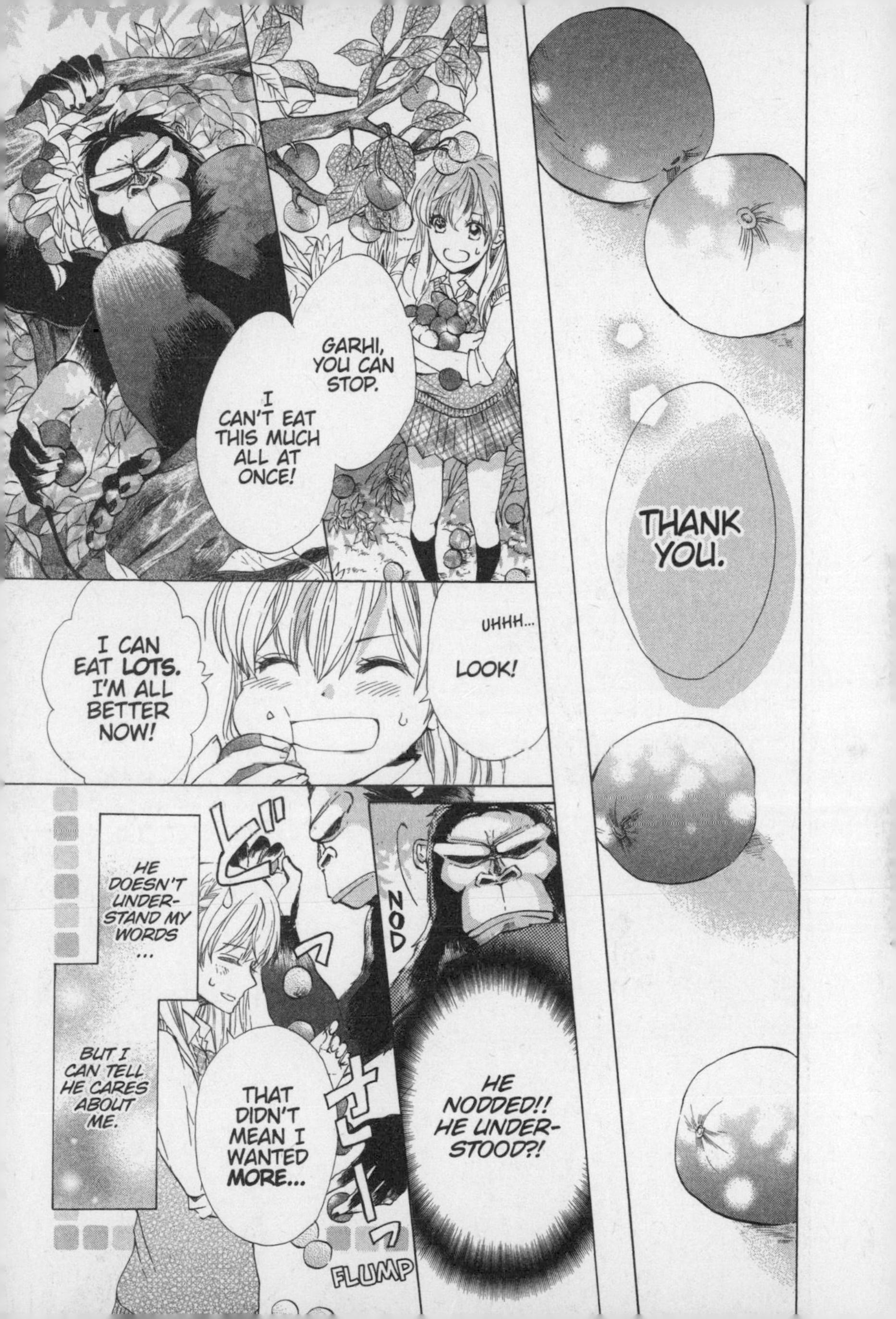
THANK YOU.
GARHI, YOU CAN STOP.
I CAN'T EAT THIS MUCH ALL AT ONCE!
UHHH...
LOOK!
I CAN EAT **LOTS**. I'M ALL BETTER NOW!
NOD
HE NODDED!! HE UNDERSTOOD?!
FLUMP
THAT DIDN'T MEAN I WANTED **MORE**...
HE DOESN'T UNDERSTAND MY WORDS ...
BUT I CAN TELL HE CARES ABOUT ME.

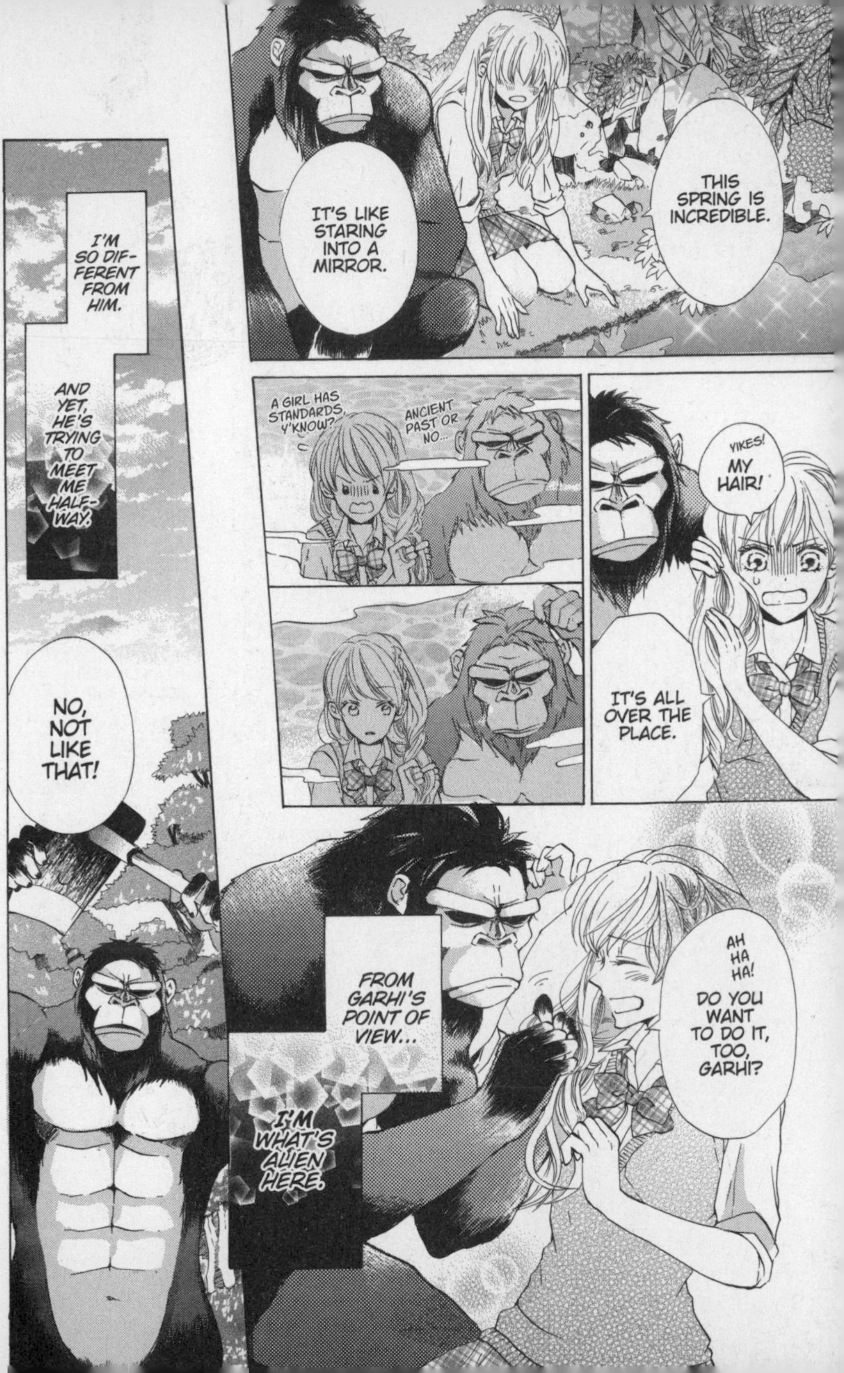
THIS SPRING IS INCREDIBLE.
IT'S LIKE STARING INTO A MIRROR.
YIKES! MY HAIR!
IT'S ALL OVER THE PLACE.
ANCIENT PAST OR NO...
A GIRL HAS STANDARDS, Y'KNOW?
AH HA HA! DO YOU WANT TO DO IT, TOO, GARHI?
FROM GARHI'S POINT OF VIEW...
I'M WHAT'S ALIEN HERE.
I'M SO DIF-FERENT FROM HIM.
AND YET, HE'S TRYING TO MEET ME HALF-WAY.
NO, NOT LIKE THAT!

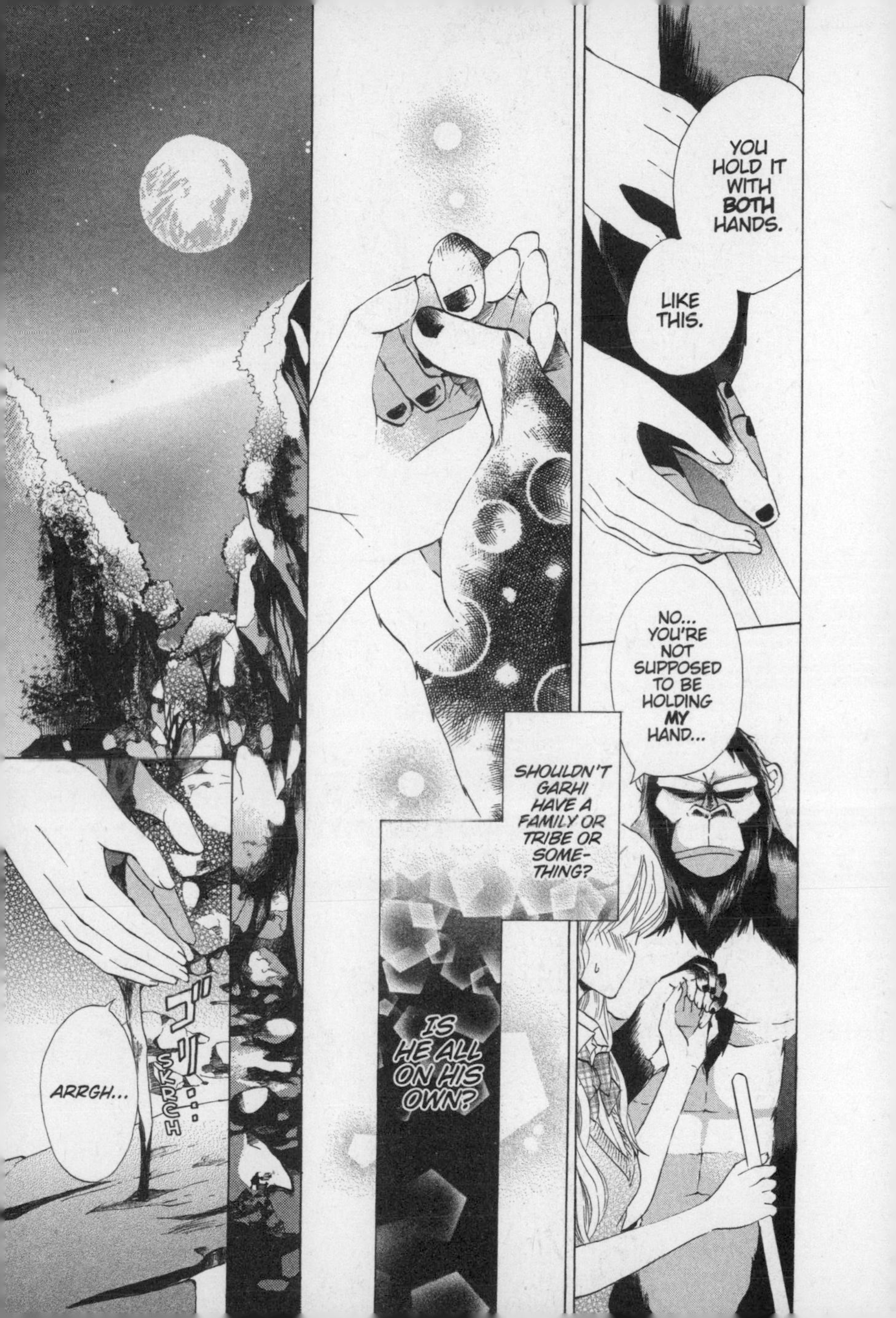
YOU HOLD IT WITH BOTH HANDS.
LIKE THIS.
NO... YOU'RE NOT SUPPOSED TO BE HOLDING MY HAND...
SHOULDN'T GARHI HAVE A FAMILY OR TRIBE OR SOMETHING?
IS HE ALL ON HIS OWN?
ゴリ・・
SKRCH
ARRGH...

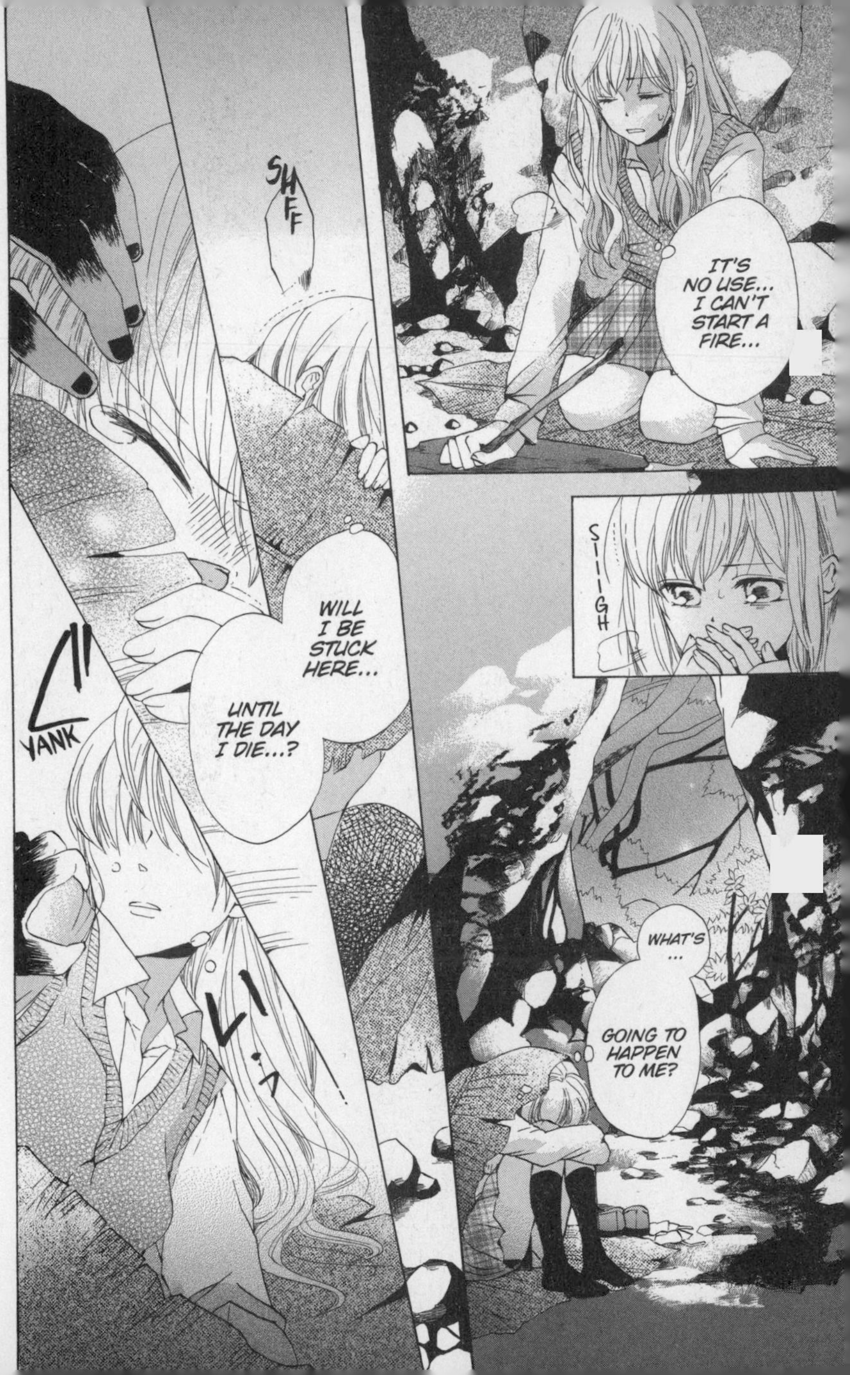
IT'S NO USE... I CAN'T START A FIRE...
SIIIGH
WHAT'S...
GOING TO HAPPEN TO ME?
SHFF
WILL I BE STUCK HERE...
UNTIL THE DAY I DIE...?
YANK

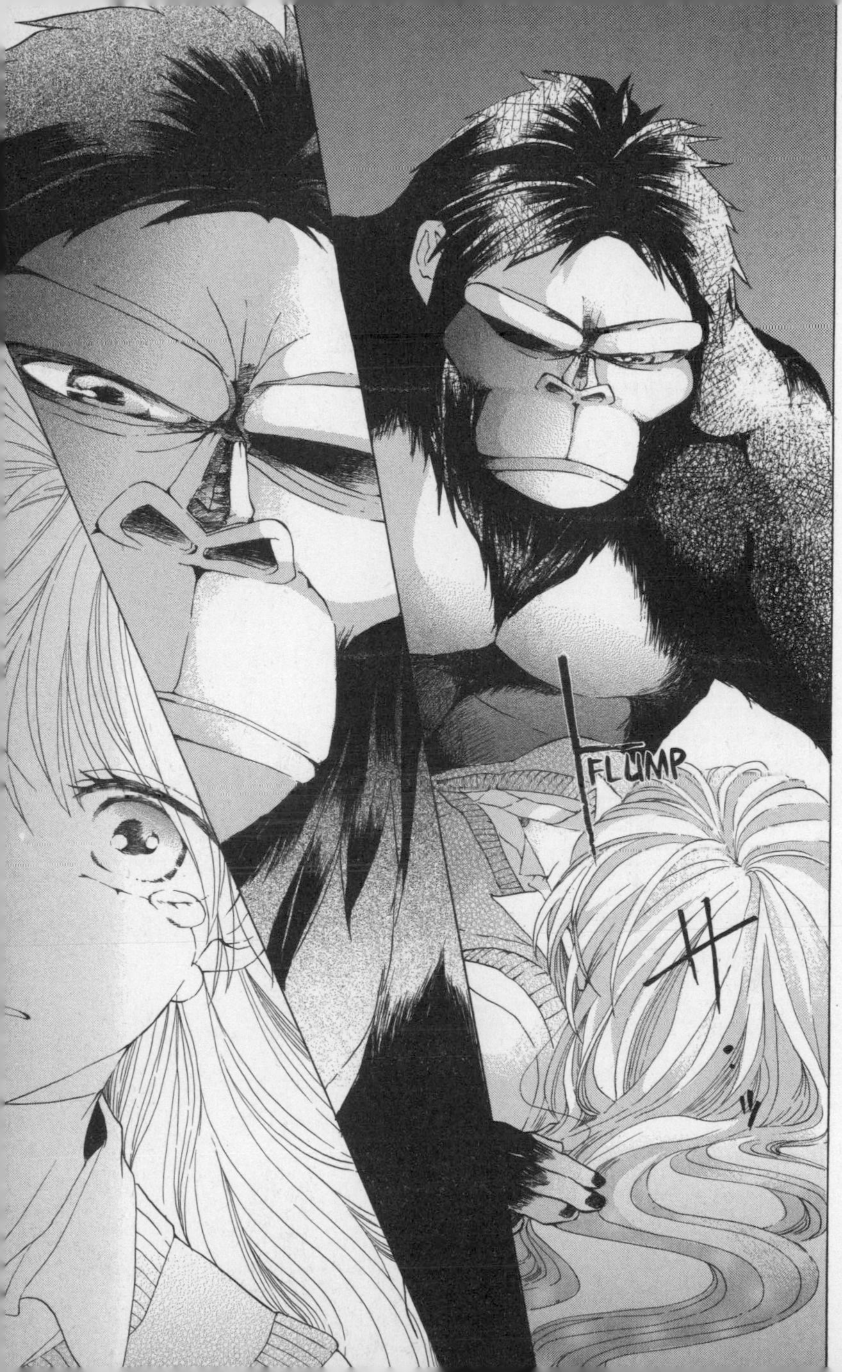
FLUMP

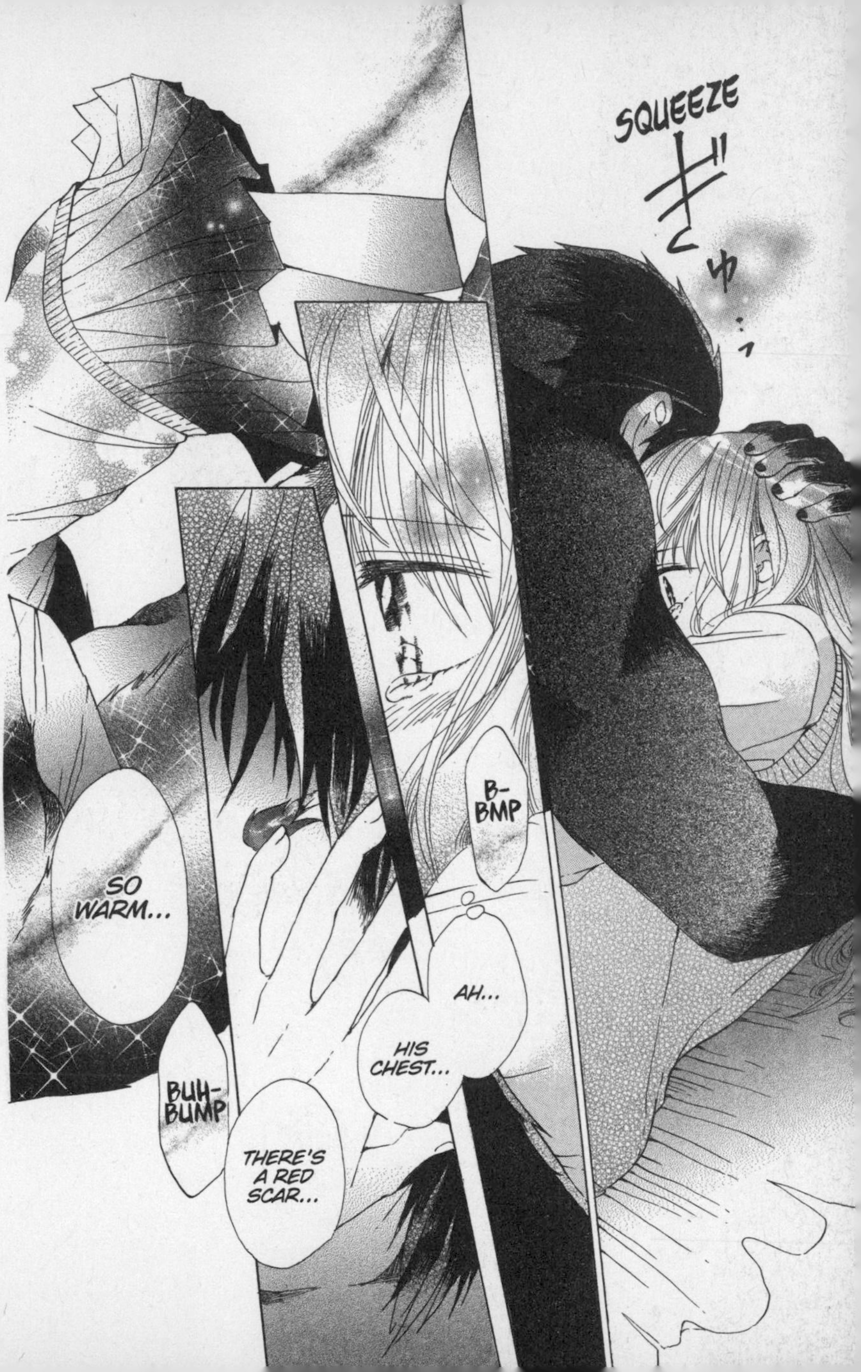
SQUEEZE
ぎゅ…っ
B-BMP
AH...
HIS CHEST...
THERE'S A RED SCAR...
BUH-BUMP
SO WARM...

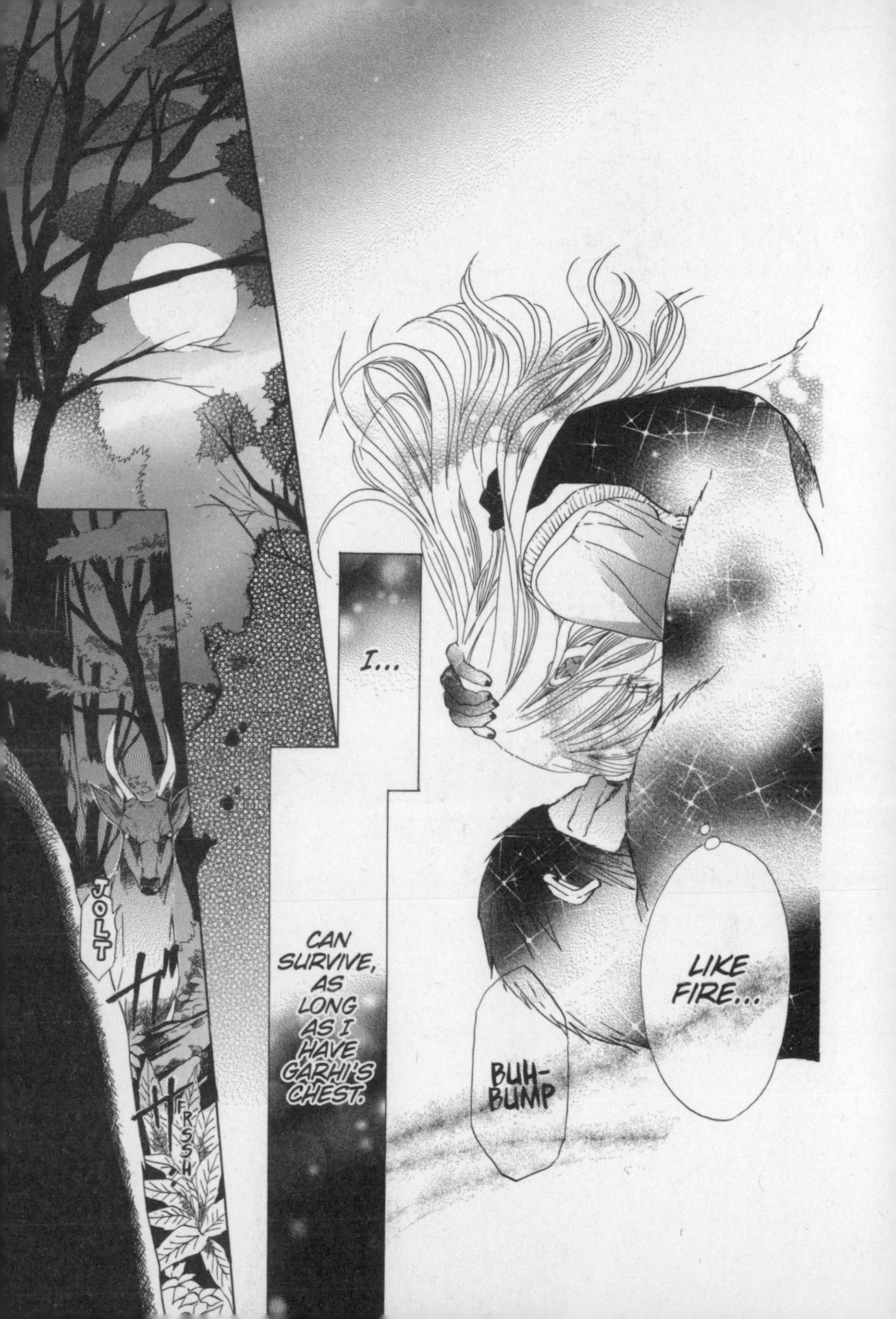
LIKE FIRE...
BUH-BUMP
I...
CAN SURVIVE, AS LONG AS I HAVE GARHI'S CHEST.
JOLT
FRSSH

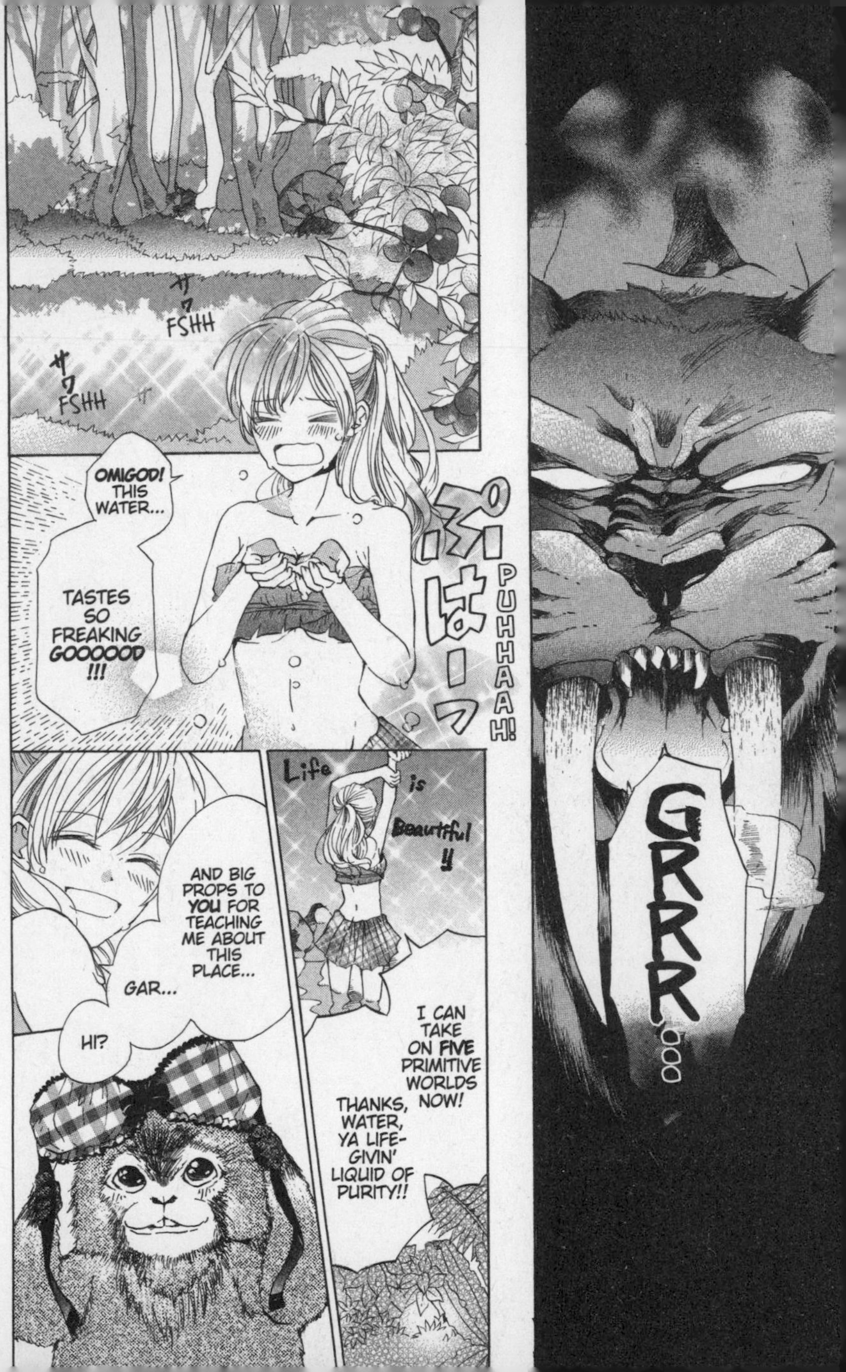
GRRR...
サワ
FSHH
サワ
FSHH
ぷはーっ
PUHHAAH!
OMIGOD! THIS WATER...
TASTES SO FREAKING GOOOOOD!!!
Life is Beautiful!!
I CAN TAKE ON FIVE PRIMITIVE WORLDS NOW!
THANKS, WATER, YA LIFE-GIVIN' LIQUID OF PURITY!!
AND BIG PROPS TO YOU FOR TEACHING ME ABOUT THIS PLACE...
GAR...
HI?

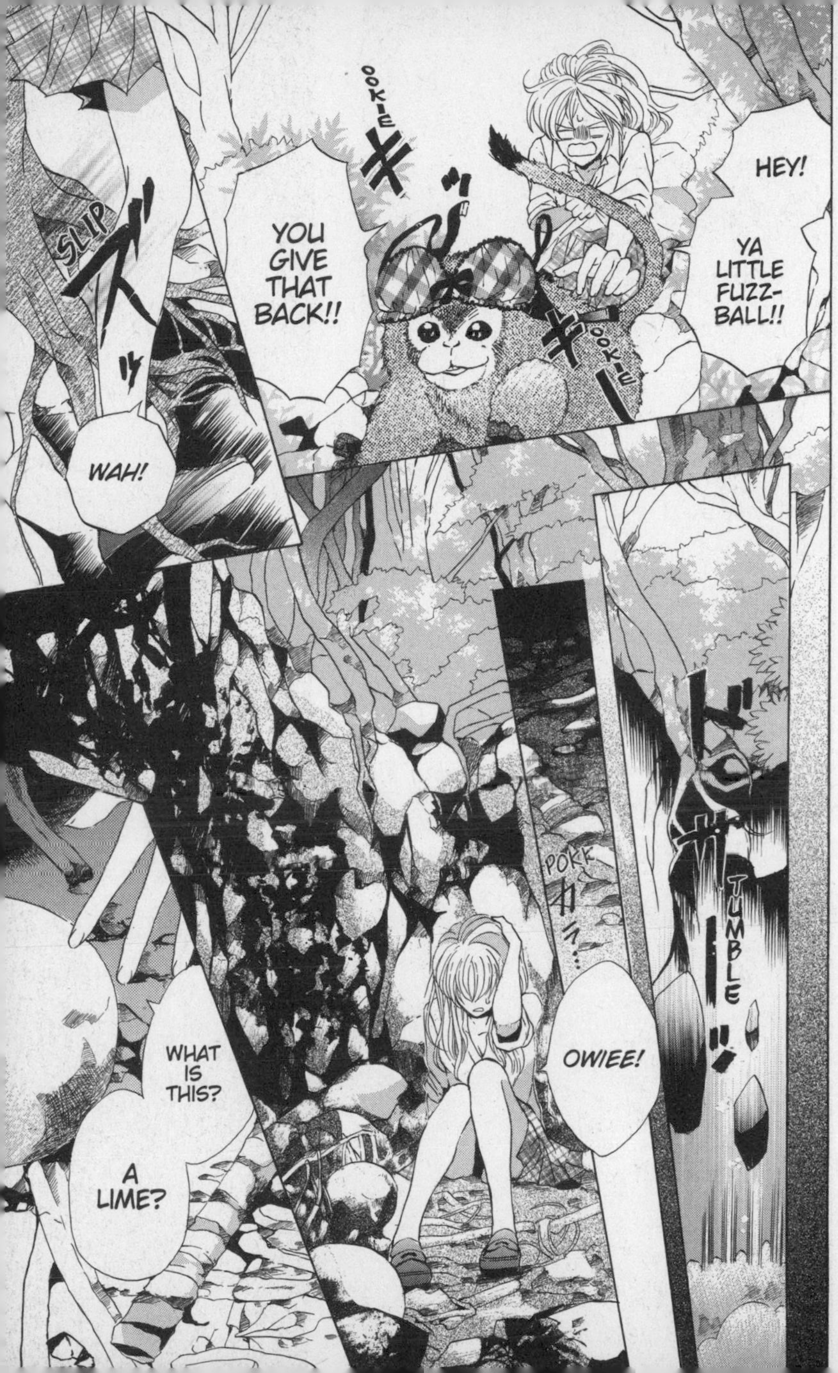
HEY!
OOKIE
YA LITTLE FUZZ-BALL!!
YOU GIVE THAT BACK!!
OOKIE
SLIP
WAH!
TUMBLE
POKK
OWIEE!
WHAT IS THIS?
A LIME?

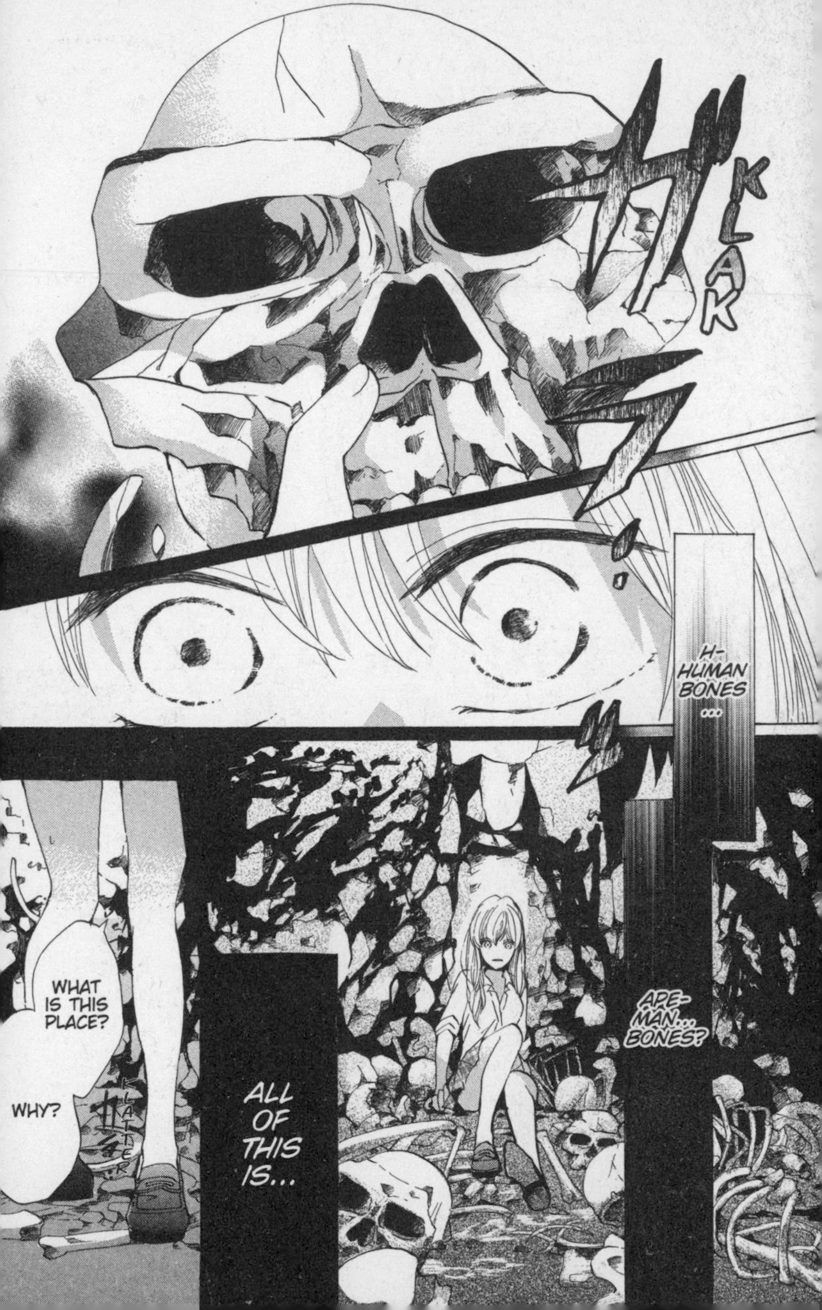
KLAK
H-HUMAN BONES...
APE-MAN... BONES?
ALL OF THIS IS...
WHAT IS THIS PLACE?
WHY?
KLATTER

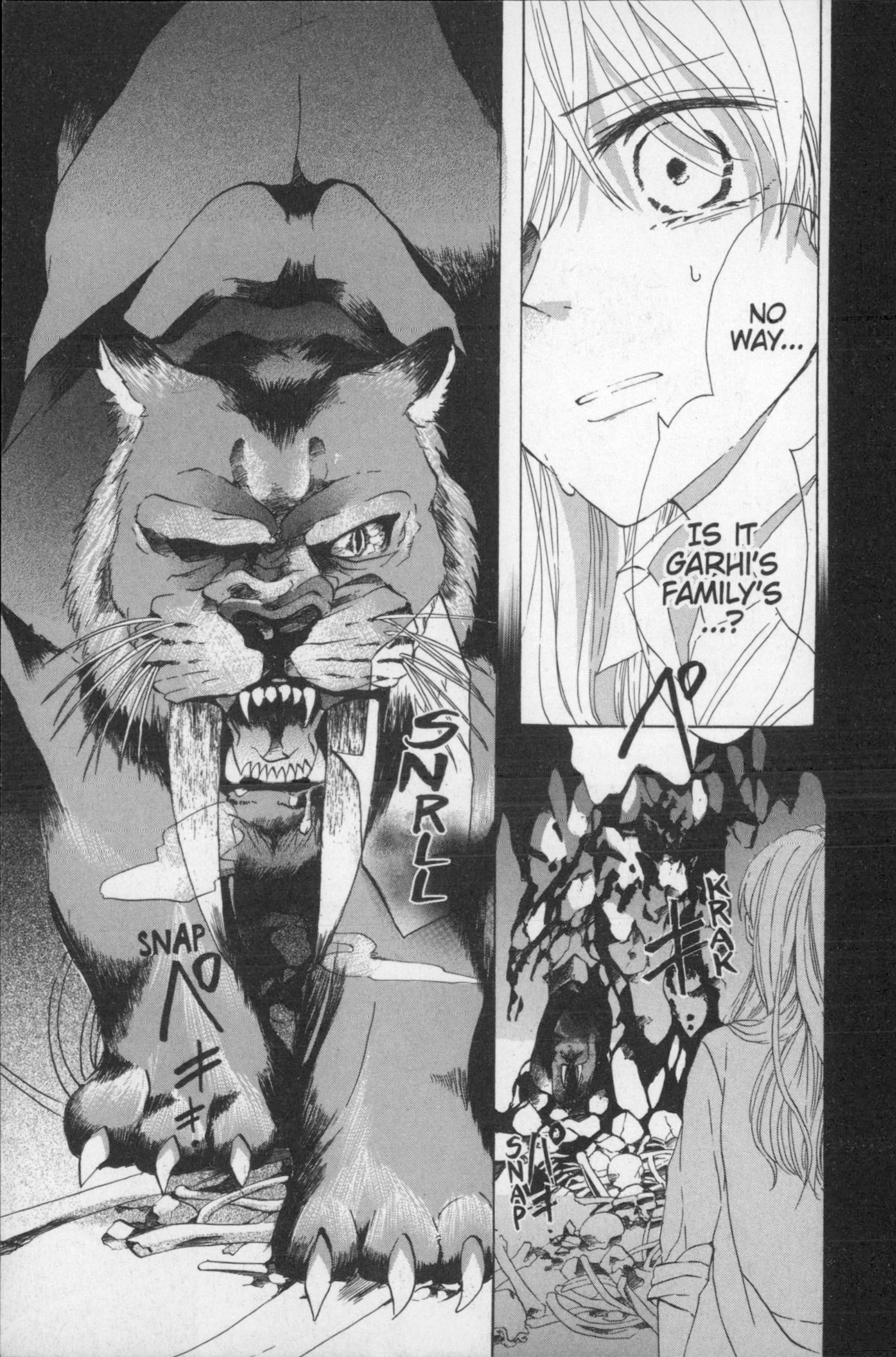
NO WAY...
IS IT GARHI'S FAMILY'S ...?
KRAK
SNAP
SNRLL
SNAP

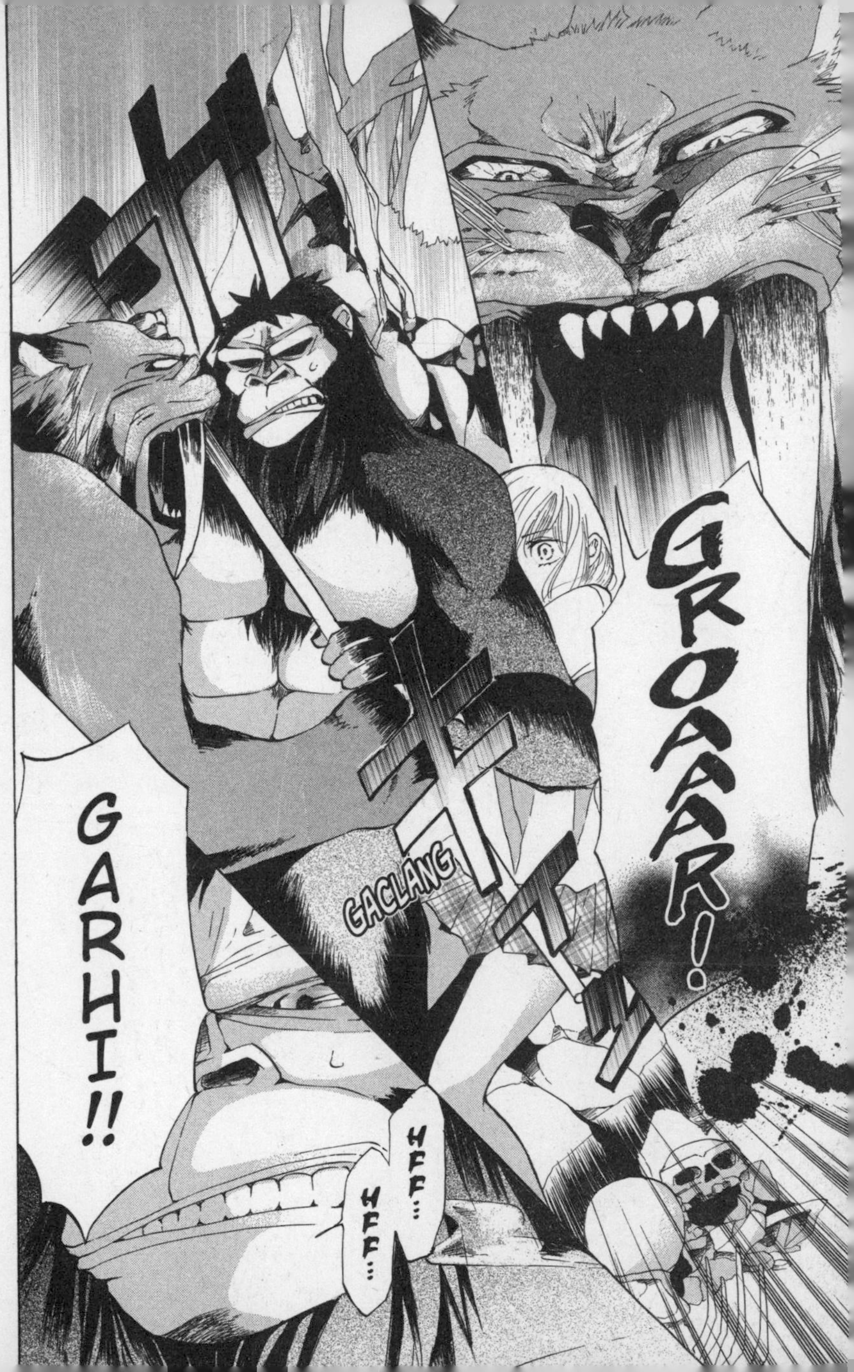
GROAAAR!
GACLANG
GARHI!!
HFF... HFF...

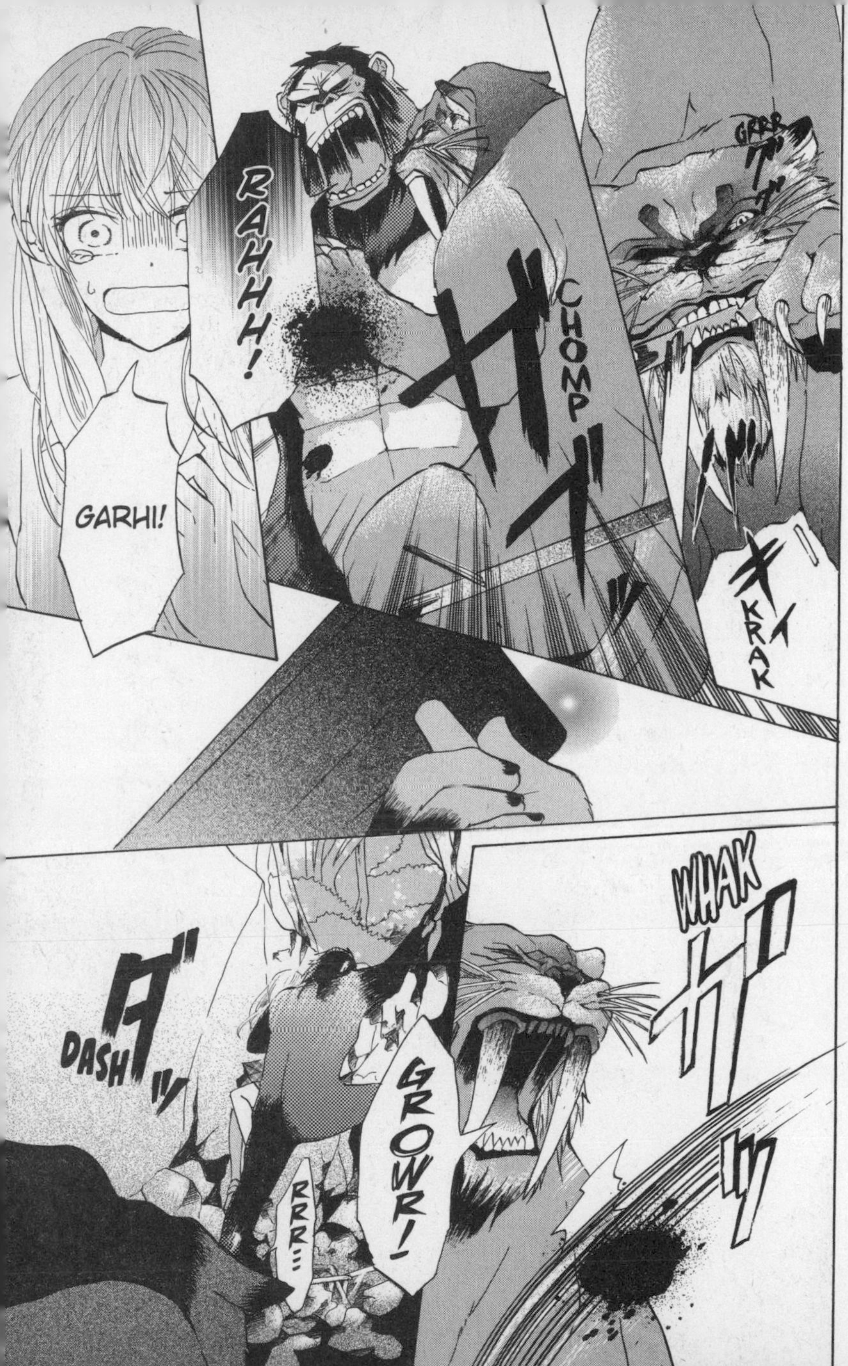
GRRR
KRAK
CHOMP
RAHHH!
GARHI!
WHAK
GROWR!
RRR...
DASH

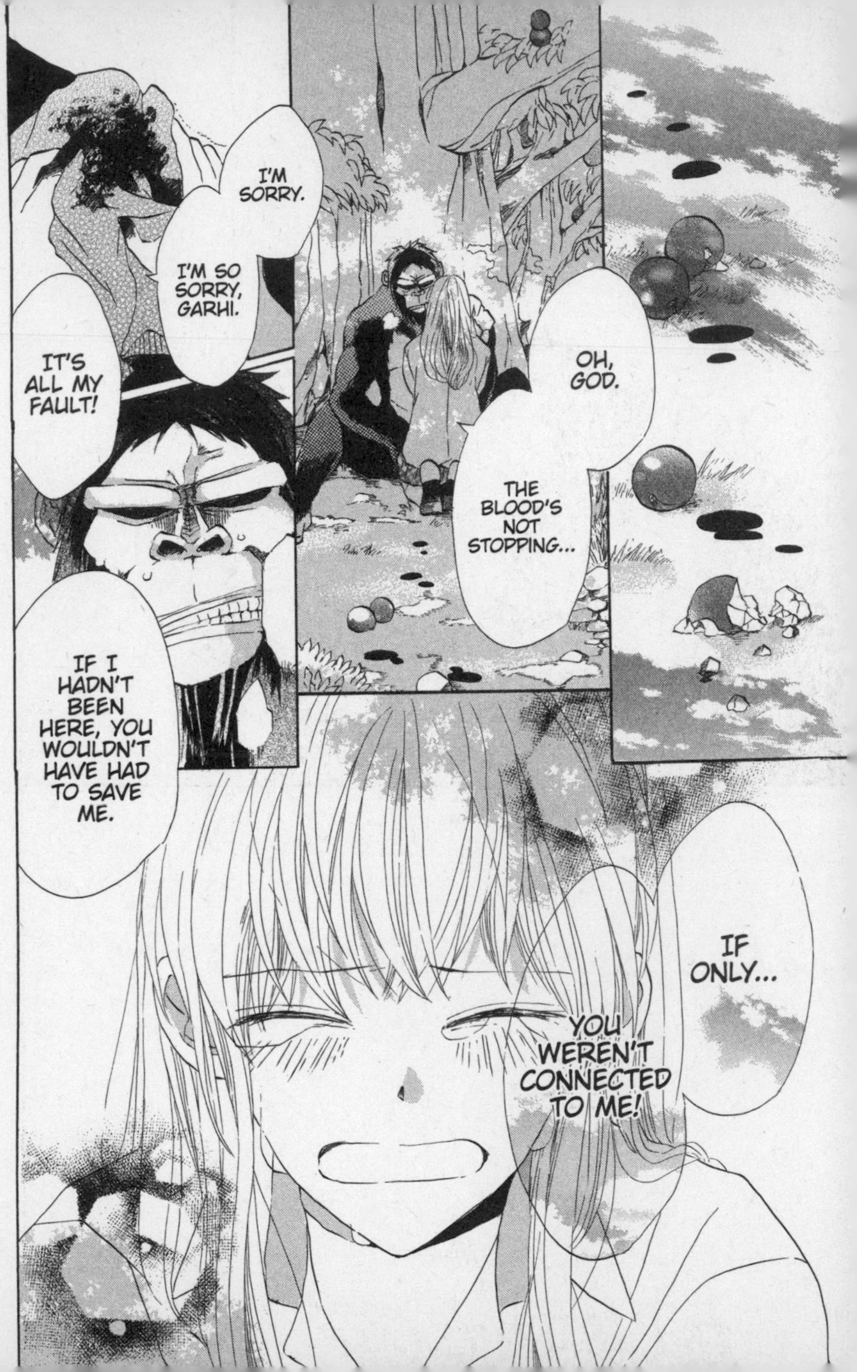
OH, GOD.
THE BLOOD'S NOT STOPPING...
I'M SORRY.
I'M SO SORRY, GARHI.
IT'S ALL MY FAULT!
IF I HADN'T BEEN HERE, YOU WOULDN'T HAVE HAD TO SAVE ME.
IF ONLY...
YOU WEREN'T CONNECTED TO ME!

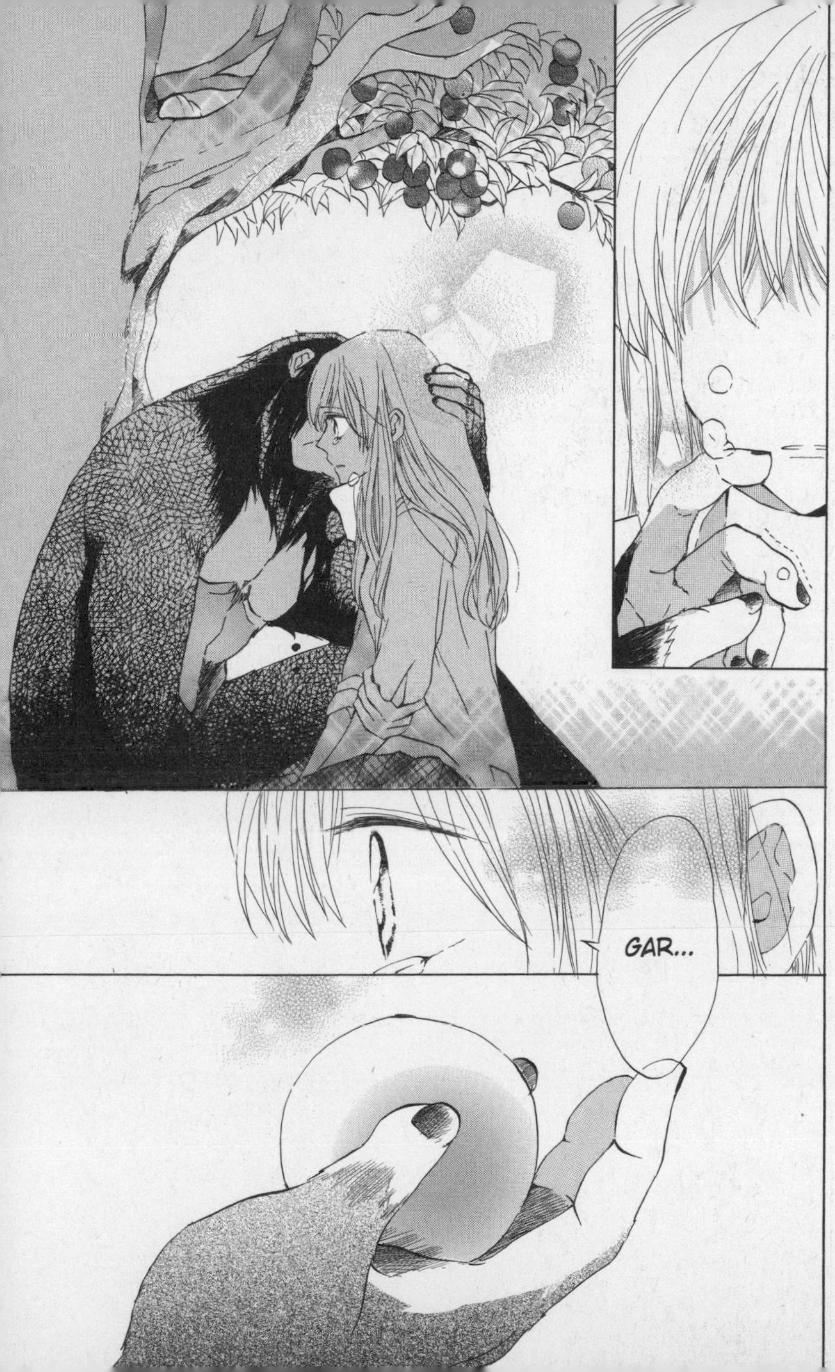
GAR...

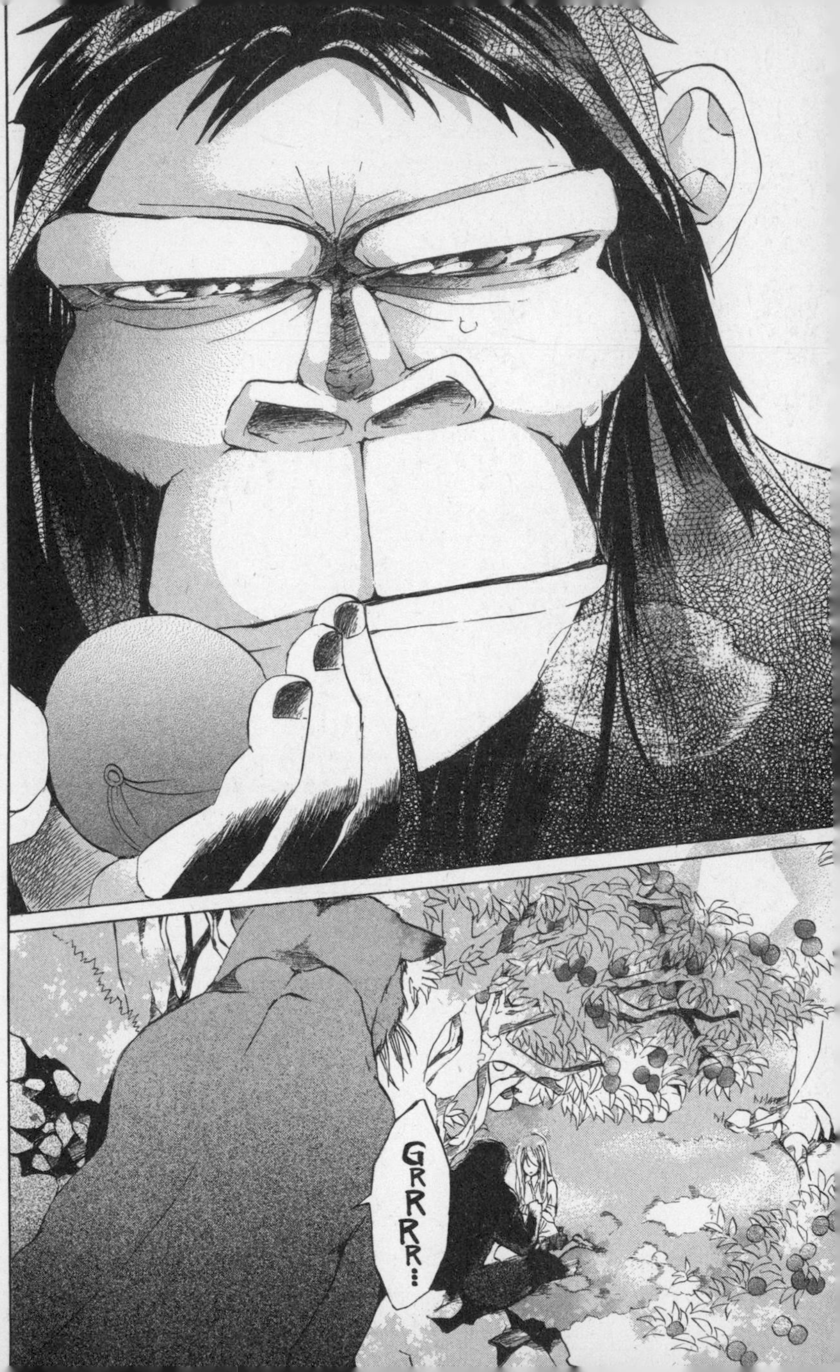
GRRRR..

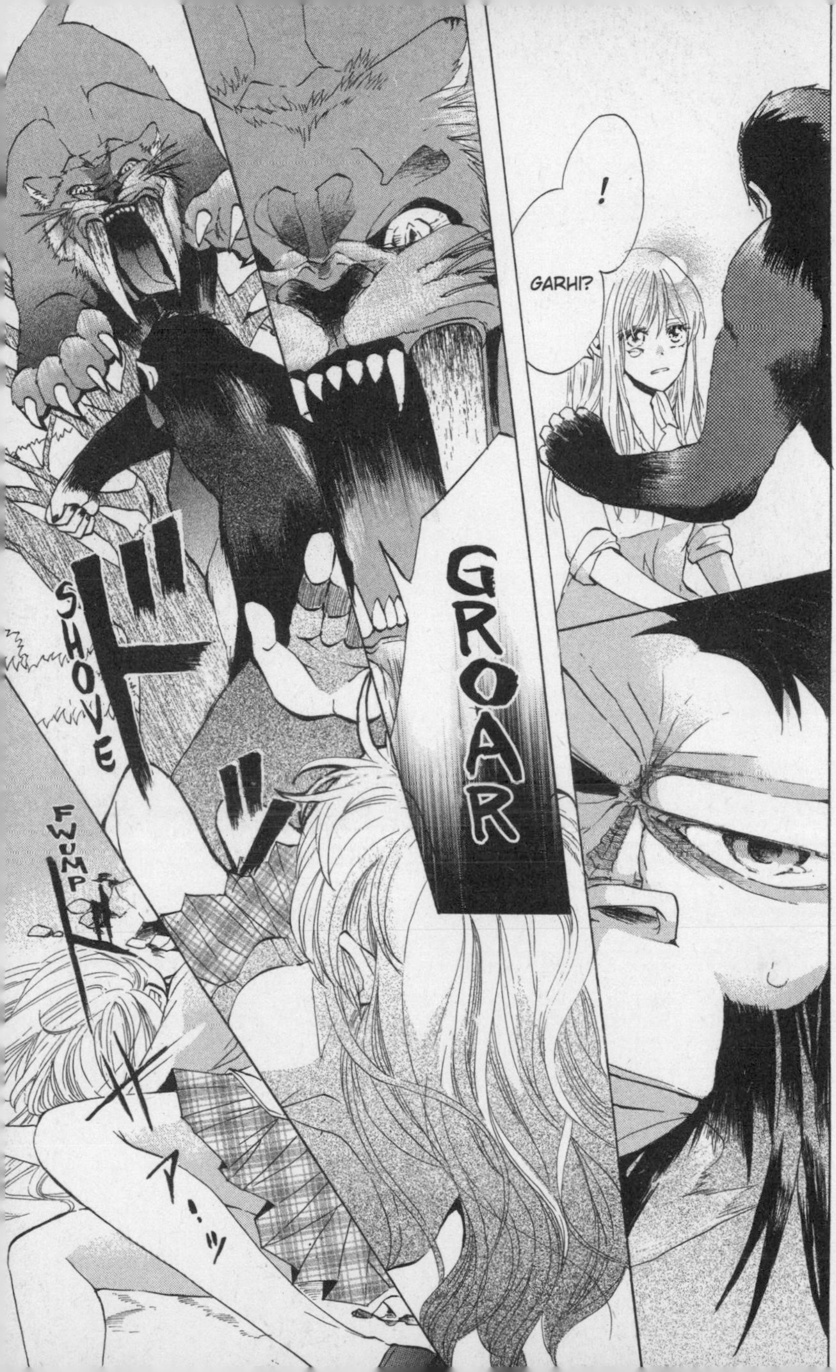
!
GARHI?
GROAR
SHOVE
FWUMP

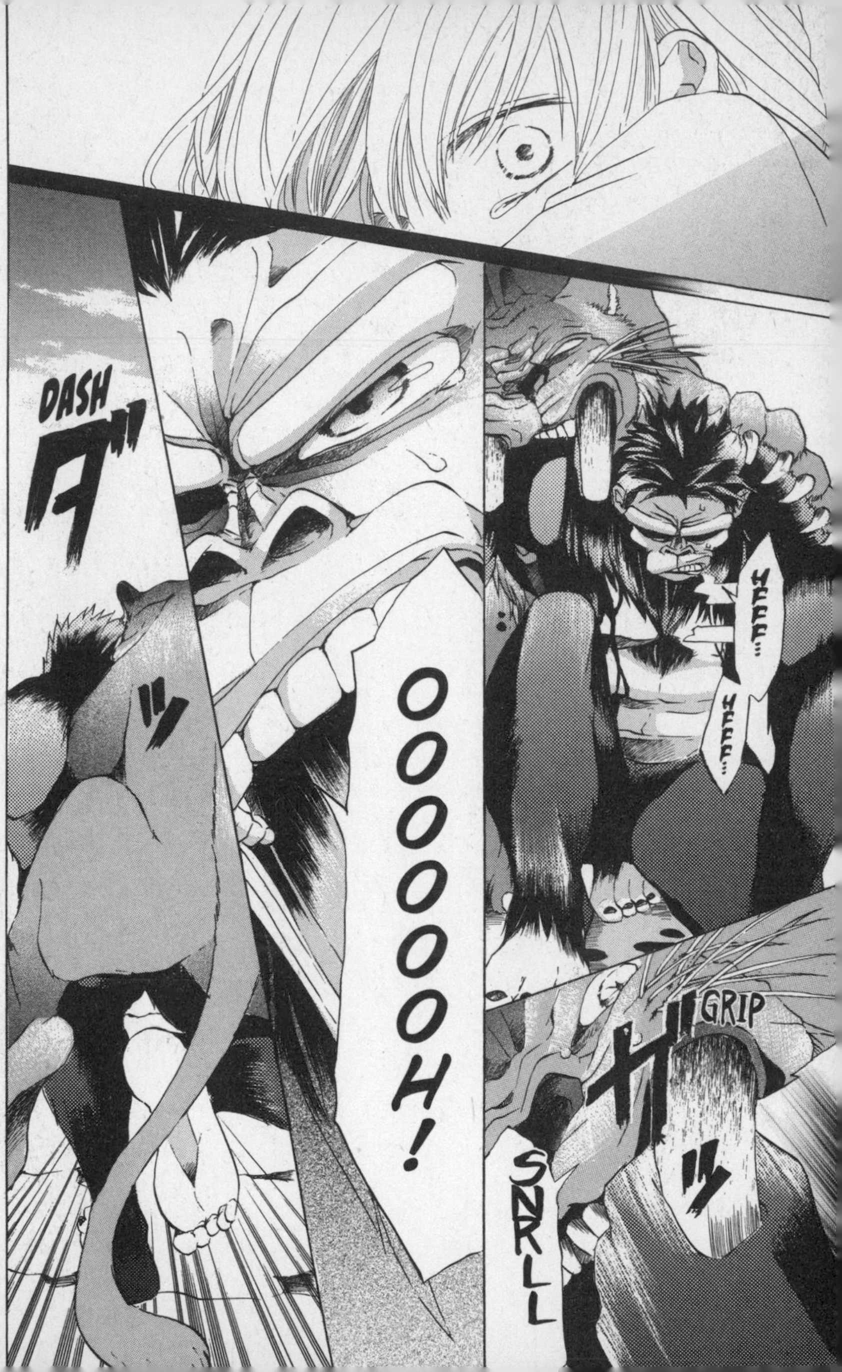
HEFF...
HEFF...
GRIP
SNRLL
OOOOOOOH!
DASH

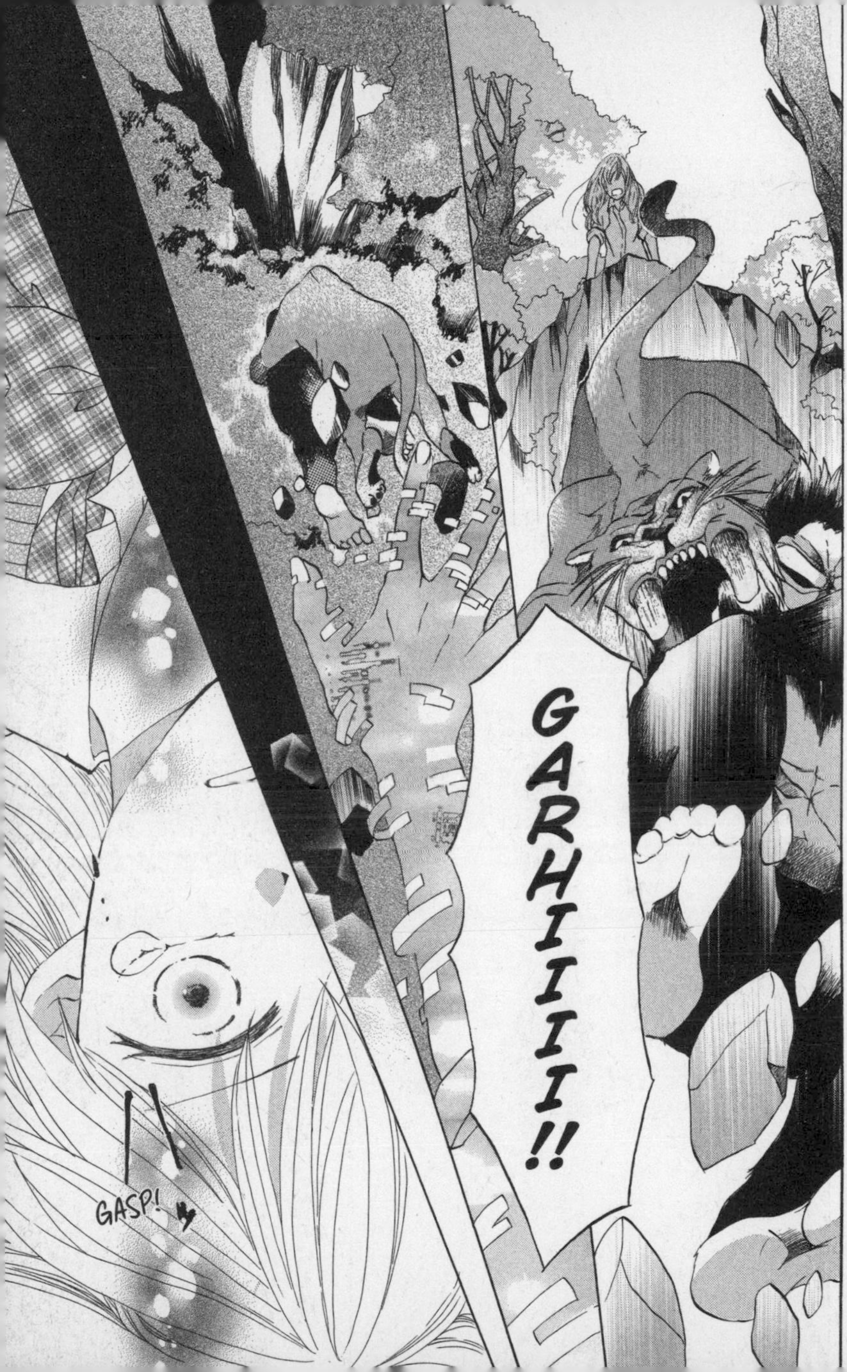
GARHIIIII!!
GASP!

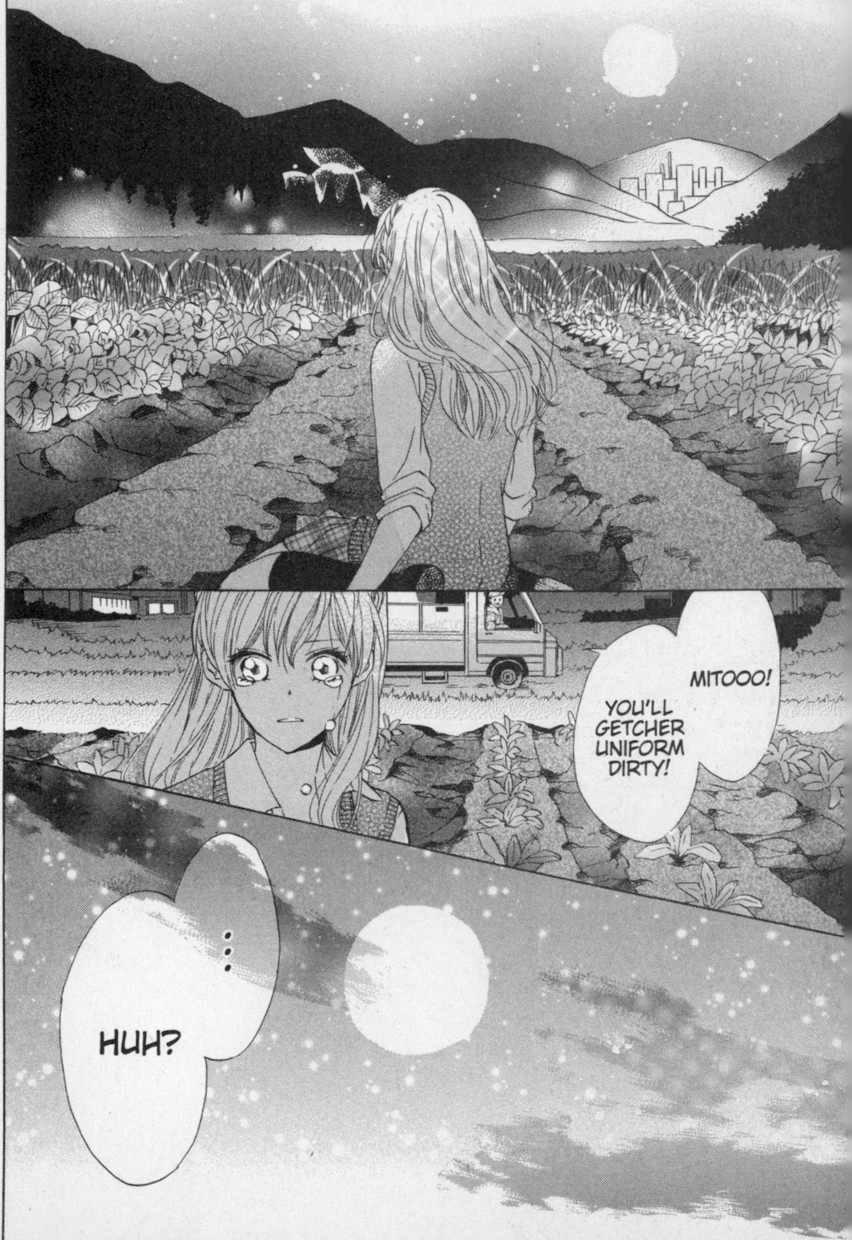
MITOOO!
YOU'LL GETCHER UNIFORM DIRTY!
...
HUH?

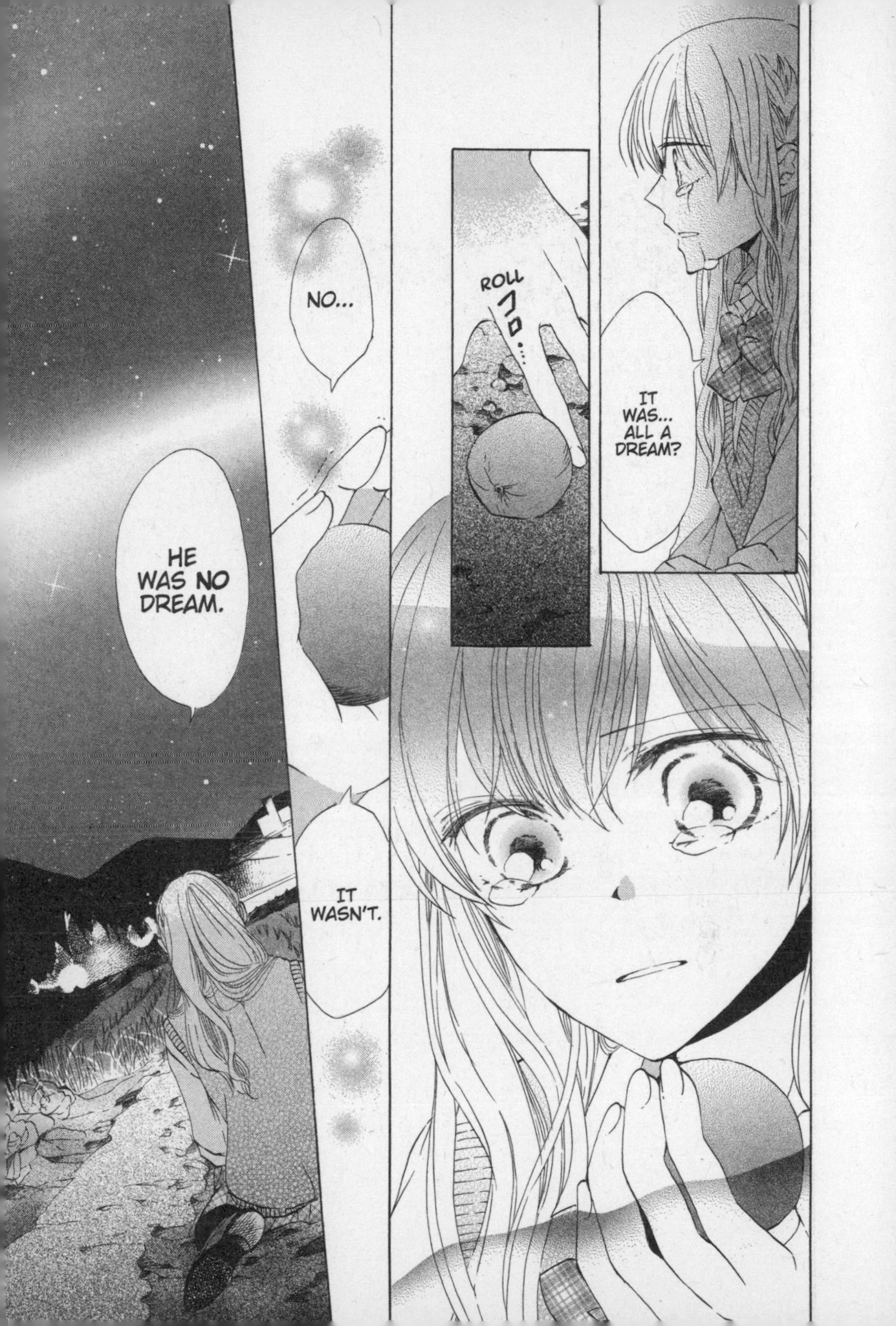
IT WAS... ALL A DREAM?
ROLL
コロ...
NO...
IT WASN'T.
HE WAS NO DREAM.

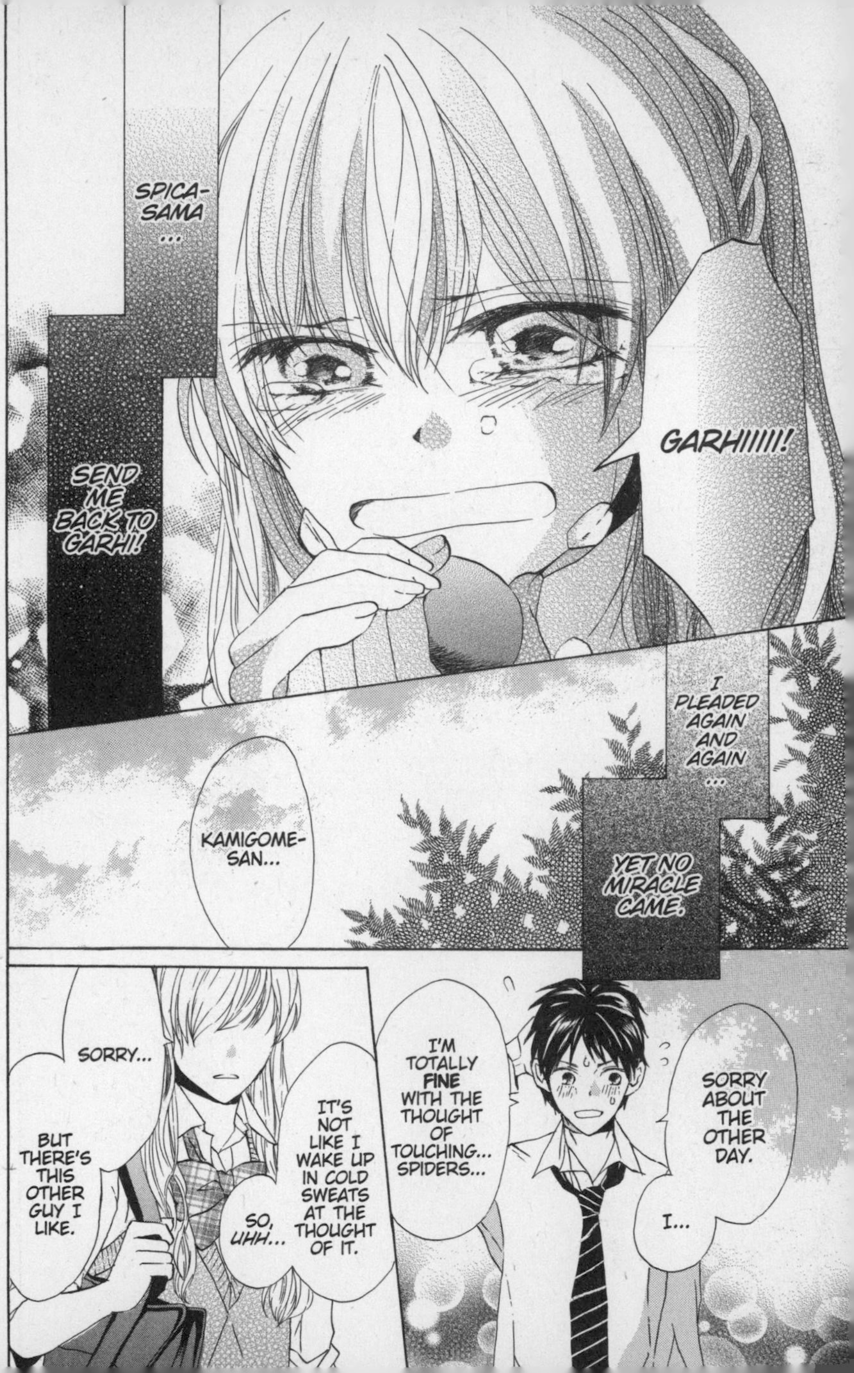
GARHIIIIII!
SPICA-SAMA...
SEND ME BACK TO GARHI!
I PLEADED AGAIN AND AGAIN...
YET NO MIRACLE CAME.
KAMIGOME-SAN...
SORRY ABOUT THE OTHER DAY.
I...
I'M TOTALLY FINE WITH THE THOUGHT OF TOUCHING... SPIDERS...
IT'S NOT LIKE I WAKE UP IN COLD SWEATS AT THE THOUGHT OF IT.
SO, UHH...
SORRY...
BUT THERE'S THIS OTHER GUY I LIKE.

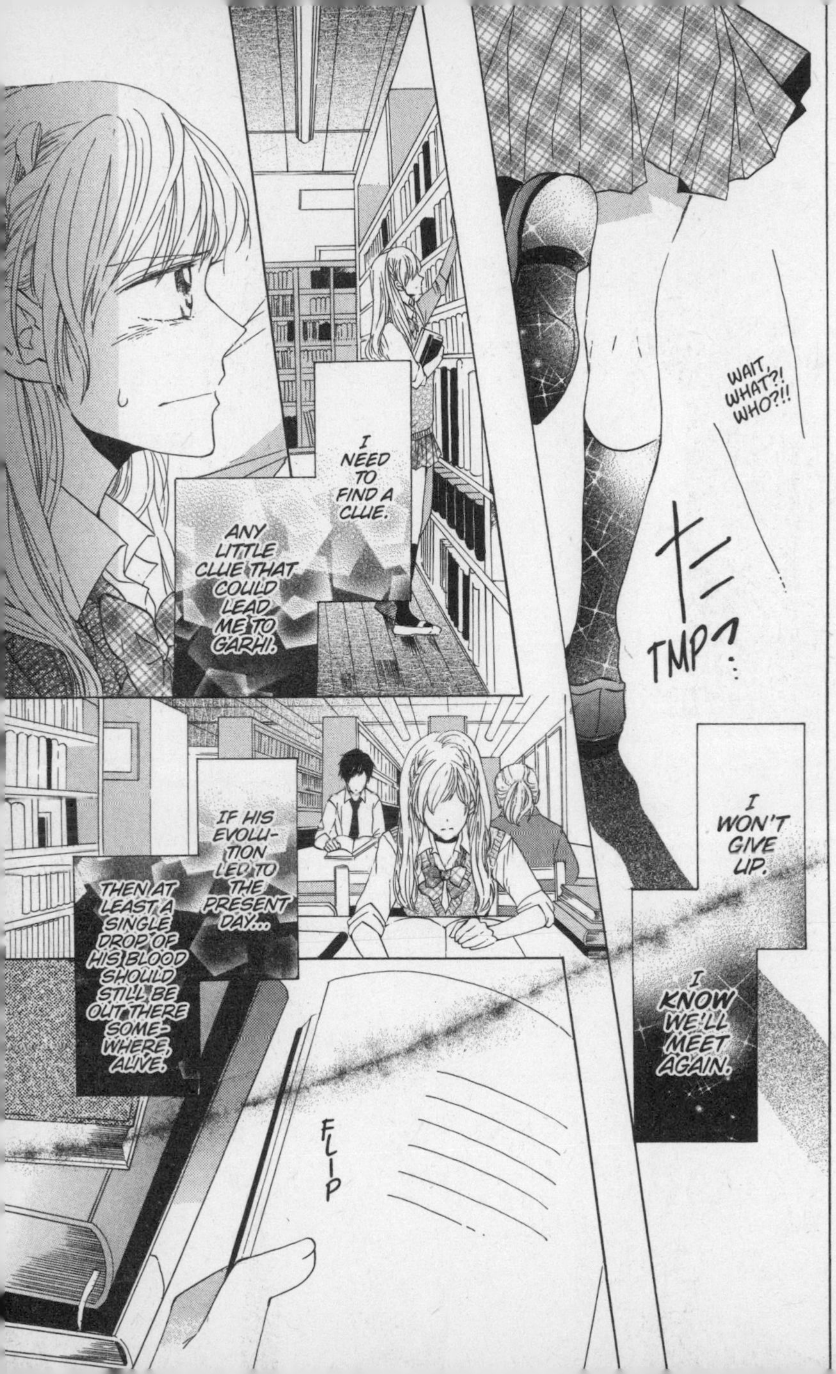
WAIT, WHAT?! WHO?!!
TMP
I WON'T GIVE UP.
I KNOW WE'LL MEET AGAIN.
I NEED TO FIND A CLUE.
ANY LITTLE CLUE THAT COULD LEAD ME TO GARHI.
IF HIS EVOLUTION LED TO THE PRESENT DAY...
THEN AT LEAST A SINGLE DROP OF HIS BLOOD SHOULD STILL BE OUT THERE SOMEWHERE, ALIVE.
FLIP

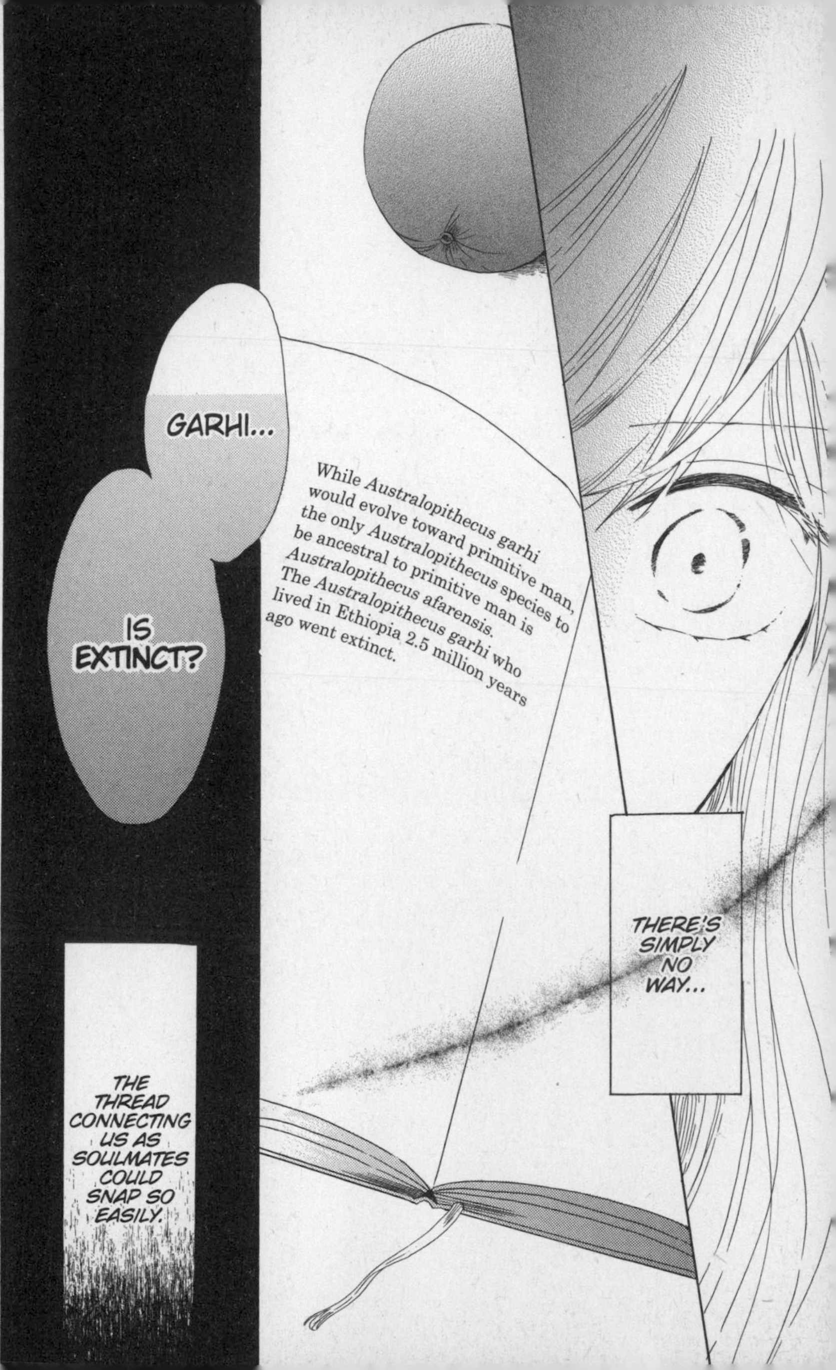
While Australopithecus garhi would evolve toward primitive man, the only Australopithecus species to be ancestral to primitive man is Australopithecus afarensis. The Australopithecus garhi who lived in Ethiopia 2.5 million years ago went extinct.
THERE'S SIMPLY NO WAY...
GARHI...
IS EXTINCT?
THE THREAD CONNECTING US AS SOULMATES COULD SNAP SO EASILY.

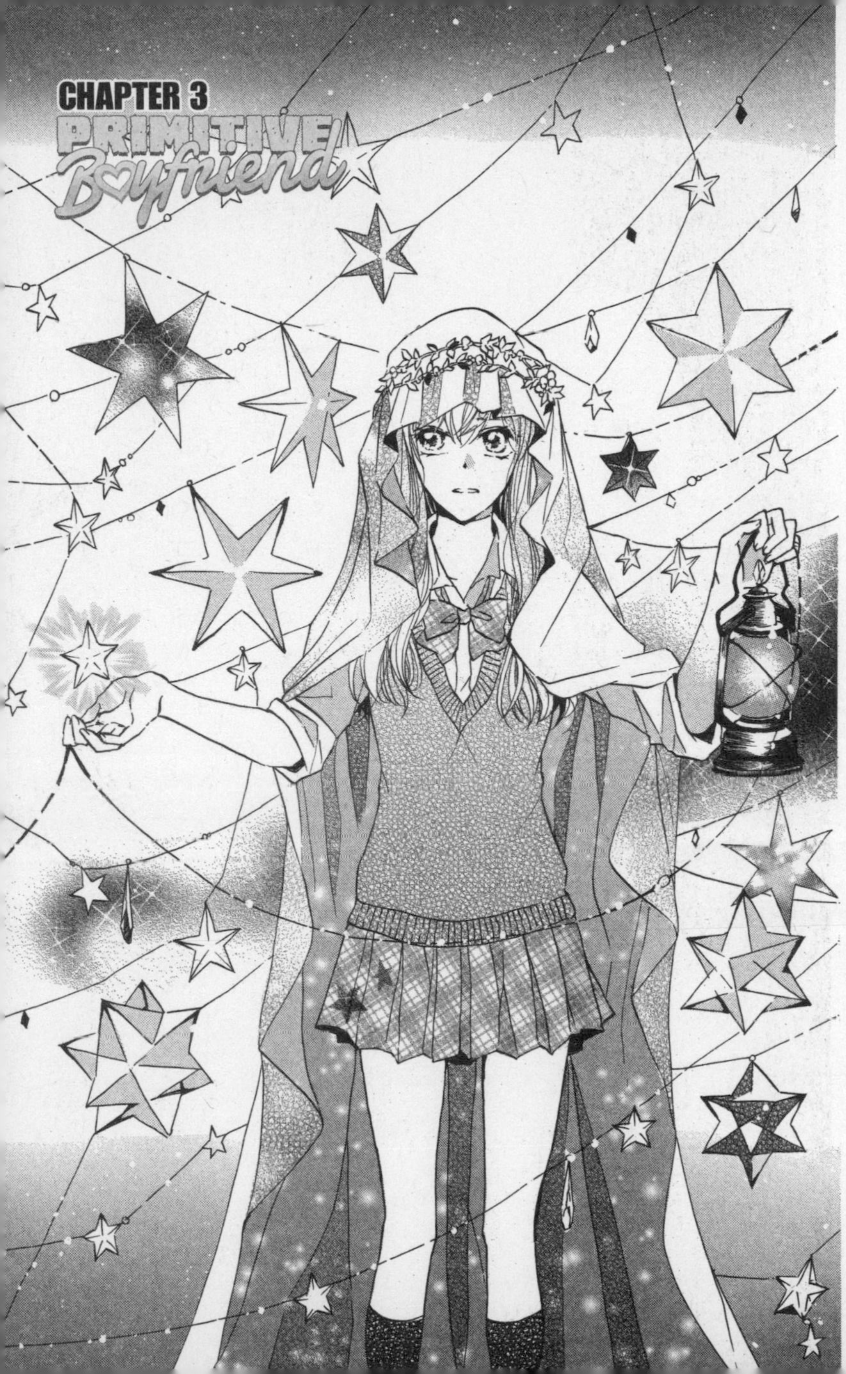
CHAPTER 3
PRIMITIVE
Boyfriend

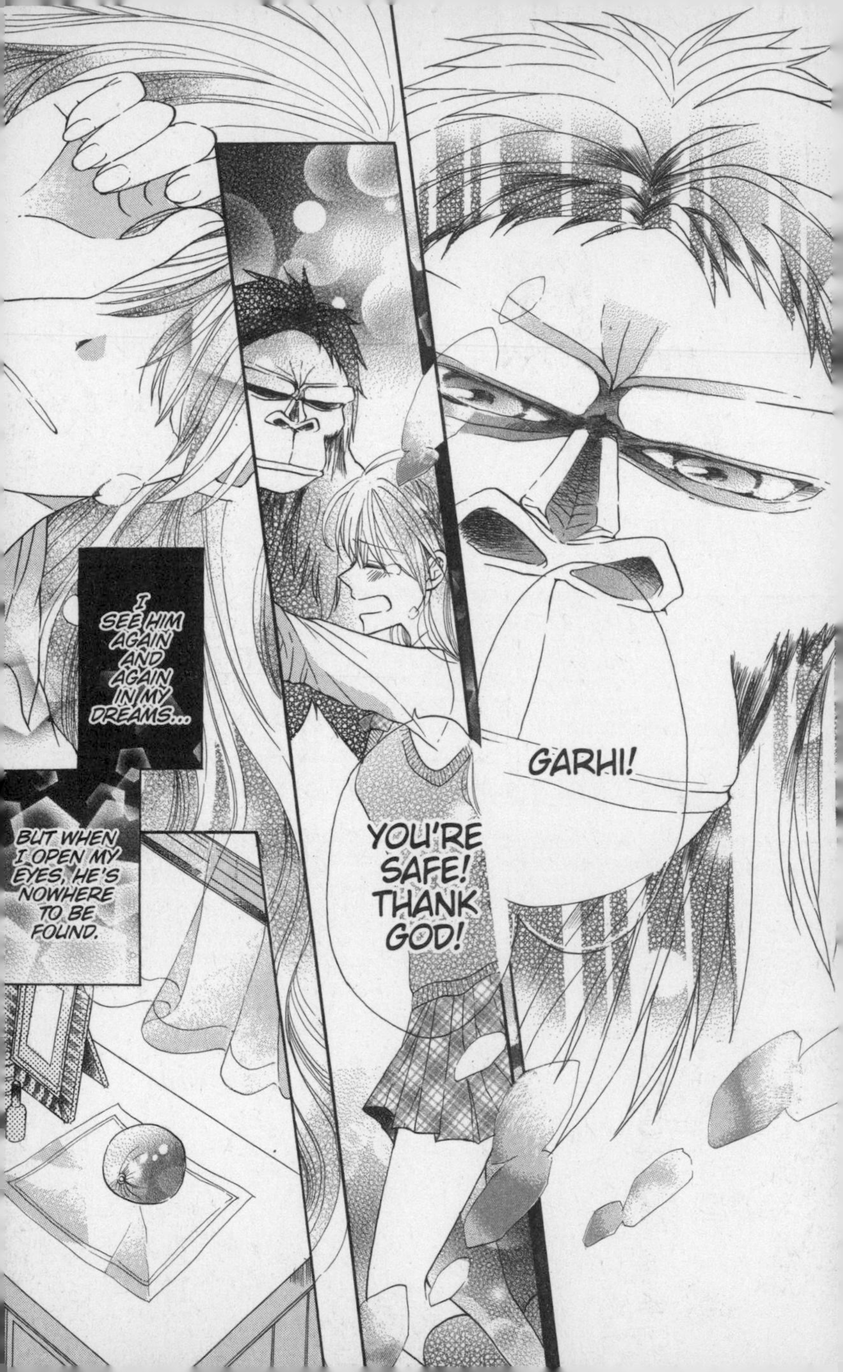
GARHI!
YOU'RE SAFE! THANK GOD!
I SEE HIM AGAIN AND AGAIN IN MY DREAMS...
BUT WHEN I OPEN MY EYES, HE'S NOWHERE TO BE FOUND.

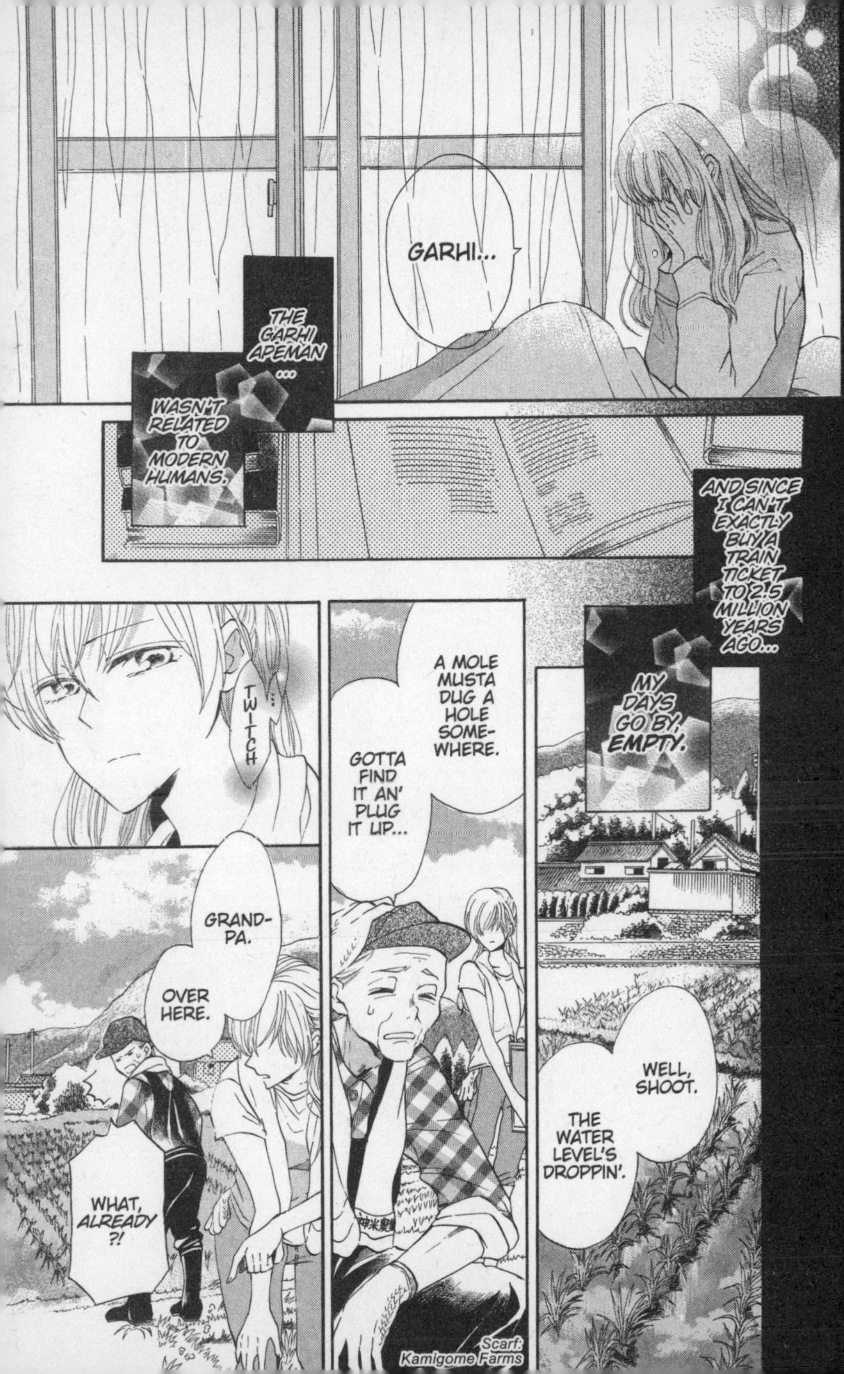
GARHI...
THE GARHI APEMAN...
WASN'T RELATED TO MODERN HUMANS.
AND SINCE I CAN'T EXACTLY BUY A TRAIN TICKET TO 2.5 MILLION YEARS AGO...
MY DAYS GO BY, EMPTY.
WELL, SHOOT.
THE WATER LEVEL'S DROPPIN'.
A MOLE MUSTA DUG A HOLE SOME-WHERE.
GOTTA FIND IT AN' PLUG IT UP...
TWITCH
GRAND-PA.
OVER HERE.
WHAT, ALREADY?!
Scarf: Kamigome Farms

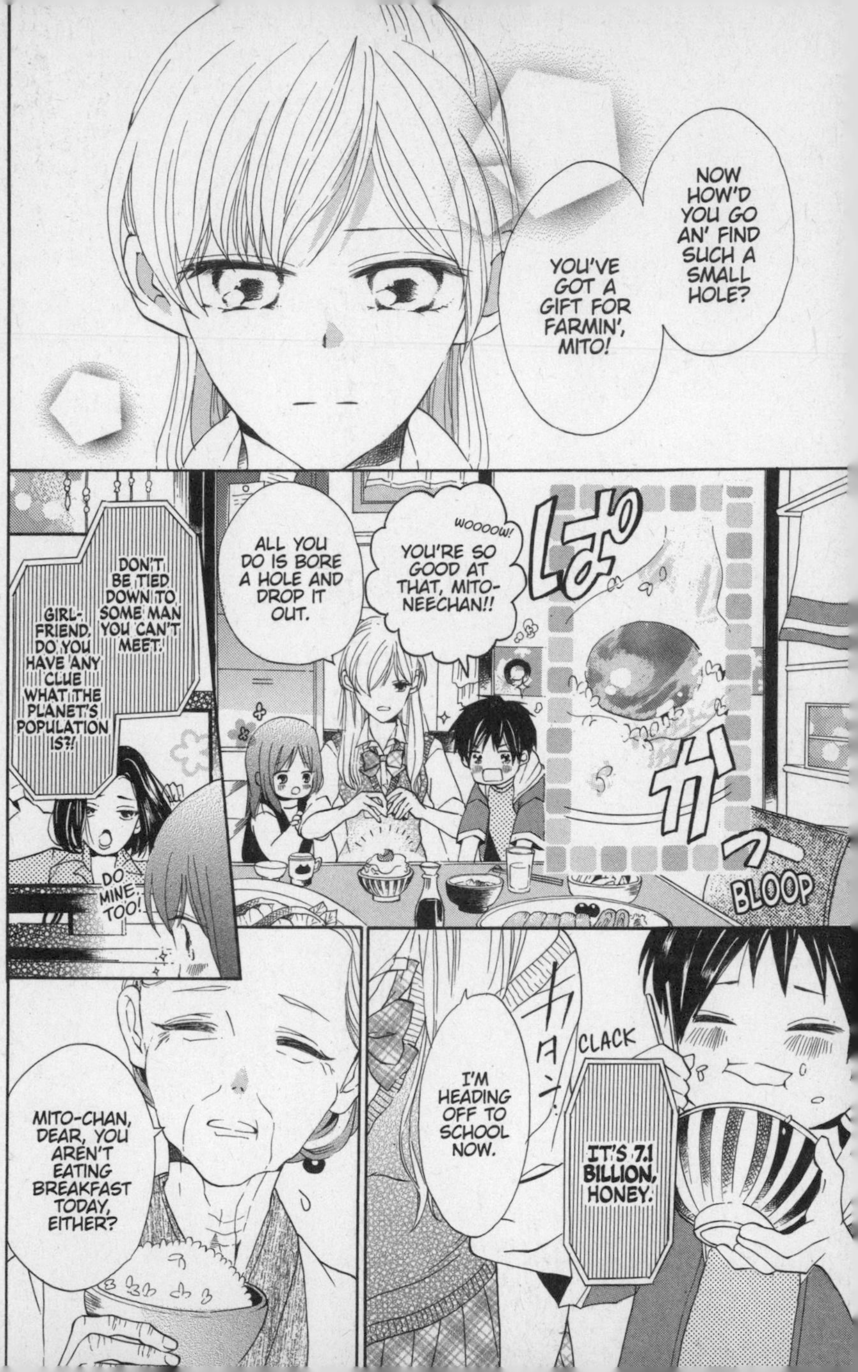
NOW HOW'D YOU GO AN' FIND SUCH A SMALL HOLE?
YOU'VE GOT A GIFT FOR FARMIN', MITO!
BLOOP
WOOOOW!
YOU'RE SO GOOD AT THAT, MITO-NEECHAN!!
ALL YOU DO IS BORE A HOLE AND DROP IT OUT.
DON'T BE TIED DOWN TO SOME MAN YOU CAN'T MEET.
GIRL-FRIEND, DO YOU HAVE ANY CLUE WHAT THE PLANET'S POPULATION IS?!
DO MINE TOO!
CLACK
IT'S 7.1 BILLION, HONEY.
I'M HEADING OFF TO SCHOOL NOW.
MITO-CHAN, DEAR, YOU AREN'T EATING BREAKFAST TODAY, EITHER?

Sign: History Museum

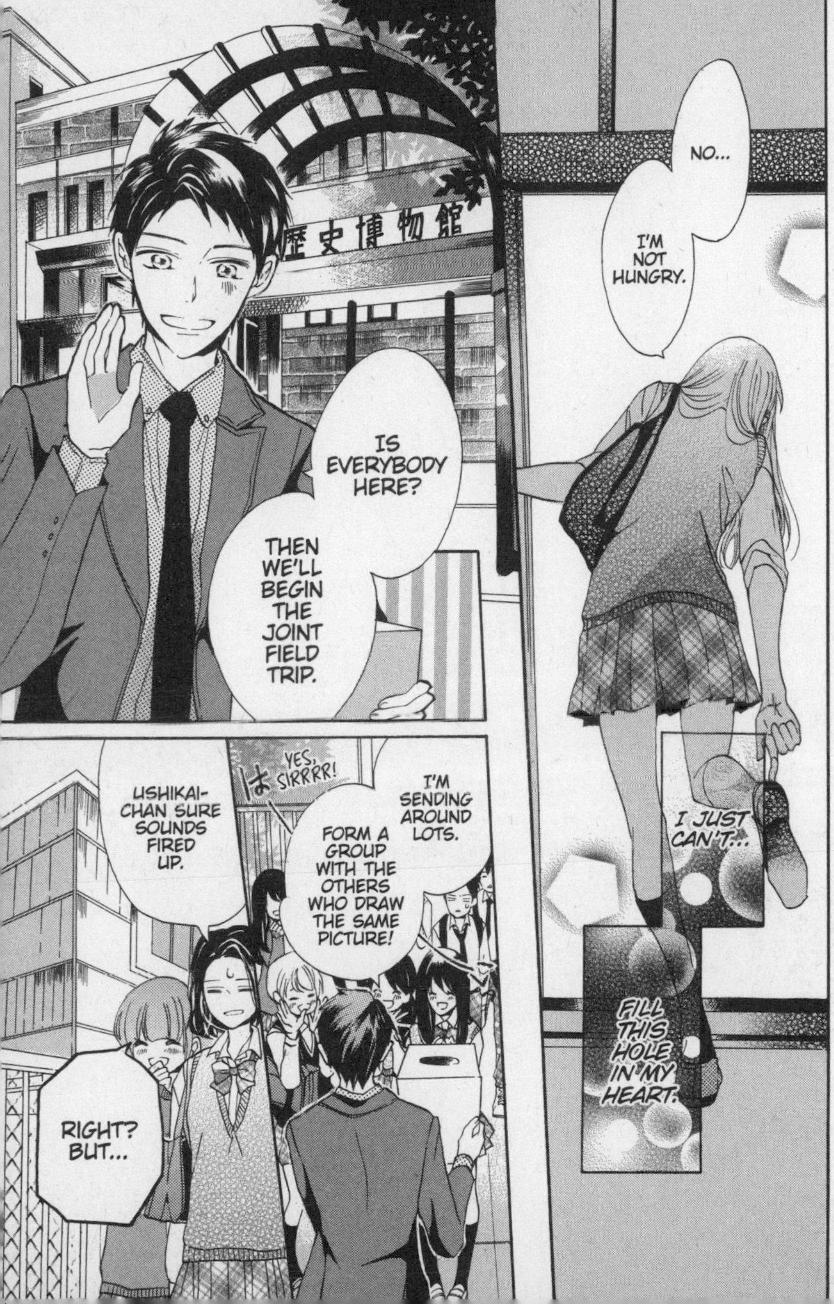
NO...
I'M NOT HUNGRY.
I JUST CAN'T...
FILL THIS HOLE IN MY HEART.
歴史博物館
IS EVERYBODY HERE?
THEN WE'LL BEGIN THE JOINT FIELD TRIP.
I'M SENDING AROUND LOTS.
FORM A GROUP WITH THE OTHERS WHO DRAW THE SAME PICTURE!
は YES, SIRRRR!
USHIKAI-CHAN SURE SOUNDS FIRED UP.
RIGHT? BUT...

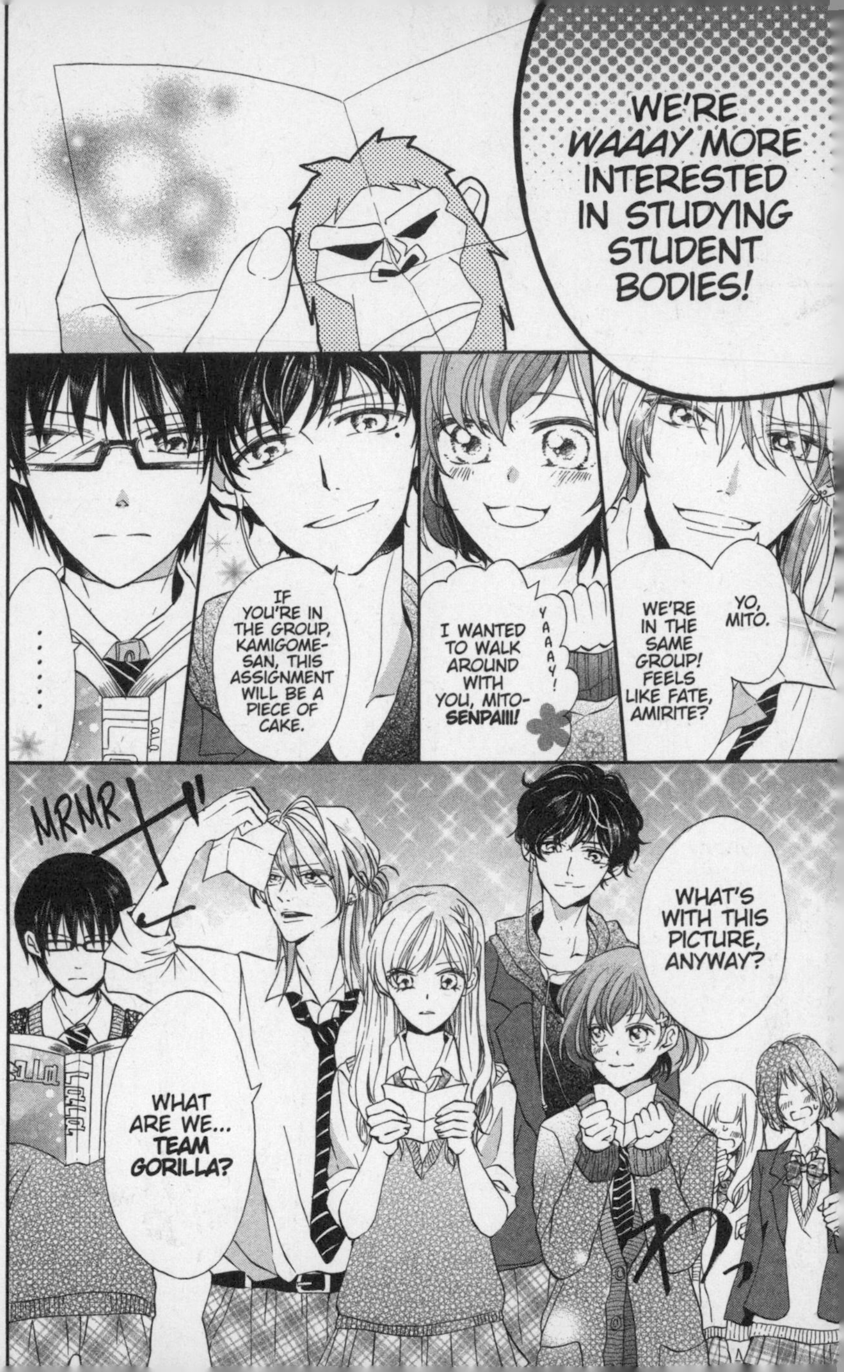
WE'RE *WAAAY* MORE INTERESTED IN STUDYING STUDENT BODIES!
YO, MITO.
WE'RE IN THE SAME GROUP! FEELS LIKE FATE, AMIRITE?
YAAAY!
I WANTED TO WALK AROUND WITH YOU, MITO-**SENPAIII!**
IF YOU'RE IN THE GROUP, KAMIGOME-SAN, THIS ASSIGNMENT WILL BE A PIECE OF CAKE.
......
WHAT'S WITH THIS PICTURE, ANYWAY?
MRMR
WHAT ARE WE... **TEAM GORILLA?**

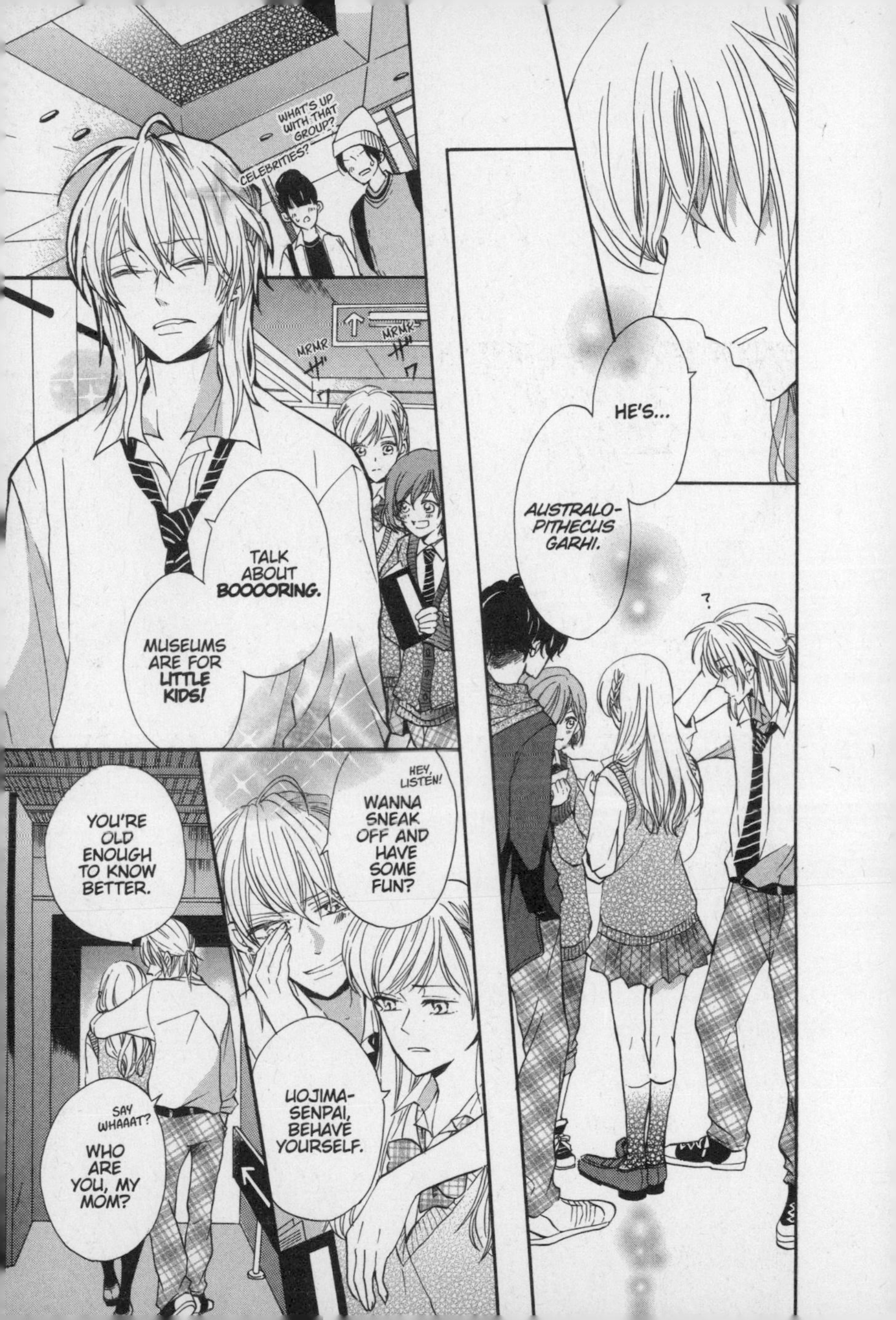
HE'S...
AUSTRALO-PITHECUS GARHI.
?
WHAT'S UP WITH THAT GROUP?
CELEBRITIES?
MRMR
MRMR
TALK ABOUT BOOOORING.
MUSEUMS ARE FOR LITTLE KIDS!
HEY, LISTEN!
WANNA SNEAK OFF AND HAVE SOME FUN?
UOJIMA-SENPAI, BEHAVE YOURSELF.
YOU'RE OLD ENOUGH TO KNOW BETTER.
SAY WHAAAT?
WHO ARE YOU, MY MOM?

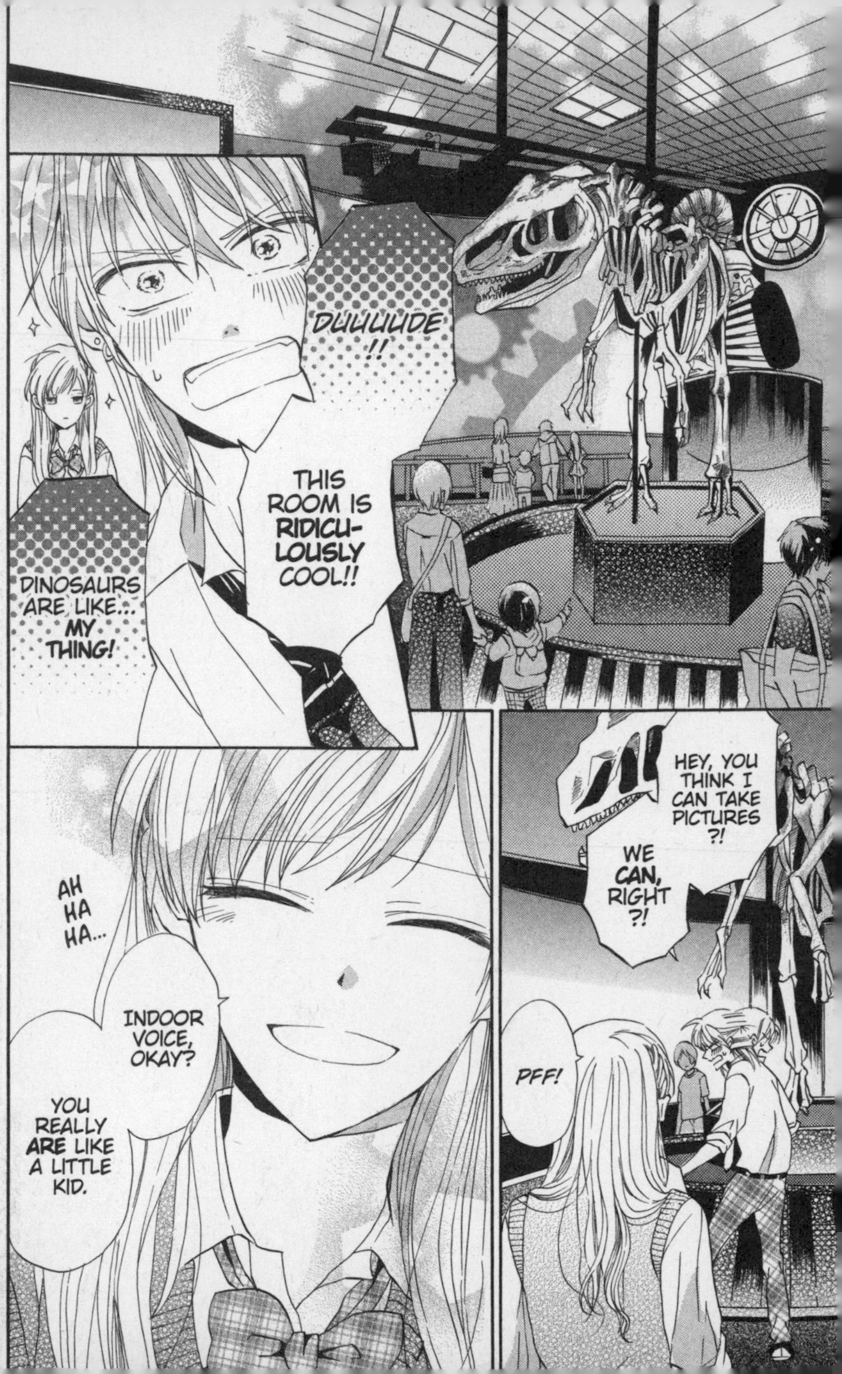
DUUUUDE!!
THIS ROOM IS RIDICULOUSLY COOL!!
DINOSAURS ARE LIKE... MY THING!
HEY, YOU THINK I CAN TAKE PICTURES?!
WE CAN, RIGHT?!
PFF!
AH HA HA...
INDOOR VOICE, OKAY?
YOU REALLY ARE LIKE A LITTLE KID.

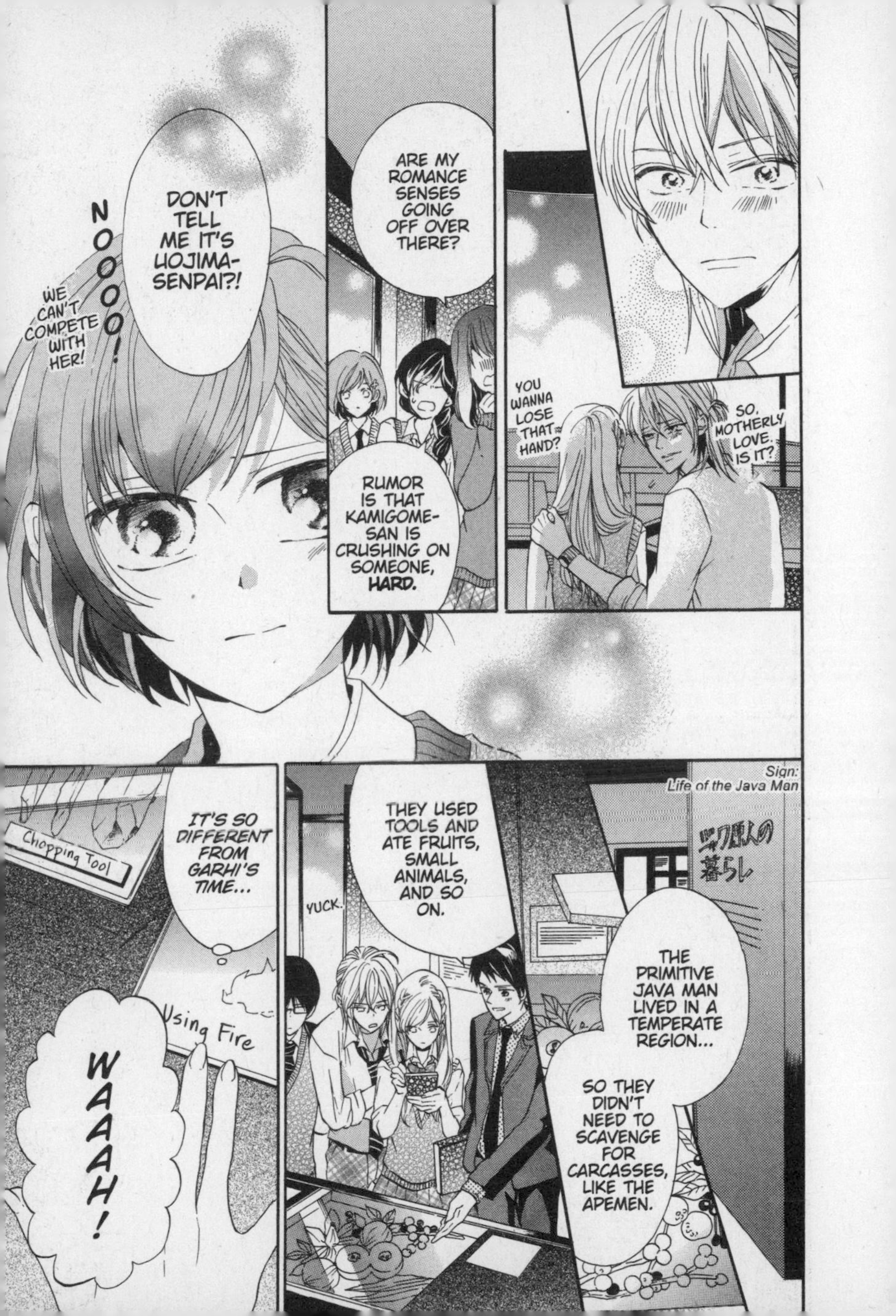
SO, MOTHERLY LOVE. IS IT?
YOU WANNA LOSE THAT HAND?
ARE MY ROMANCE SENSES GOING OFF OVER THERE?
RUMOR IS THAT KAMIGOME-SAN IS CRUSHING ON SOMEONE, **HARD.**
DON'T TELL ME IT'S UOJIMA-SENPAI?!
NOOOOO!
WE CAN'T COMPETE WITH HER!
Sign:
Life of the Java Man
ジャワ原人の暮らし
THEY USED TOOLS AND ATE FRUITS, SMALL ANIMALS, AND SO ON.
THE PRIMITIVE JAVA MAN LIVED IN A TEMPERATE REGION...
SO THEY DIDN'T NEED TO SCAVENGE FOR CARCASSES, LIKE THE APEMEN.
YUCK.
Chopping Tool
IT'S SO DIFFERENT FROM GARHI'S TIME...
Using Fire
WAAAAH!

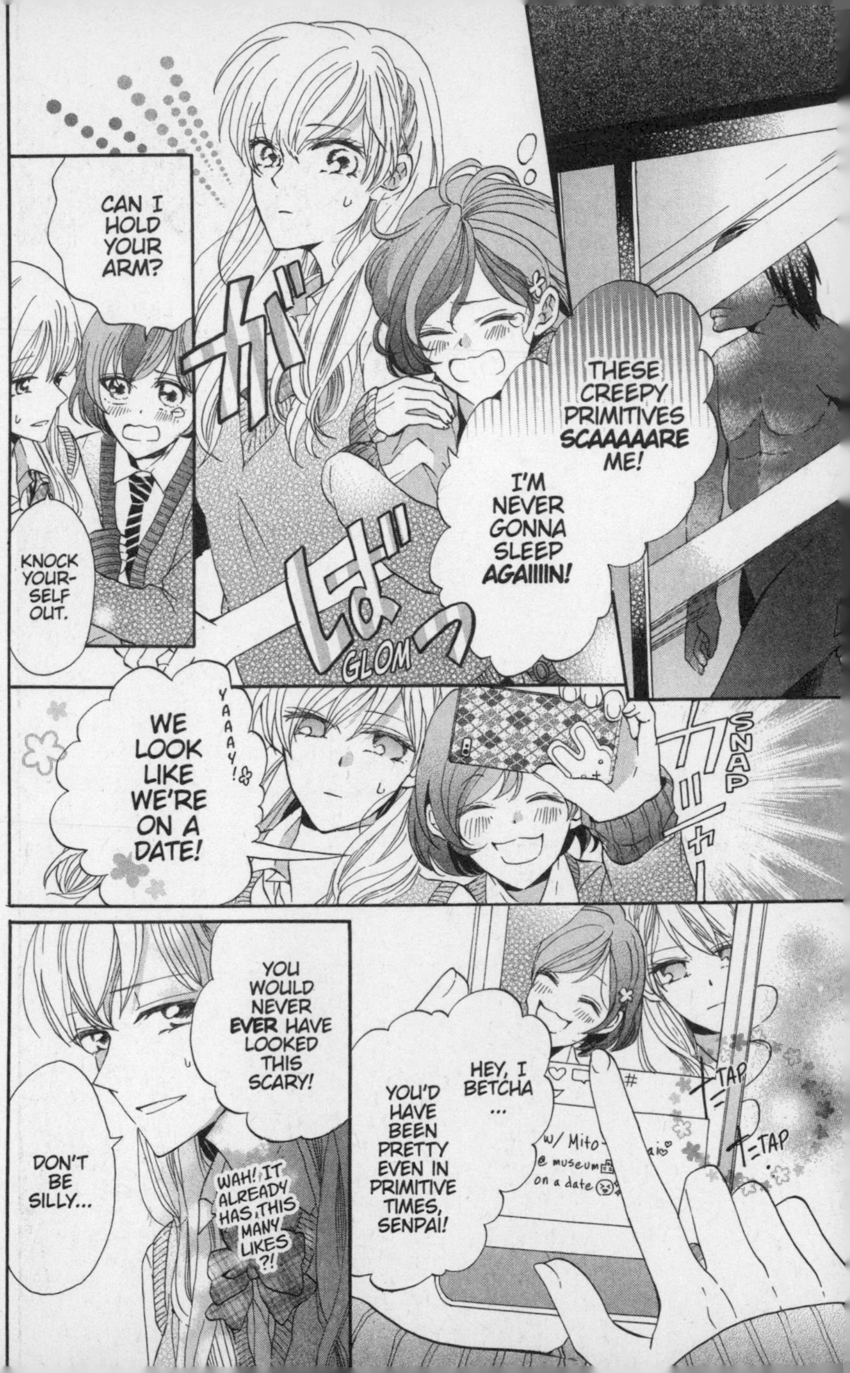
THESE CREEPY PRIMITIVES SCAAAAARE ME!
I'M NEVER GONNA SLEEP AGAIIIIN!
GLOM
CAN I HOLD YOUR ARM?
KNOCK YOURSELF OUT.
SNAP
YAAAAY!
WE LOOK LIKE WE'RE ON A DATE!
TAP
TAP
w/ Mito-
@ museum
on a date
HEY, I BETCHA...
YOU'D HAVE BEEN PRETTY EVEN IN PRIMITIVE TIMES, SENPAI!
YOU WOULD NEVER EVER HAVE LOOKED THIS SCARY!
WAH! IT ALREADY HAS THIS MANY LIKES?!
DON'T BE SILLY...

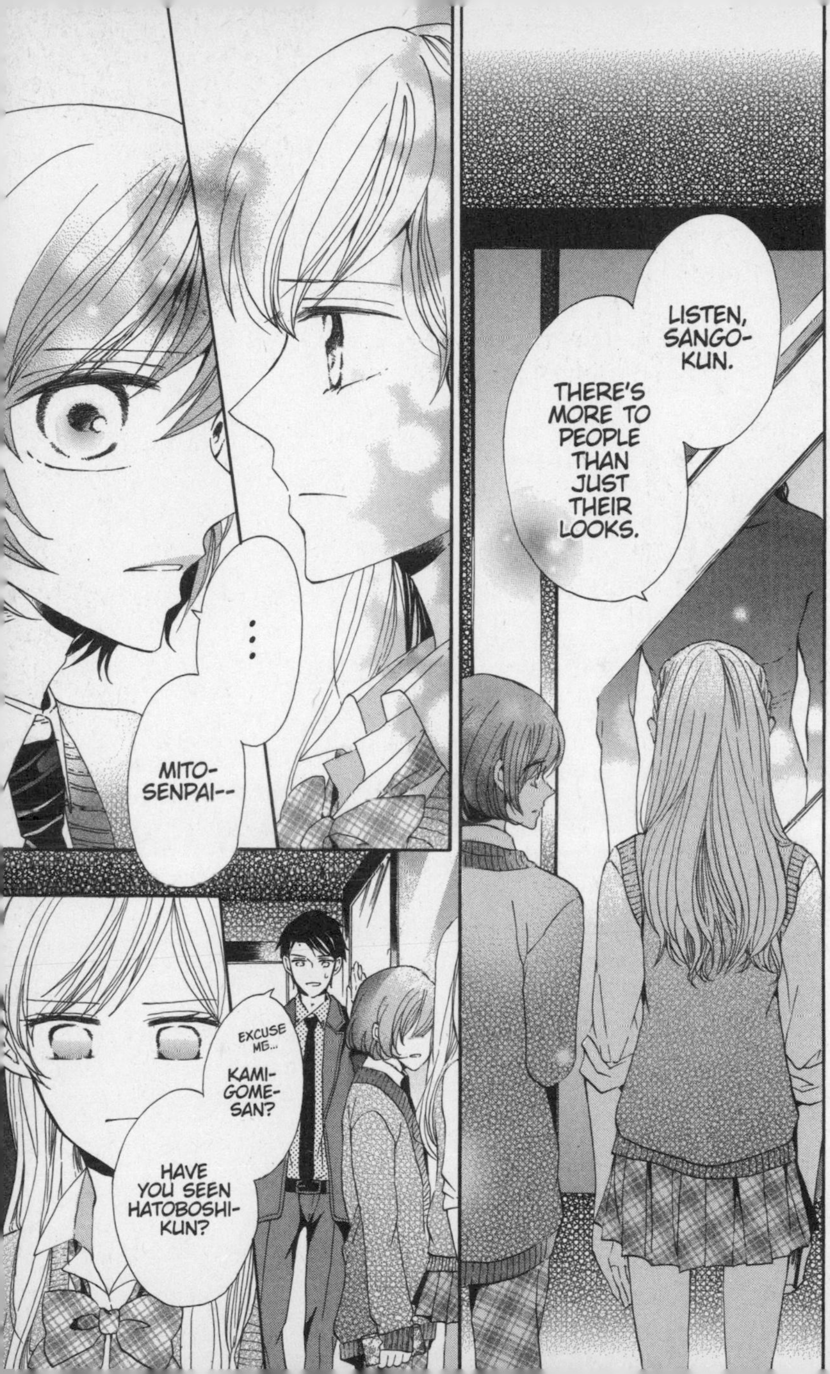
LISTEN, SANGO-KUN.
THERE'S MORE TO PEOPLE THAN JUST THEIR LOOKS.
...
MITO-SENPAI--
EXCUSE ME...
KAMI-GOME-SAN?
HAVE YOU SEEN HATOBOSHI-KUN?

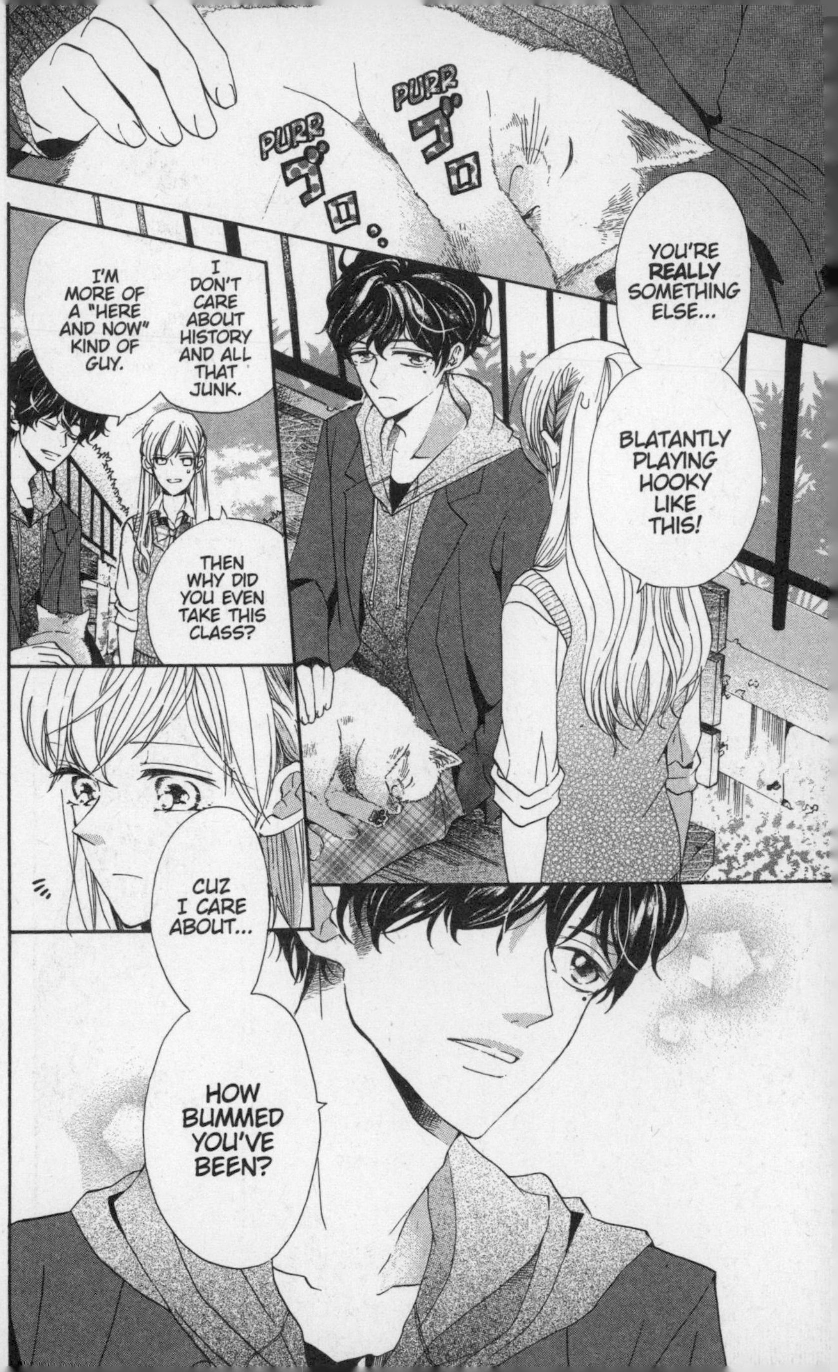
PURR ゴロ
PURR ゴロ…
YOU'RE REALLY SOMETHING ELSE...
BLATANTLY PLAYING HOOKY LIKE THIS!
I DON'T CARE ABOUT HISTORY AND ALL THAT JUNK.
I'M MORE OF A "HERE AND NOW" KIND OF GUY.
THEN WHY DID YOU EVEN TAKE THIS CLASS?
CUZ I CARE ABOUT...
HOW BUMMED YOU'VE BEEN?

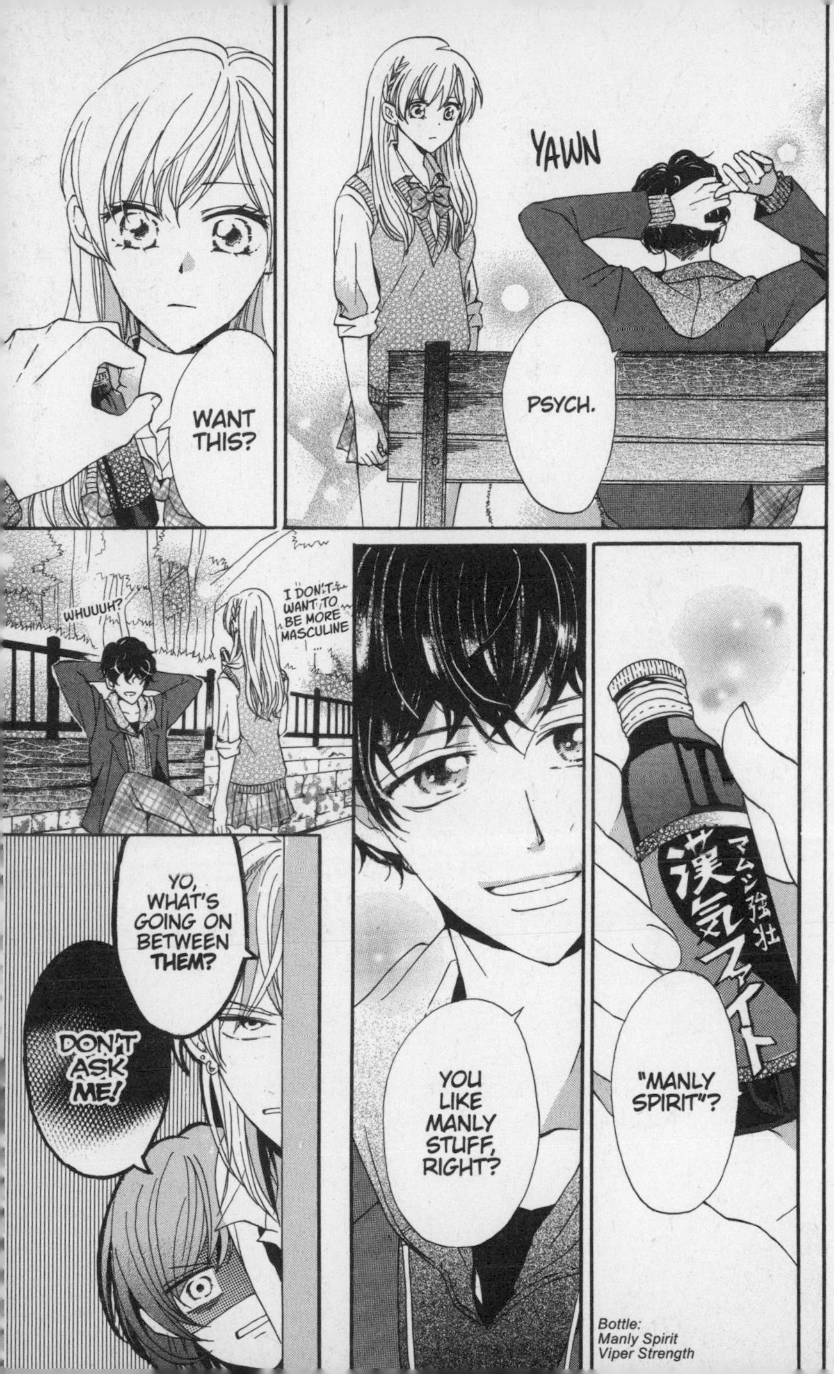
YAWN
PSYCH.
WANT THIS?
マムシ強壮
漢気ファイト
"MANLY SPIRIT"?
Bottle:
Manly Spirit
Viper Strength
YOU LIKE MANLY STUFF, RIGHT?
I DON'T WANT TO BE MORE MASCULINE...
WHUUUH?
YO, WHAT'S GOING ON BETWEEN THEM?
DON'T ASK ME!

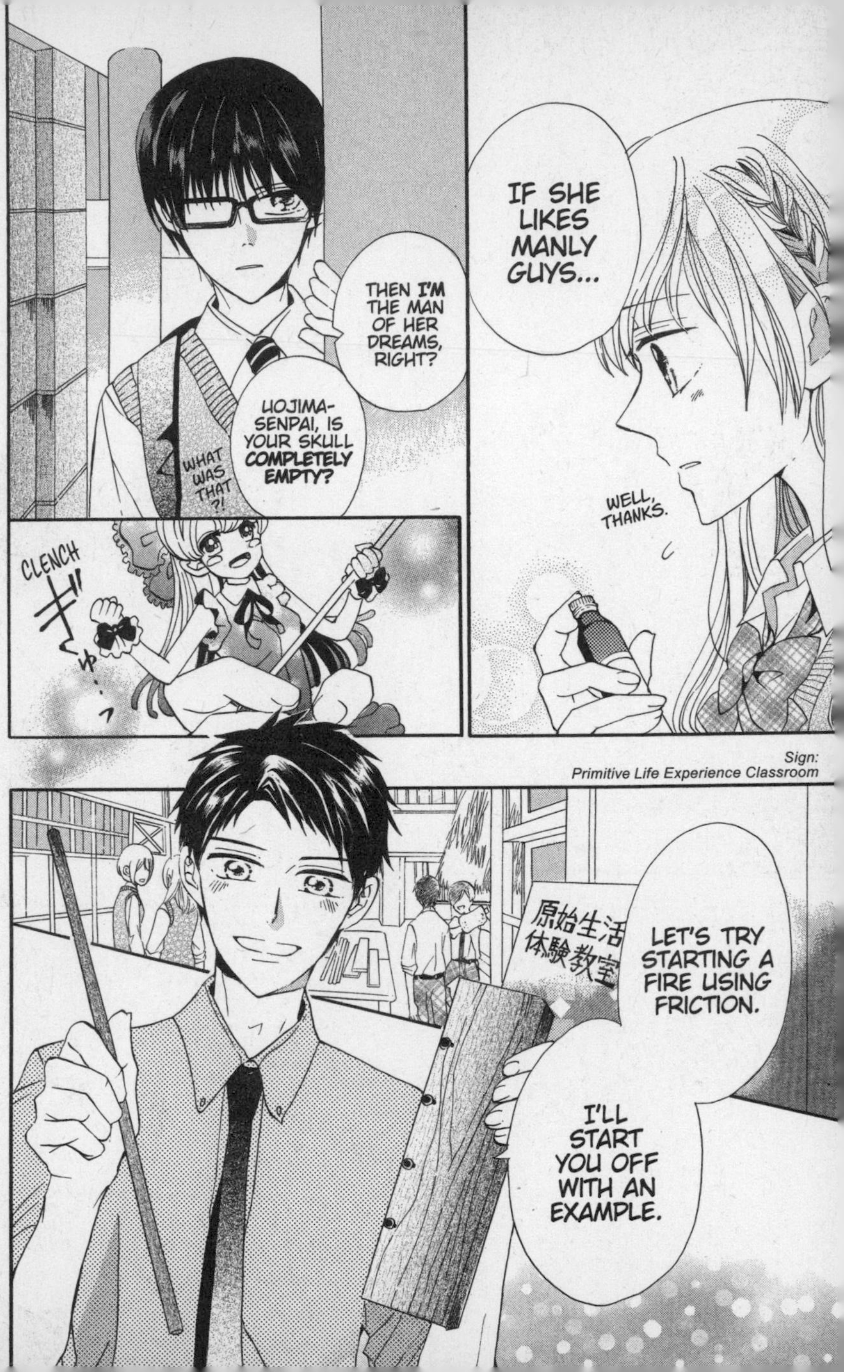
IF SHE LIKES MANLY GUYS...
WELL, THANKS.
THEN I'M THE MAN OF HER DREAMS, RIGHT?
UOJIMA-SENPAI, IS YOUR SKULL COMPLETELY EMPTY?
WHAT WAS THAT?!
CLENCH
ぎゅ…っ
原始生活体験教室
LET'S TRY STARTING A FIRE USING FRICTION.
I'LL START YOU OFF WITH AN EXAMPLE.
Sign: Primitive Life Experience Classroom

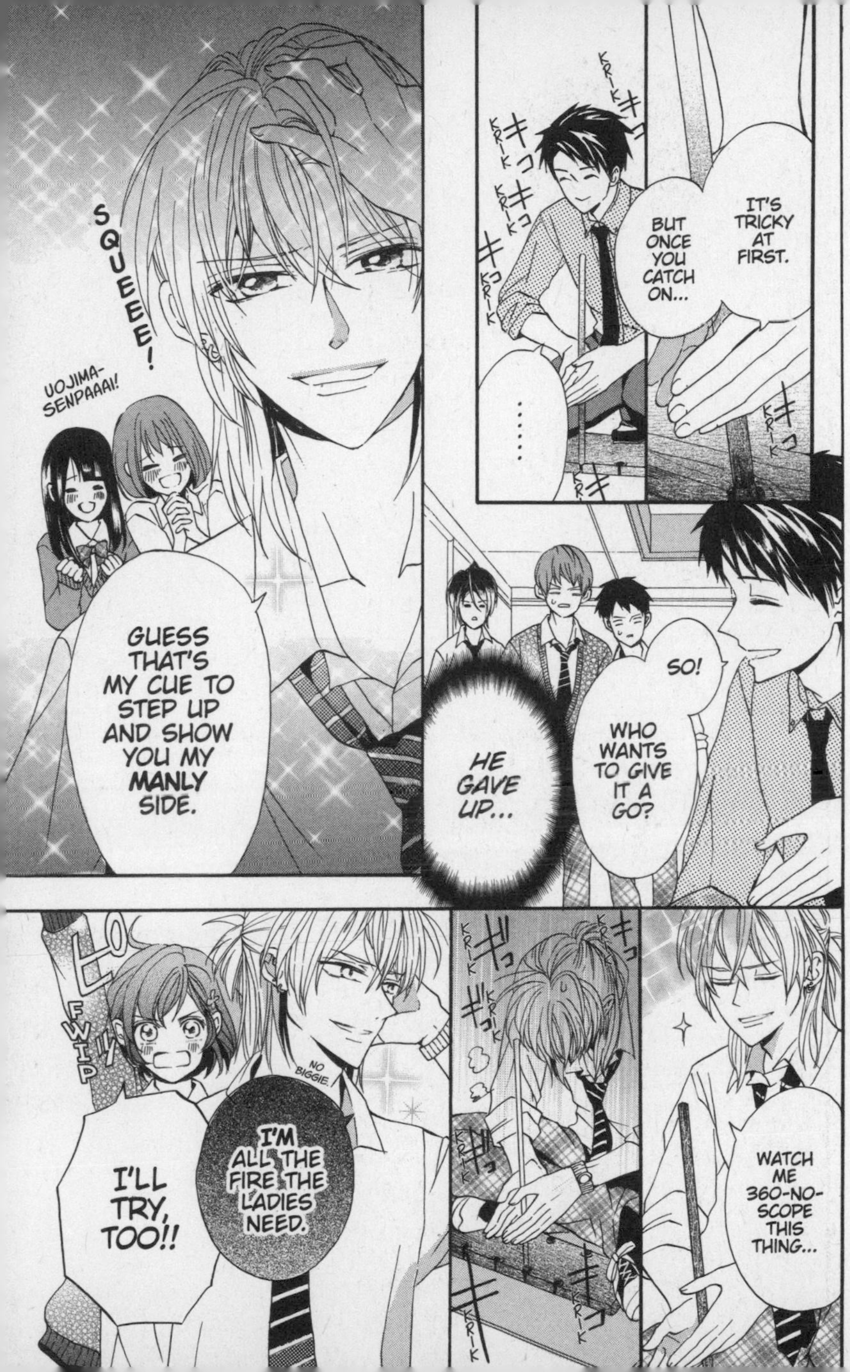
IT'S TRICKY AT FIRST.
BUT ONCE YOU CATCH ON...
KRIK
KRIK
KRIK
KRIK
KRIK
......
SO!
WHO WANTS TO GIVE IT A GO?
HE GAVE UP...
SQUEEEE!
UOJIMA-SENPAAAI!
GUESS THAT'S MY CUE TO STEP UP AND SHOW YOU MY MANLY SIDE.
WATCH ME 360-NO-SCOPE THIS THING...
KRIK
KRIK
KRIK
KRIK
KRIK
KRIK
FWIP
NO BIGGIE.
I'M ALL THE FIRE THE LADIES NEED.
I'LL TRY, TOO!!

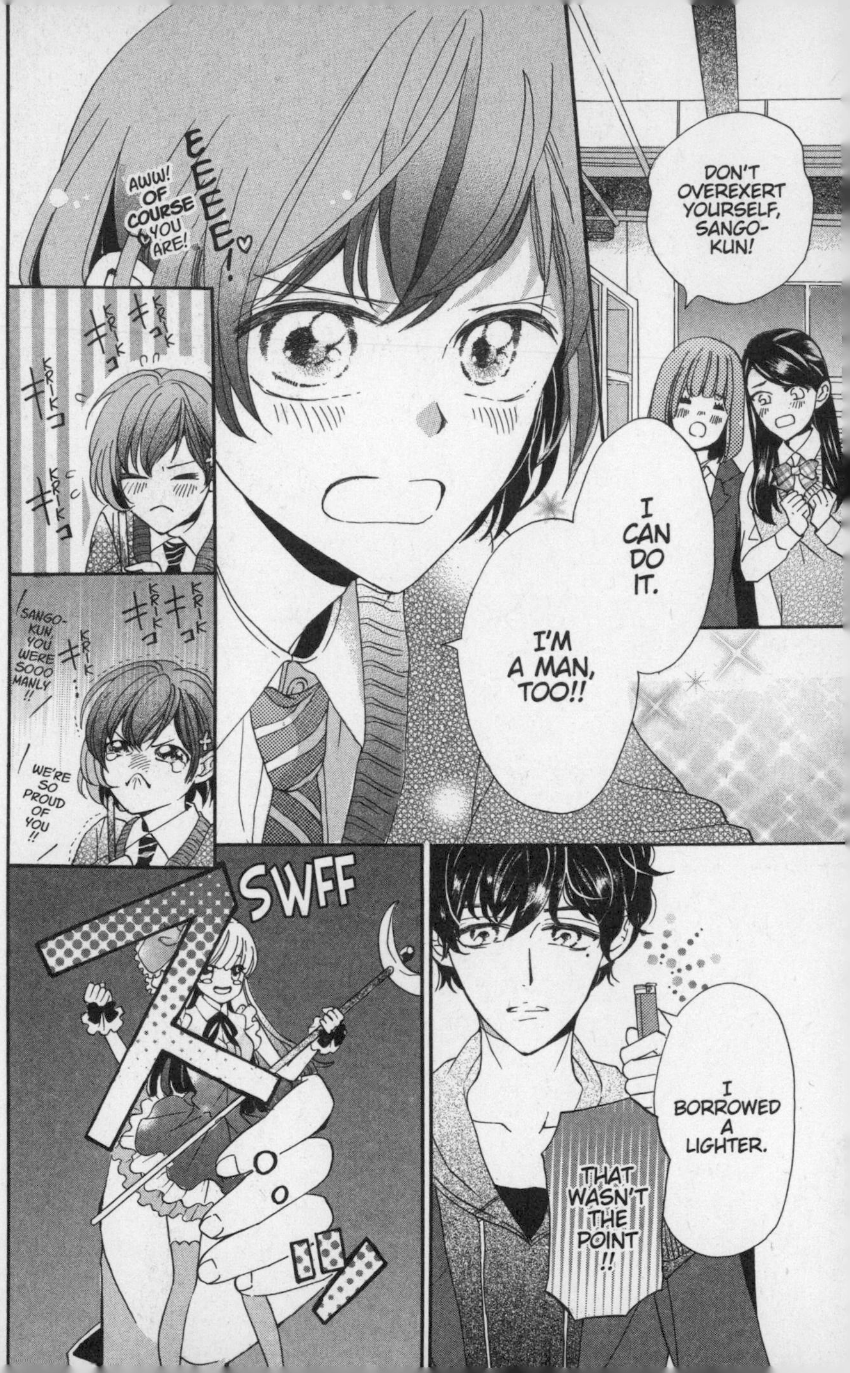
DON'T OVEREXERT YOURSELF, SANGO-KUN!
I CAN DO IT.
I'M A MAN, TOO!!
AWW! OF COURSE YOU ARE!
EEEEEE!♡
KRIK KRIK
KRIK KRIK
KRIK KRIK KRIK
SANGO-KUN YOU WERE SOOO MANLY!!
WE'RE SO PROUD OF YOU!!
I BORROWED A LIGHTER.
THAT WASN'T THE POINT!!
SWFF

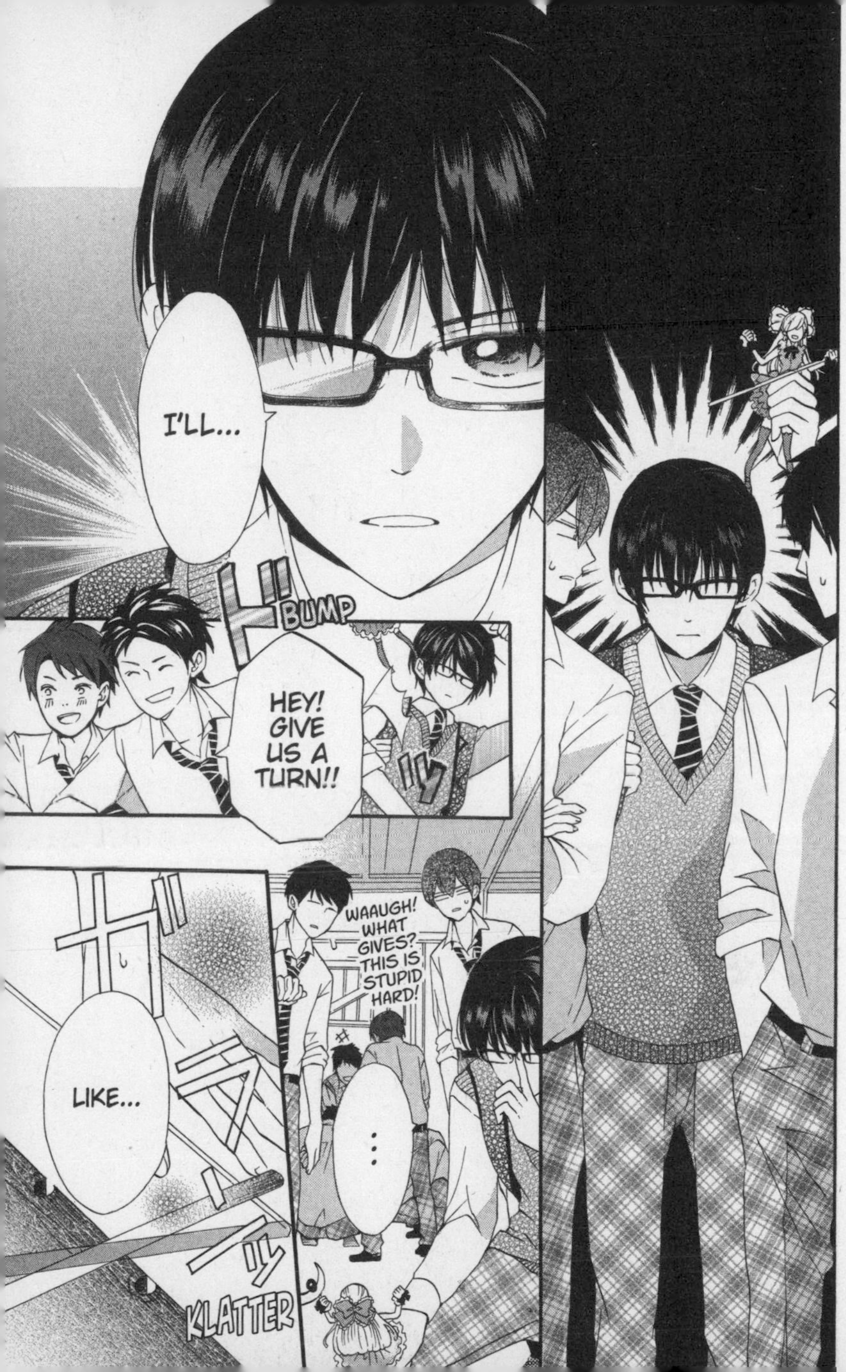
I'LL...
BUMP
HEY! GIVE US A TURN!!
WAAUGH! WHAT GIVES? THIS IS STUPID HARD!
...
LIKE...
KLATTER

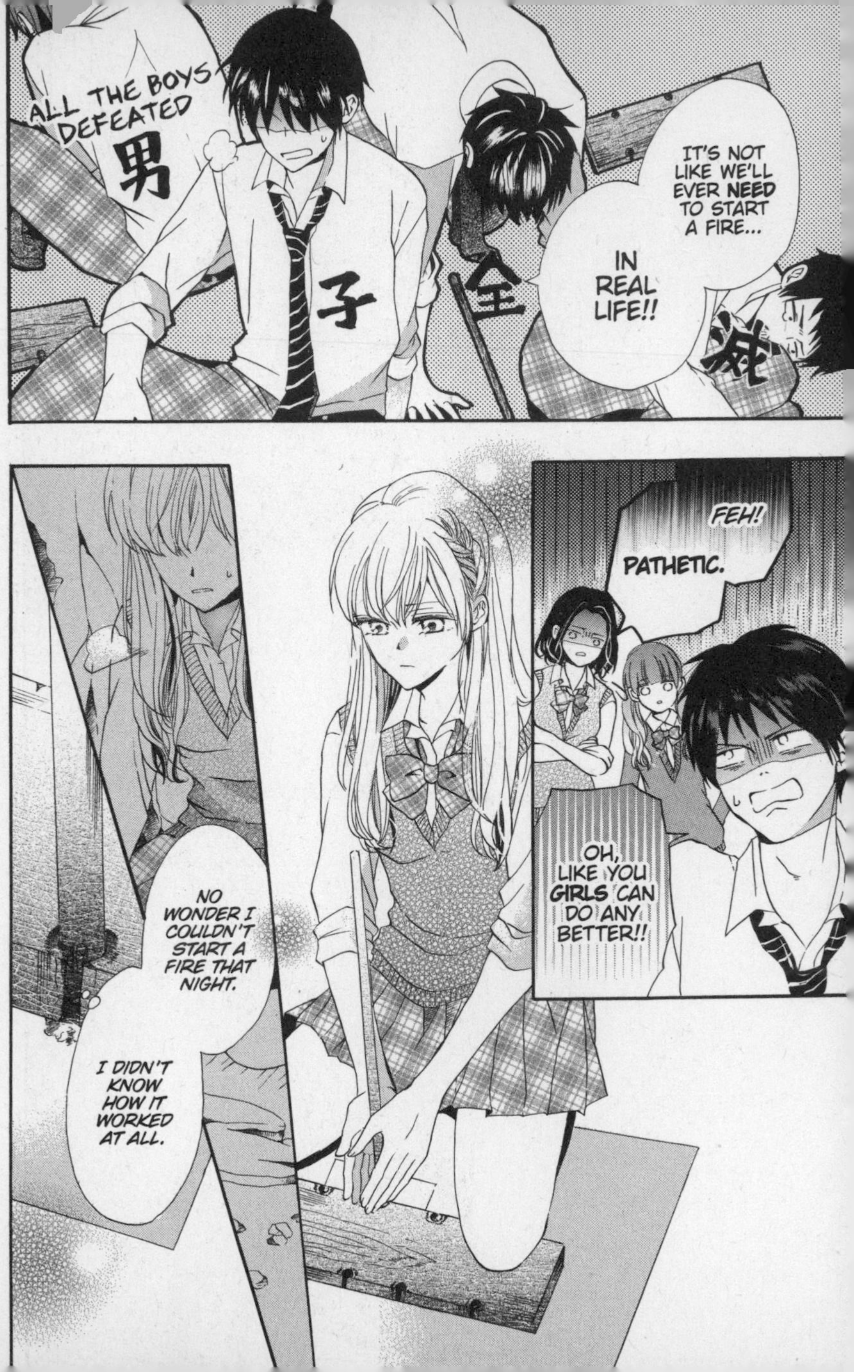
IT'S NOT LIKE WE'LL EVER NEED TO START A FIRE...
IN REAL LIFE!!
ALL THE BOYS DEFEATED
男子全滅
FEH!
PATHETIC.
OH, LIKE YOU GIRLS CAN DO ANY BETTER!!
NO WONDER I COULDN'T START A FIRE THAT NIGHT.
I DIDN'T KNOW HOW IT WORKED AT ALL.

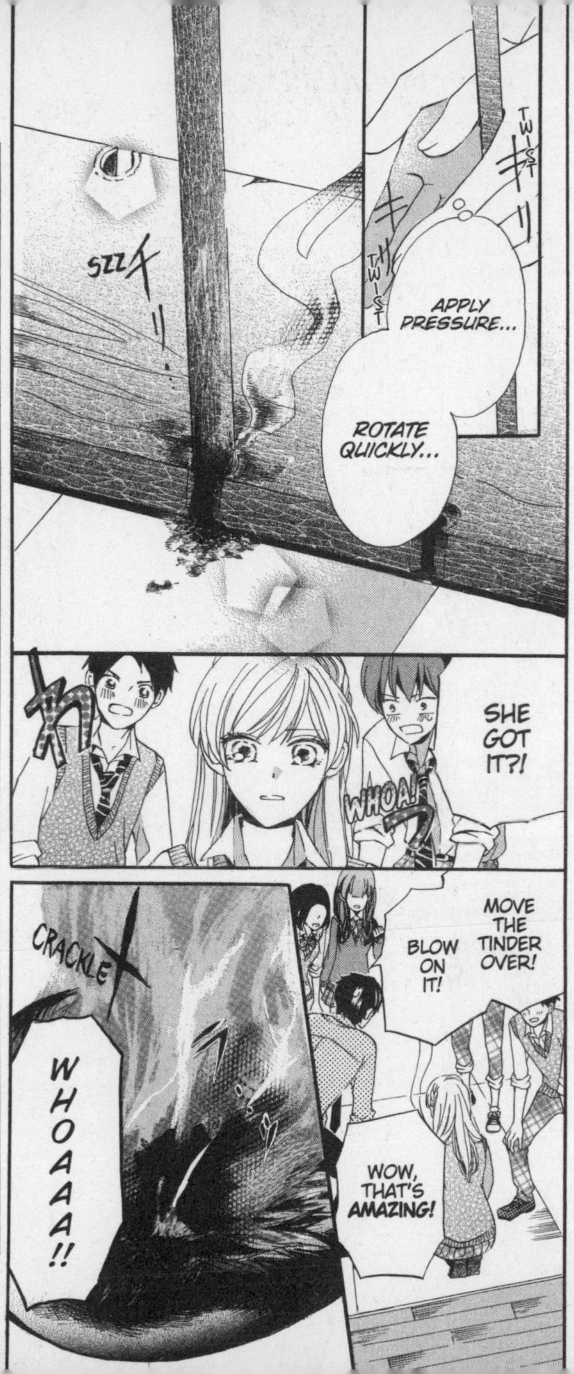
TWIST
TWIST
SZZ
APPLY PRESSURE...
ROTATE QUICKLY...
SHE GOT IT?!
WHOA!
MOVE THE TINDER OVER!
BLOW ON IT!
CRACKLE
WHOAAAA!!
WOW, THAT'S AMAZING!

3

I USED THE NATIONAL MUSEUM OF SCIENCE AND NATURE IN UENO, TOKYO AS THE MODEL FOR THE CHAPTER 3 MUSEUM.

I WENT THERE ON MY LONESOME TO LOOK FOR MATERIAL AND SUCH, BUT I ENDED UP HAVING SO MUCH FUN THAT I STAYED AT THE MUSEUM RIGHT UP UNTIL CLOSING TIME.

IT WAS SUUUUPER FUN!!! SO I'D LIKE TO GO BACK AGAIN AND AGAIN. I WILL BE BACK.

(A DECLARATION!)

THAT DAY, MY DINNER WAS THE ASTRONAUT ICE CREAM I BOUGHT AT THE MUSEUM.

SO WHITE YOU COULD ALMOST HEAR IT SAY, "I AM WHITENESS ITSELF." IT FELT LIKE A LUXURY FOOD ONLY THE UPPER ECHELONS COULD GET THEIR HANDS ON IN A POST-APOCALYPTIC WORLD.

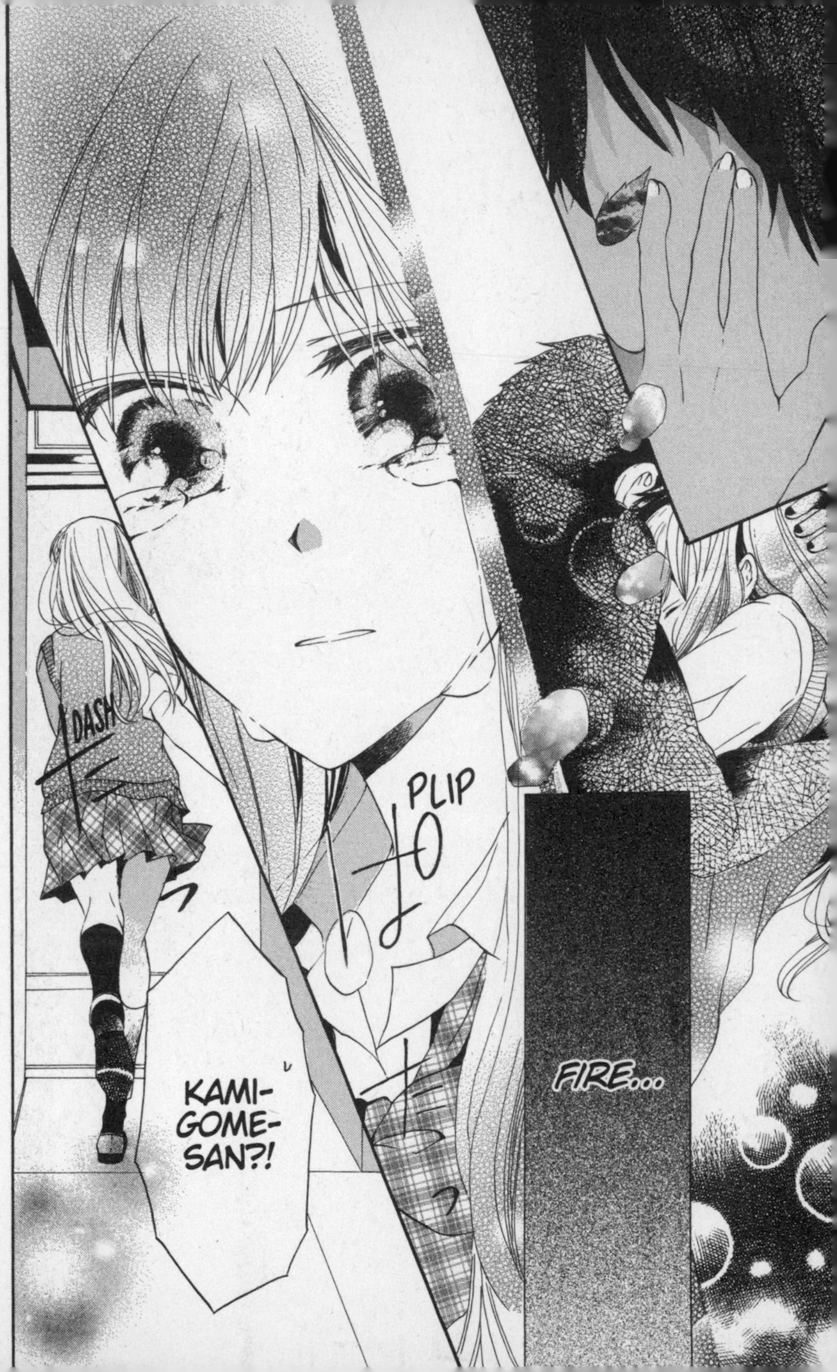
FIRE...
PLIP
KAMI-GOME-SAN?!
DASH

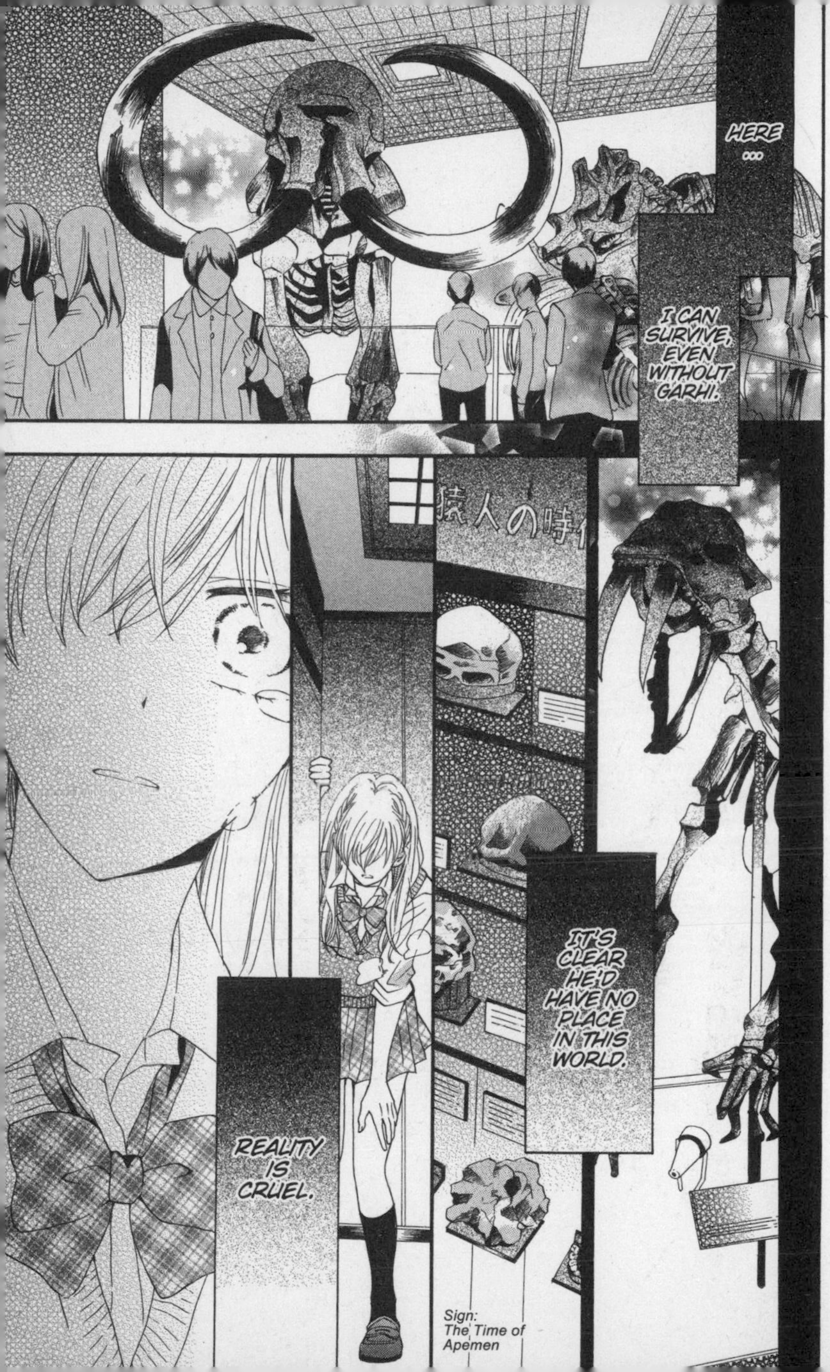
HERE...
I CAN SURVIVE, EVEN WITHOUT GARHI.
猿人の時
IT'S CLEAR HE'D HAVE NO PLACE IN THIS WORLD.
REALITY IS CRUEL.
Sign: The Time of Apemen

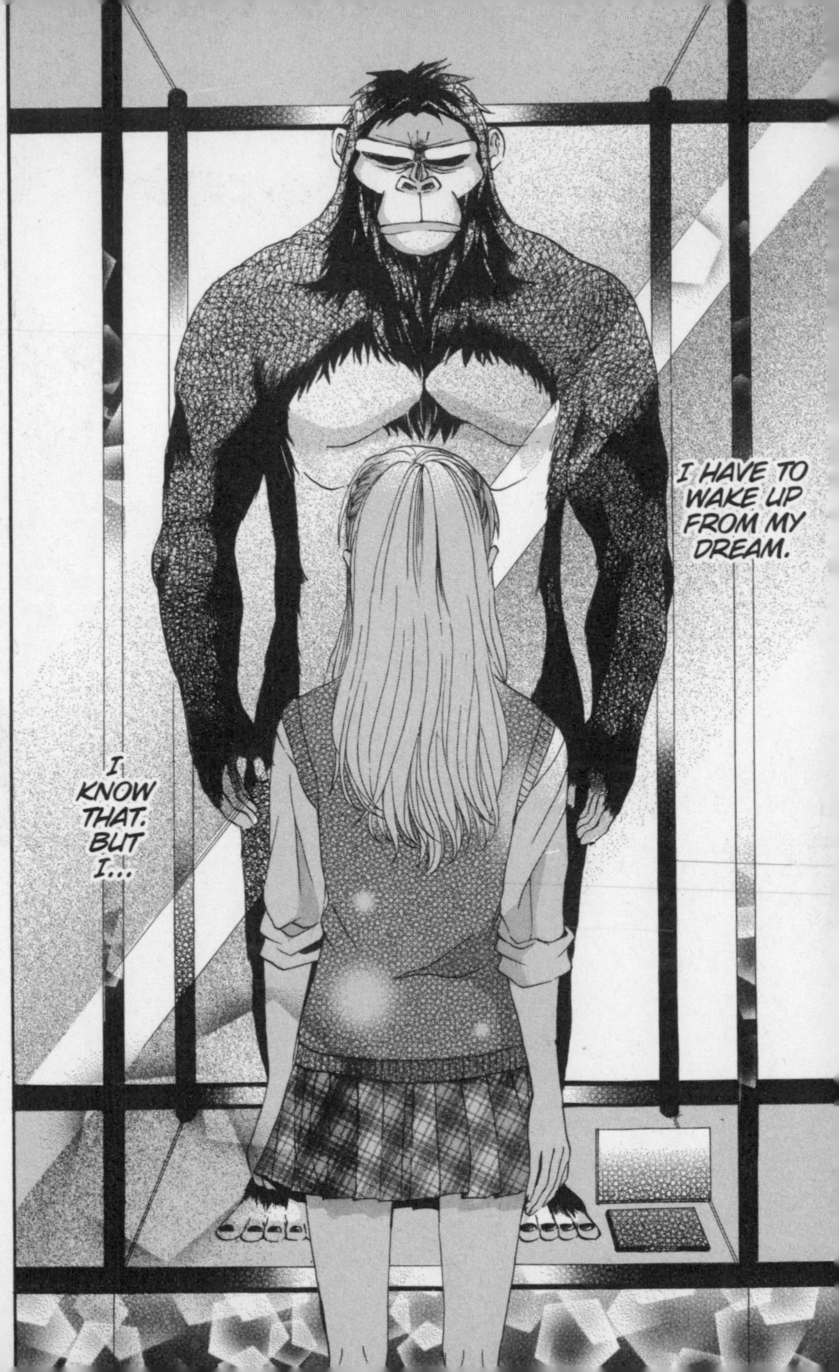
I HAVE TO WAKE UP FROM MY DREAM.
I KNOW THAT. BUT I...

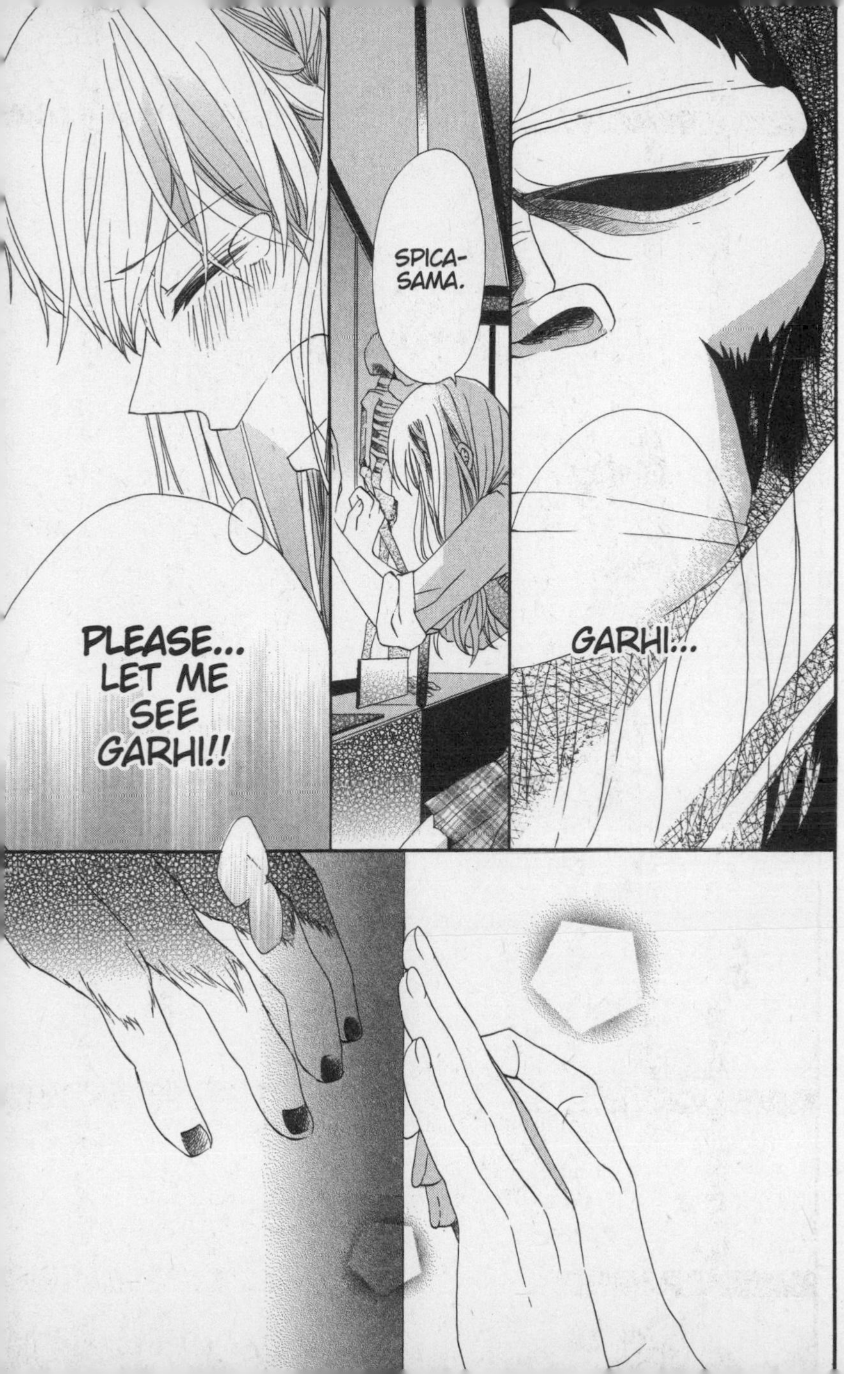
GARHI...
SPICA-SAMA.
PLEASE... LET ME SEE GARHI!!

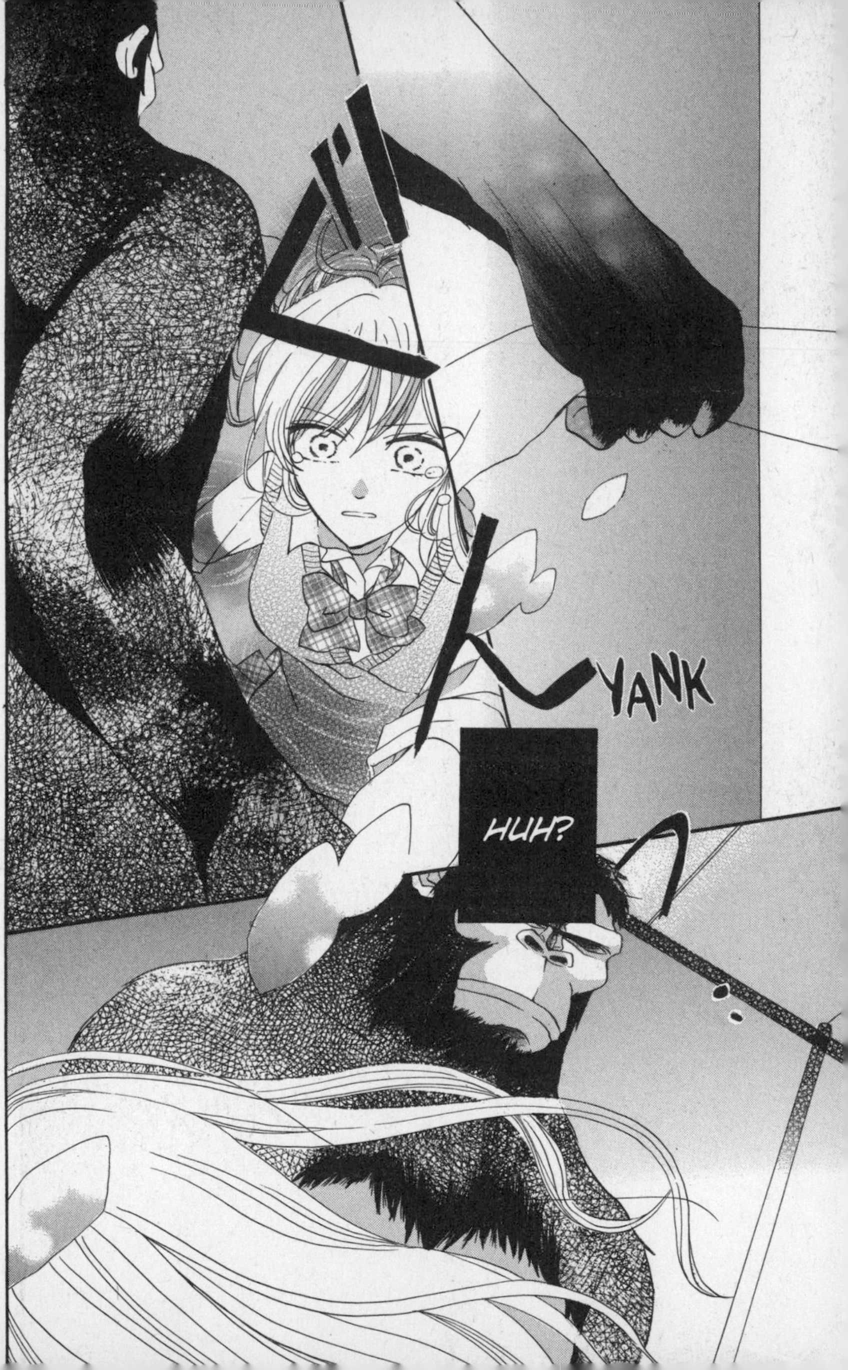
YANK
HUH?

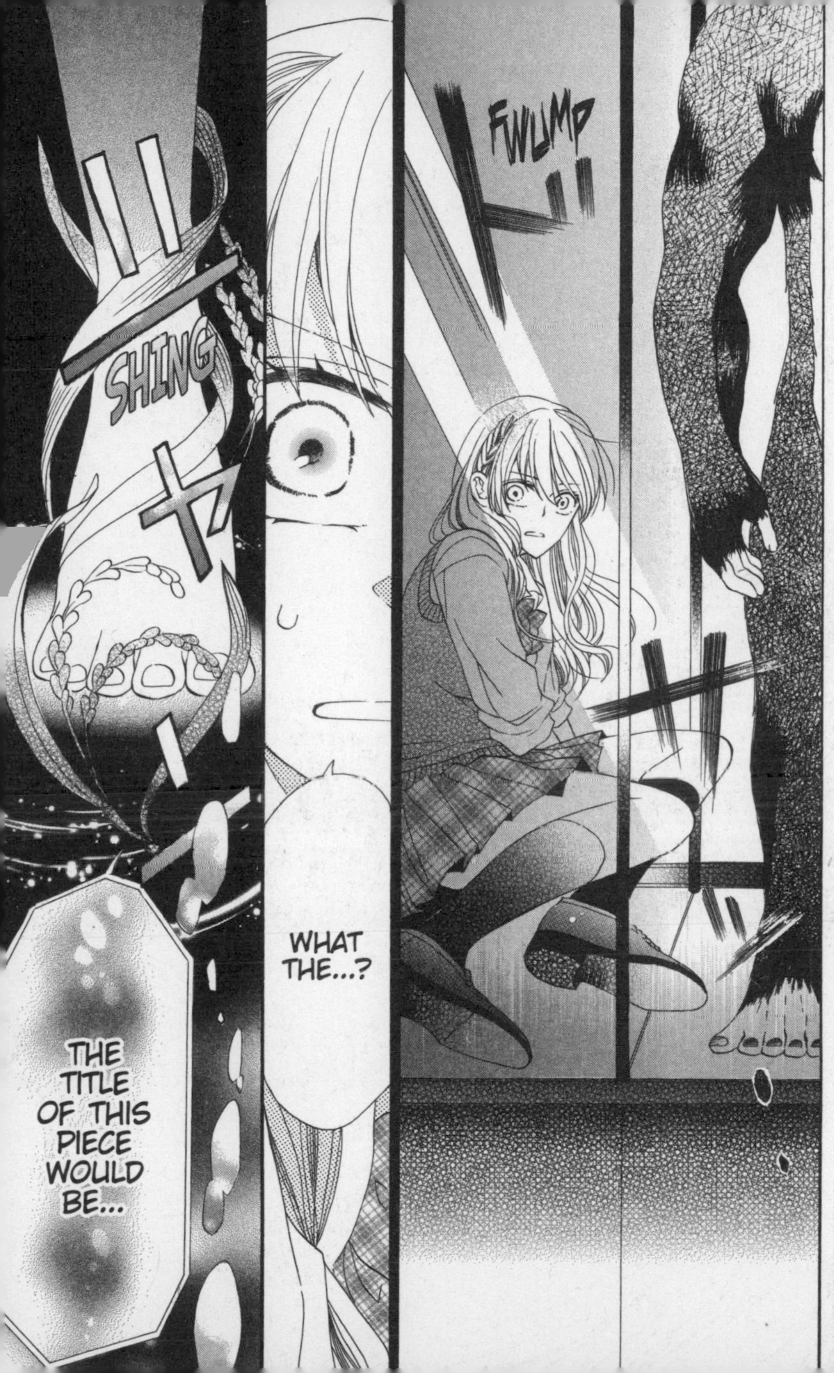
FWUMP
WHAT THE...?
SHING
THE TITLE OF THIS PIECE WOULD BE...

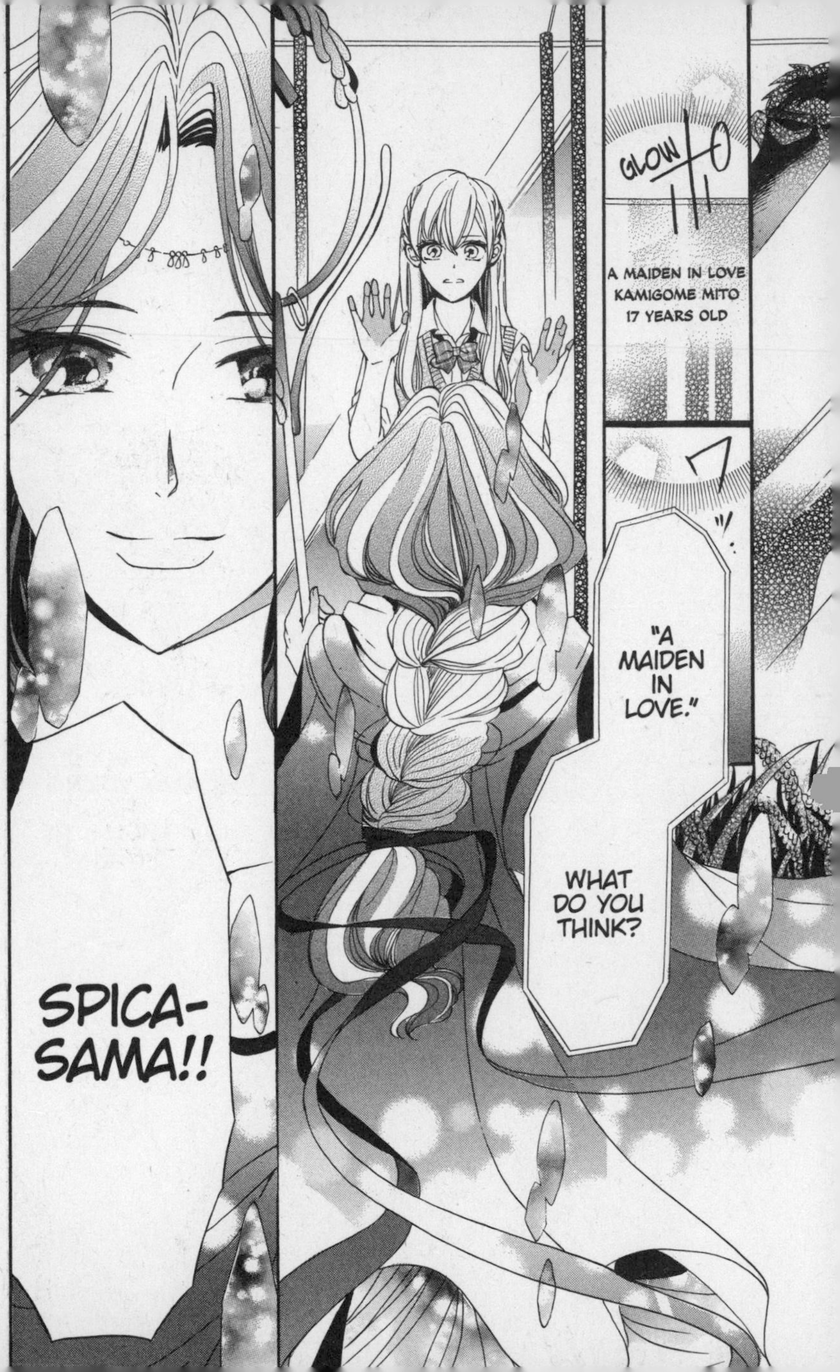
GLOW
A MAIDEN IN LOVE
KAMIGOME MITO
17 YEARS OLD
"A MAIDEN IN LOVE."
WHAT DO YOU THINK?
SPICA-SAMA!!

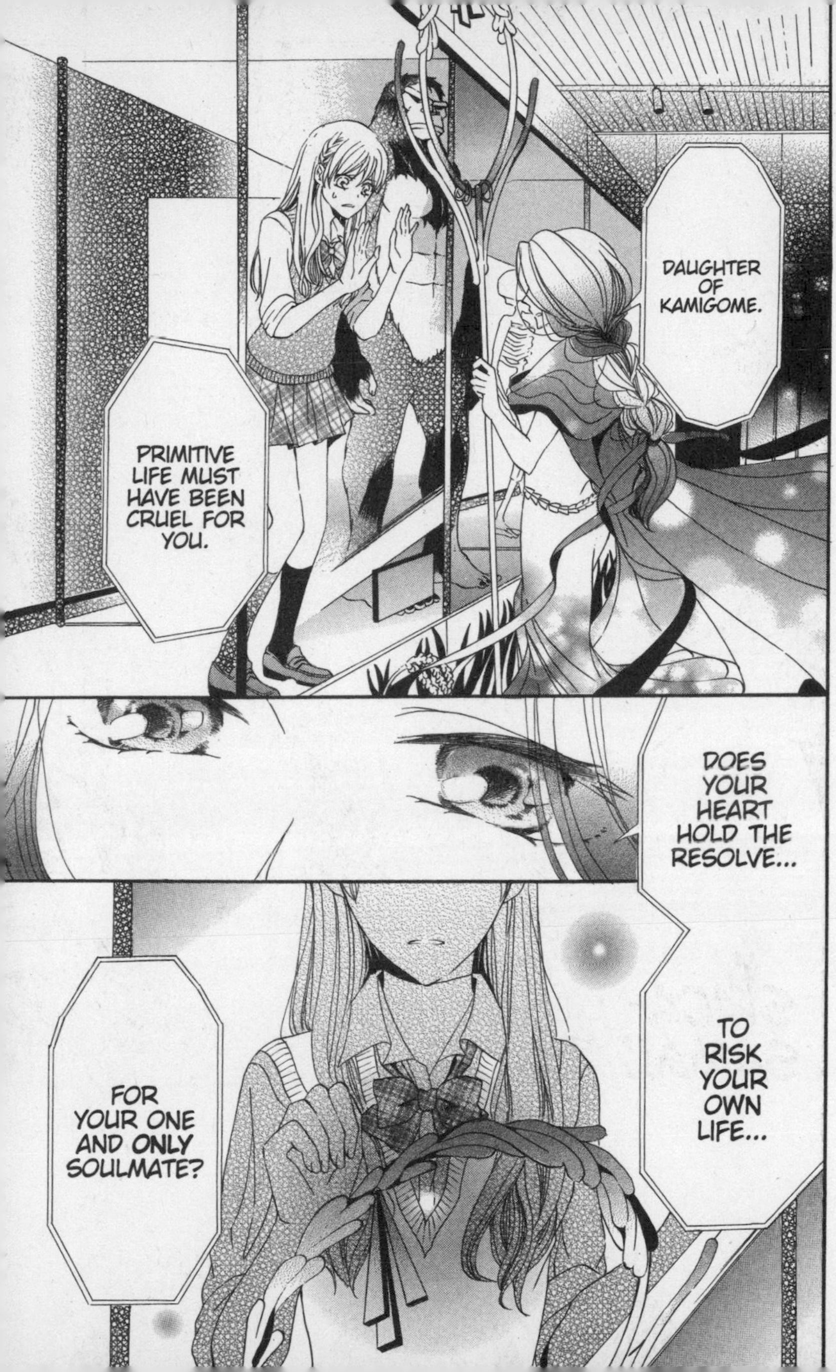
DAUGHTER OF KAMIGOME.
PRIMITIVE LIFE MUST HAVE BEEN CRUEL FOR YOU.
DOES YOUR HEART HOLD THE RESOLVE...
TO RISK YOUR OWN LIFE...
FOR YOUR ONE AND ONLY SOULMATE?

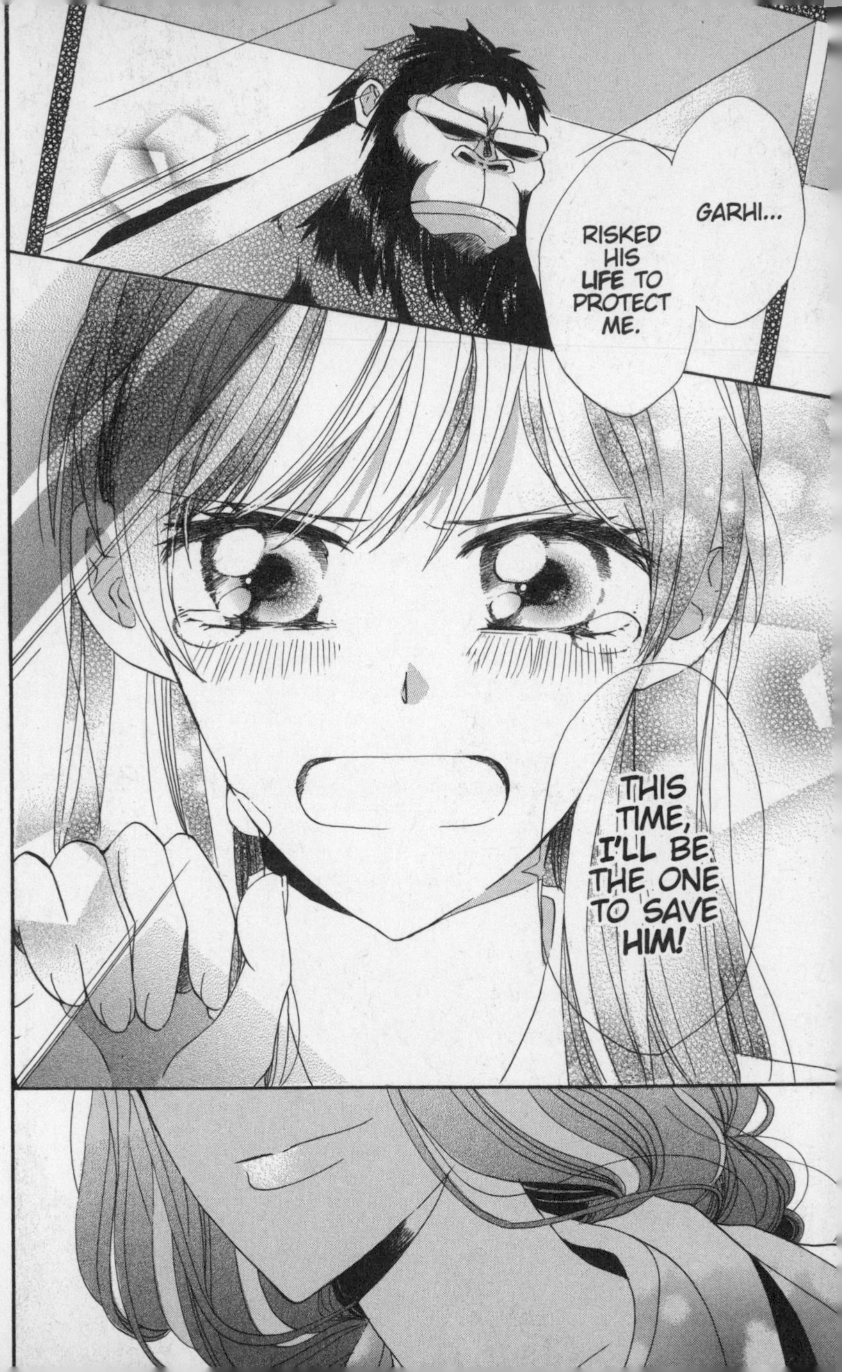
GARHI... RISKED HIS LIFE TO PROTECT ME.
THIS TIME, I'LL BE THE ONE TO SAVE HIM!

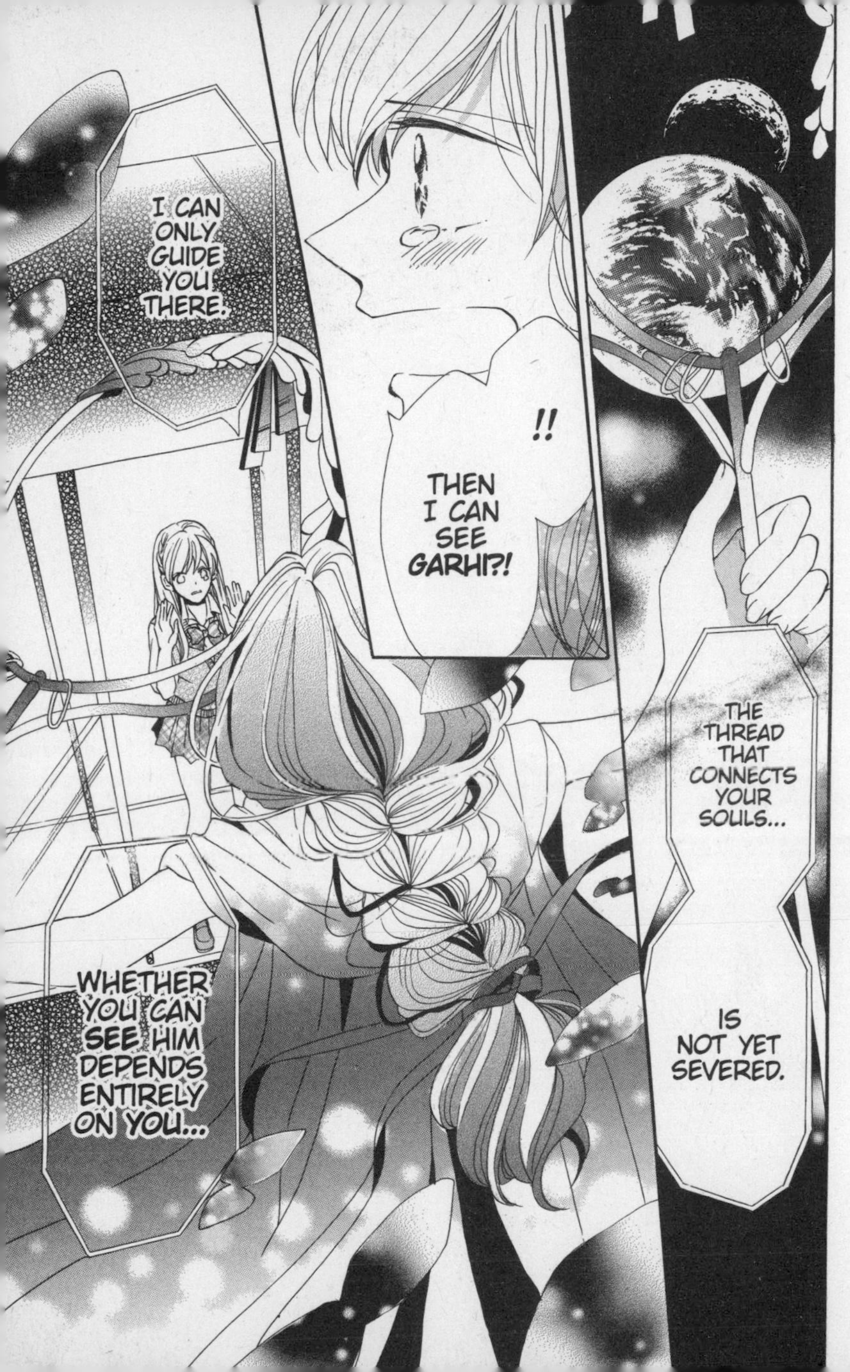
THE THREAD THAT CONNECTS YOUR SOULS...
IS NOT YET SEVERED.
!!
THEN I CAN SEE GARHI?!
I CAN ONLY GUIDE YOU THERE.
WHETHER YOU CAN SEE HIM DEPENDS ENTIRELY ON YOU...

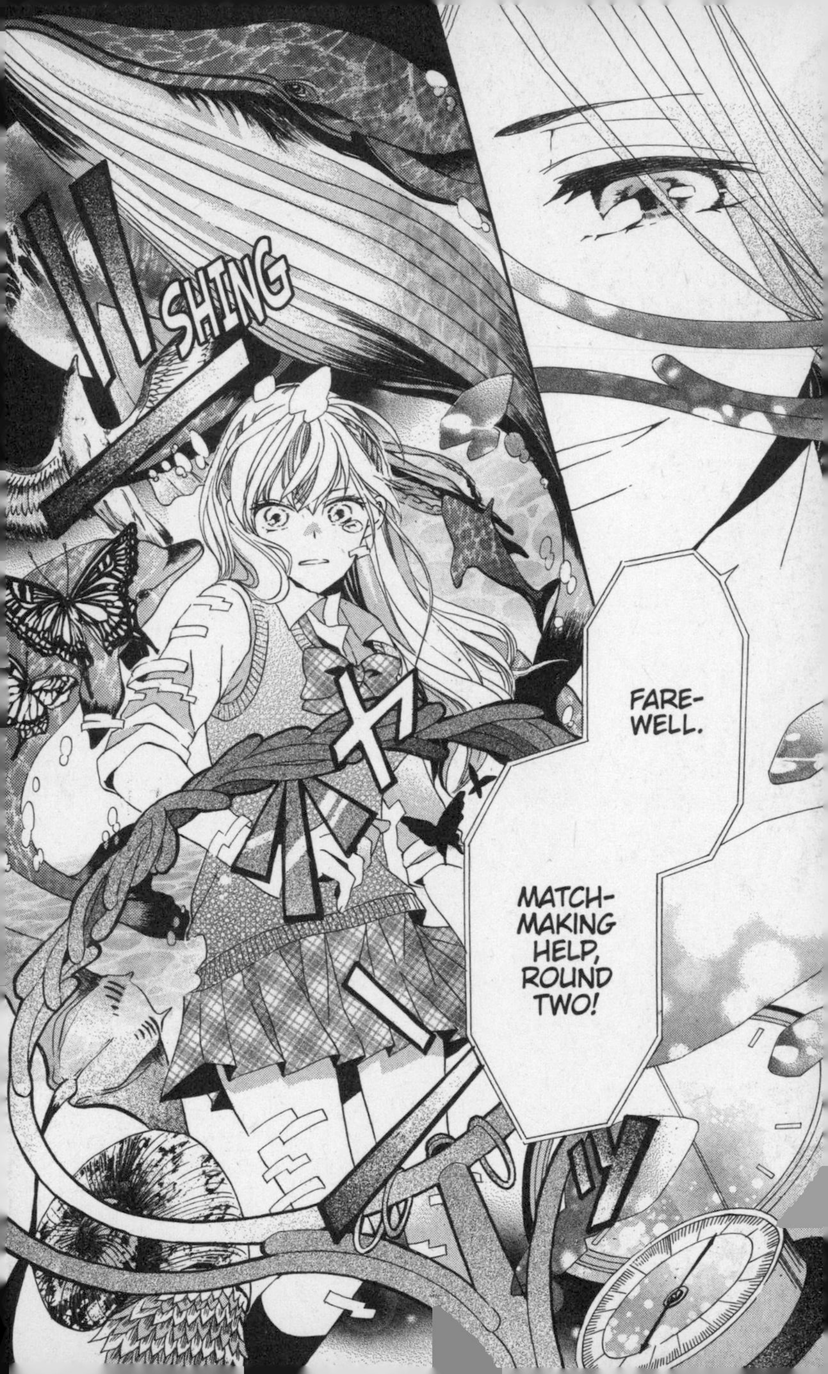
SHING
FARE-WELL.
MATCH-MAKING HELP, ROUND TWO!

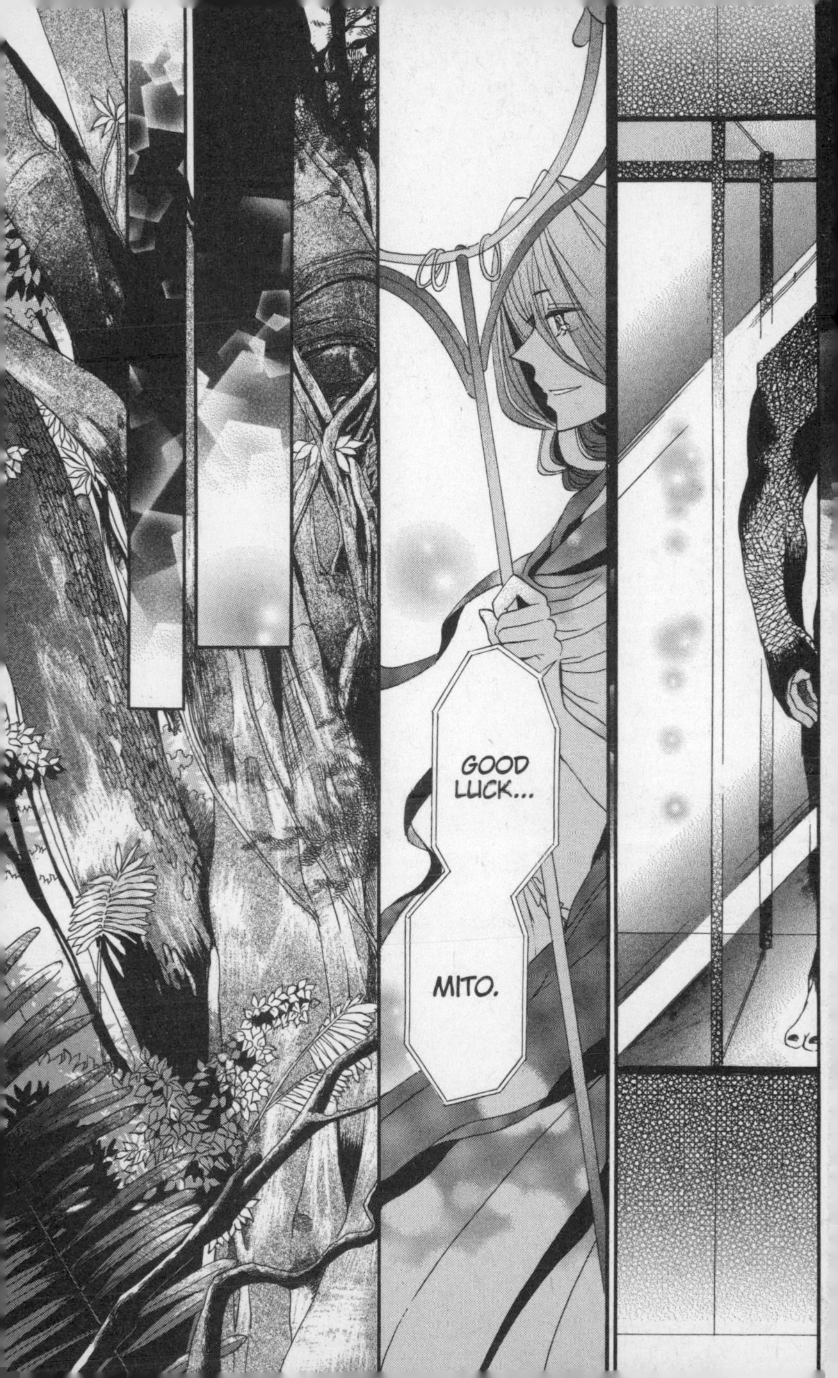
GOOD LUCK...
MITO.

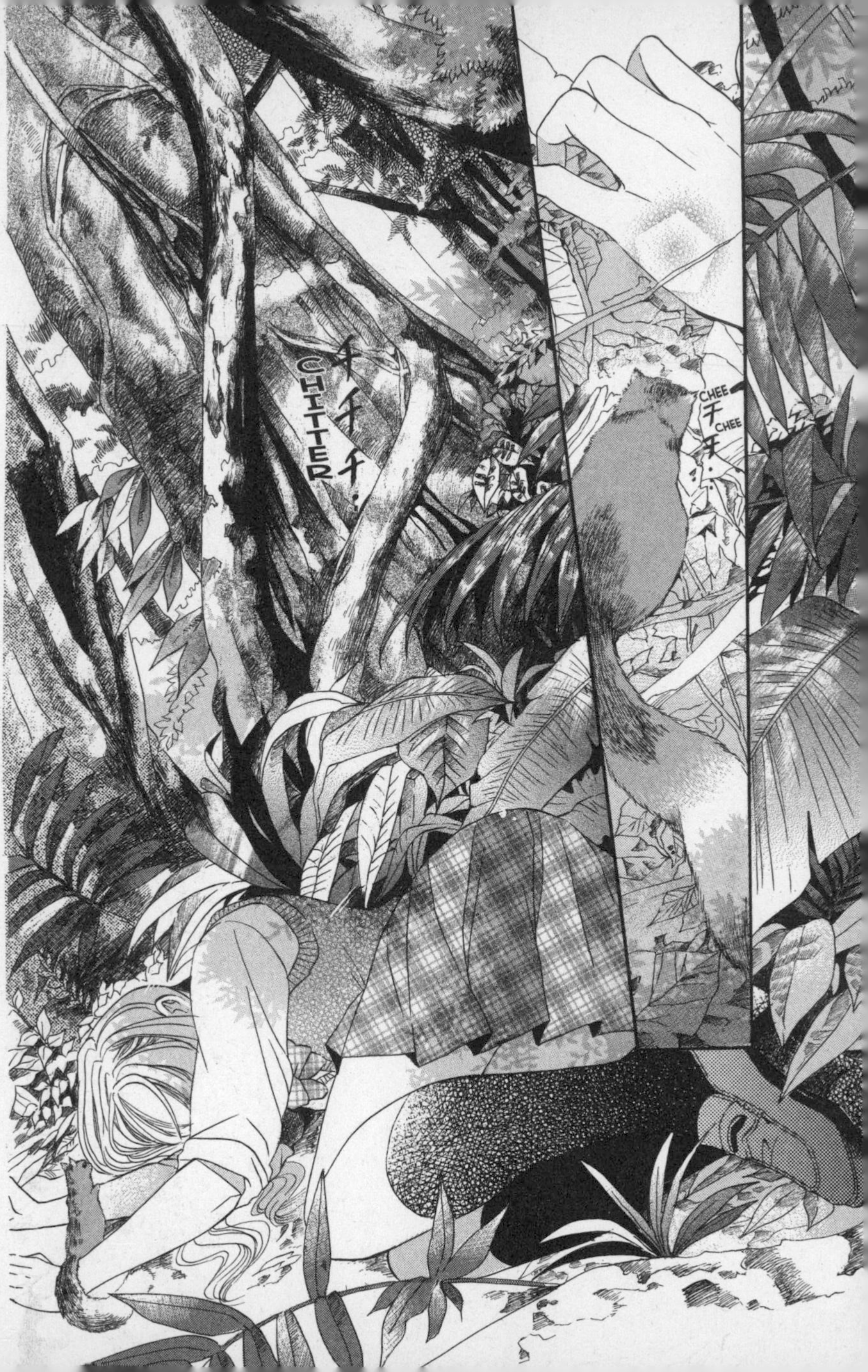
チ CHEE チ CHEE…
チチチ… CHITTER

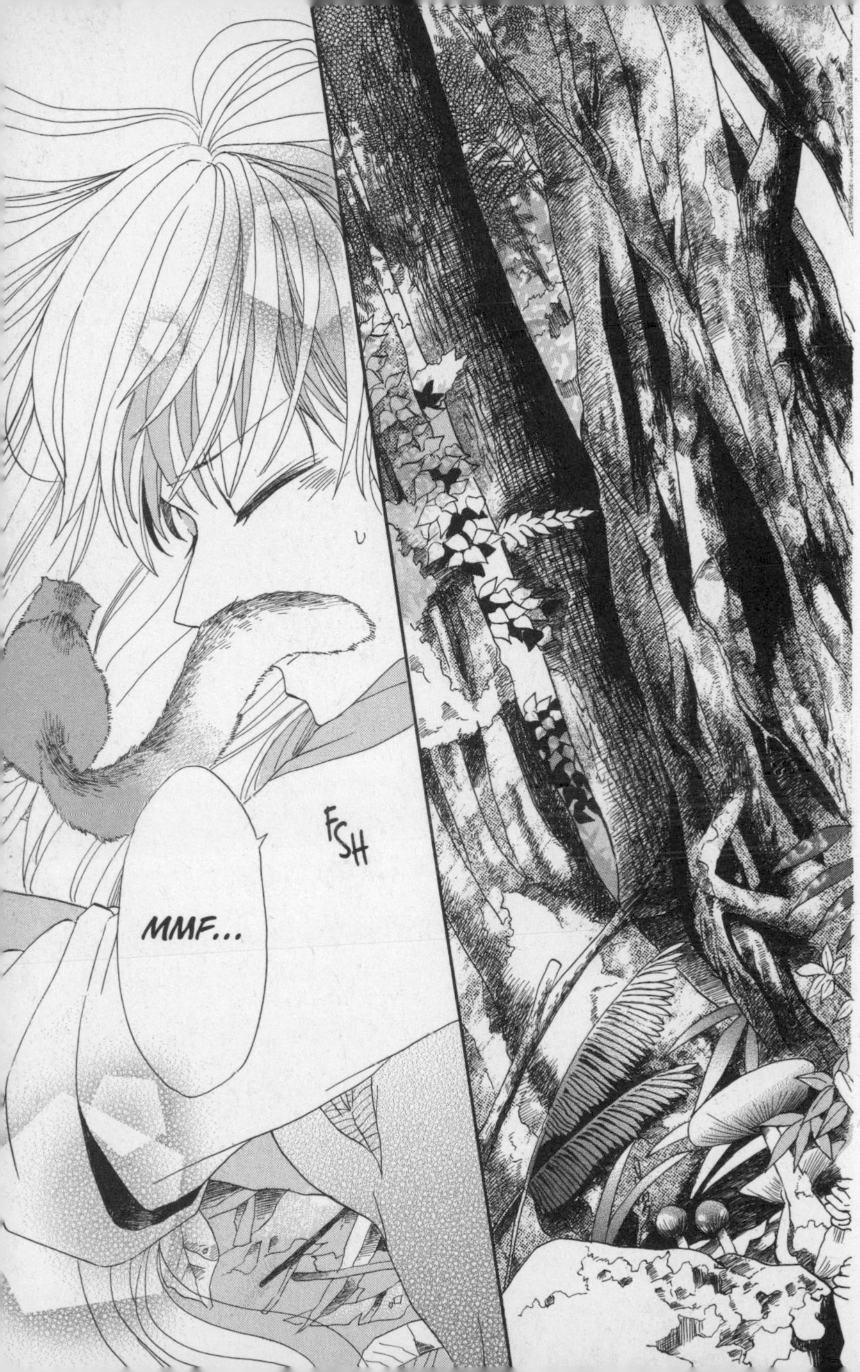
FSH
MMF...

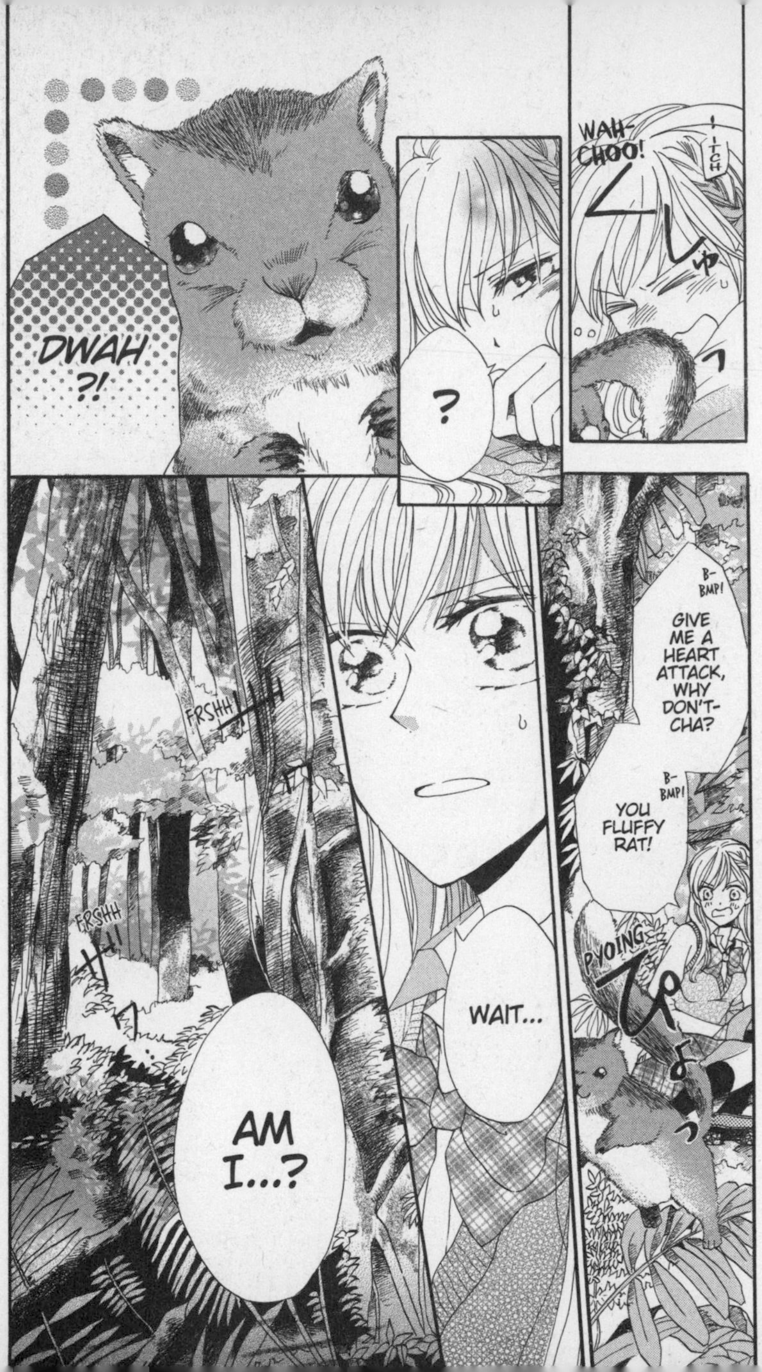
WAH-CHOO!
ITCH
?
DWAH?!
B-BMP!
GIVE ME A HEART ATTACK, WHY DON'T-CHA?
B-BMP!
YOU FLUFFY RAT!
PYOING
WAIT...
AM I...?
FRSHH
FRSHH

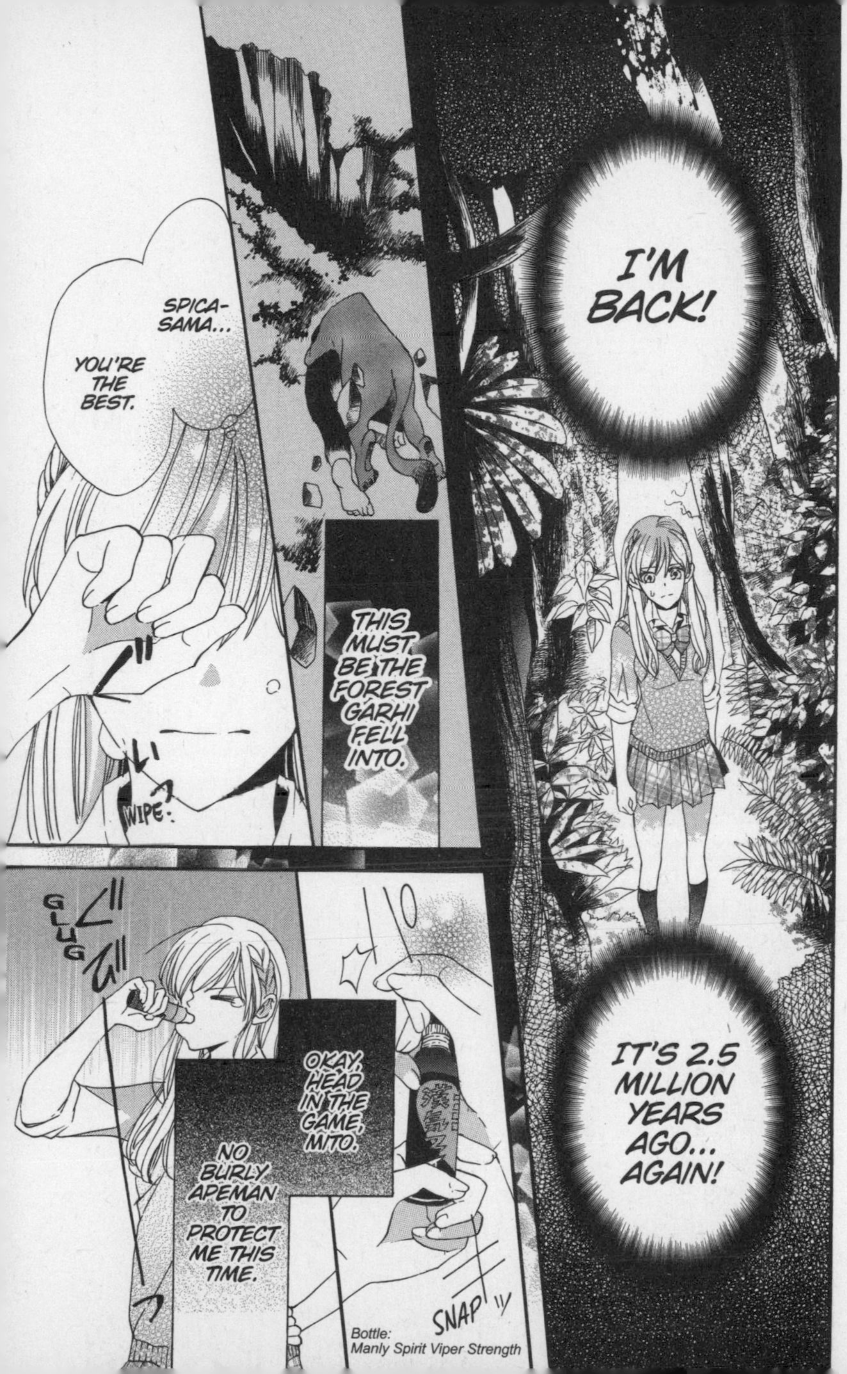
I'M BACK!
IT'S 2.5 MILLION YEARS AGO... AGAIN!
THIS MUST BE THE FOREST GARHI FELL INTO.
SPICA-SAMA...
YOU'RE THE BEST.
WIPE
OKAY, HEAD IN THE GAME, MITO.
NO BURLY APEMAN TO PROTECT ME THIS TIME.
SNAP
Bottle: Manly Spirit Viper Strength
GLUG

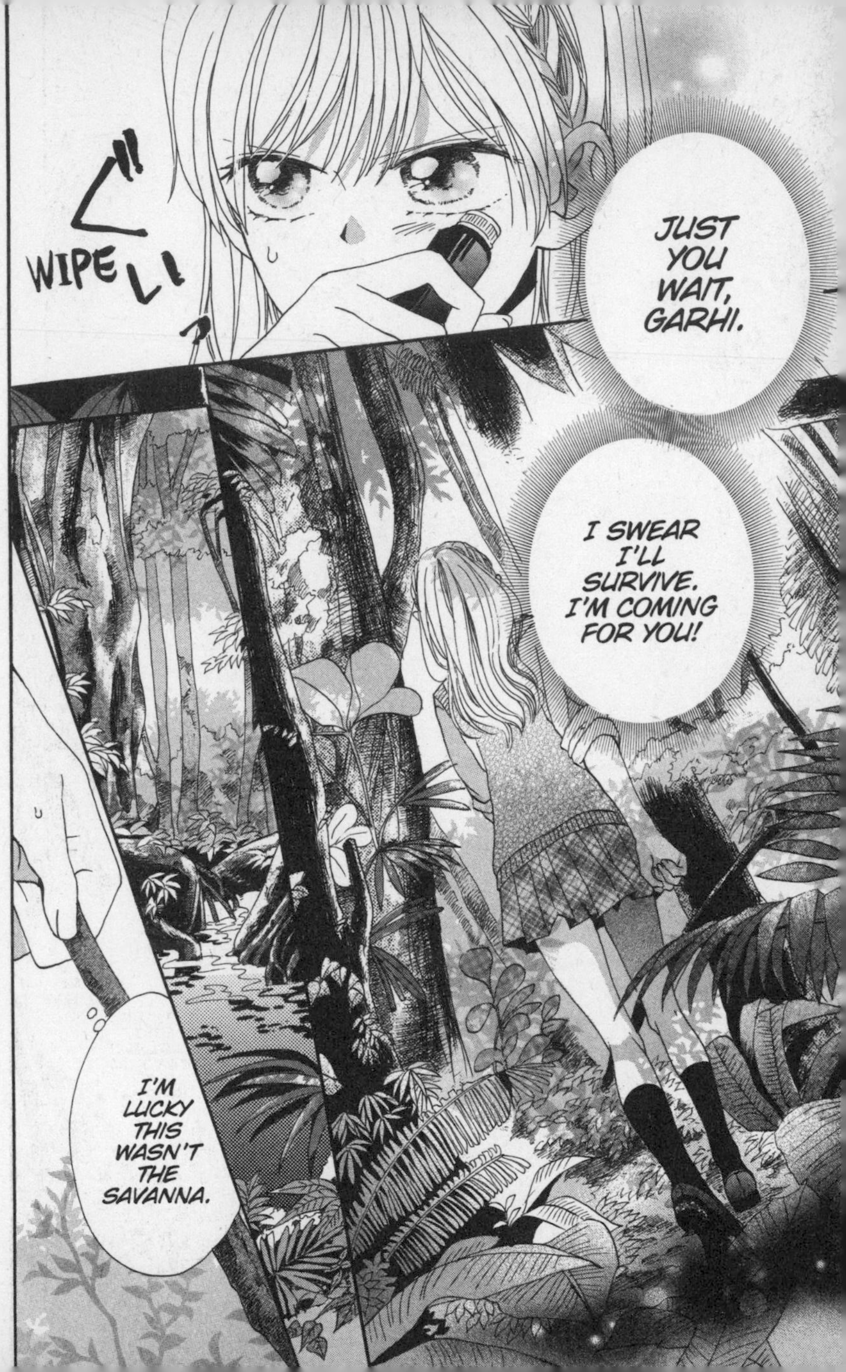
WIPE
JUST YOU WAIT, GARHI.
I SWEAR I'LL SURVIVE. I'M COMING FOR YOU!
I'M LUCKY THIS WASN'T THE SAVANNA.

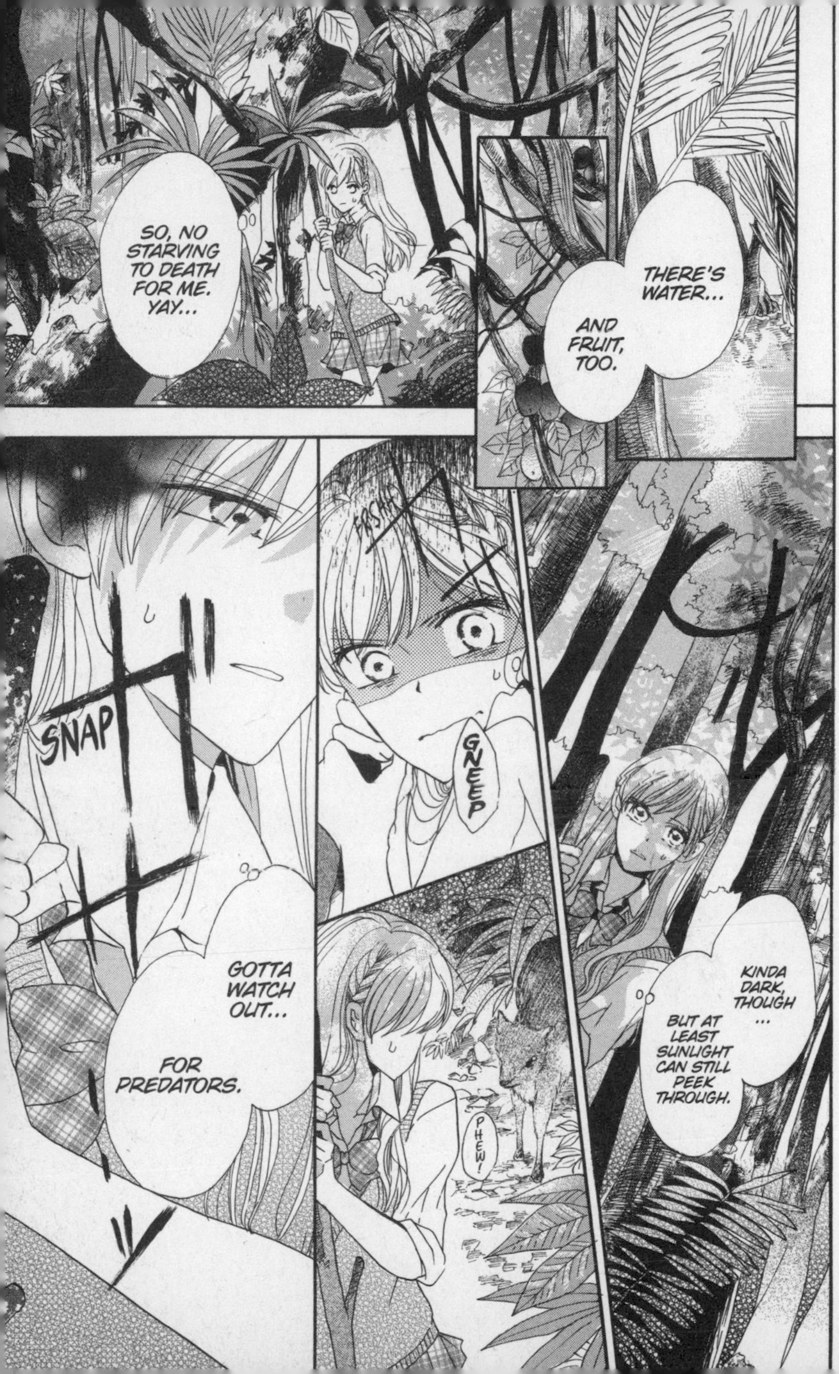
THERE'S WATER...
AND FRUIT, TOO.
SO, NO STARVING TO DEATH FOR ME. YAY...
KINDA DARK, THOUGH ...
BUT AT LEAST SUNLIGHT CAN STILL PEEK THROUGH.
GNEEP
PHEW!
SNAP
GOTTA WATCH OUT...
FOR PREDATORS.

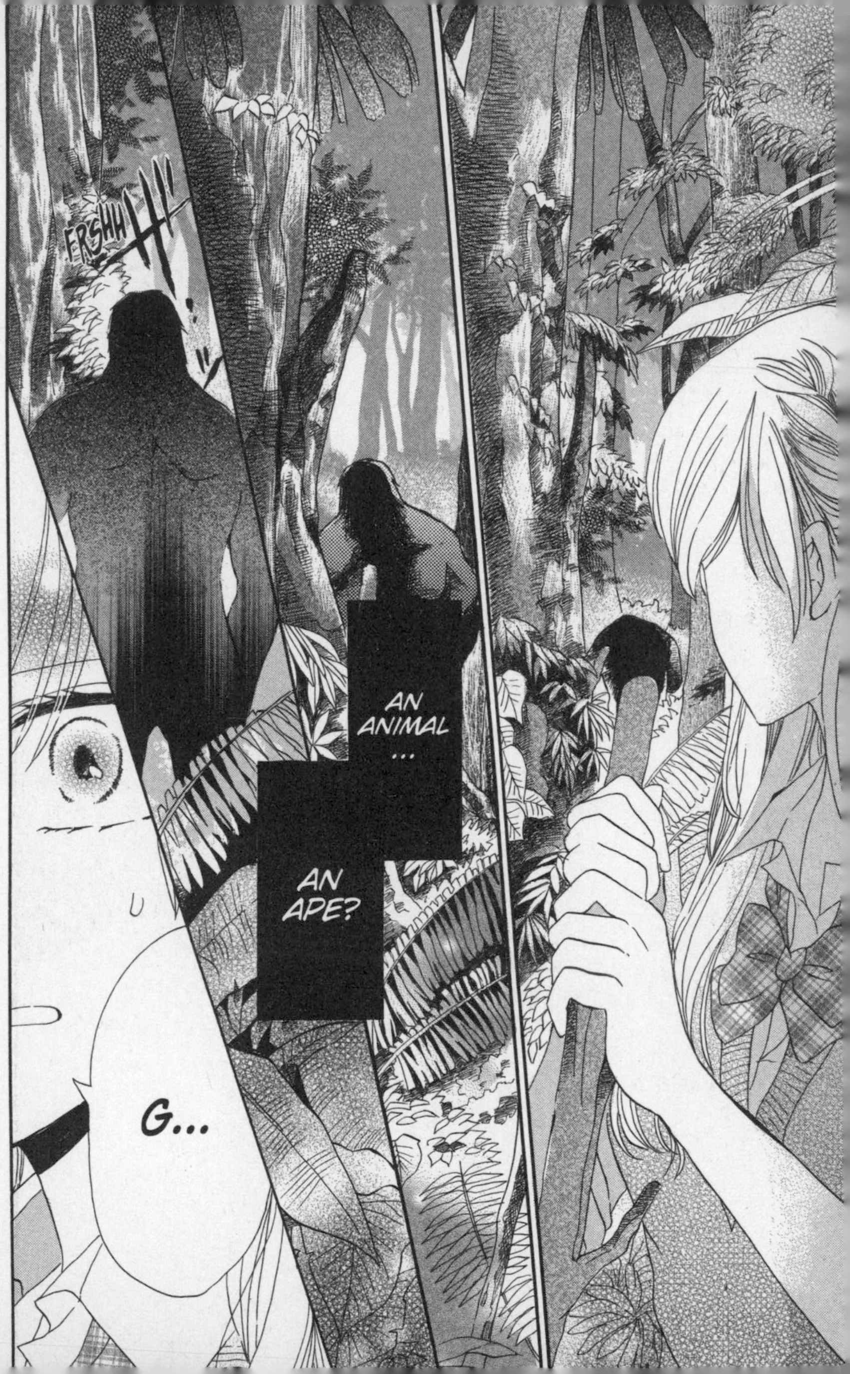
FRSHH
AN ANIMAL...
AN APE?
G...

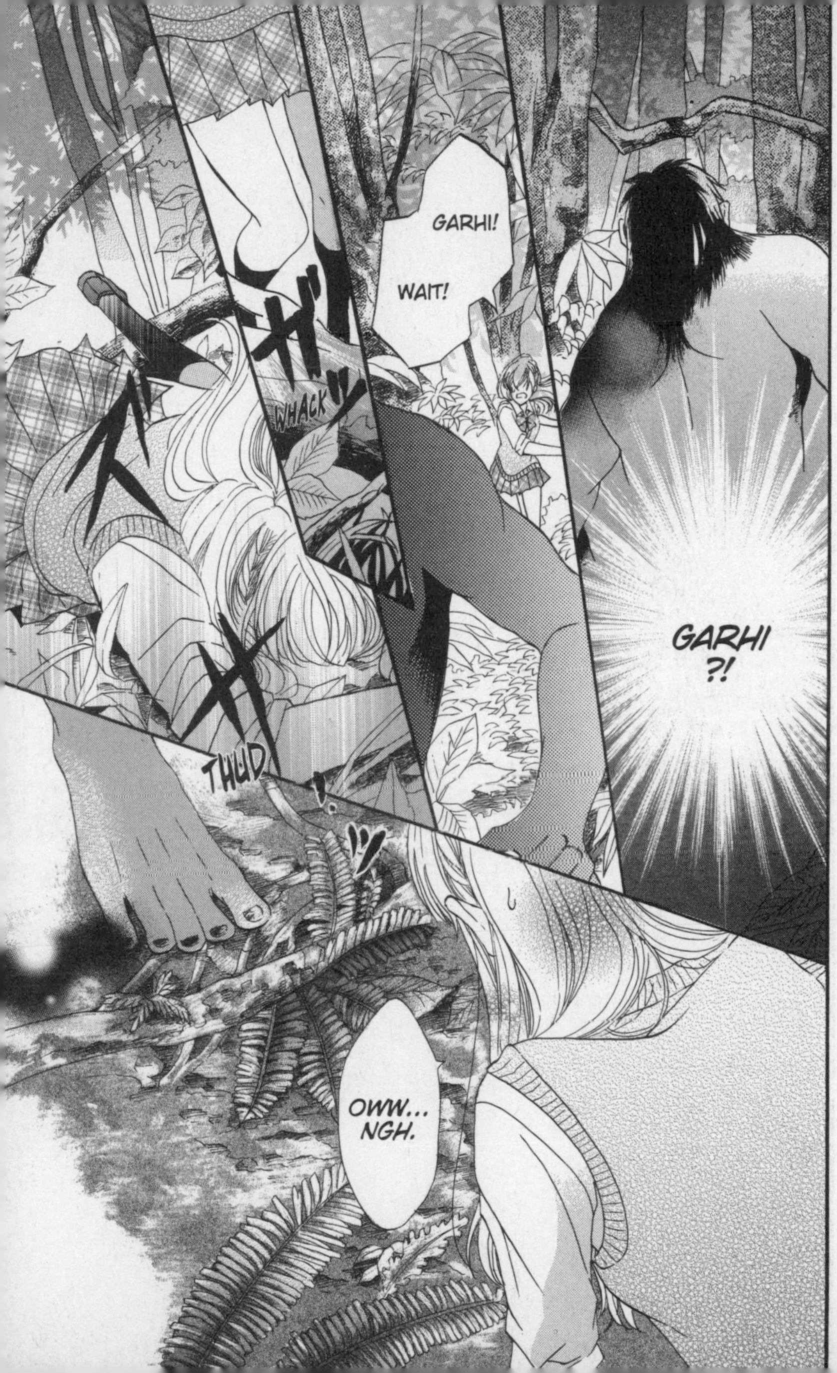
GARHI ?!
GARHI!
WAIT!
WHACK
THUD
OWW... NGH.

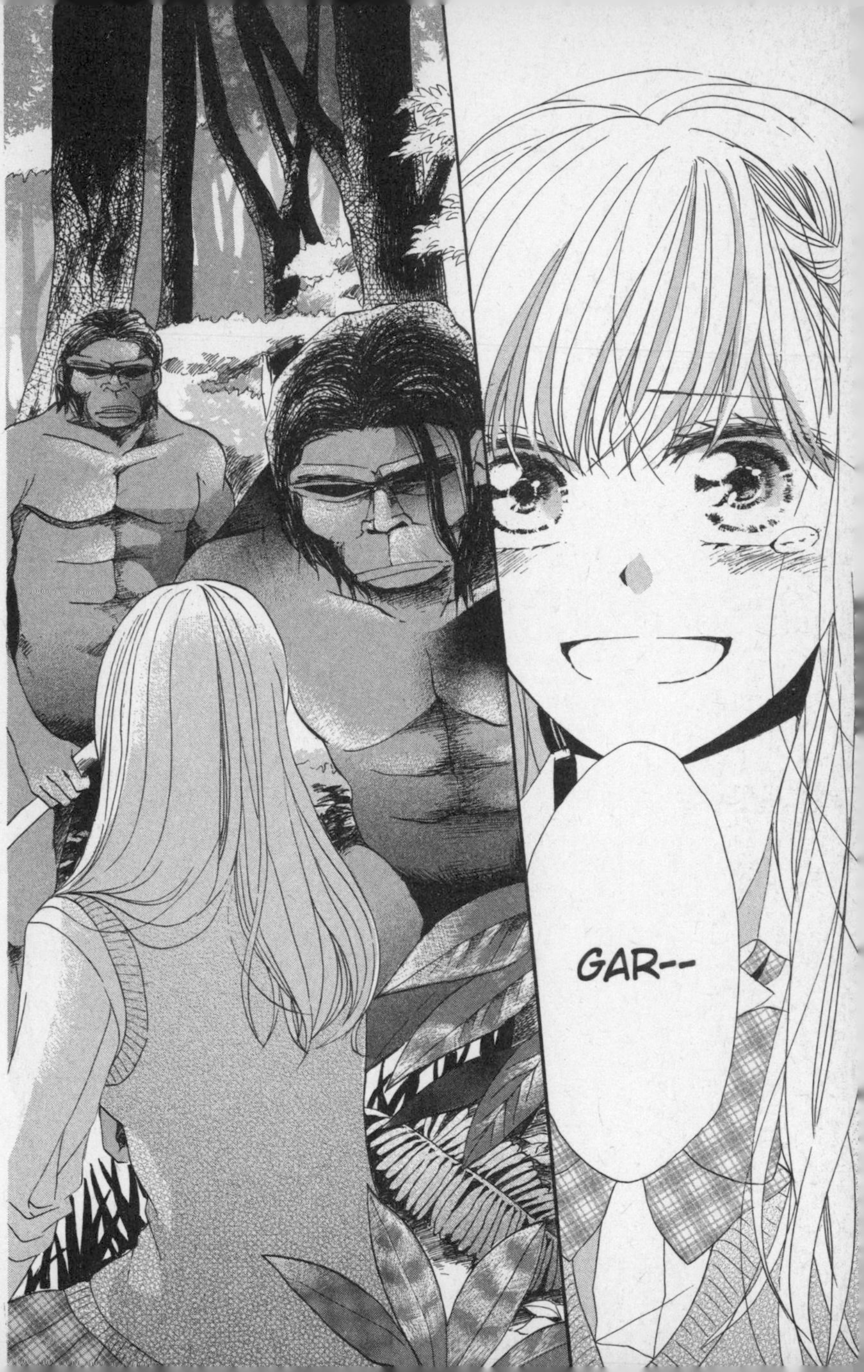
GAR--

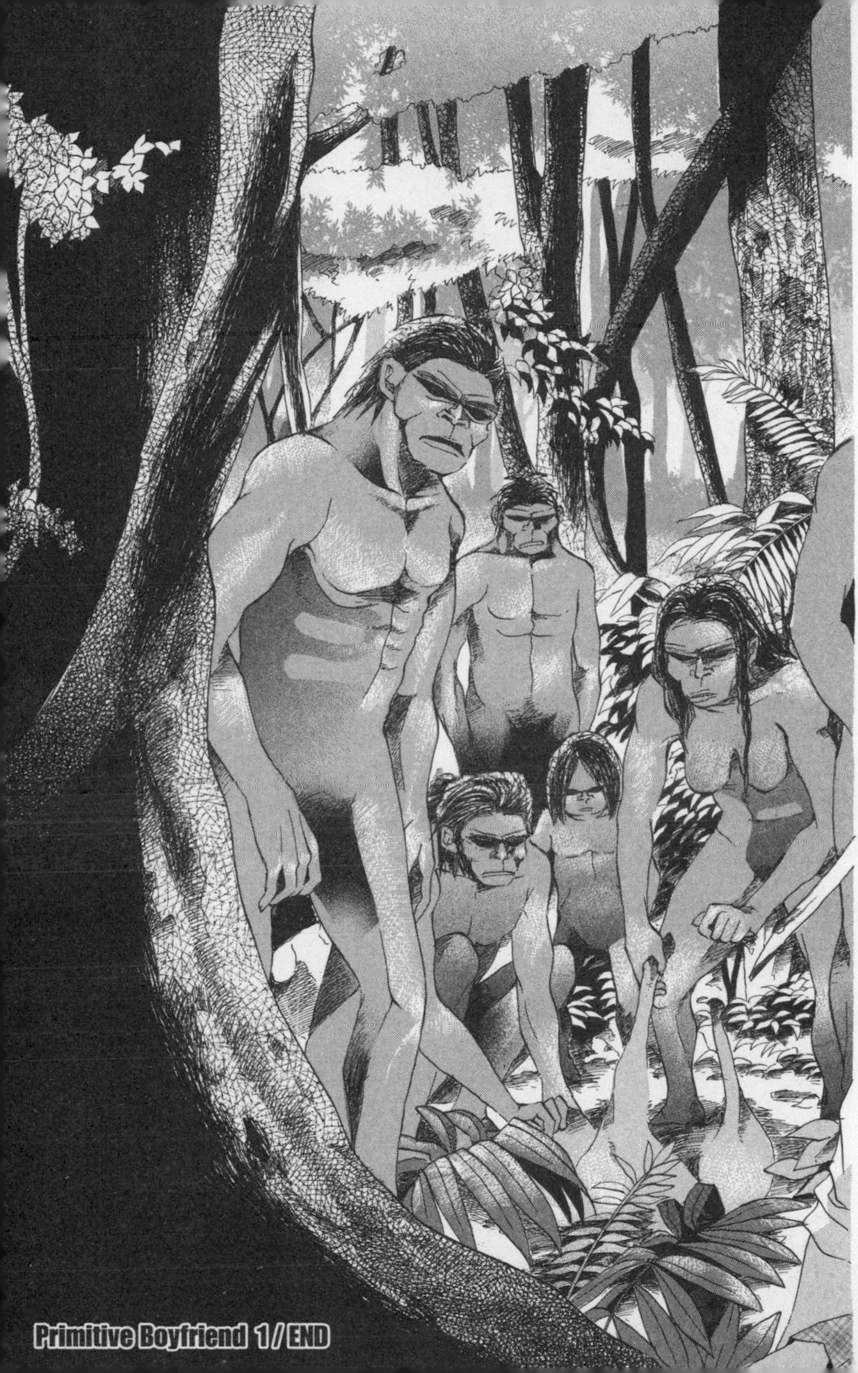

Primitive Boyfriend 1 / END

Giselle's Flash

THIS WAS MY FIRST ONE-SHOT AFTER WINNING A NEWCOMER'S AWARD. AT FIRST, THE STORY WASN'T FOCUSED ON BALLET; IT WAS ABOUT MAHIRU (A BALLERINA) AND YUU (AN ASPIRING COOK), AND IT FOCUSED ON THE COOKING.

IN THE SELECTION PROCESS, IT GOT REJECTED, AND THEY GAVE ME A SECOND CHANCE TO REDRAW IT, IF IT FOCUSED ON BALLET. I STRUGGLED WITH REDOING MY ROUGH DRAFT OVER AND OVER. BUT THEN, WHEN RURIKO'S CHARACTER SUDDENLY CAME TO ME, EVERYTHING FELL INTO PLACE.

I HAD NO FAMILIARITY WITH BALLET AND ITS DEEP RULES AND FORMALITIES, SO THIS WAS COMPLETELY NEW TERRITORY FOR ME, BUT MY BRIEF BRUSH WITH THE WORLD OF BALLET, AND ITS PHILOSOPHY OF LIFTING YOUR HEAD AND IMPROVING YOURSELF MORE AND MORE, MADE THIS STORY ONE THAT GAVE ME COURAGE MYSELF.

I HOPE YOU ENJOY IT!

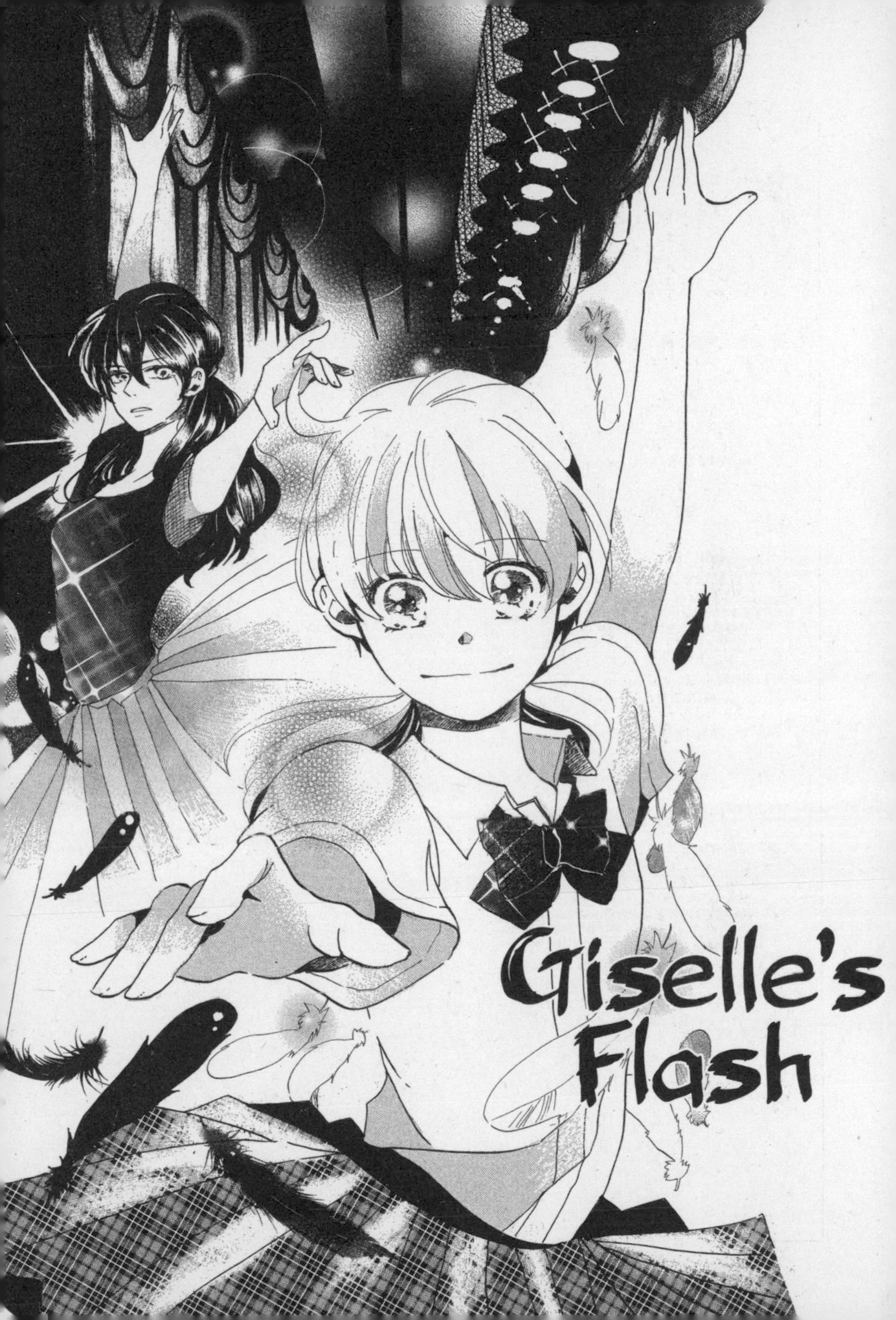
Giselle's
Flash

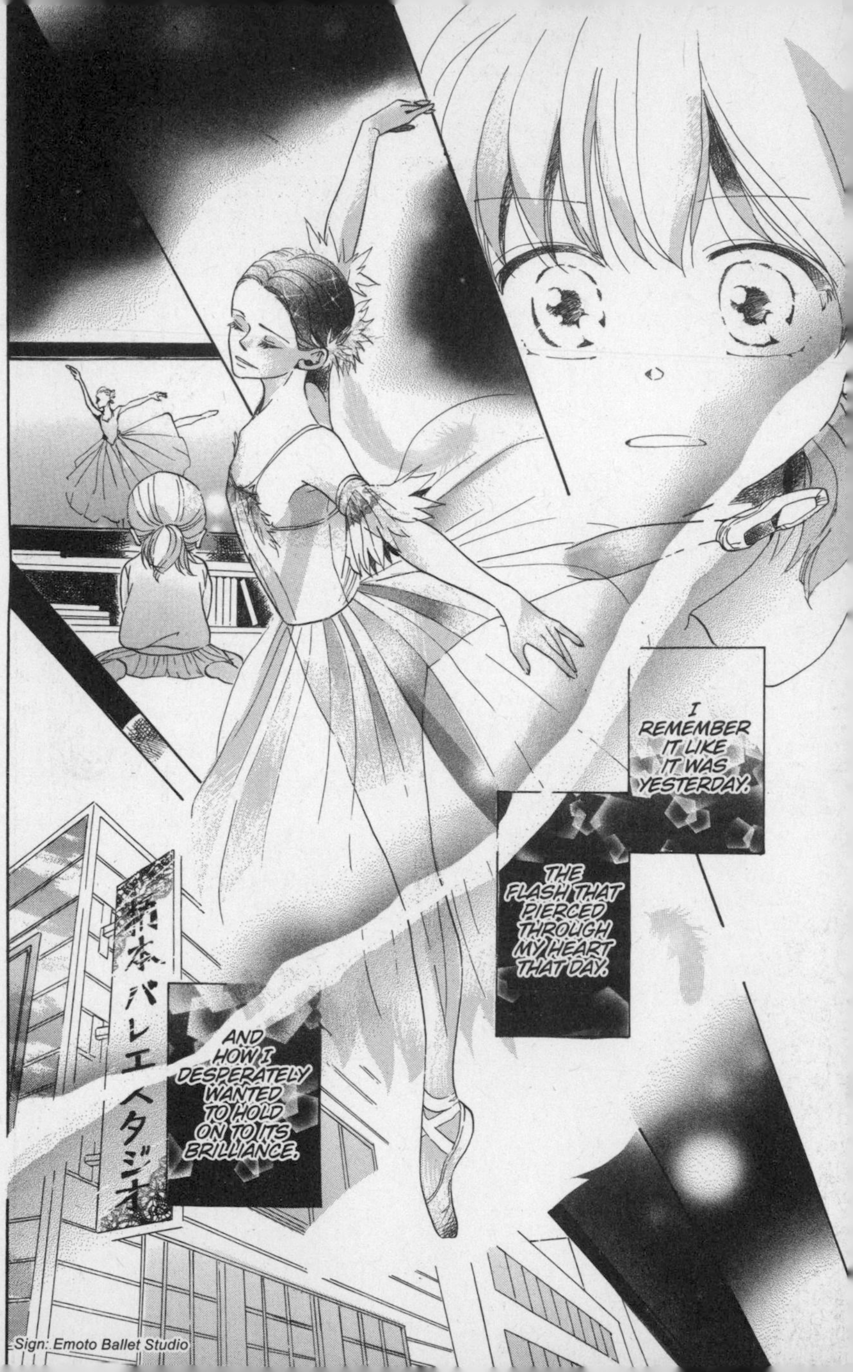
I REMEMBER IT LIKE IT WAS YESTERDAY.
THE FLASH THAT PIERCED THROUGH MY HEART THAT DAY.
AND HOW I DESPERATELY WANTED TO HOLD ON TO ITS BRILLIANCE.
江本バレエスタジオ
Sign: Emoto Ballet Studio

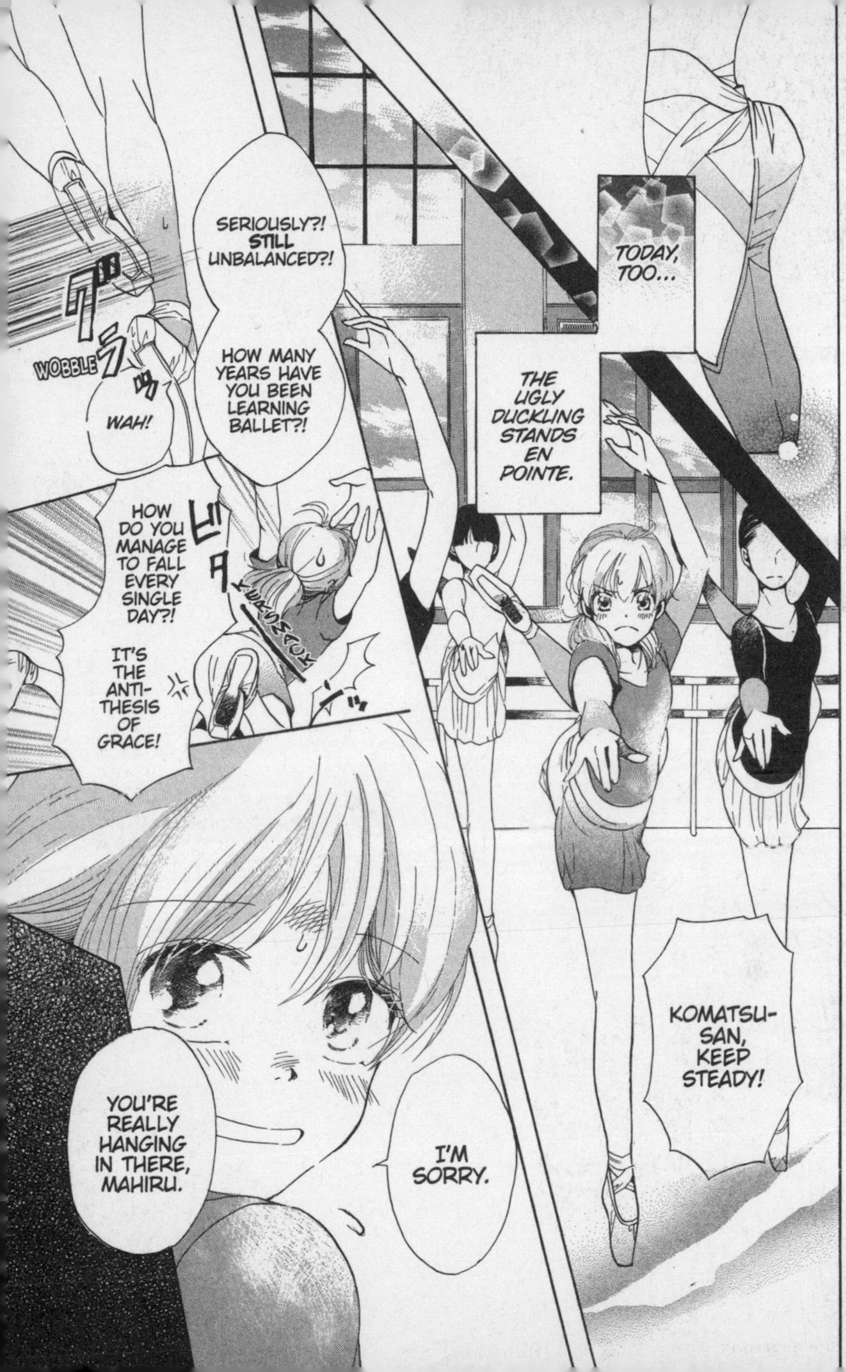
TODAY, TOO...
THE UGLY DUCKLING STANDS EN POINTE.
KOMATSU-SAN, KEEP STEADY!
SERIOUSLY?! STILL UNBALANCED?!
HOW MANY YEARS HAVE YOU BEEN LEARNING BALLET?!
WOBBLE
WAH!
HOW DO YOU MANAGE TO FALL EVERY SINGLE DAY?!
IT'S THE ANTI-THESIS OF GRACE!
I'M SORRY.
YOU'RE REALLY HANGING IN THERE, MAHIRU.

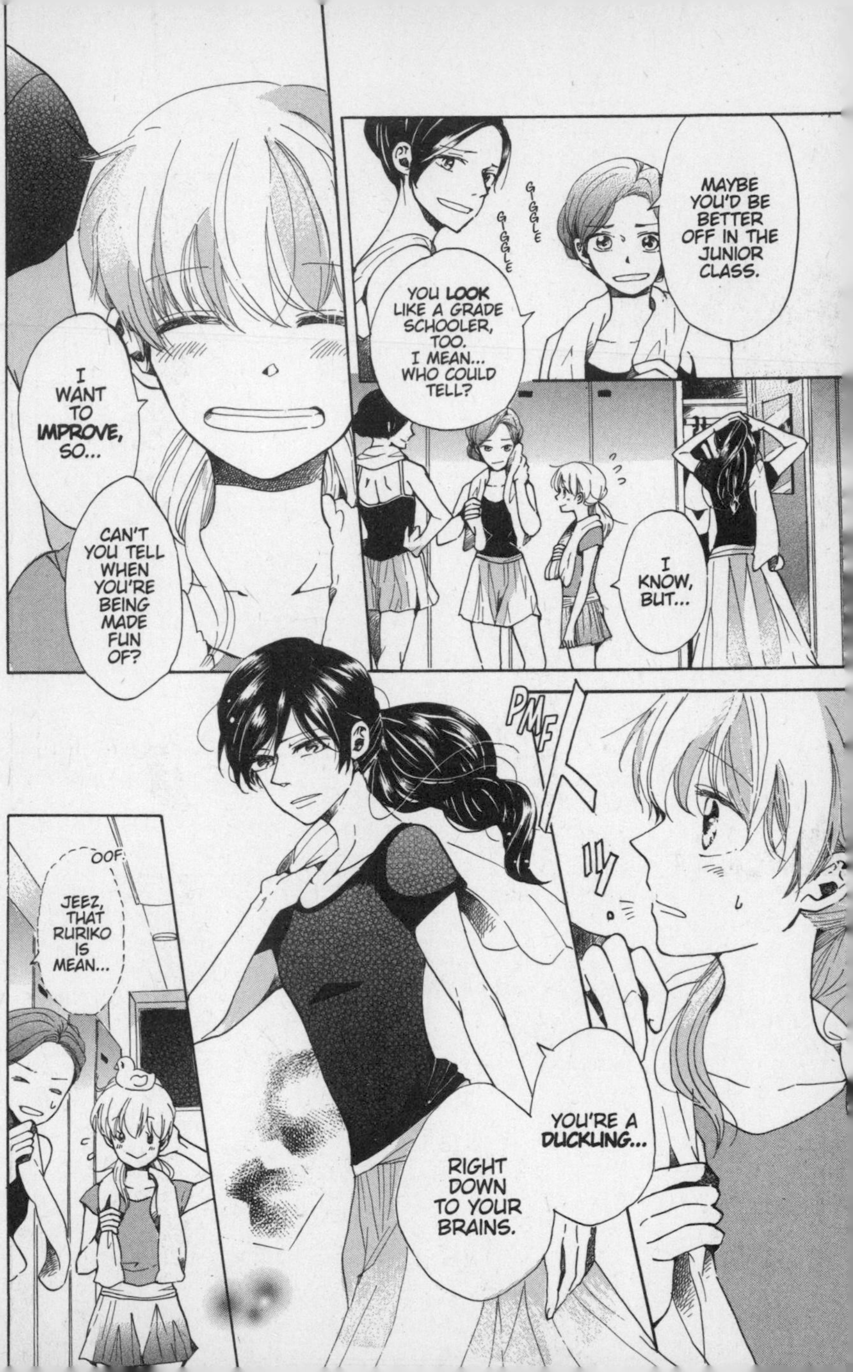
MAYBE YOU'D BE BETTER OFF IN THE JUNIOR CLASS.
GIGGLE GIGGLE
YOU LOOK LIKE A GRADE SCHOOLER, TOO. I MEAN... WHO COULD TELL?
I KNOW, BUT...
I WANT TO IMPROVE, SO...
CAN'T YOU TELL WHEN YOU'RE BEING MADE FUN OF?
PMF
YOU'RE A DUCKLING...
RIGHT DOWN TO YOUR BRAINS.
OOF
JEEZ, THAT RURIKO IS MEAN...

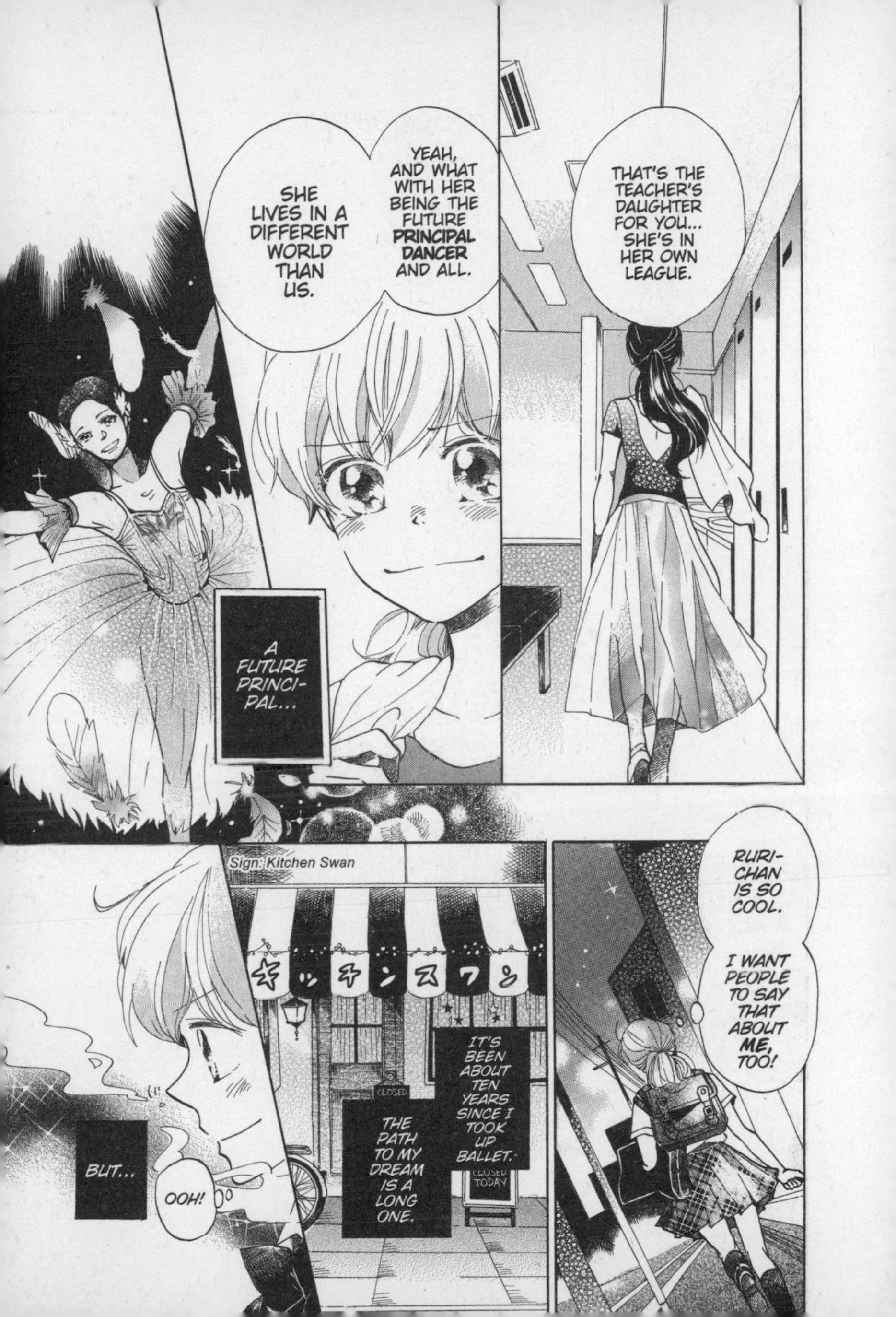
THAT'S THE TEACHER'S DAUGHTER FOR YOU... SHE'S IN HER OWN LEAGUE.
YEAH, AND WHAT WITH HER BEING THE FUTURE PRINCIPAL DANCER AND ALL.
SHE LIVES IN A DIFFERENT WORLD THAN US.
A FUTURE PRINCIPAL...
RURI-CHAN IS SO COOL.
I WANT PEOPLE TO SAY THAT ABOUT ME, TOO!
Sign: Kitchen Swan
CLOSED
IT'S BEEN ABOUT TEN YEARS SINCE I TOOK UP BALLET.
CLOSED TODAY
THE PATH TO MY DREAM IS A LONG ONE.
BUT...
OOH!

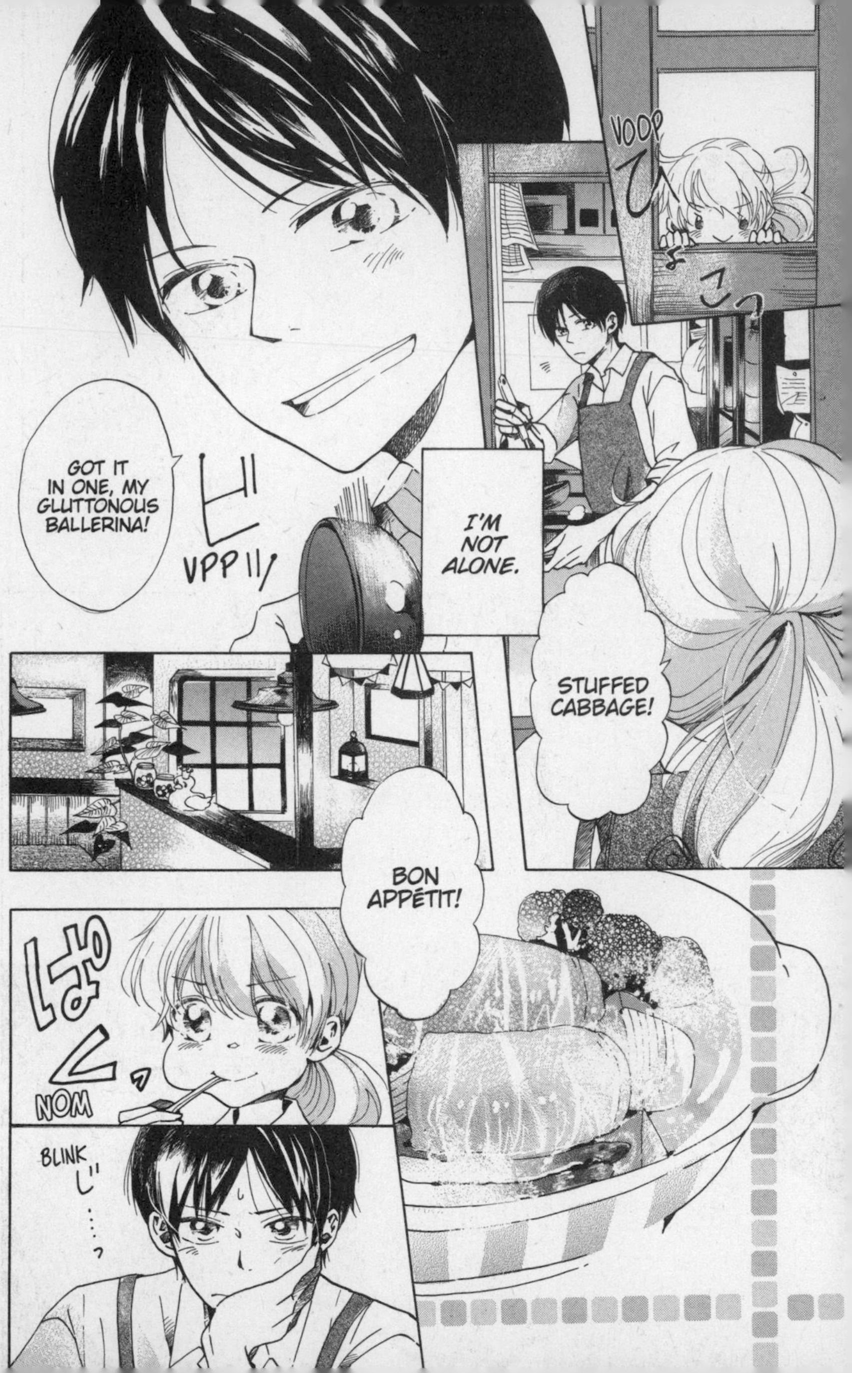

VOOP
I'M NOT ALONE.
GOT IT IN ONE, MY GLUTTONOUS BALLERINA!
VPP
STUFFED CABBAGE!
BON APPÉTIT!
NOM
BLINK

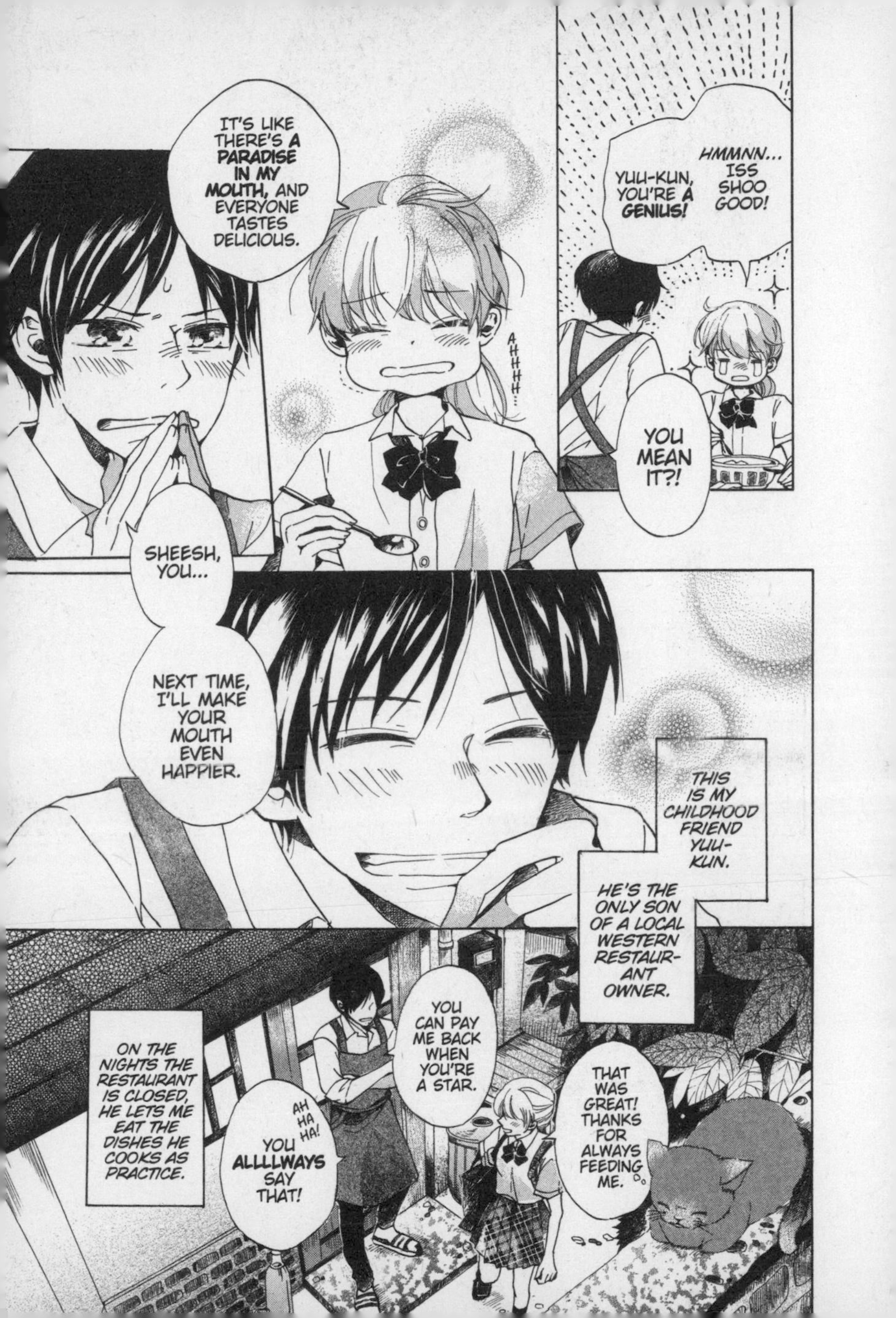
HMMNN... ISS SHOO GOOD! YUU-KUN, YOU'RE A GENIUS!
YOU MEAN IT?!
IT'S LIKE THERE'S A PARADISE IN MY MOUTH, AND EVERYONE TASTES DELICIOUS.
AHHHHH...
SHEESH, YOU...
NEXT TIME, I'LL MAKE YOUR MOUTH EVEN HAPPIER.
THIS IS MY CHILDHOOD FRIEND YUU-KUN.
HE'S THE ONLY SON OF A LOCAL WESTERN RESTAUR-ANT OWNER.
THAT WAS GREAT! THANKS FOR ALWAYS FEEDING ME.
YOU CAN PAY ME BACK WHEN YOU'RE A STAR.
AH HA HA!
YOU ALLLLWAYS SAY THAT!
ON THE NIGHTS THE RESTAURANT IS CLOSED, HE LETS ME EAT THE DISHES HE COOKS AS PRACTICE.

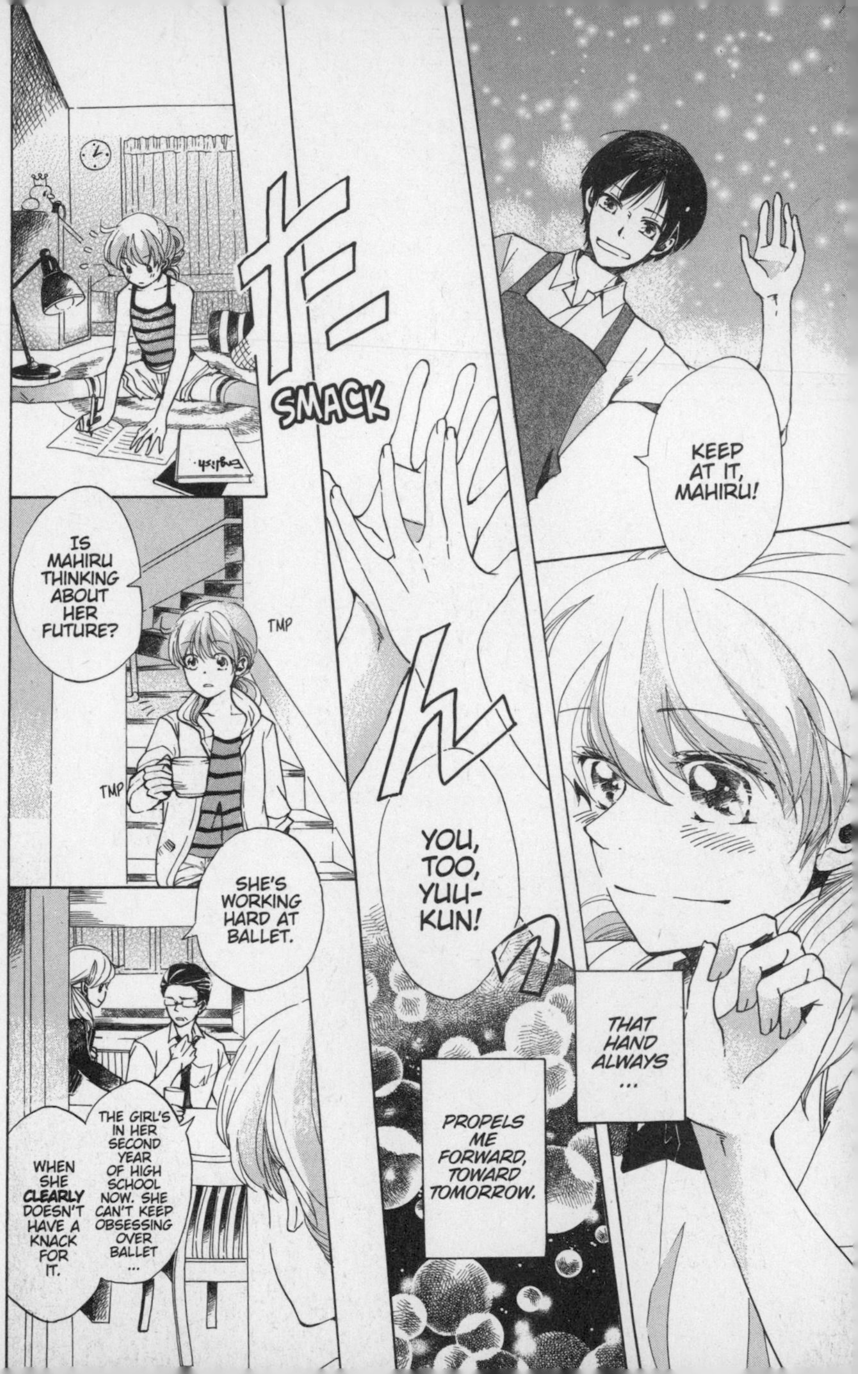
KEEP AT IT, MAHIRU!
SMACK
YOU, TOO, YUU-KUN!
THAT HAND ALWAYS ...
PROPELS ME FORWARD, TOWARD TOMORROW.
English
IS MAHIRU THINKING ABOUT HER FUTURE?
TMP
TMP
SHE'S WORKING HARD AT BALLET.
THE GIRL'S IN HER SECOND YEAR OF HIGH SCHOOL NOW. SHE CAN'T KEEP OBSESSING OVER BALLET ...
WHEN SHE **CLEARLY** DOESN'T HAVE A KNACK FOR IT.

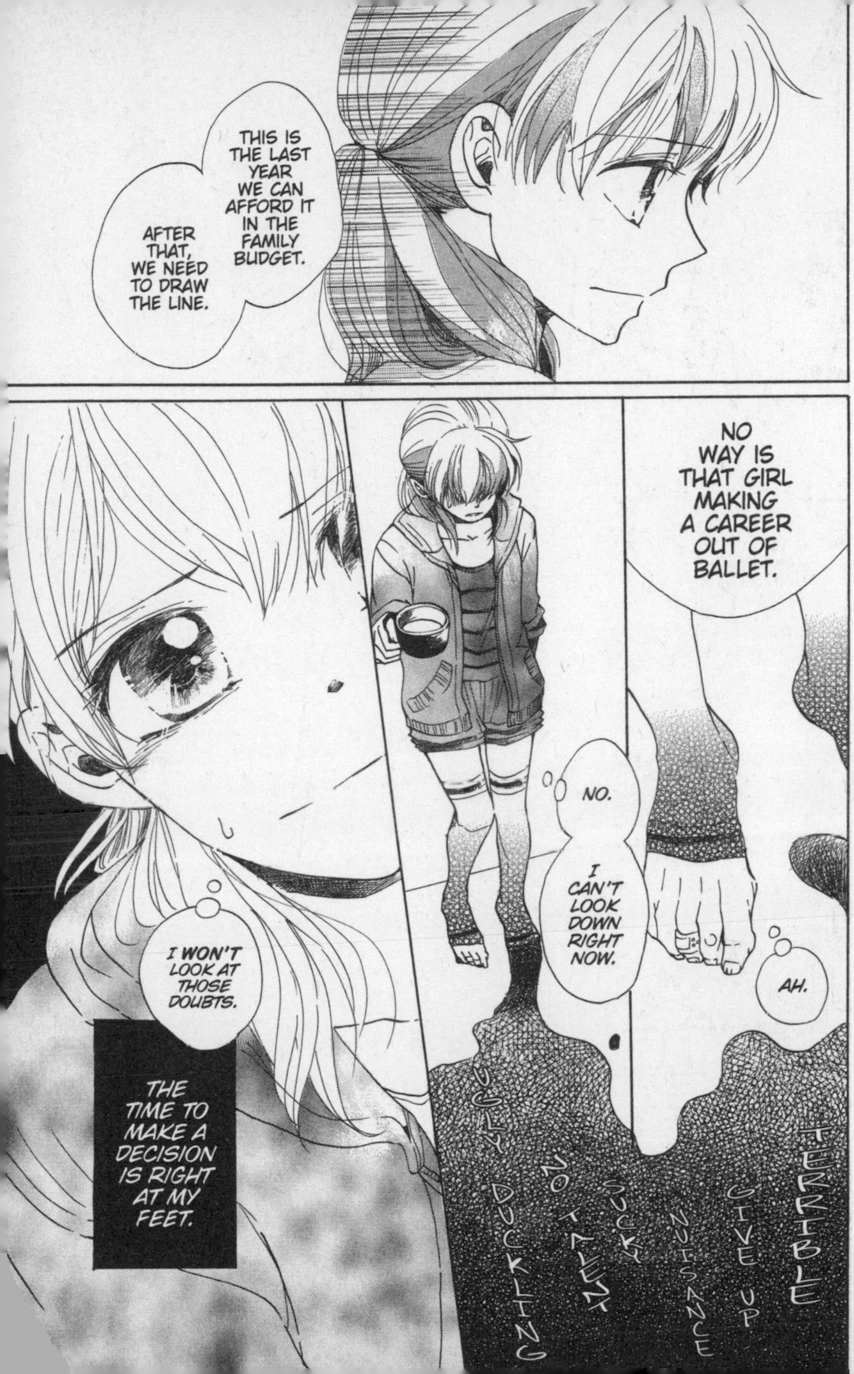
THIS IS THE LAST YEAR WE CAN AFFORD IT IN THE FAMILY BUDGET.
AFTER THAT, WE NEED TO DRAW THE LINE.
NO WAY IS THAT GIRL MAKING A CAREER OUT OF BALLET.
AH.
TERRIBLE
GIVE UP
NUISANCE
SUCKY
NO TALENT
UGLY DUCKLING
NO.
I CAN'T LOOK DOWN RIGHT NOW.
I WON'T LOOK AT THOSE DOUBTS.
THE TIME TO MAKE A DECISION IS RIGHT AT MY FEET.

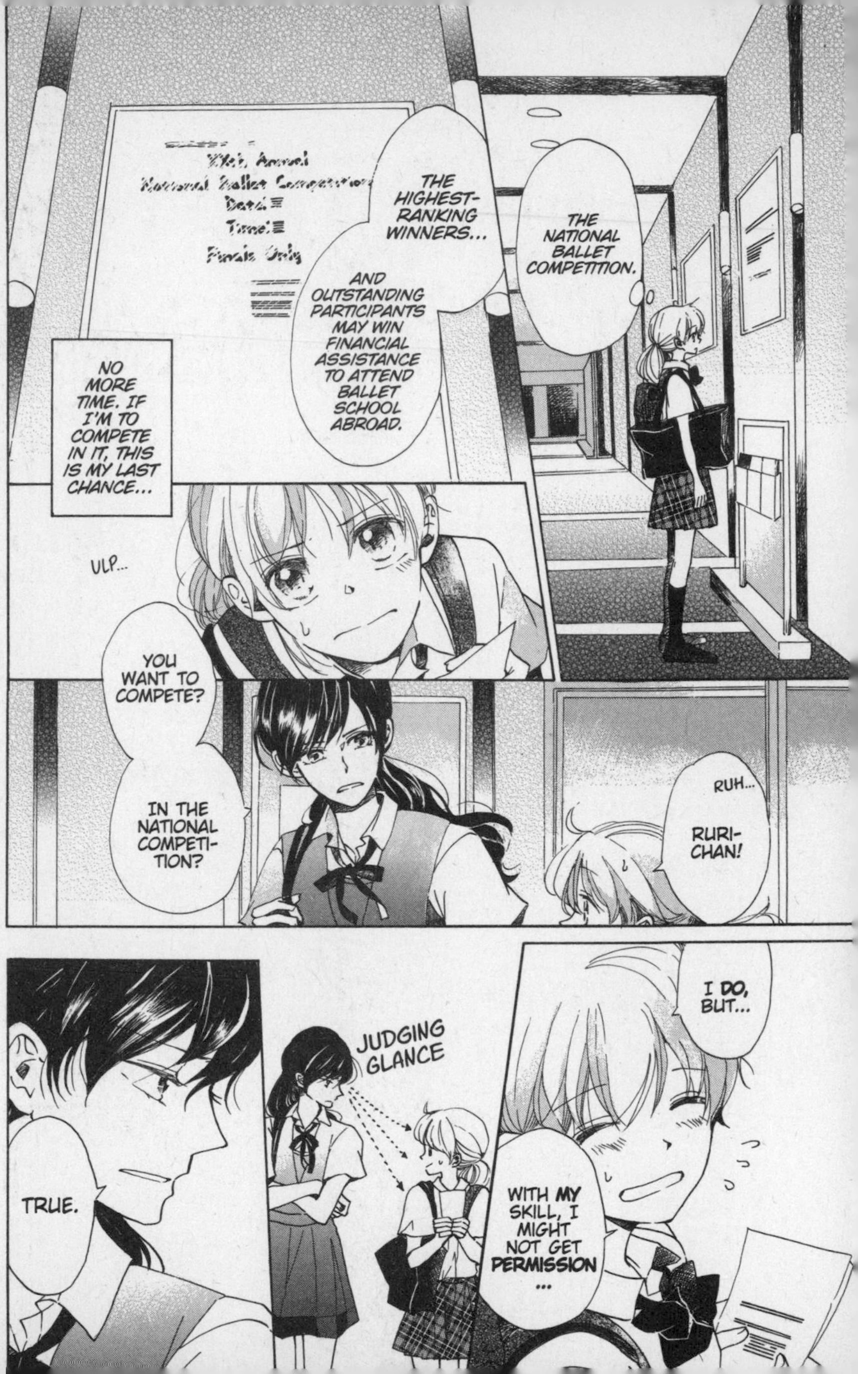
THE NATIONAL BALLET COMPETITION.
THE HIGHEST-RANKING WINNERS...
AND OUTSTANDING PARTICIPANTS MAY WIN FINANCIAL ASSISTANCE TO ATTEND BALLET SCHOOL ABROAD.
NO MORE TIME. IF I'M TO COMPETE IN IT, THIS IS MY LAST CHANCE...
ULP...
RUH...
RURI-CHAN!
YOU WANT TO COMPETE?
IN THE NATIONAL COMPETITION?
I DO, BUT...
WITH MY SKILL, I MIGHT NOT GET PERMISSION ...
JUDGING GLANCE
TRUE.

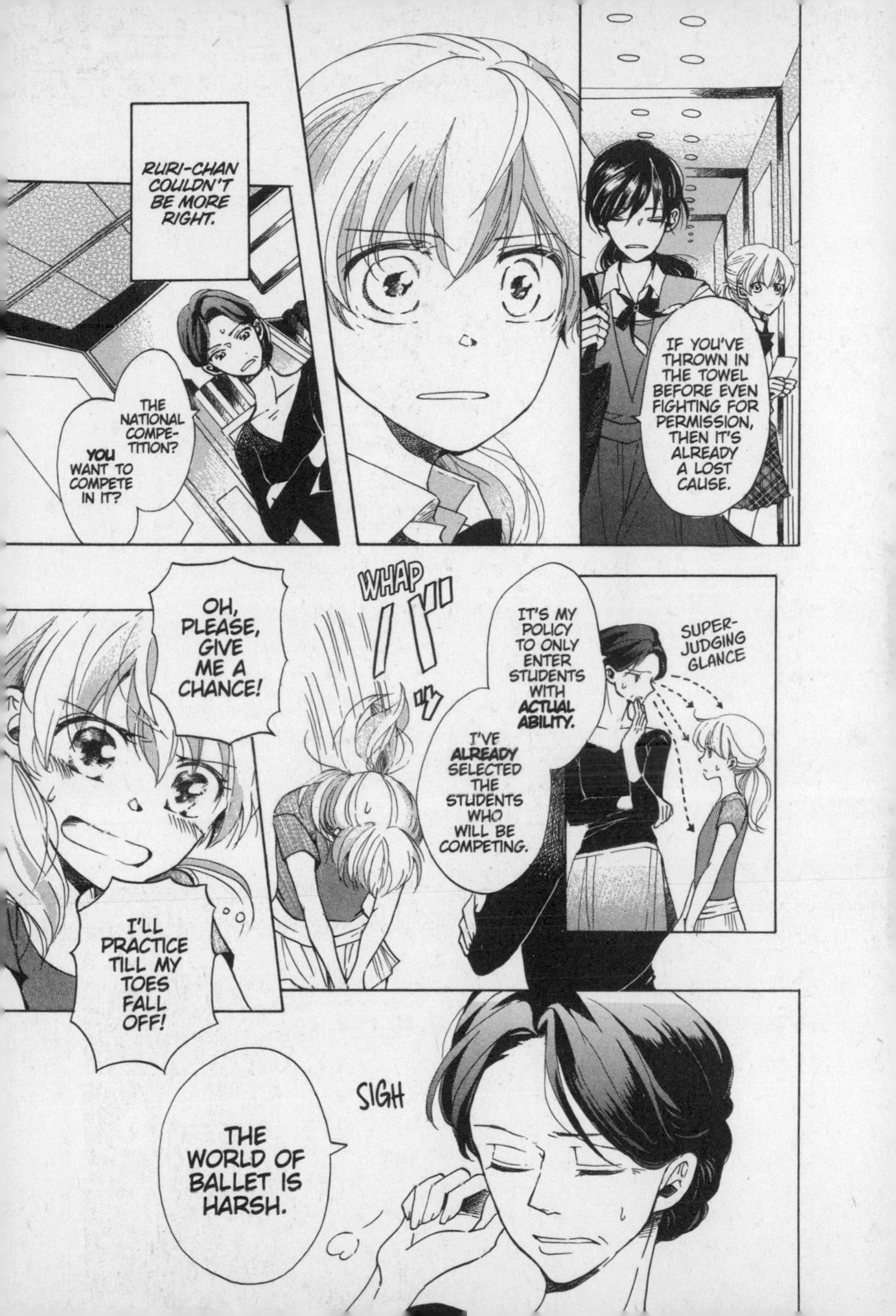
IF YOU'VE THROWN IN THE TOWEL BEFORE EVEN FIGHTING FOR PERMISSION, THEN IT'S ALREADY A LOST CAUSE.
RURI-CHAN COULDN'T BE MORE RIGHT.
THE NATIONAL COMPETITION? YOU WANT TO COMPETE IN IT?
IT'S MY POLICY TO ONLY ENTER STUDENTS WITH ACTUAL ABILITY.
I'VE ALREADY SELECTED THE STUDENTS WHO WILL BE COMPETING.
SUPER-JUDGING GLANCE
WHAP
OH, PLEASE, GIVE ME A CHANCE!
I'LL PRACTICE TILL MY TOES FALL OFF!
SIGH
THE WORLD OF BALLET IS HARSH.

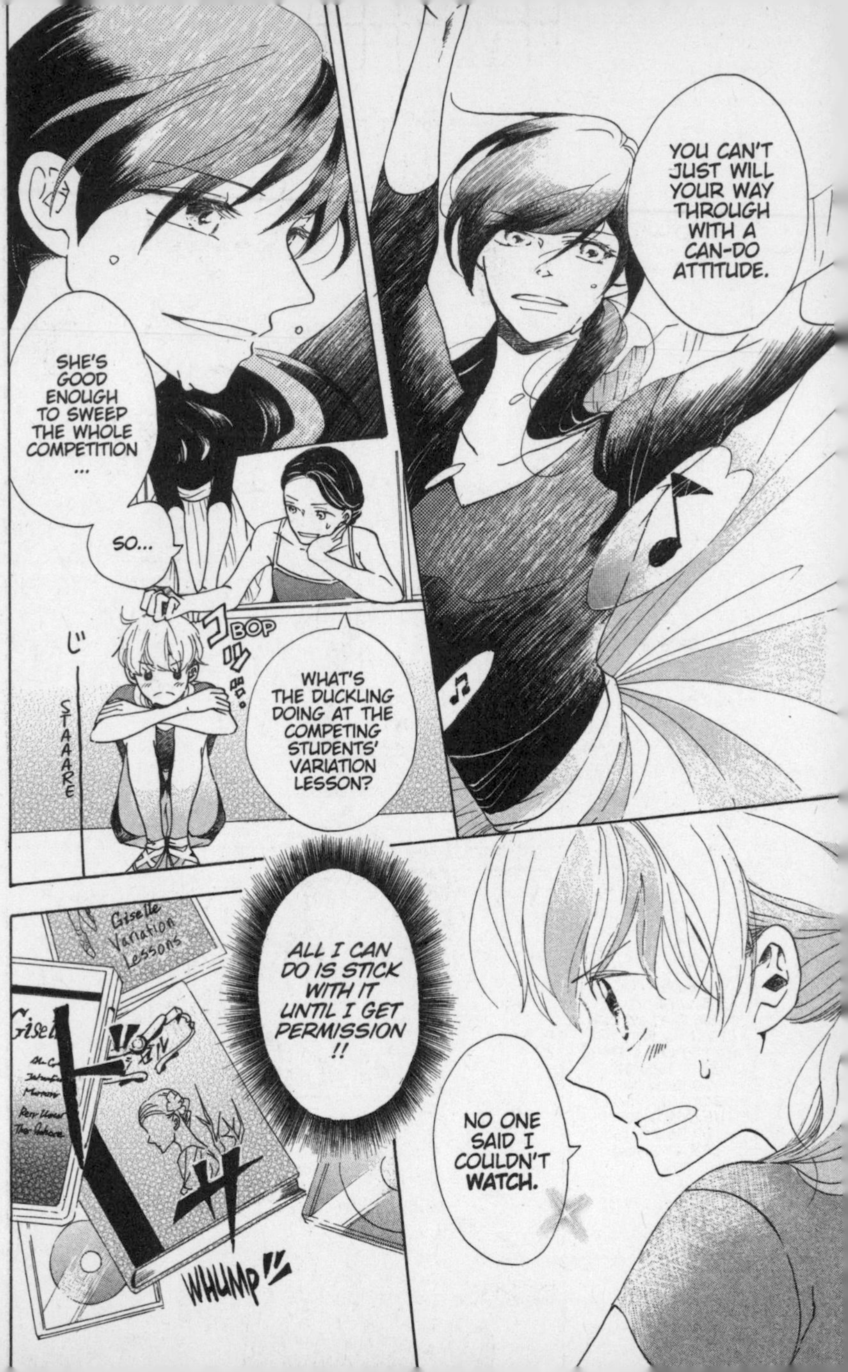
YOU CAN'T JUST WILL YOUR WAY THROUGH WITH A CAN-DO ATTITUDE.
SHE'S GOOD ENOUGH TO SWEEP THE WHOLE COMPETITION ...
SO...
ゴツ
BOP
WHAT'S THE DUCKLING DOING AT THE COMPETING STUDENTS' VARIATION LESSON?
じ
STAAAARE
NO ONE SAID I COULDN'T WATCH.
ALL I CAN DO IS STICK WITH IT UNTIL I GET PERMISSION !!
Giselle Variation Lessons
WHUMP!!

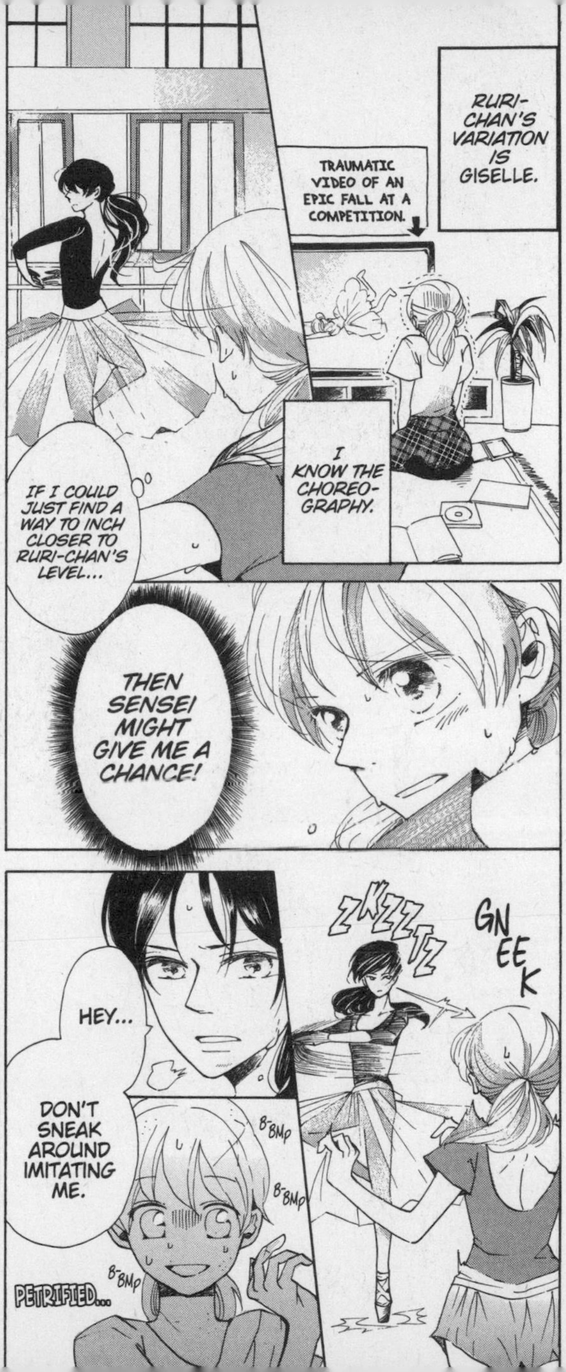
RURI-CHAN'S VARIATION IS GISELLE.
TRAUMATIC VIDEO OF AN EPIC FALL AT A COMPETITION.
I KNOW THE CHOREOGRAPHY.
IF I COULD JUST FIND A WAY TO INCH CLOSER TO RURI-CHAN'S LEVEL...
THEN SENSEI MIGHT GIVE ME A CHANCE!
GNEEK
ZKZZTZ
HEY...
DON'T SNEAK AROUND IMITATING ME.
B-BMP
B-BMP
B-BMP
PETRIFIED...

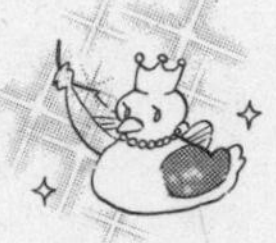

4

GISELLE'S FLASH

I PACKED THIS STORY WITH THE LITTLE OBJECTS/PROPS I USED IN THE REJECTED ROUGH DRAFT, HA HA.

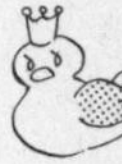

KITCHEN SWAN'S MASCOT

MYSTERIOUS CAT

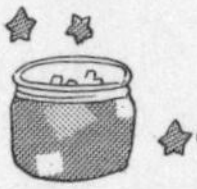

STAR-SHAPED CARROTS IN YUU'S SOUP

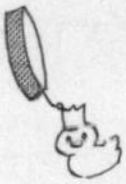

MAHIRU'S CELL PHONE STRAP

ETC.

IT MIGHT ONLY BE A PERSONAL THING THAT NO ONE (EVEN MY EDITOR) WOULD EVER NOTICE, BUT I WANTED TO SHOW MY GRATITUDE FOR THE OPPORTUNITY TO GIVE THIS STORY FORM.

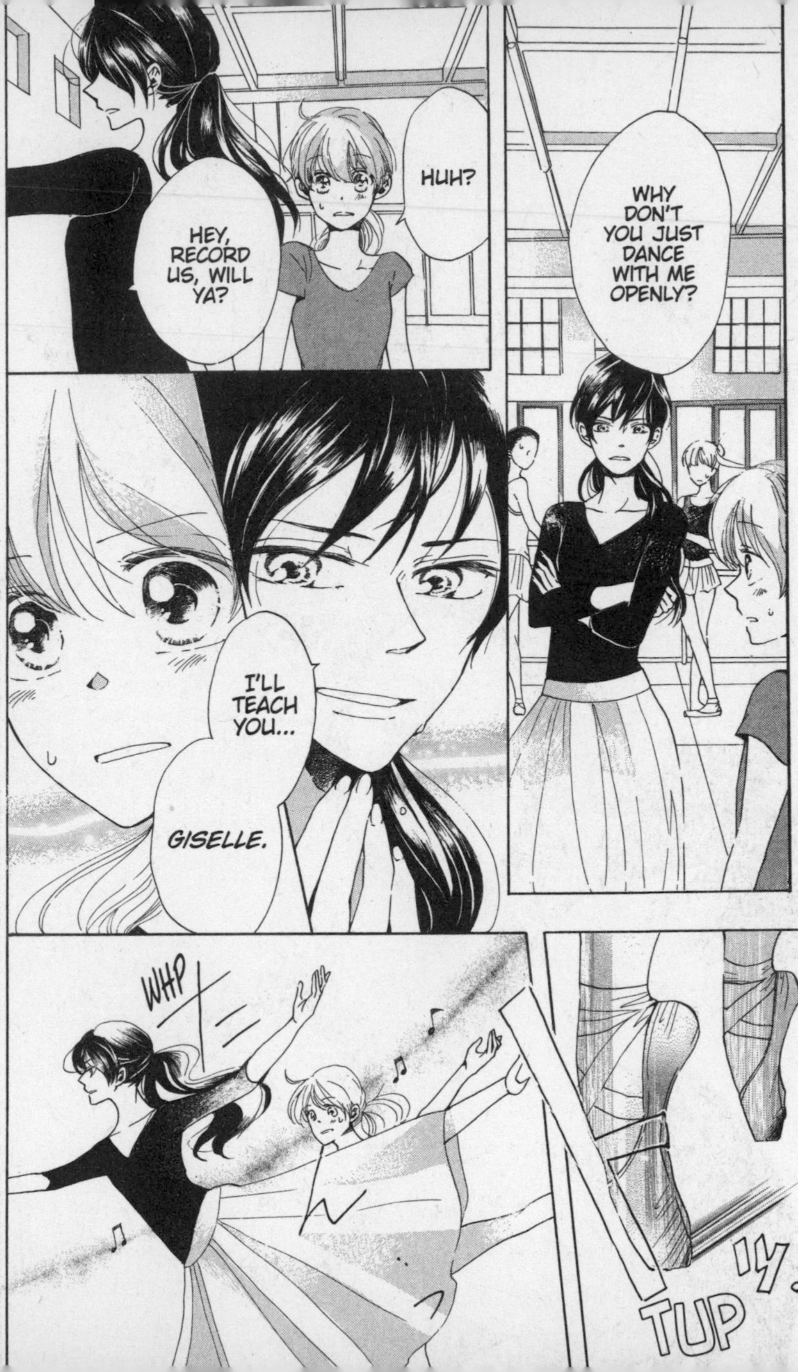
WHY DON'T YOU JUST DANCE WITH ME OPENLY?
HUH?
HEY, RECORD US, WILL YA?
I'LL TEACH YOU...
GISELLE.
TUP
WHP

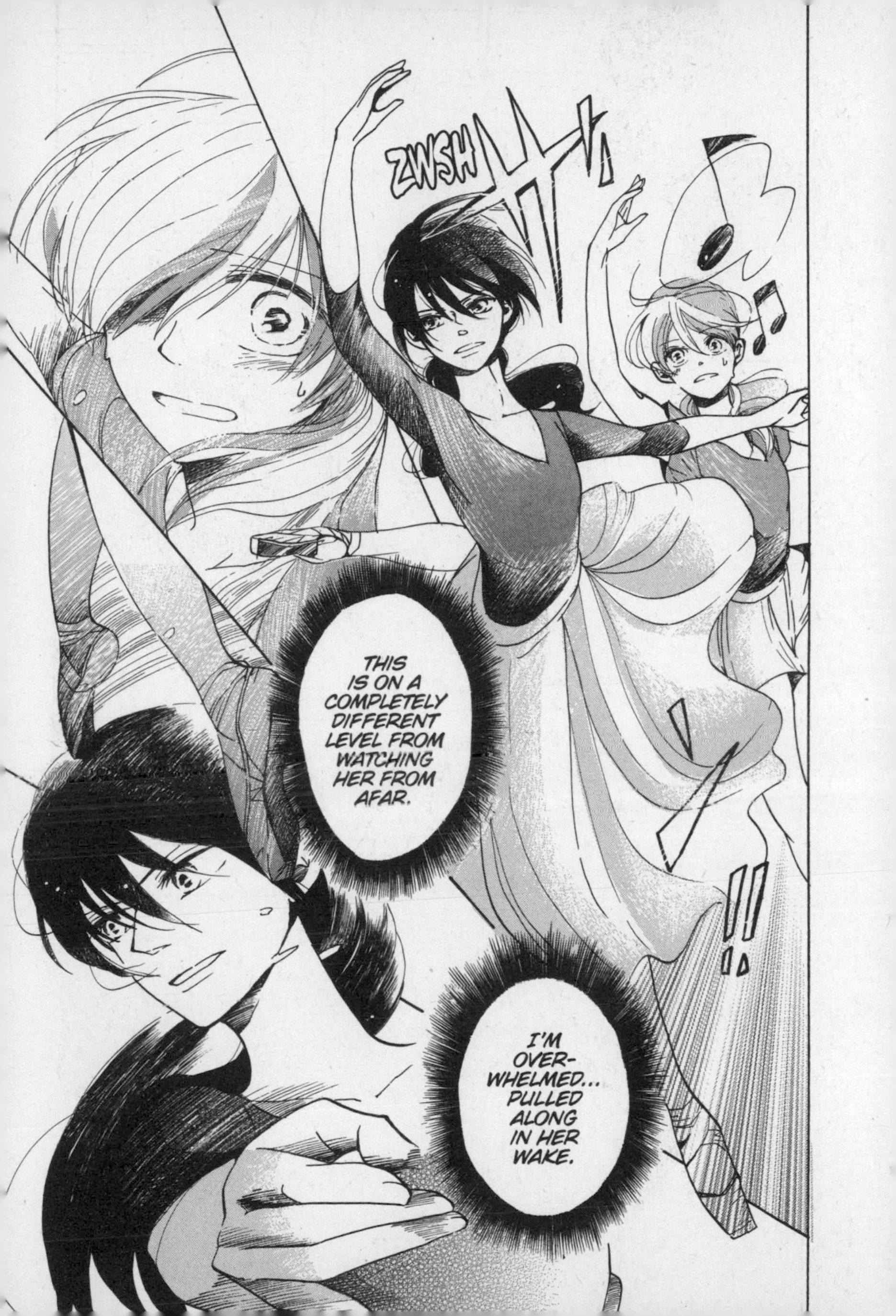
ZWSH
THIS IS ON A COMPLETELY DIFFERENT LEVEL FROM WATCHING HER FROM AFAR.
!!
I'M OVER-WHELMED... PULLED ALONG IN HER WAKE.

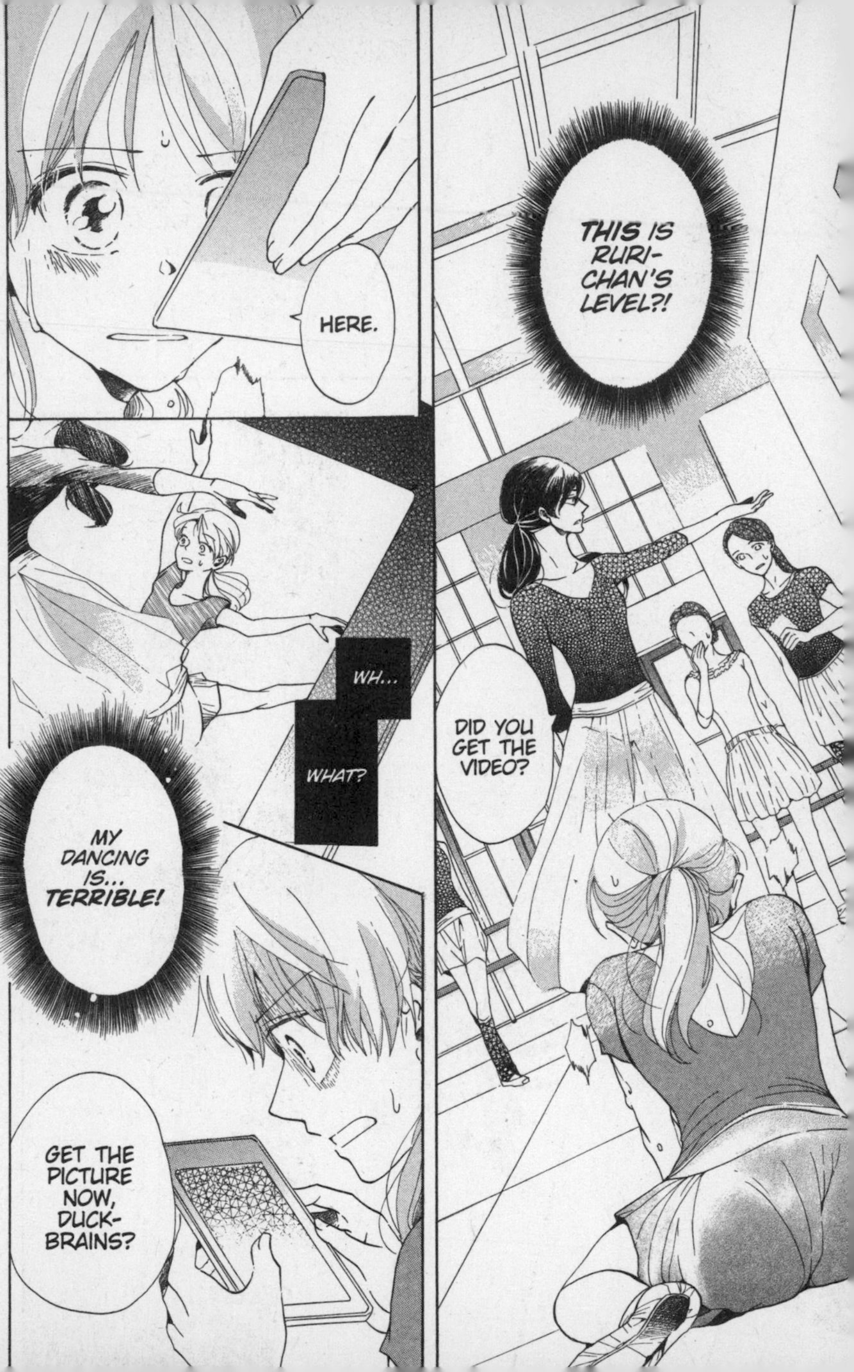
THIS IS RURI-CHAN'S LEVEL?!
DID YOU GET THE VIDEO?
HERE.
WH...
WHAT?
MY DANCING IS... TERRIBLE!
GET THE PICTURE NOW, DUCK-BRAINS?

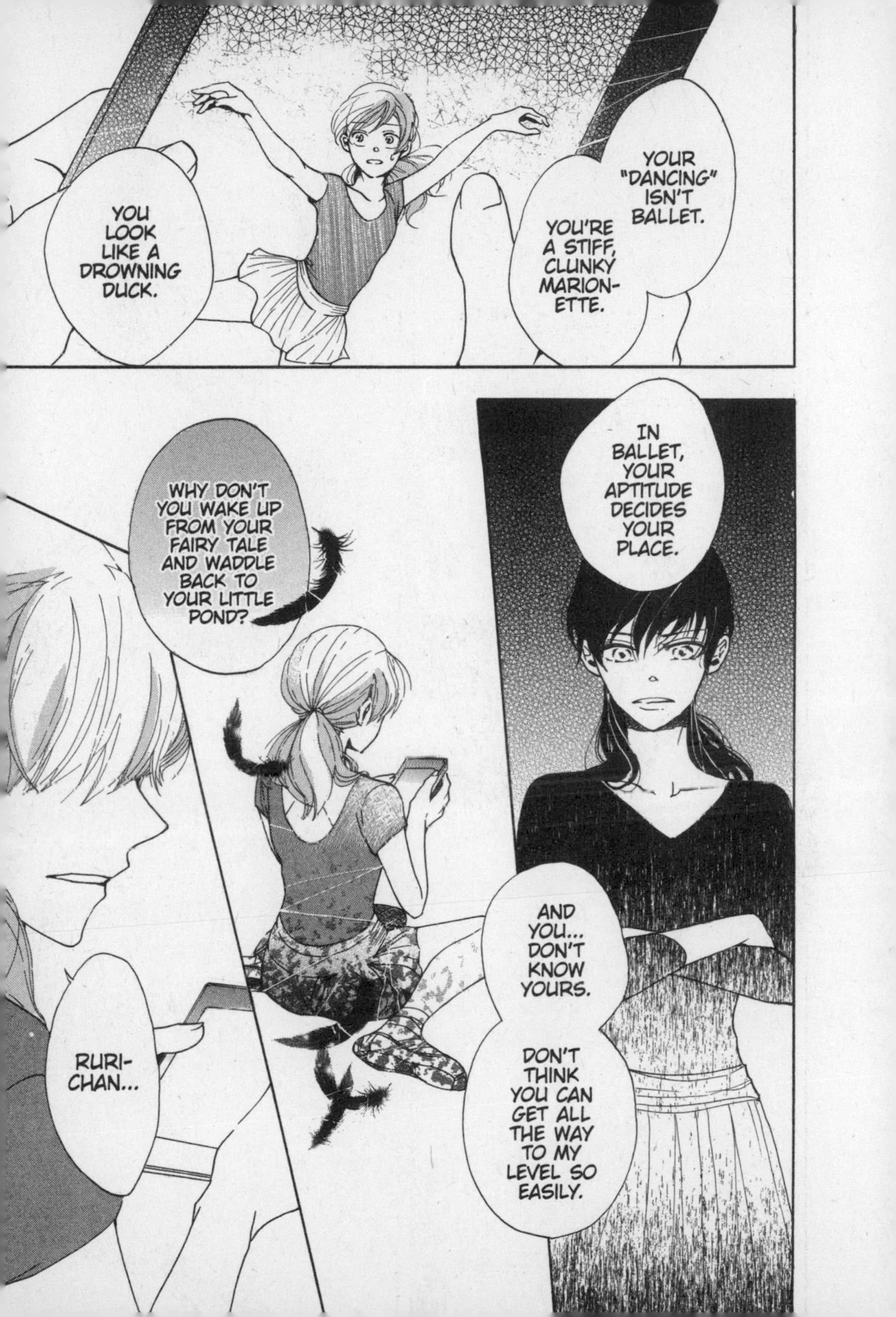
YOUR "DANCING" ISN'T BALLET.
YOU'RE A STIFF, CLUNKY MARIONETTE.
YOU LOOK LIKE A DROWNING DUCK.
IN BALLET, YOUR APTITUDE DECIDES YOUR PLACE.
AND YOU... DON'T KNOW YOURS.
DON'T THINK YOU CAN GET ALL THE WAY TO MY LEVEL SO EASILY.
WHY DON'T YOU WAKE UP FROM YOUR FAIRY TALE AND WADDLE BACK TO YOUR LITTLE POND?
RURI-CHAN...

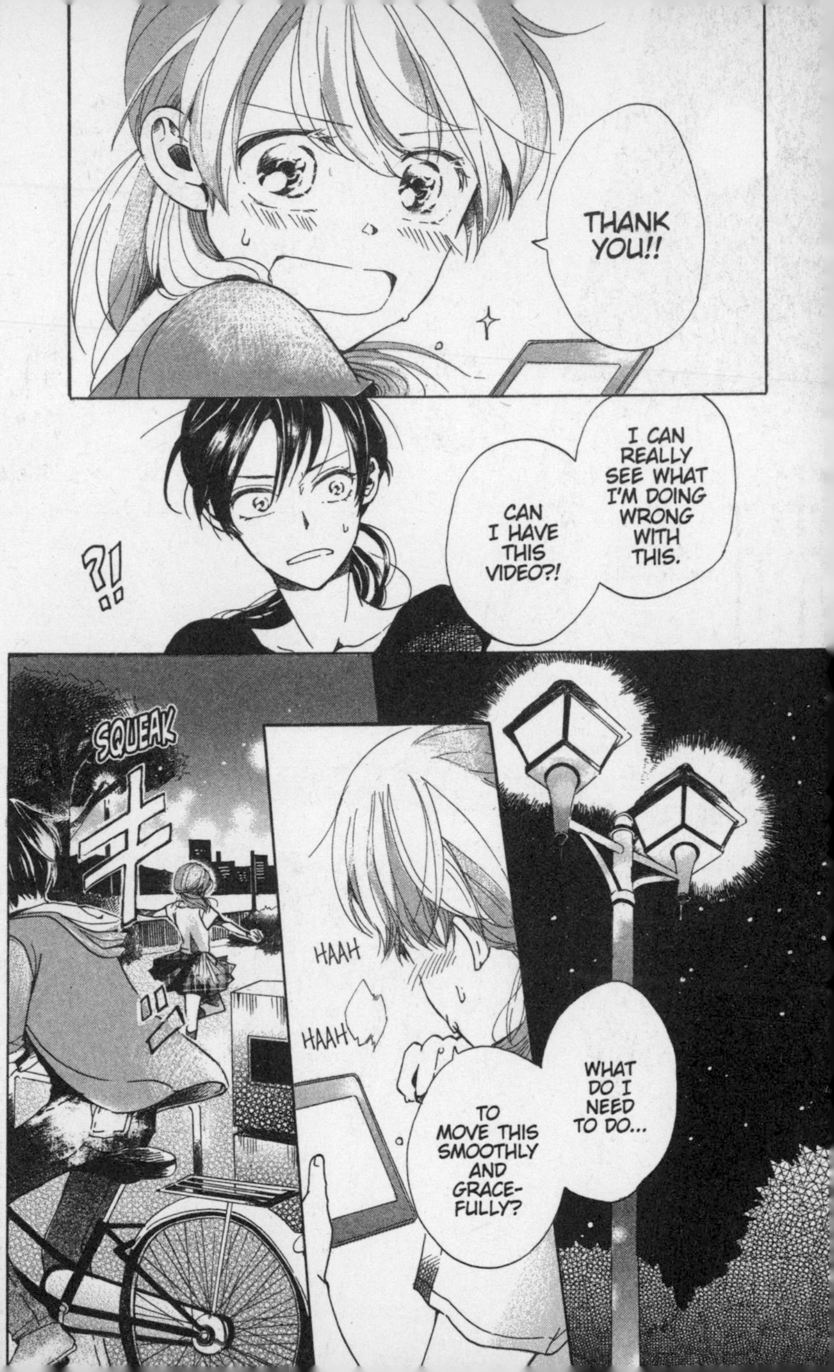
THANK YOU!!
I CAN REALLY SEE WHAT I'M DOING WRONG WITH THIS.
CAN I HAVE THIS VIDEO?!
?!
HAAH
HAAH
WHAT DO I NEED TO DO...
TO MOVE THIS SMOOTHLY AND GRACE-FULLY?
SQUEAK

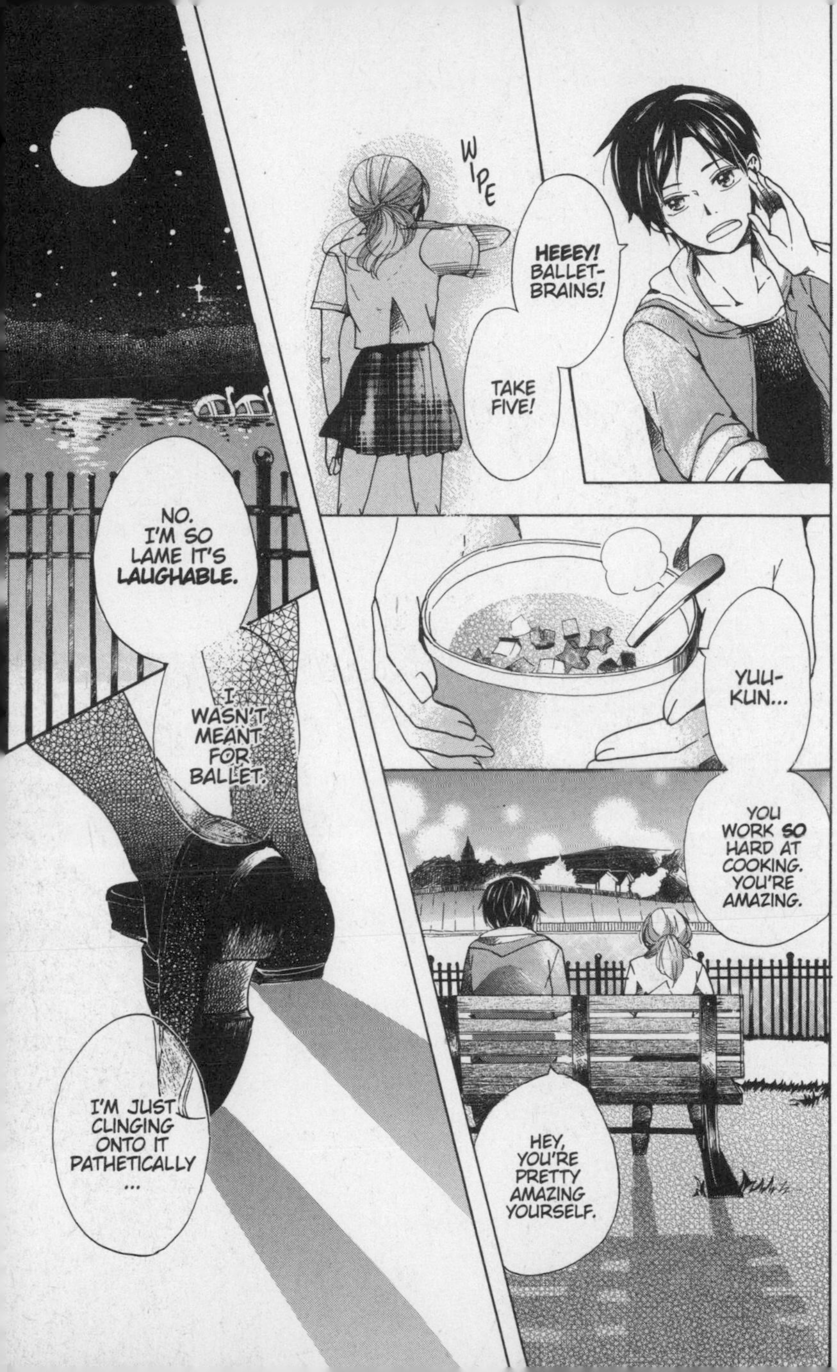
HEEEY! BALLET-BRAINS!
TAKE FIVE!
WIPE
YUU-KUN...
YOU WORK SO HARD AT COOKING. YOU'RE AMAZING.
HEY, YOU'RE PRETTY AMAZING YOURSELF.
NO. I'M SO LAME IT'S LAUGHABLE.
I WASN'T MEANT FOR BALLET.
I'M JUST CLINGING ONTO IT PATHETICALLY ...

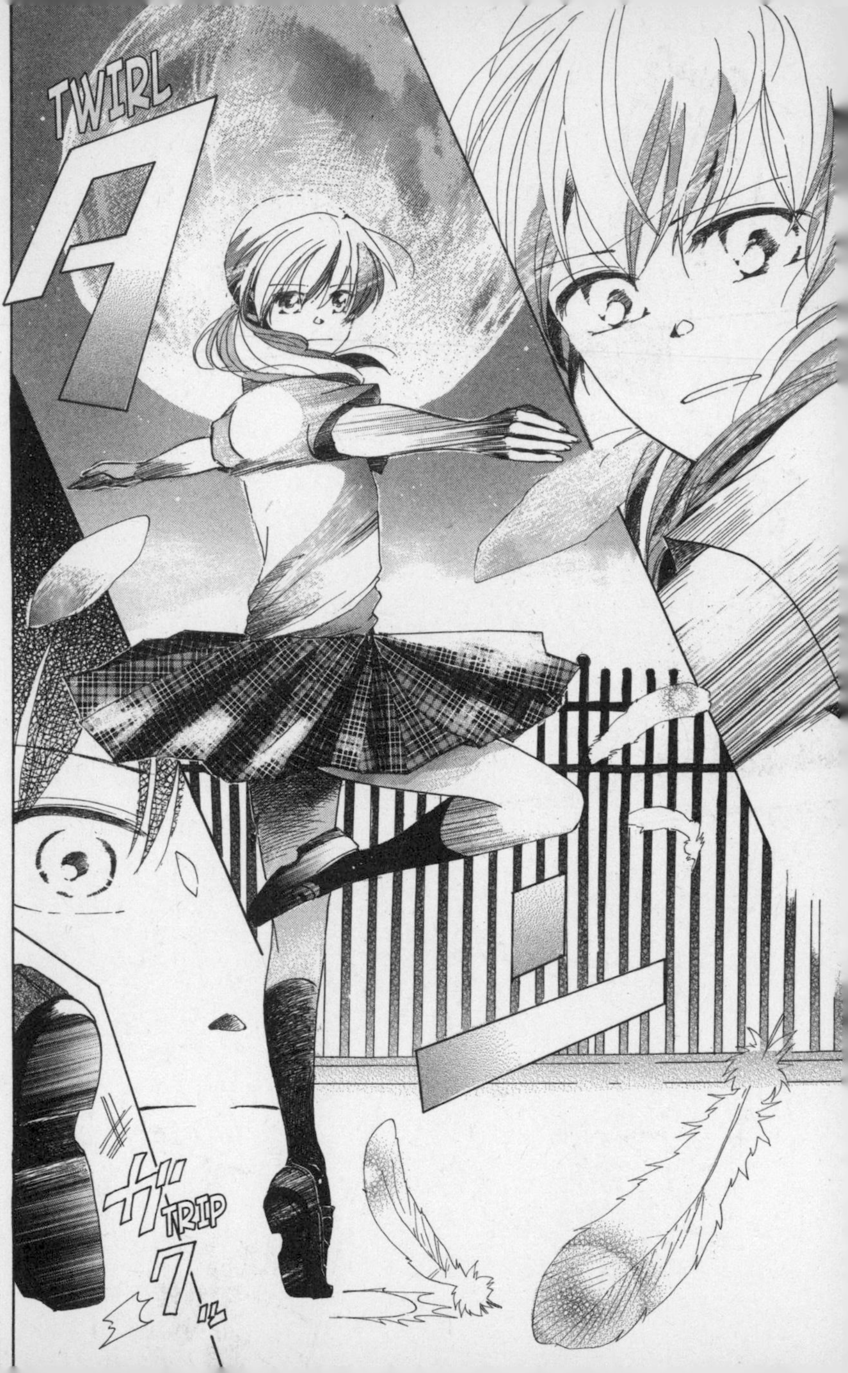
TWIRL
TRIP

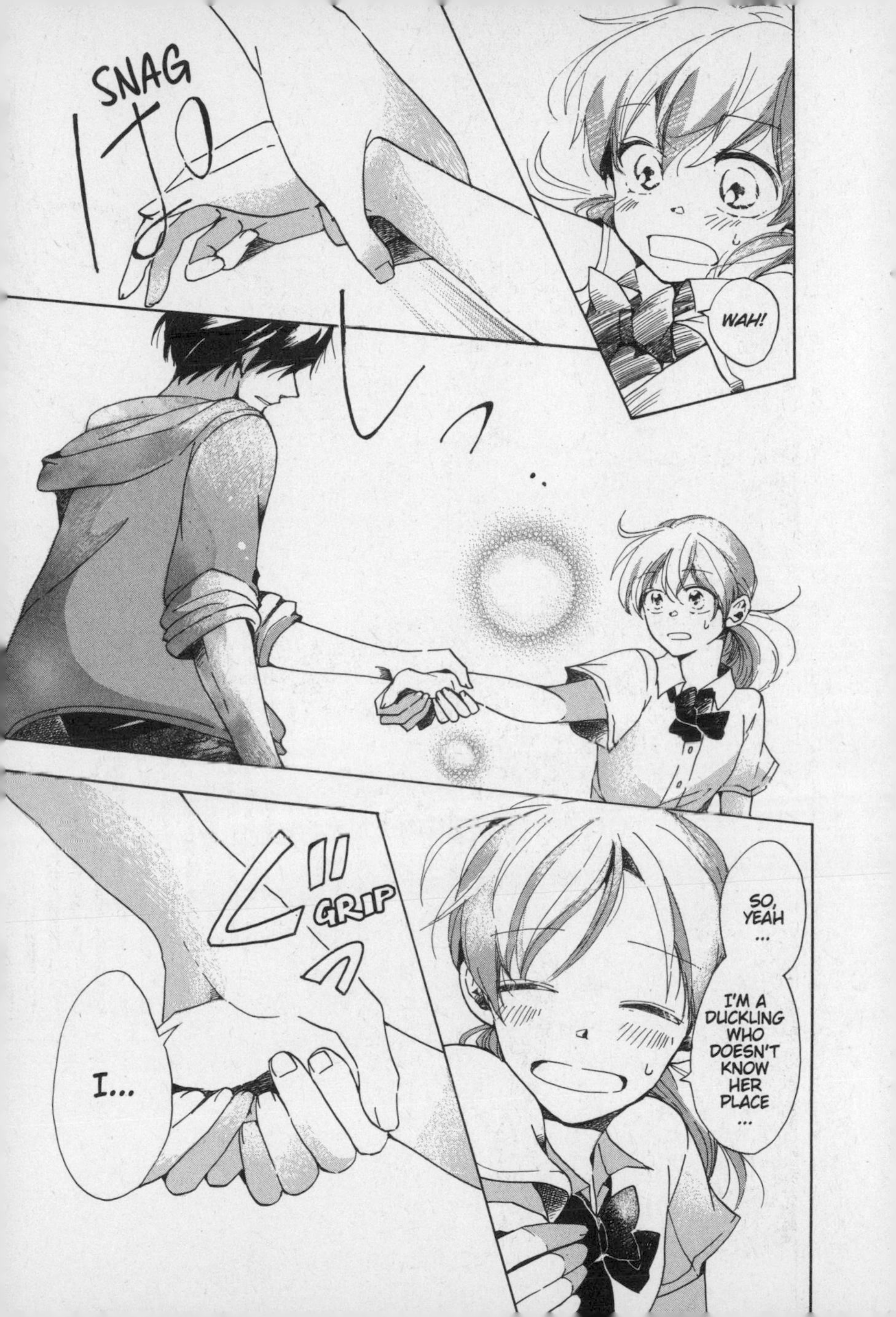
WAH!
SNAG
SO, YEAH ...
I'M A DUCKLING WHO DOESN'T KNOW HER PLACE ...
GRIP
I...

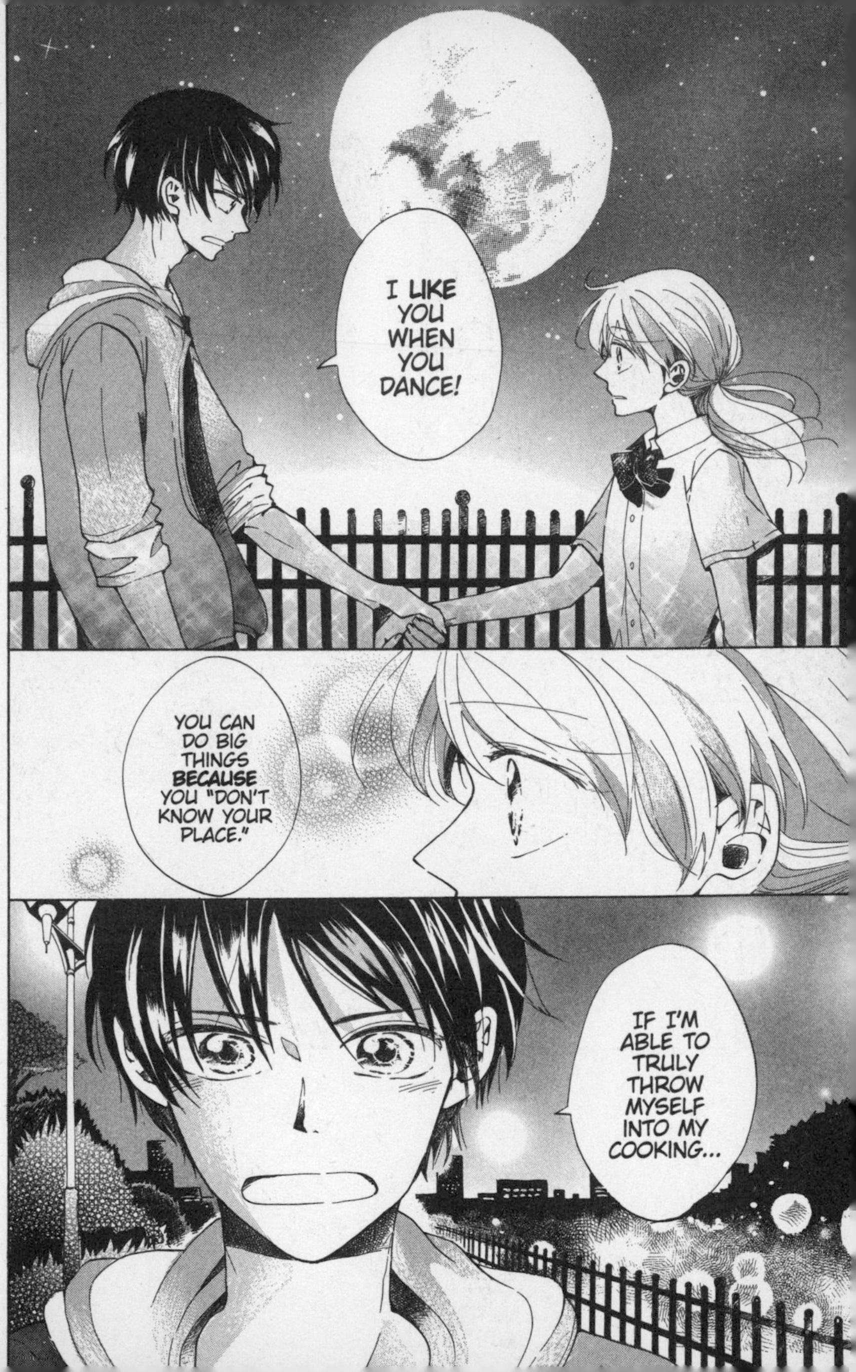
I LIKE YOU WHEN YOU DANCE!
YOU CAN DO BIG THINGS BECAUSE YOU "DON'T KNOW YOUR PLACE."
IF I'M ABLE TO TRULY THROW MYSELF INTO MY COOKING...

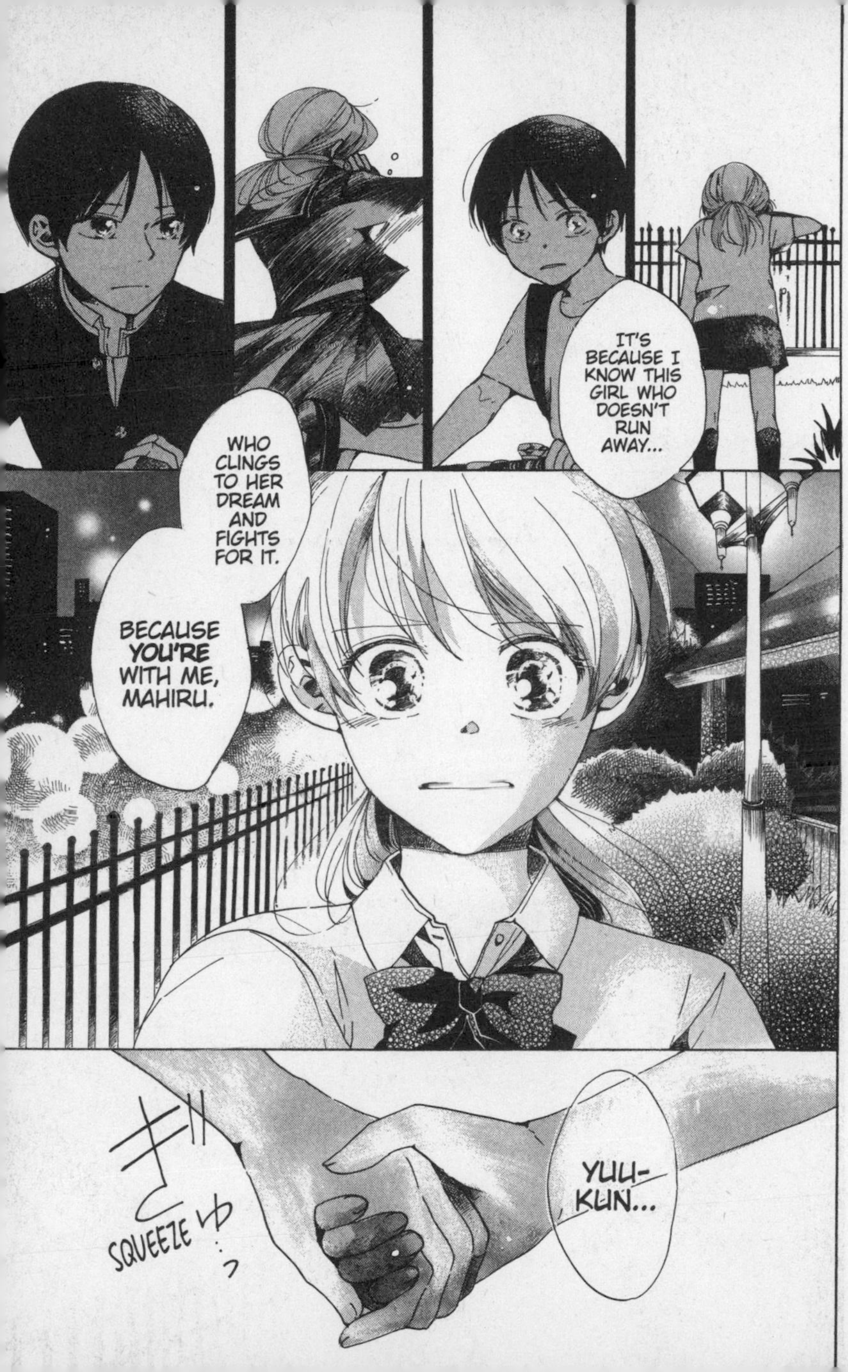
IT'S BECAUSE I KNOW THIS GIRL WHO DOESN'T RUN AWAY...
WHO CLINGS TO HER DREAM AND FIGHTS FOR IT.
BECAUSE YOU'RE WITH ME, MAHIRU.
YUU-KUN...
SQUEEZE

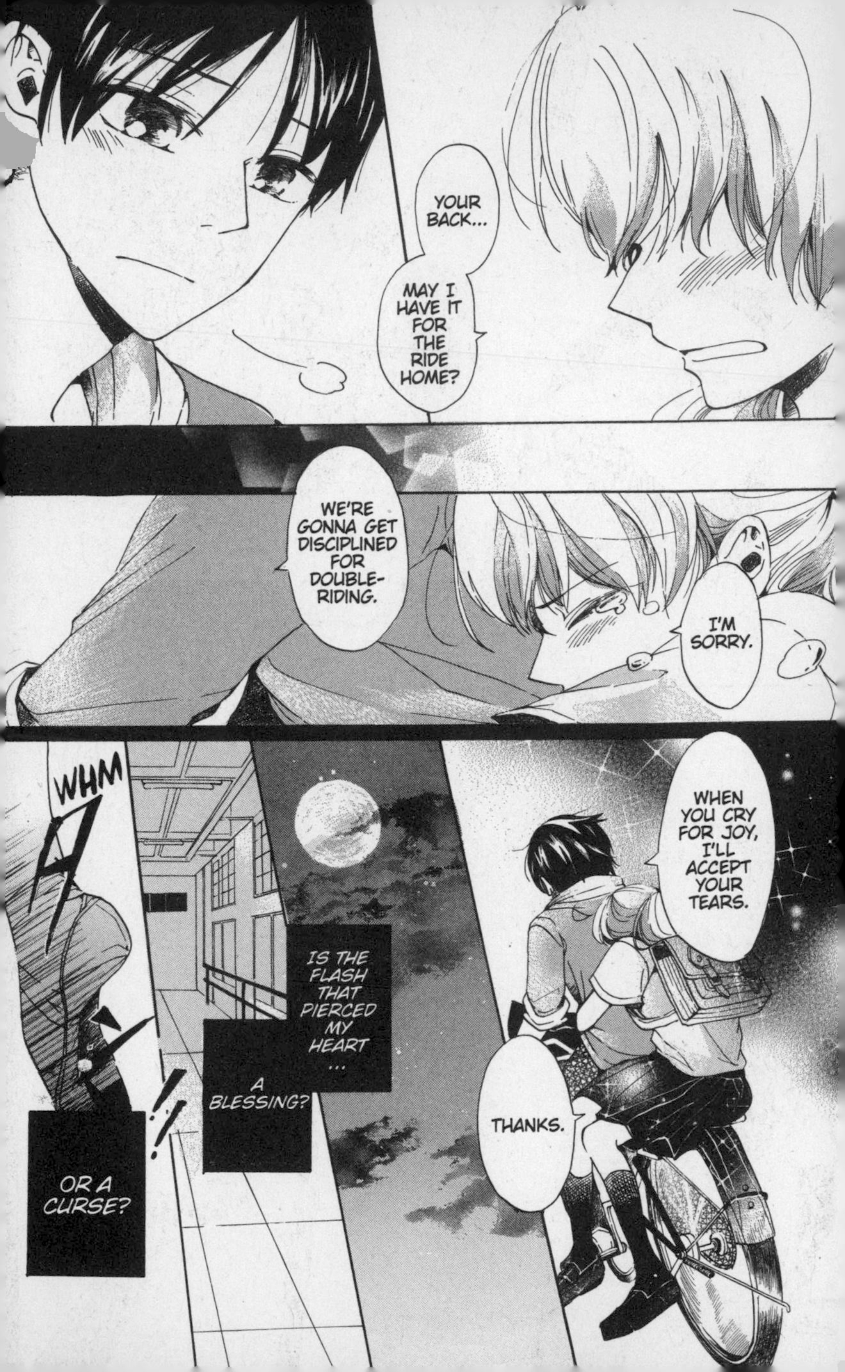
YOUR BACK...
MAY I HAVE IT FOR THE RIDE HOME?
I'M SORRY.
WE'RE GONNA GET DISCIPLINED FOR DOUBLE-RIDING.
WHEN YOU CRY FOR JOY, I'LL ACCEPT YOUR TEARS.
THANKS.
IS THE FLASH THAT PIERCED MY HEART ...
A BLESSING?
WHM
OR A CURSE?

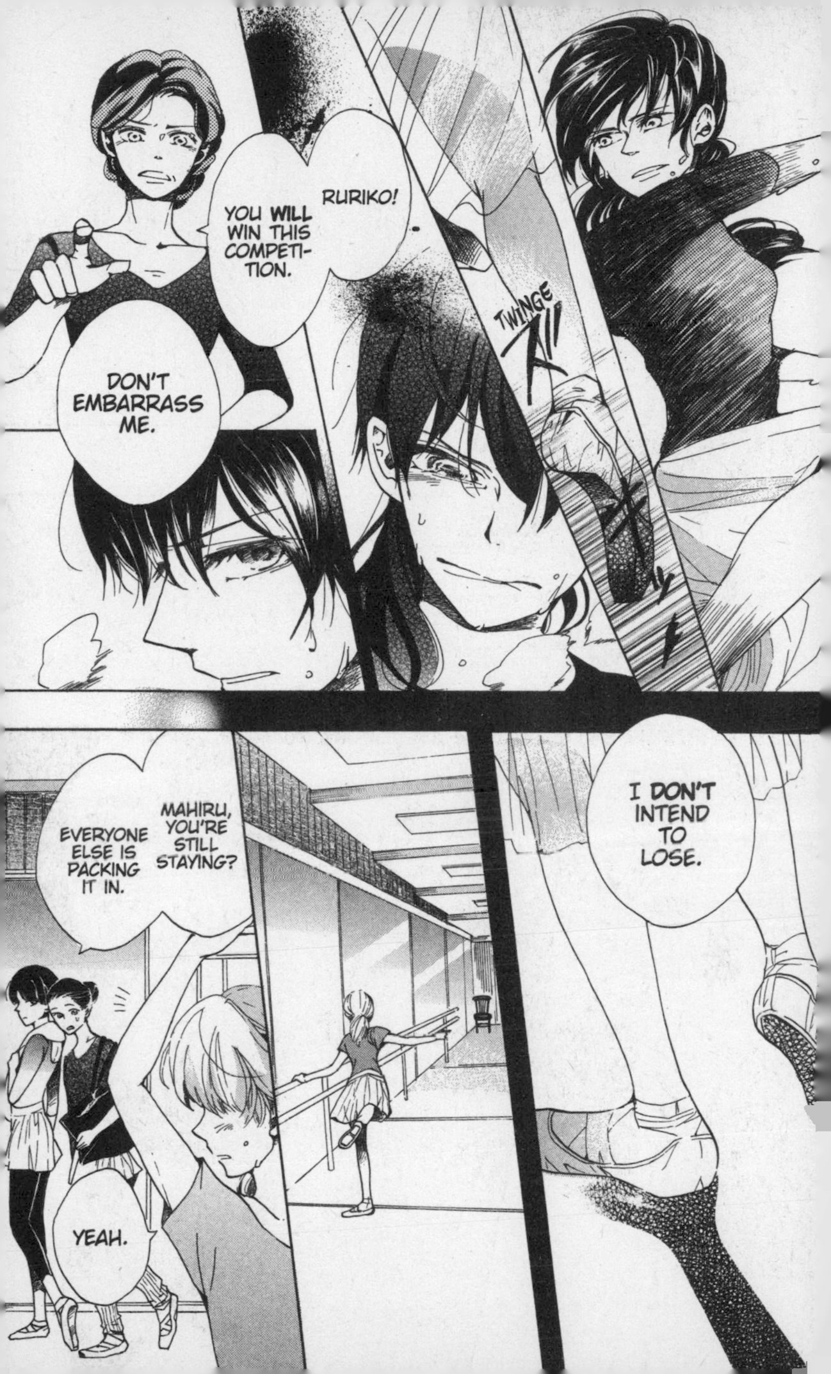
TWINGE
RURIKO!
YOU WILL WIN THIS COMPETITION.
DON'T EMBARRASS ME.
I DON'T INTEND TO LOSE.
MAHIRU, YOU'RE STILL STAYING?
EVERYONE ELSE IS PACKING IT IN.
YEAH.

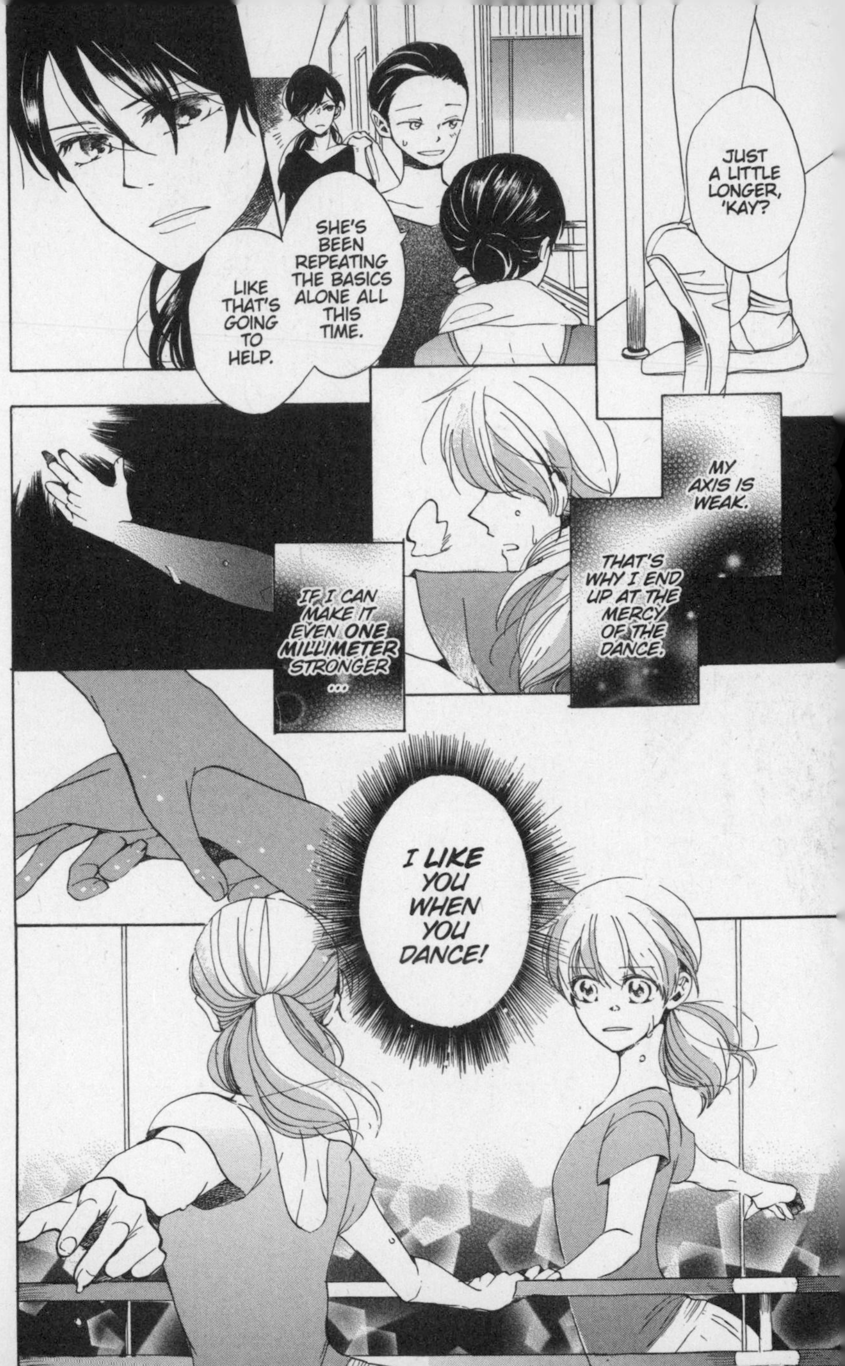
JUST A LITTLE LONGER, 'KAY?
SHE'S BEEN REPEATING THE BASICS ALONE ALL THIS TIME.
LIKE THAT'S GOING TO HELP.
MY AXIS IS WEAK.
THAT'S WHY I END UP AT THE MERCY OF THE DANCE.
IF I CAN MAKE IT EVEN ONE MILLIMETER STRONGER...
I LIKE YOU WHEN YOU DANCE!

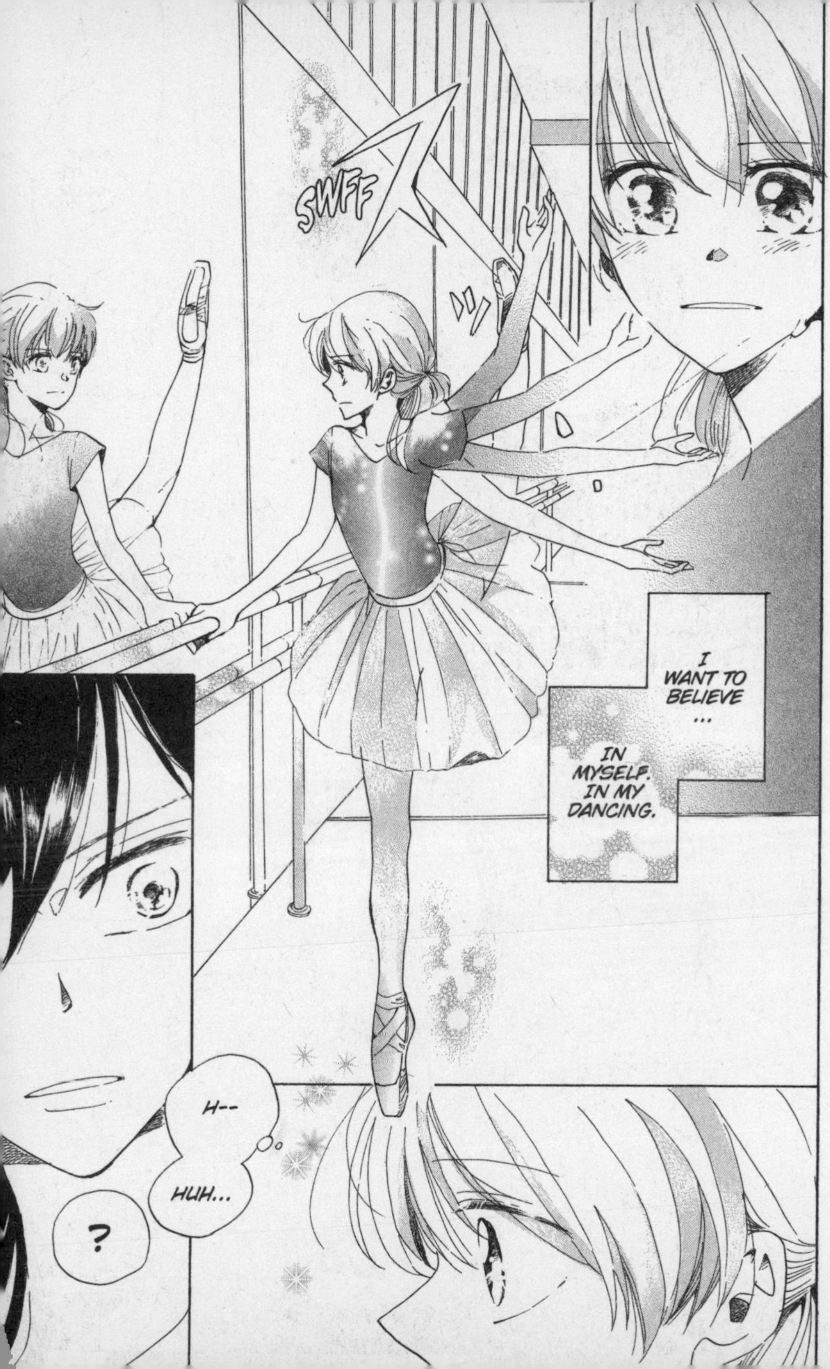
SWFF
I WANT TO BELIEVE ...
IN MYSELF. IN MY DANCING.
H--
HUH...
?

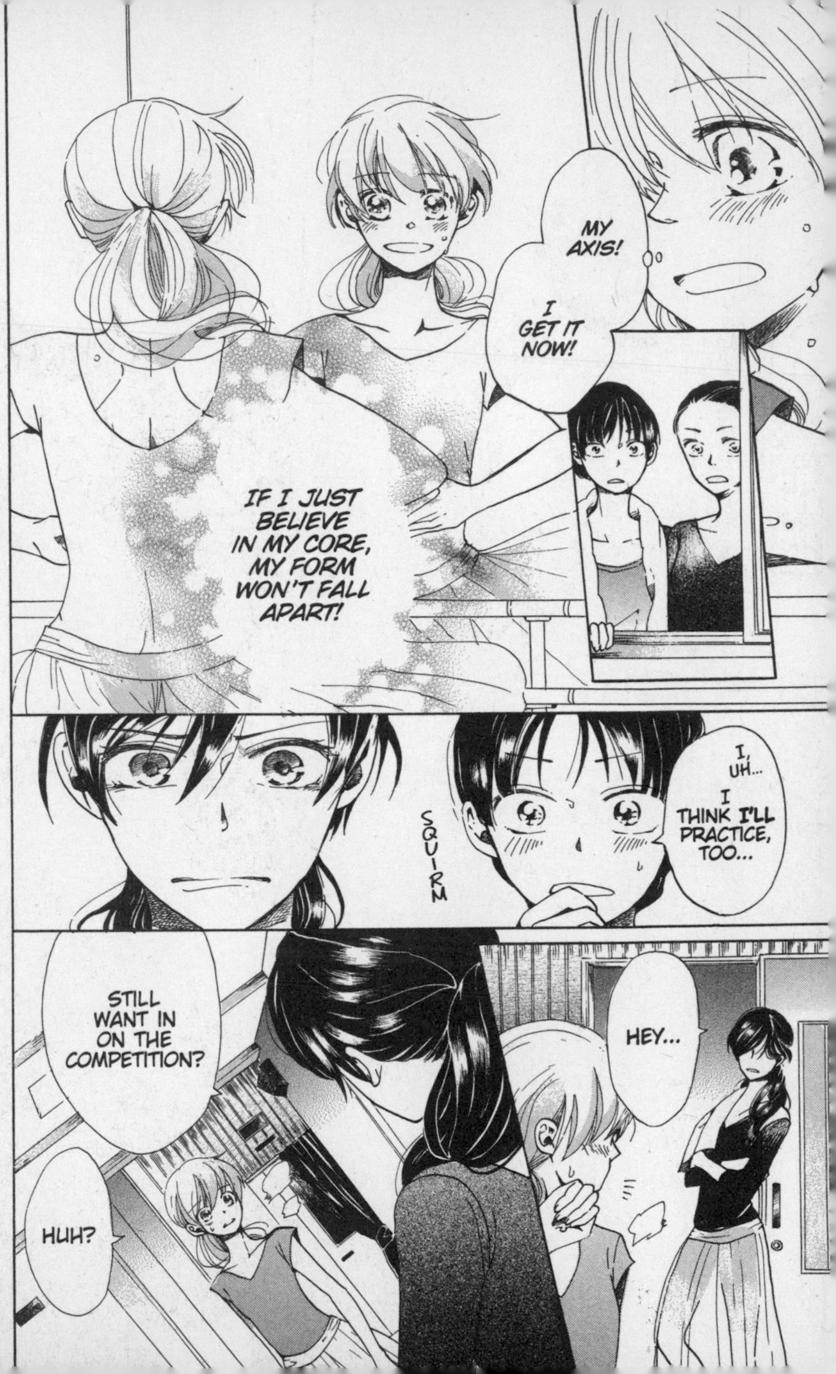
MY AXIS!
I GET IT NOW!
IF I JUST BELIEVE IN MY CORE, MY FORM WON'T FALL APART!
I, UH... I THINK I'LL PRACTICE, TOO...
SQUIRM
HEY...
STILL WANT IN ON THE COMPETITION?
HUH?

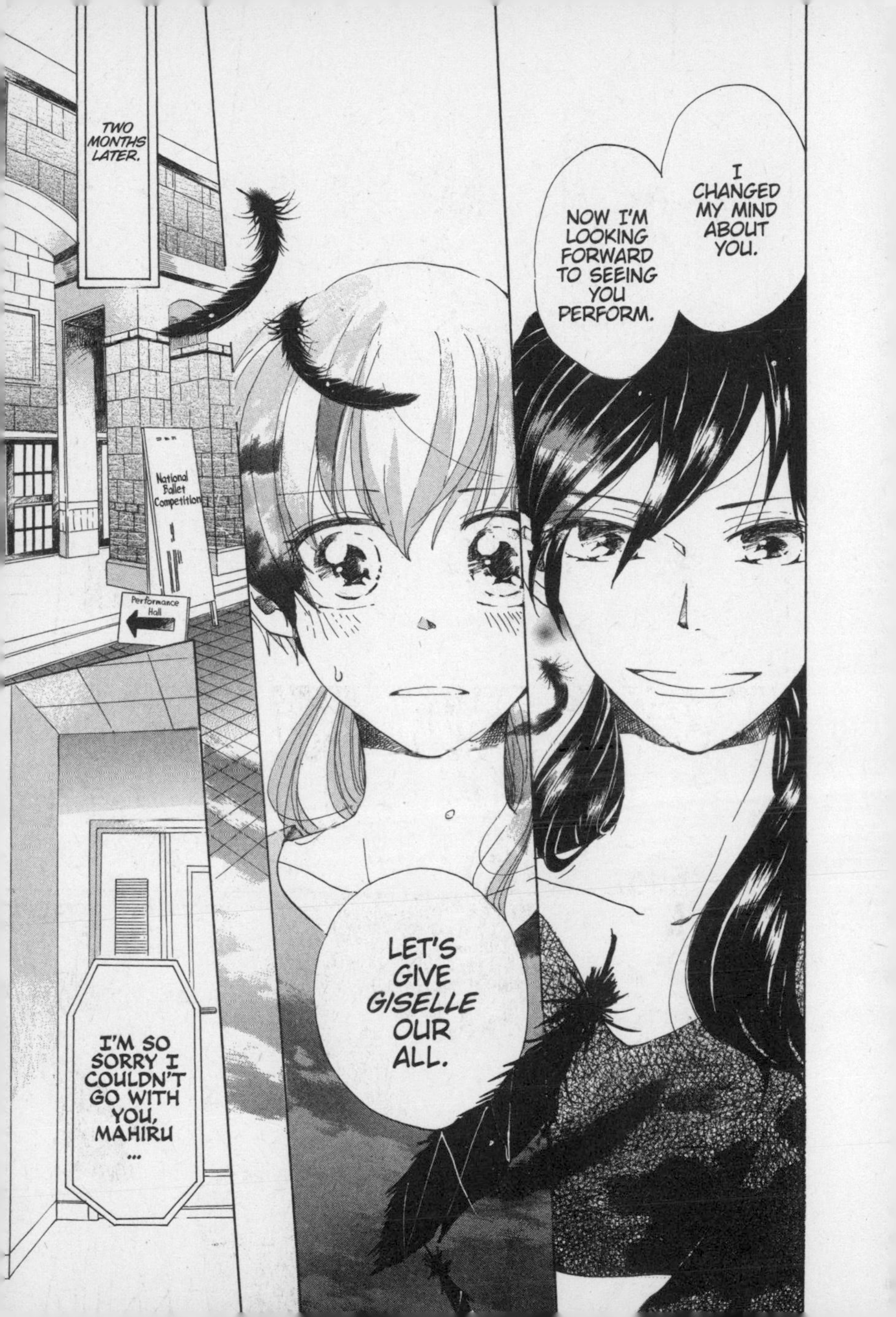
I CHANGED MY MIND ABOUT YOU.
NOW I'M LOOKING FORWARD TO SEEING YOU PERFORM.
LET'S GIVE GISELLE OUR ALL.
TWO MONTHS LATER.
National Ballet Competition
Performance Hall
I'M SO SORRY I COULDN'T GO WITH YOU, MAHIRU ...

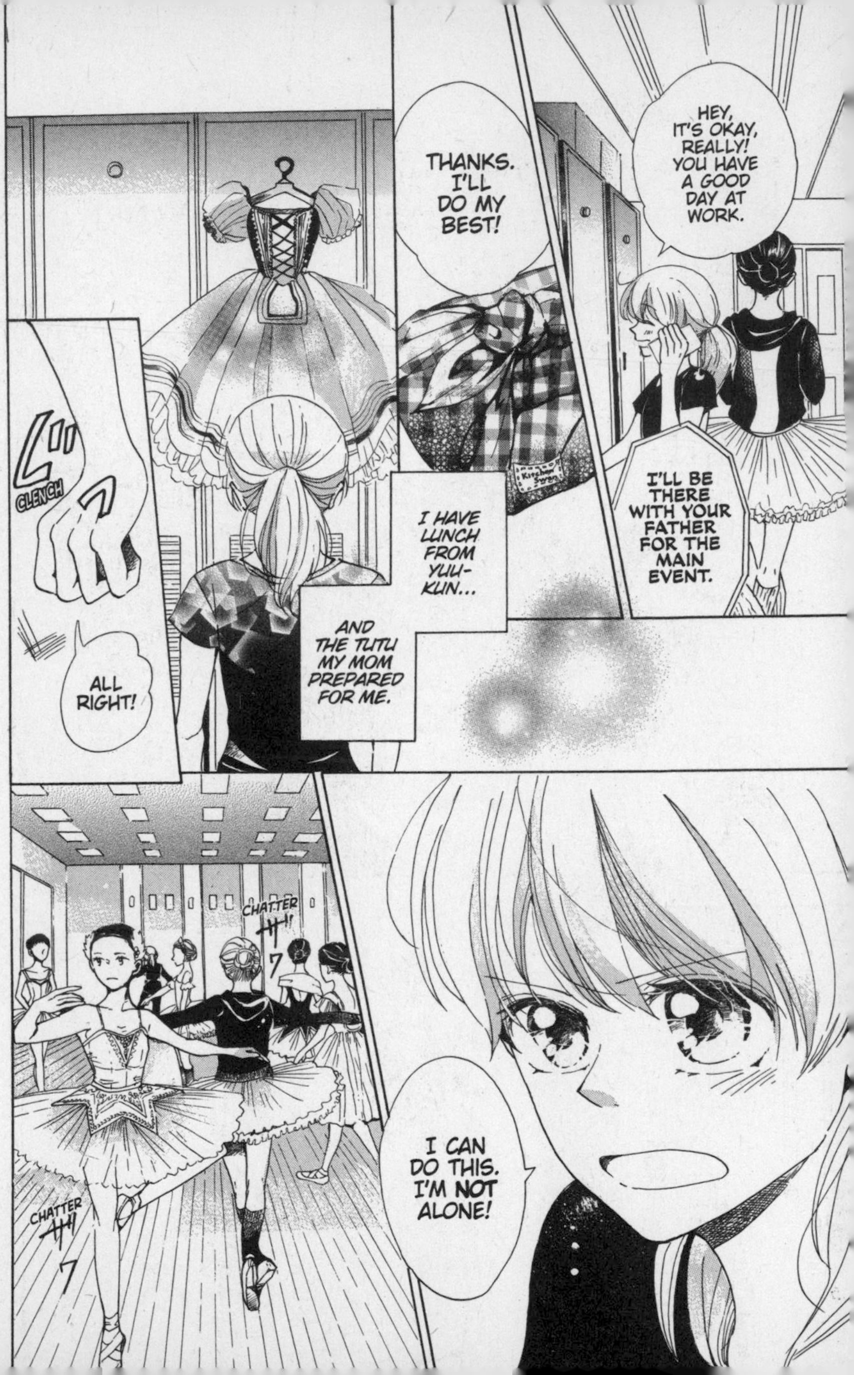
HEY, IT'S OKAY, REALLY! YOU HAVE A GOOD DAY AT WORK.
I'LL BE THERE WITH YOUR FATHER FOR THE MAIN EVENT.
THANKS. I'LL DO MY BEST!
I HAVE LUNCH FROM YUU-KUN...
AND THE TUTU MY MOM PREPARED FOR ME.
CLENCH
ALL RIGHT!
I CAN DO THIS. I'M NOT ALONE!
CHATTER
CHATTER

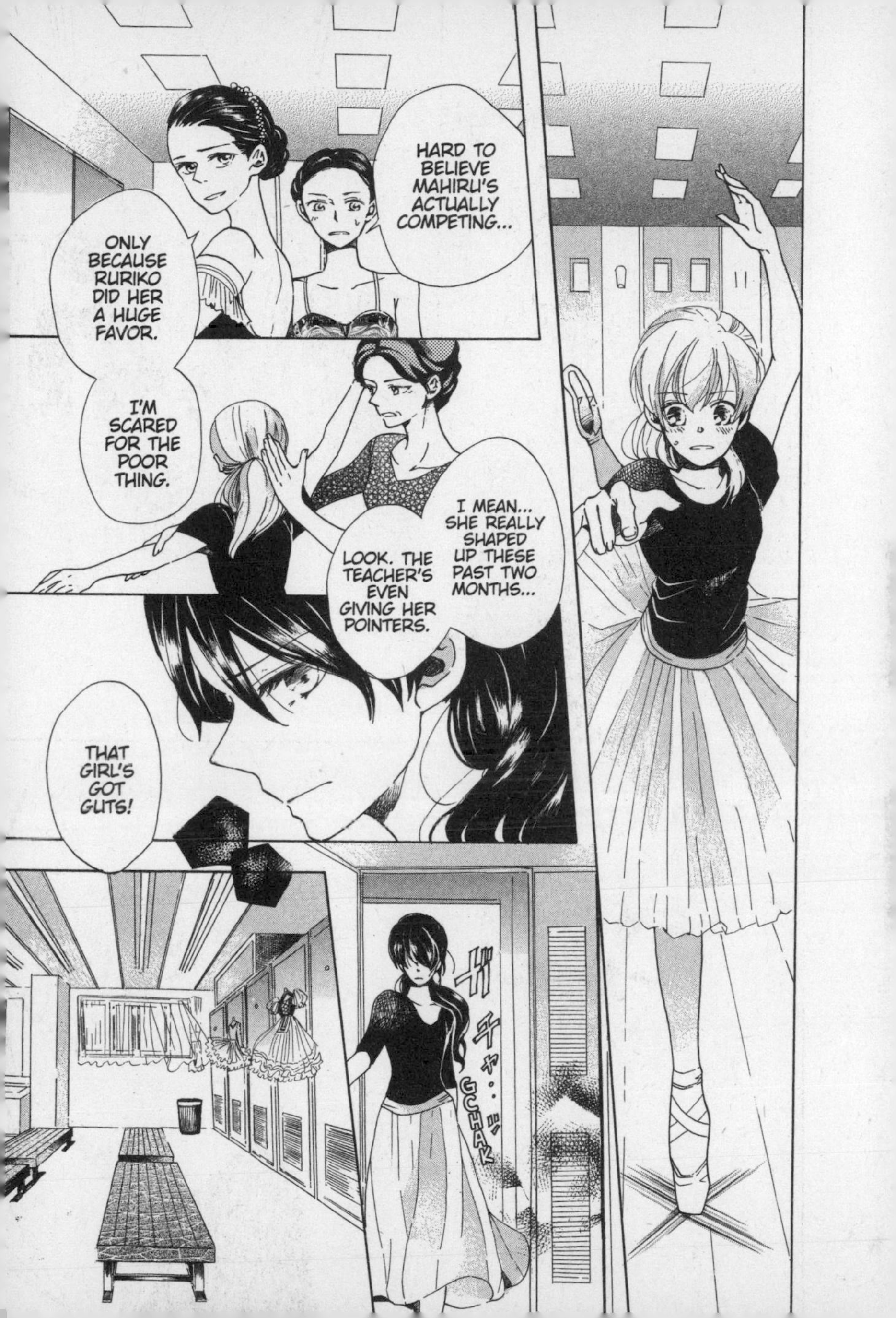
HARD TO BELIEVE MAHIRU'S ACTUALLY COMPETING...
ONLY BECAUSE RURIKO DID HER A HUGE FAVOR.
I'M SCARED FOR THE POOR THING.
I MEAN... SHE REALLY SHAPED UP THESE PAST TWO MONTHS...
LOOK. THE TEACHER'S EVEN GIVING HER POINTERS.
THAT GIRL'S GOT GUTS!
GCHAK

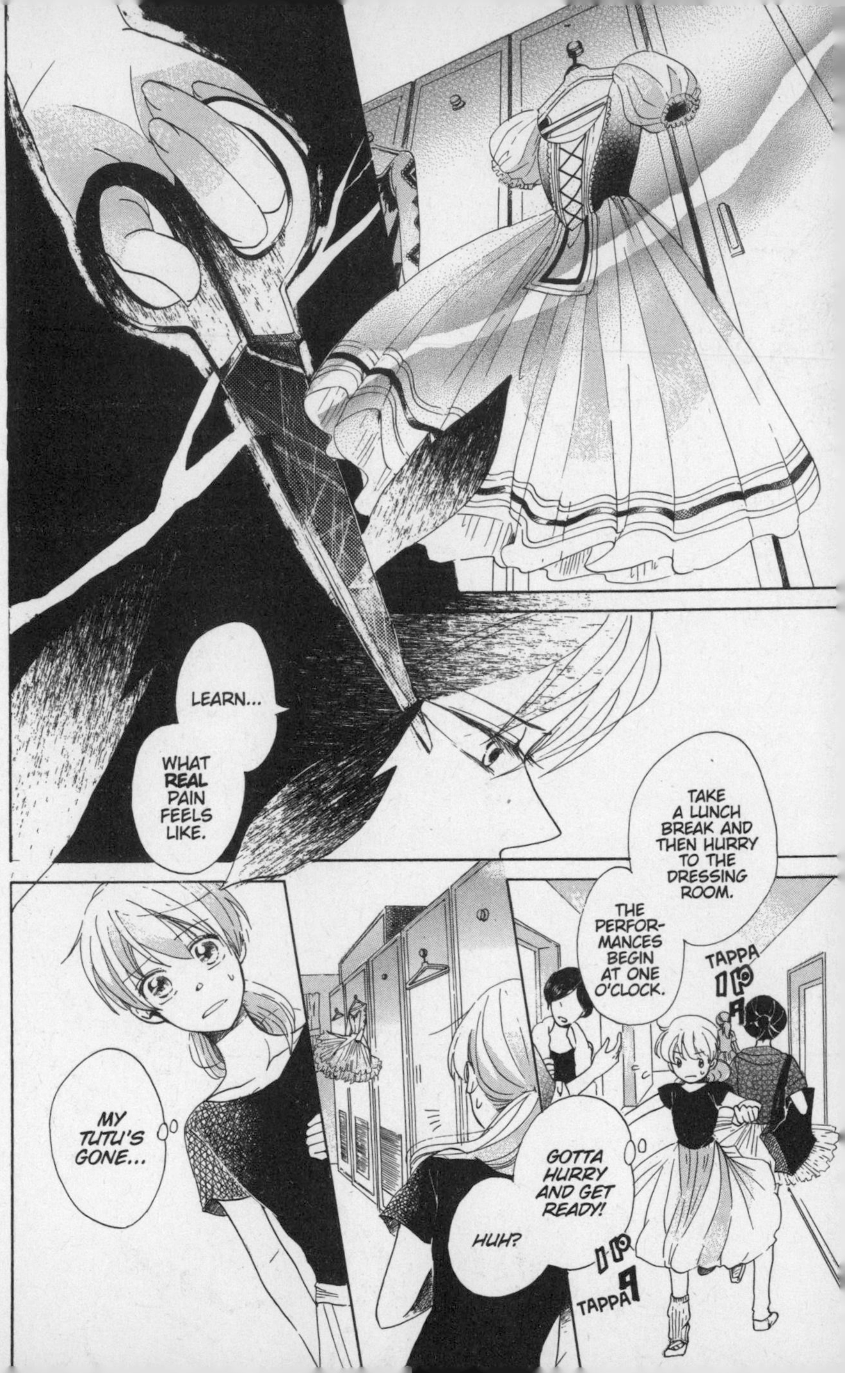
LEARN...
WHAT REAL PAIN FEELS LIKE.
TAKE A LUNCH BREAK AND THEN HURRY TO THE DRESSING ROOM.
THE PERFORMANCES BEGIN AT ONE O'CLOCK.
TAPPA
TAPPA
GOTTA HURRY AND GET READY!
HUH?
MY TUTU'S GONE...

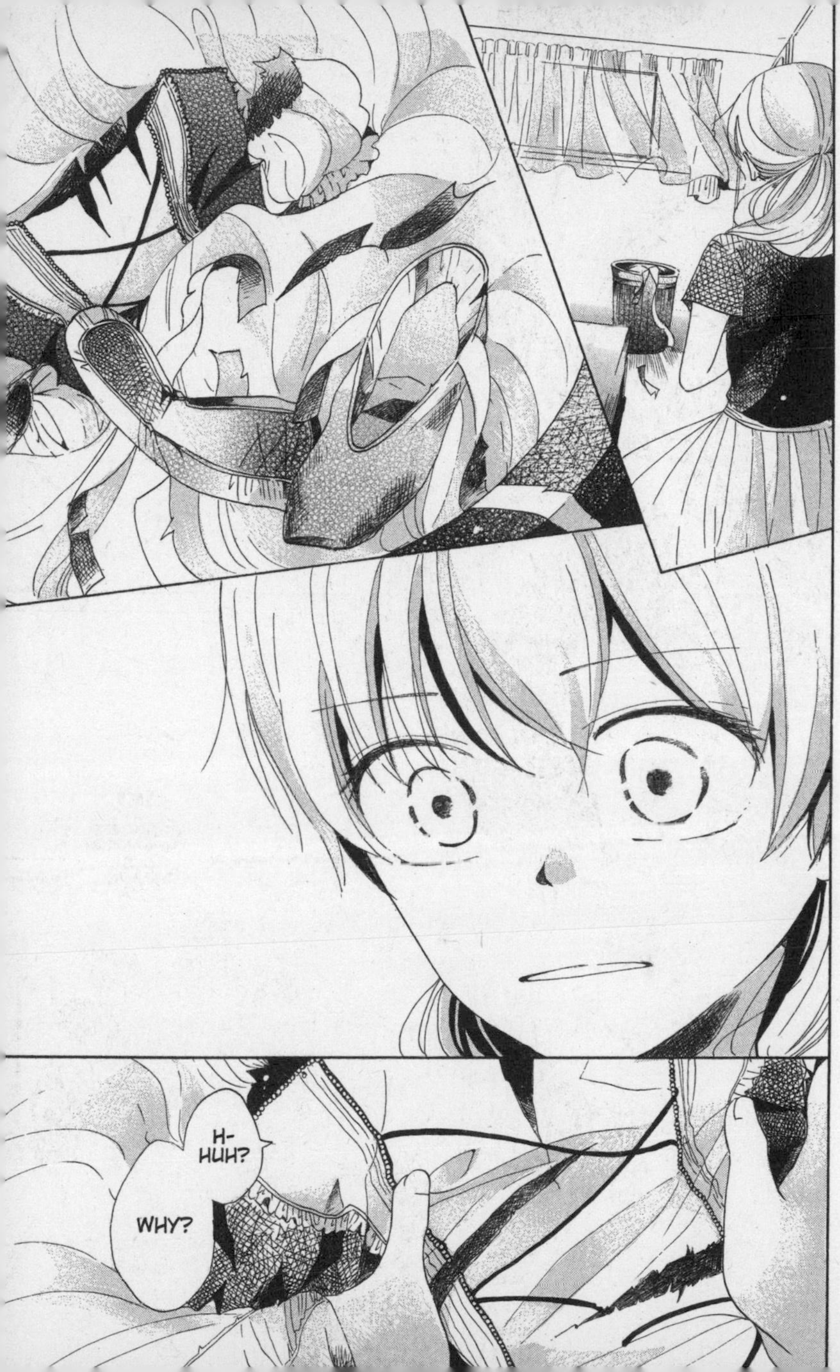
H-HUH?
WHY?

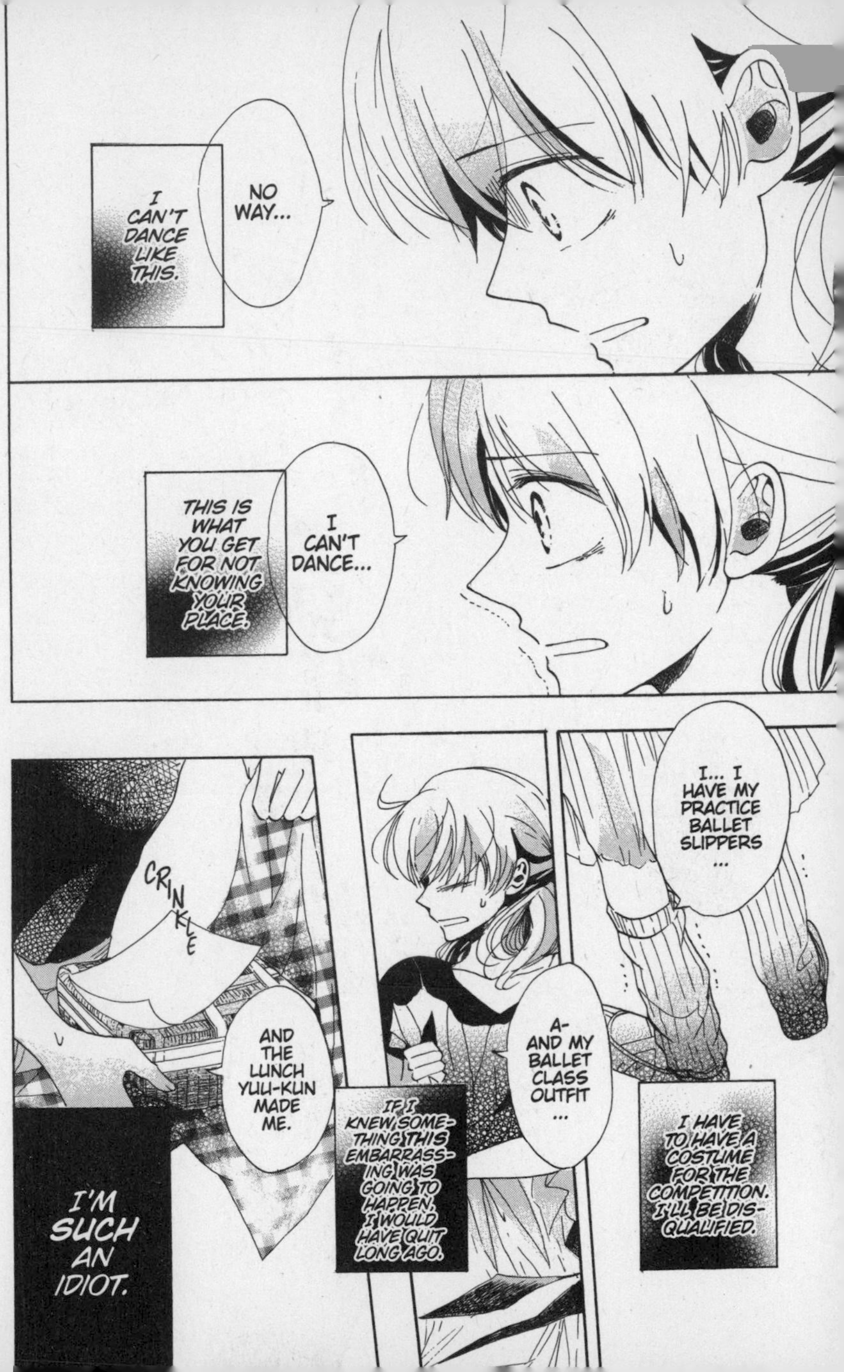
NO WAY...
I CAN'T DANCE LIKE THIS.
I CAN'T DANCE...
THIS IS WHAT YOU GET FOR NOT KNOWING YOUR PLACE.
I... I HAVE MY PRACTICE BALLET SLIPPERS ...
I HAVE TO HAVE A COSTUME FOR THE COMPETITION. I'LL BE DIS-QUALIFIED.
A- AND MY BALLET CLASS OUTFIT ...
IF I KNEW SOME-THING THIS EMBARRASS-ING WAS GOING TO HAPPEN, I WOULD HAVE QUIT LONG AGO.
CRINKLE
AND THE LUNCH YUU-KUN MADE ME.
I'M SUCH AN IDIOT.

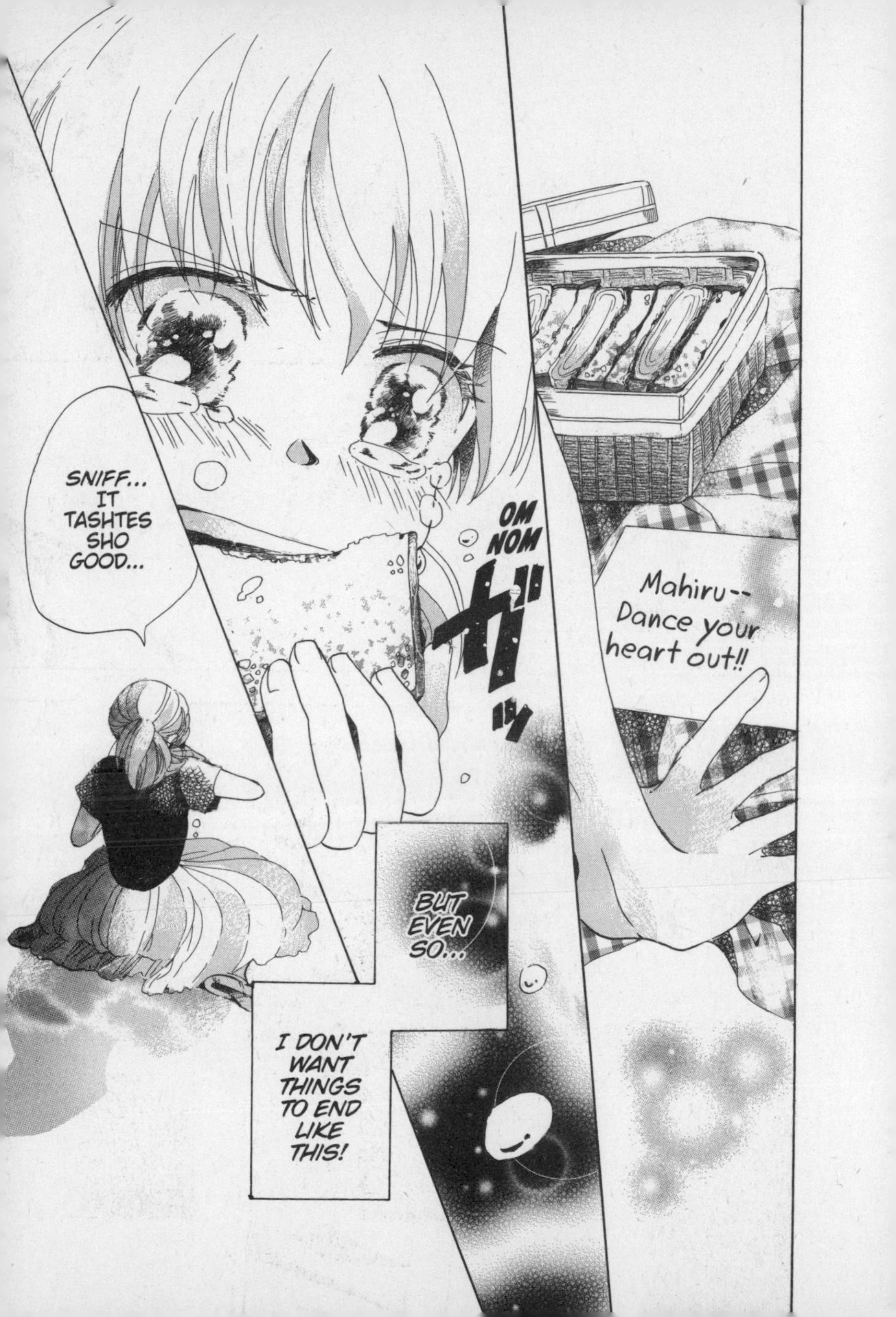
Mahiru-- Dance your heart out!!
OM NOM
SNIFF... IT TASHTES SHO GOOD...
BUT EVEN SO...
I DON'T WANT THINGS TO END LIKE THIS!

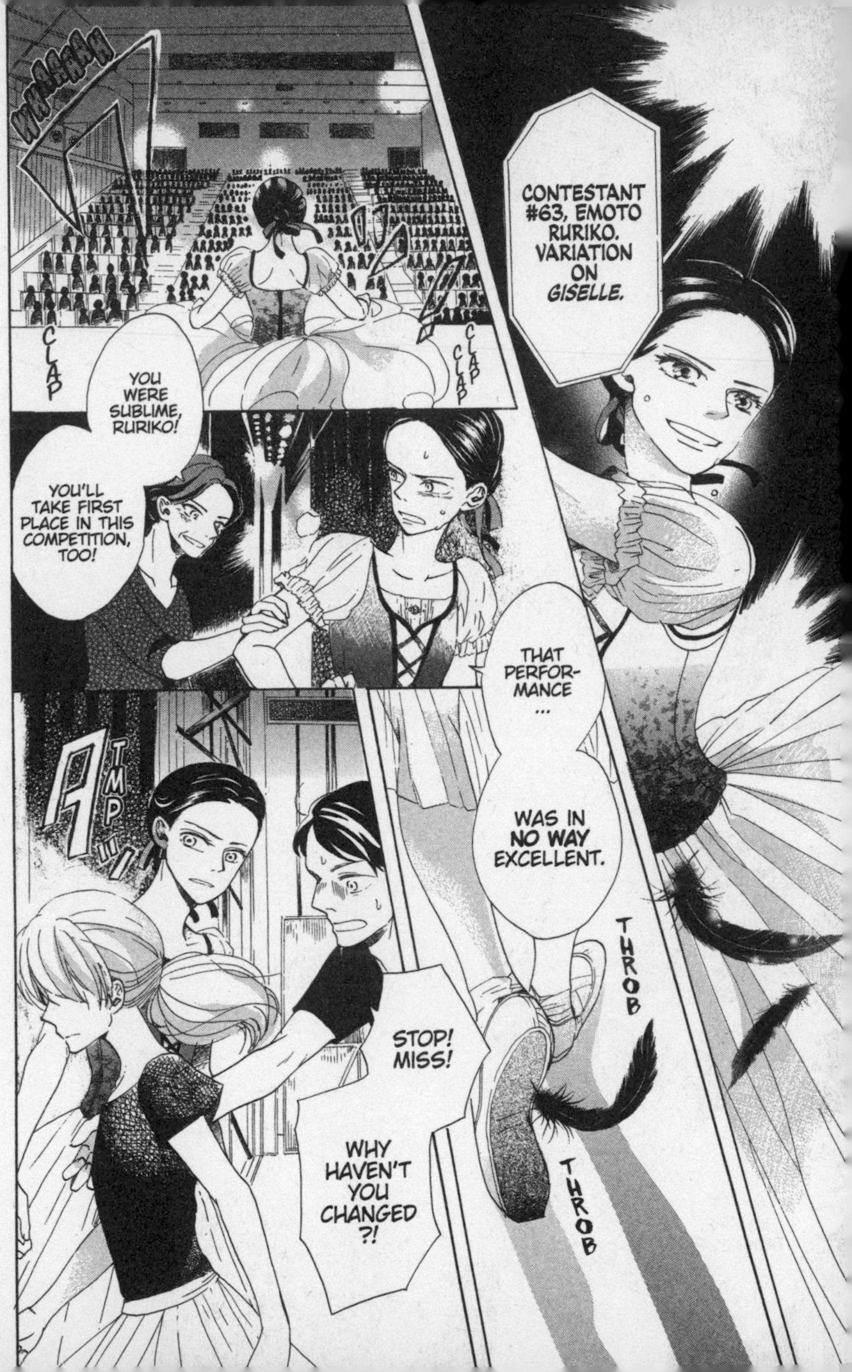
CONTESTANT #63, EMOTO RURIKO. VARIATION ON GISELLE.
THAT PERFORMANCE...
WAS IN NO WAY EXCELLENT.
THROB
THROB
WHAAAAH
CLAP CLAP
CLAP
YOU WERE SUBLIME, RURIKO!
YOU'LL TAKE FIRST PLACE IN THIS COMPETITION, TOO!
TMP
STOP! MISS!
WHY HAVEN'T YOU CHANGED?!

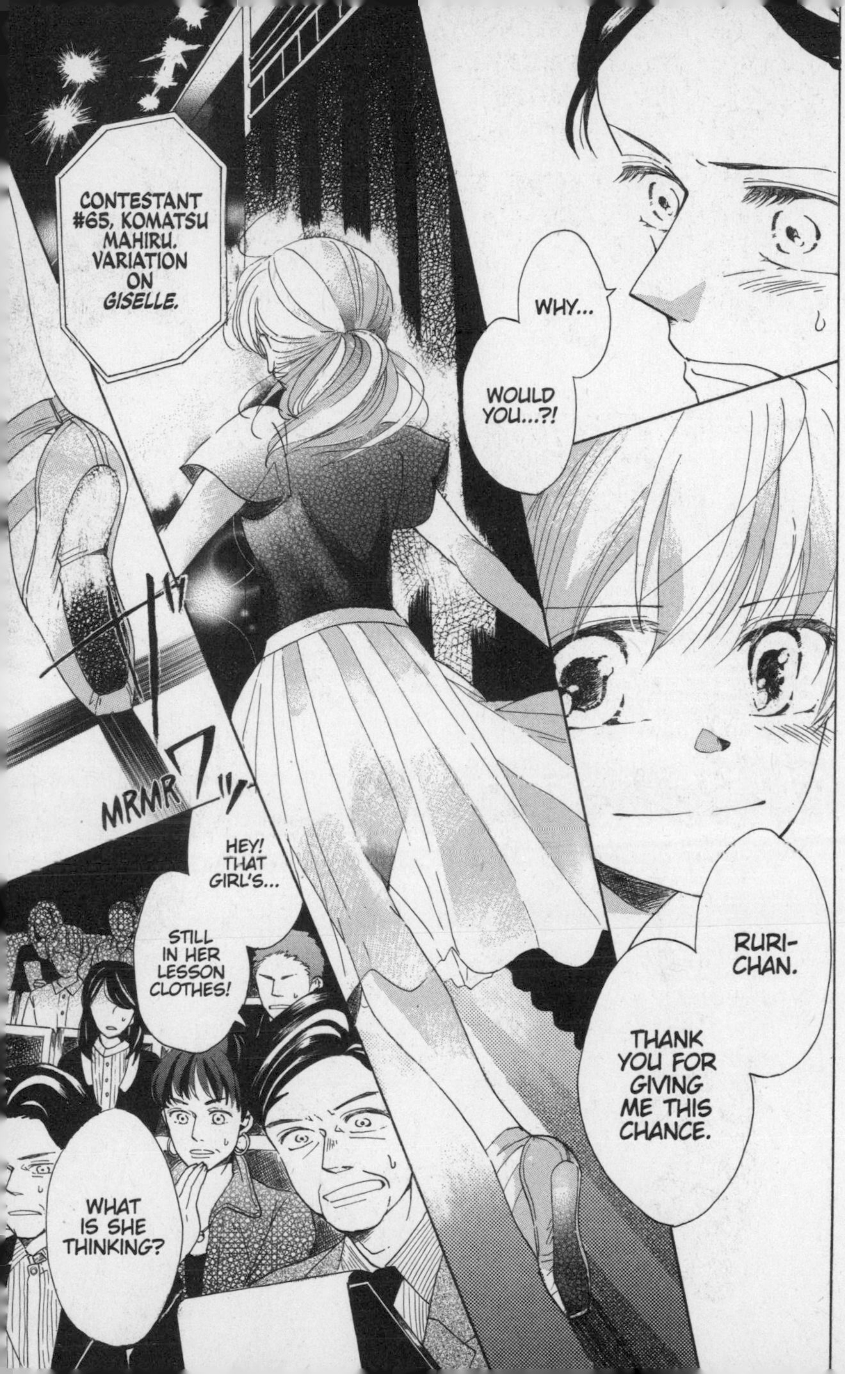
WHY...
WOULD YOU...?!
RURI-CHAN.
THANK YOU FOR GIVING ME THIS CHANCE.
CONTESTANT #65, KOMATSU MAHIRU. VARIATION ON *GISELLE.*
MRMR
HEY! THAT GIRL'S...
STILL IN HER LESSON CLOTHES!
WHAT IS SHE THINKING?

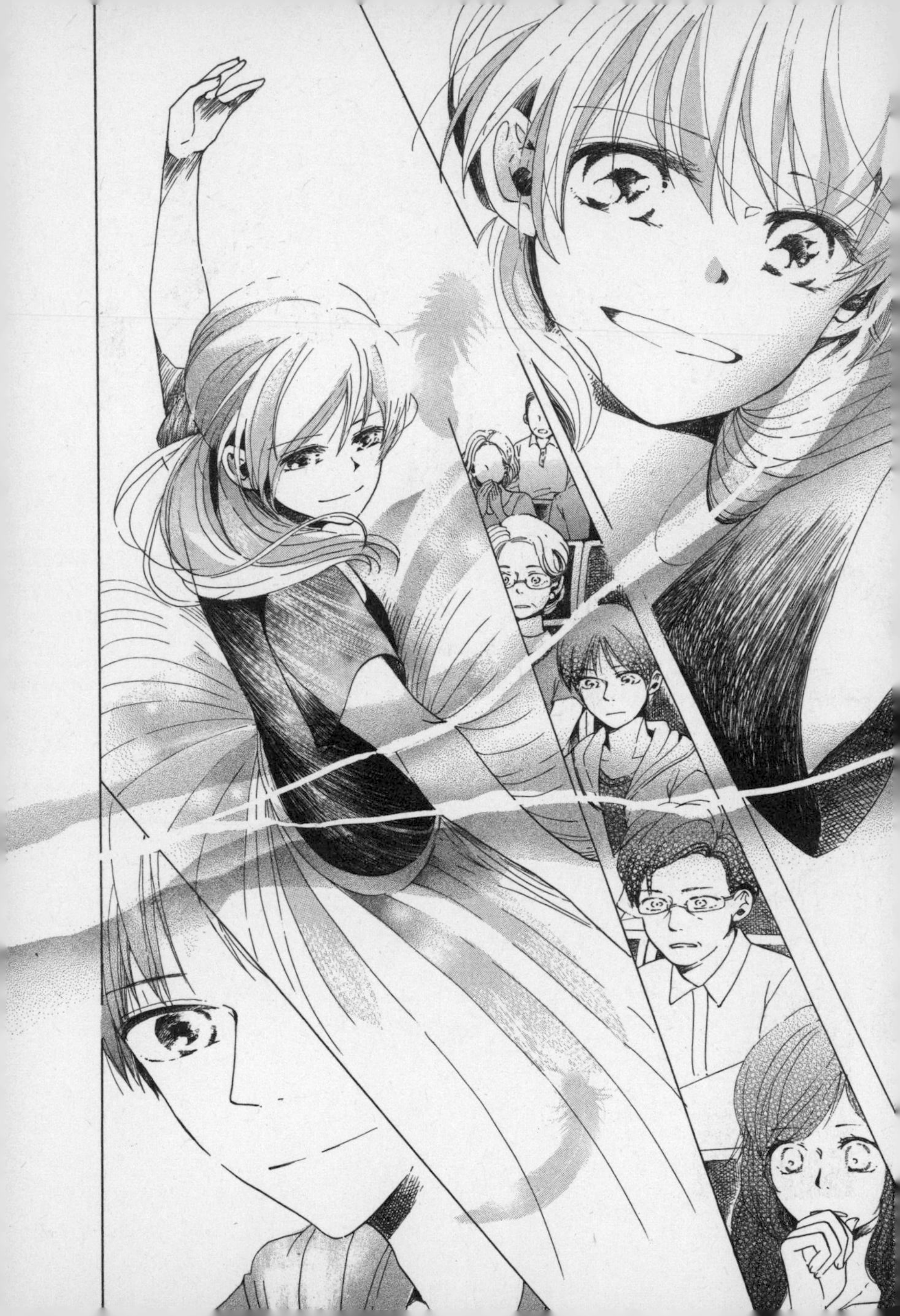

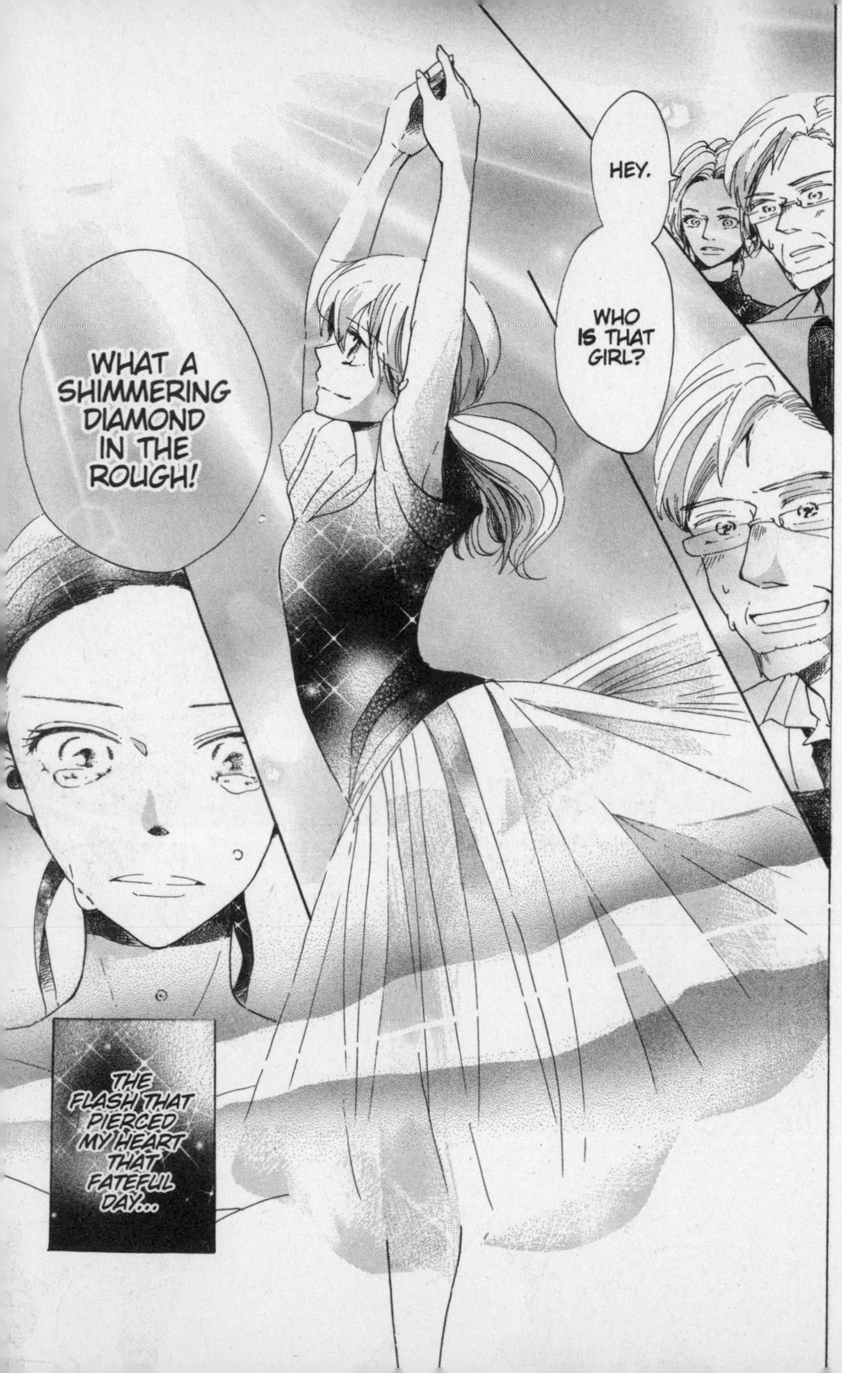
HEY.
WHO IS THAT GIRL?
WHAT A SHIMMERING DIAMOND IN THE ROUGH!
THE FLASH THAT PIERCED MY HEART THAT FATEFUL DAY...

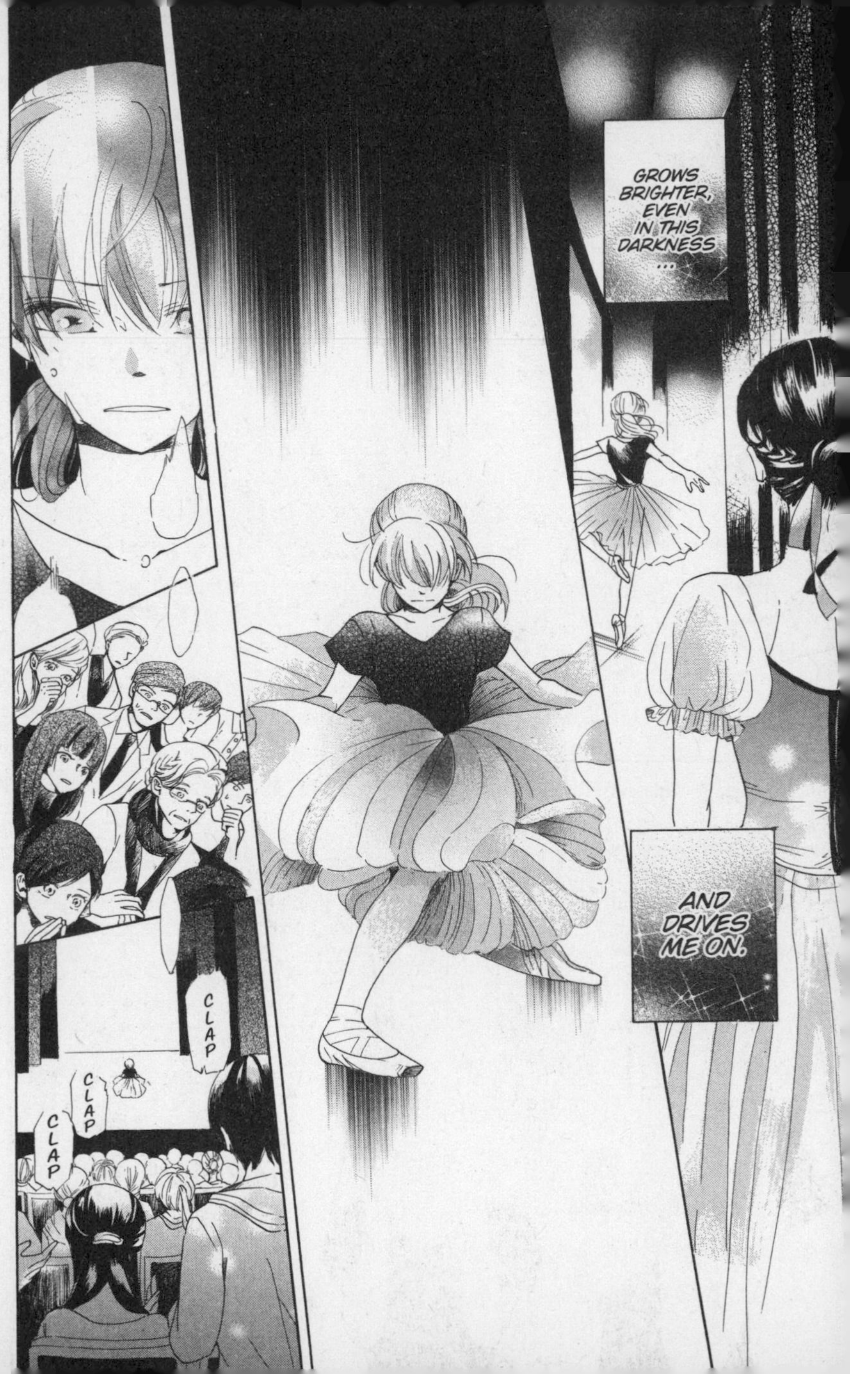
GROWS BRIGHTER, EVEN IN THIS DARKNESS ...
AND DRIVES ME ON.
CLAP
CLAP
CLAP
CLAP

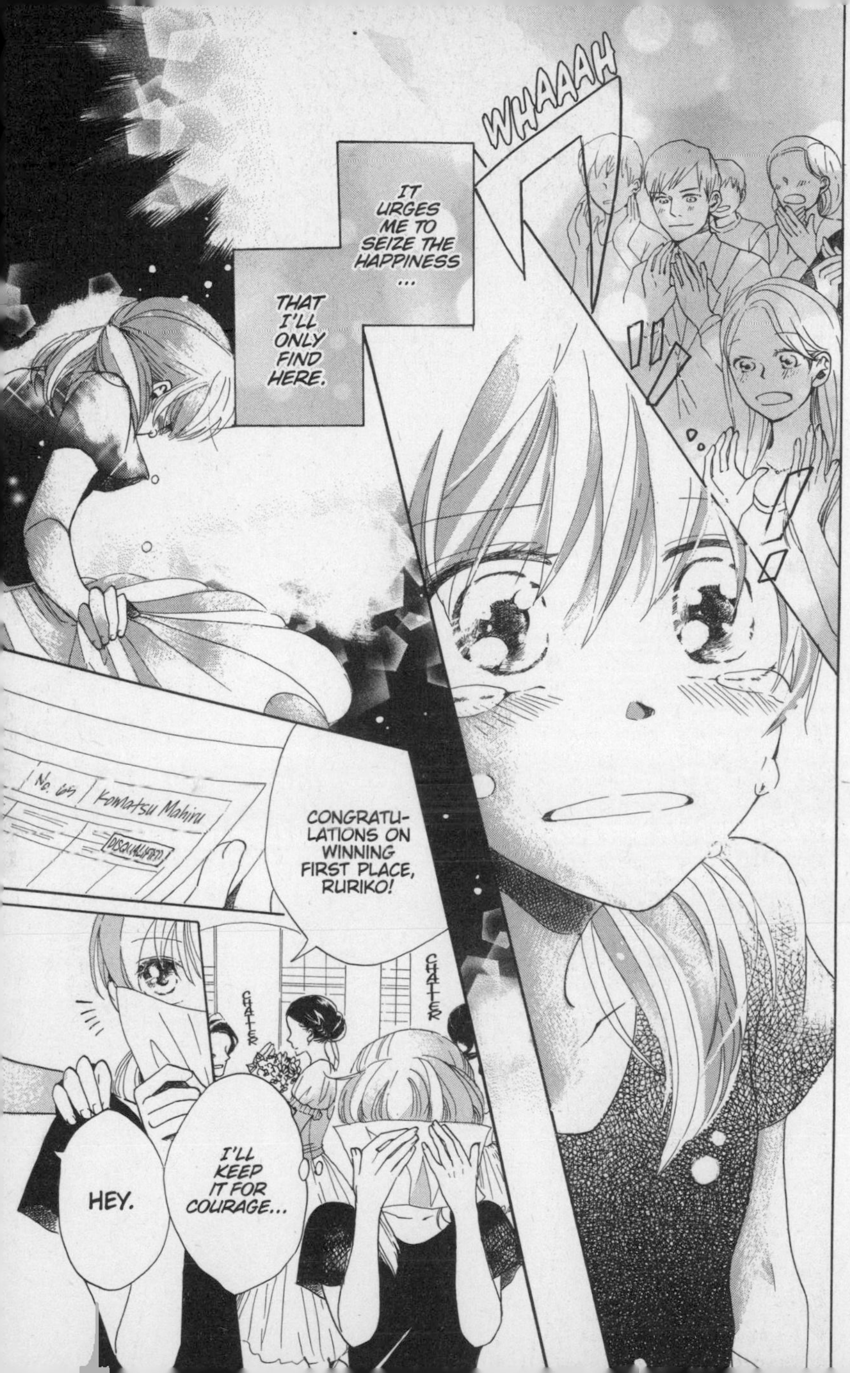
WHAAAH
IT URGES ME TO SEIZE THE HAPPINESS...
THAT I'LL ONLY FIND HERE.
CONGRATULATIONS ON WINNING FIRST PLACE, RURIKO!
CHATTER
CHATTER
No. 65
Komatsu Mahiru
I'LL KEEP IT FOR COURAGE...
HEY.

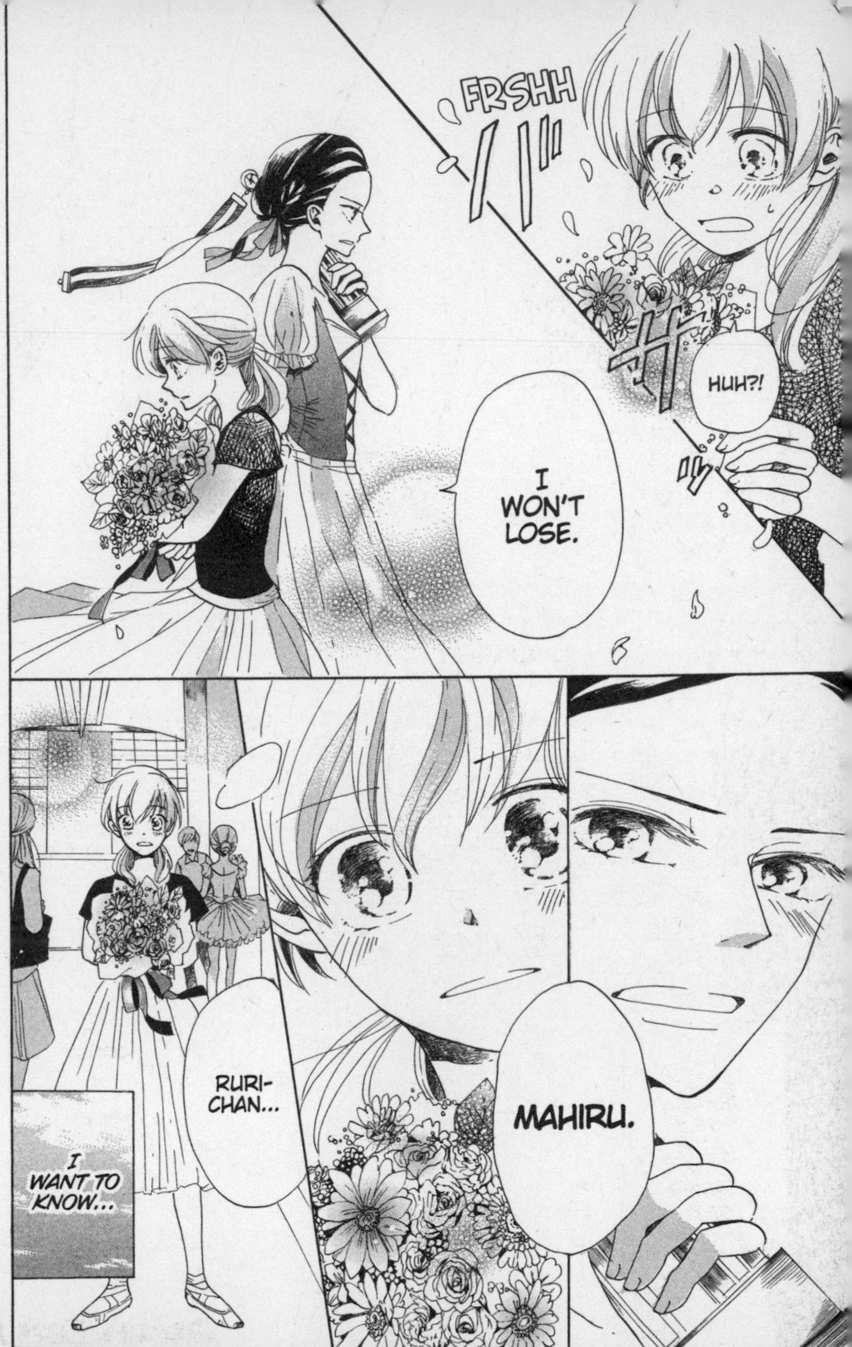
FRSHH
HUH?!
I WON'T LOSE.
MAHIRU.
RURI-CHAN...
I WANT TO KNOW...

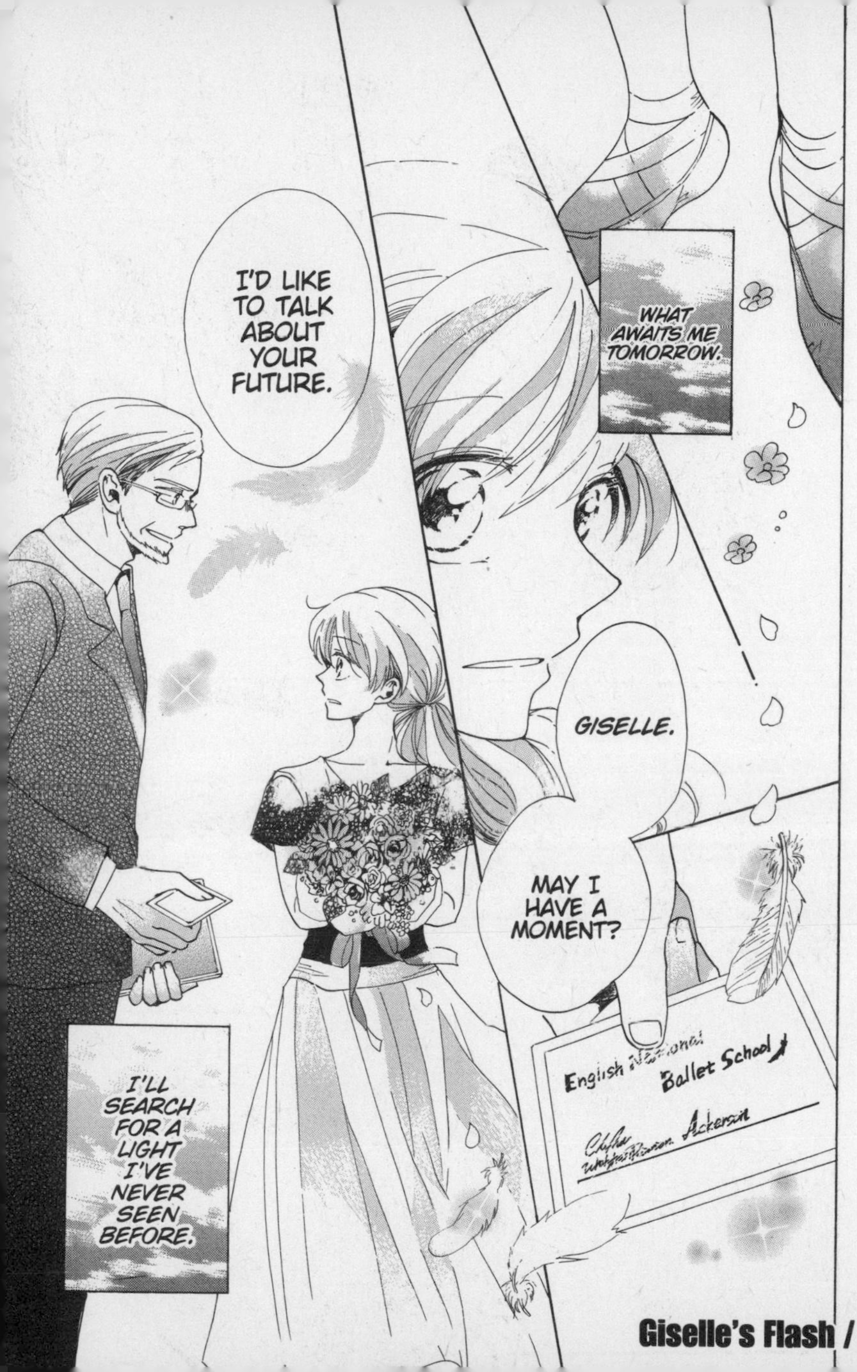
WHAT AWAITS ME TOMORROW.
GISELLE.
MAY I HAVE A MOMENT?
English National Ballet School
I'D LIKE TO TALK ABOUT YOUR FUTURE.
I'LL SEARCH FOR A LIGHT I'VE NEVER SEEN BEFORE.

Giselle's Flash / Fin

GISELLE'S FLASH: BONUS MANGA

RIGHT AFTER THE COMPETITION

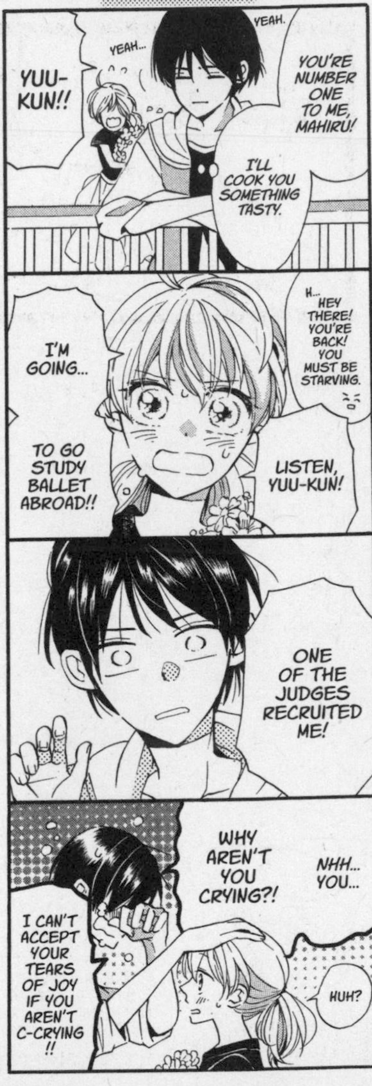
YEAH.
YOU'RE NUMBER ONE TO ME, MAHIRU!
YEAH...
YUU-KUN!!
I'LL COOK YOU SOMETHING TASTY.
H... HEY THERE! YOU'RE BACK! YOU MUST BE STARVING.
LISTEN, YUU-KUN!
I'M GOING...
TO GO STUDY BALLET ABROAD!!
ONE OF THE JUDGES RECRUITED ME!
NHH... YOU...
WHY AREN'T YOU CRYING?!
HUH?
I CAN'T ACCEPT YOUR TEARS OF JOY IF YOU AREN'T C-CRYING!!

STUDY ABROAD IN ENGLAND

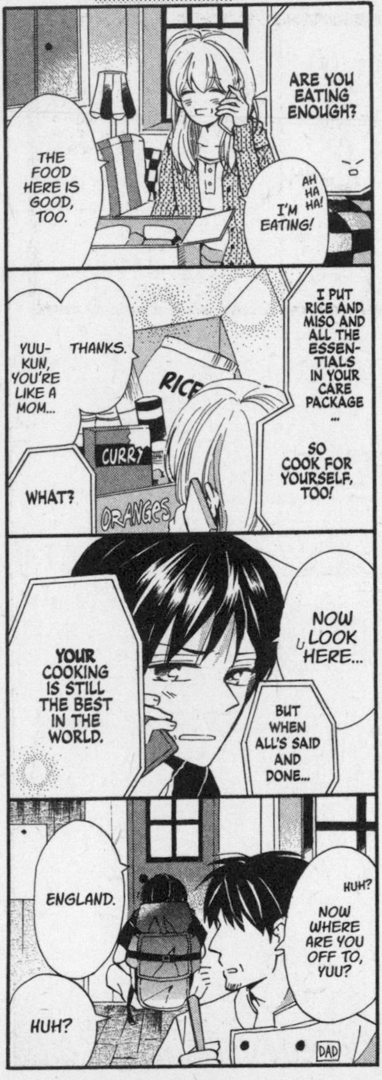
ARE YOU EATING ENOUGH?
AH HA HA! I'M EATING!
THE FOOD HERE IS GOOD, TOO.
I PUT RICE AND MISO AND ALL THE ESSENTIALS IN YOUR CARE PACKAGE...
SO COOK FOR YOURSELF, TOO!
RICE
THANKS.
YUU-KUN, YOU'RE LIKE A MOM...
CURRY
ORANGES
WHAT?
NOW LOOK HERE...
BUT WHEN ALL'S SAID AND DONE...
YOUR COOKING IS STILL THE BEST IN THE WORLD.
HUH?
NOW WHERE ARE YOU OFF TO, YUU?
ENGLAND.
HUH?
DAD

ABOUT GARHI, ETC.

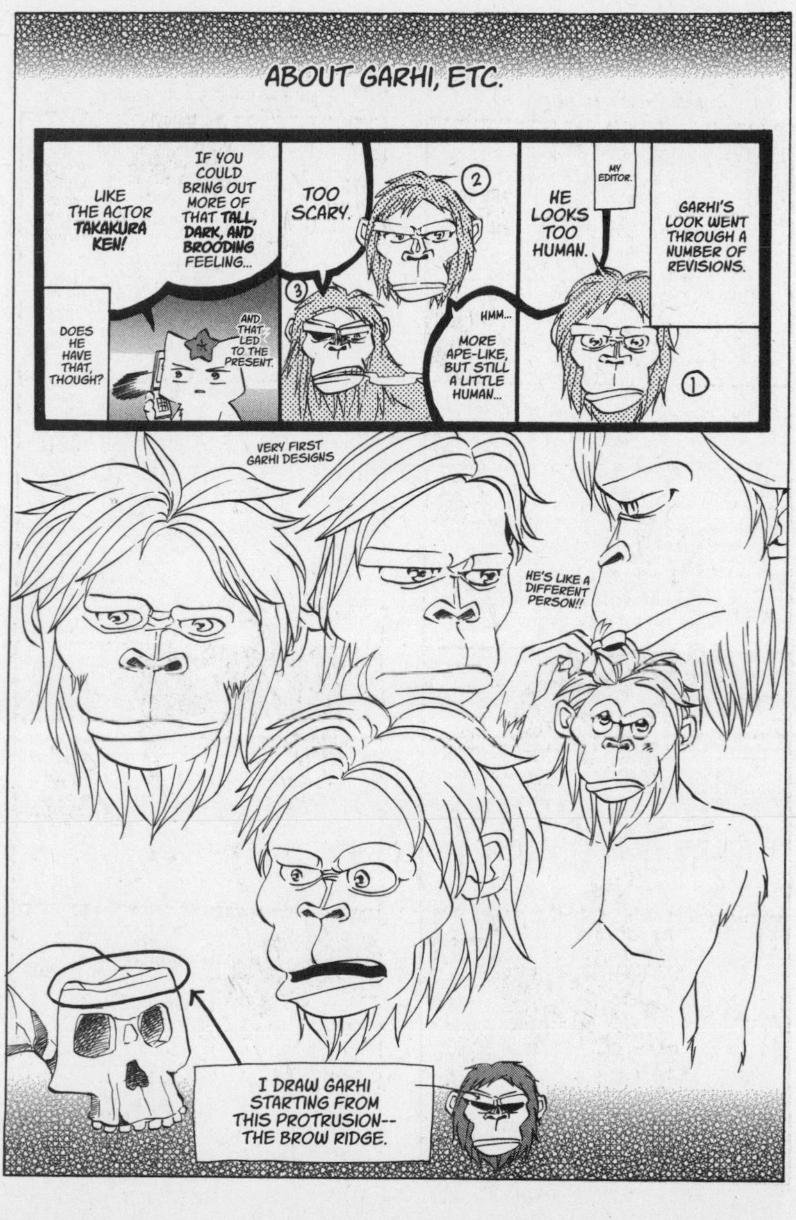
GARHI'S LOOK WENT THROUGH A NUMBER OF REVISIONS.
MY EDITOR.
HE LOOKS TOO HUMAN.
HMM... MORE APE-LIKE, BUT STILL A LITTLE HUMAN...
1
2
TOO SCARY.
3
IF YOU COULD BRING OUT MORE OF THAT TALL, DARK, AND BROODING FEELING...
LIKE THE ACTOR TAKAKURA KEN!
AND THAT LED TO THE PRESENT.
DOES HE HAVE THAT, THOUGH?
VERY FIRST GARHI DESIGNS
HE'S LIKE A DIFFERENT PERSON!!
I DRAW GARHI STARTING FROM THIS PROTRUSION--THE BROW RIDGE.

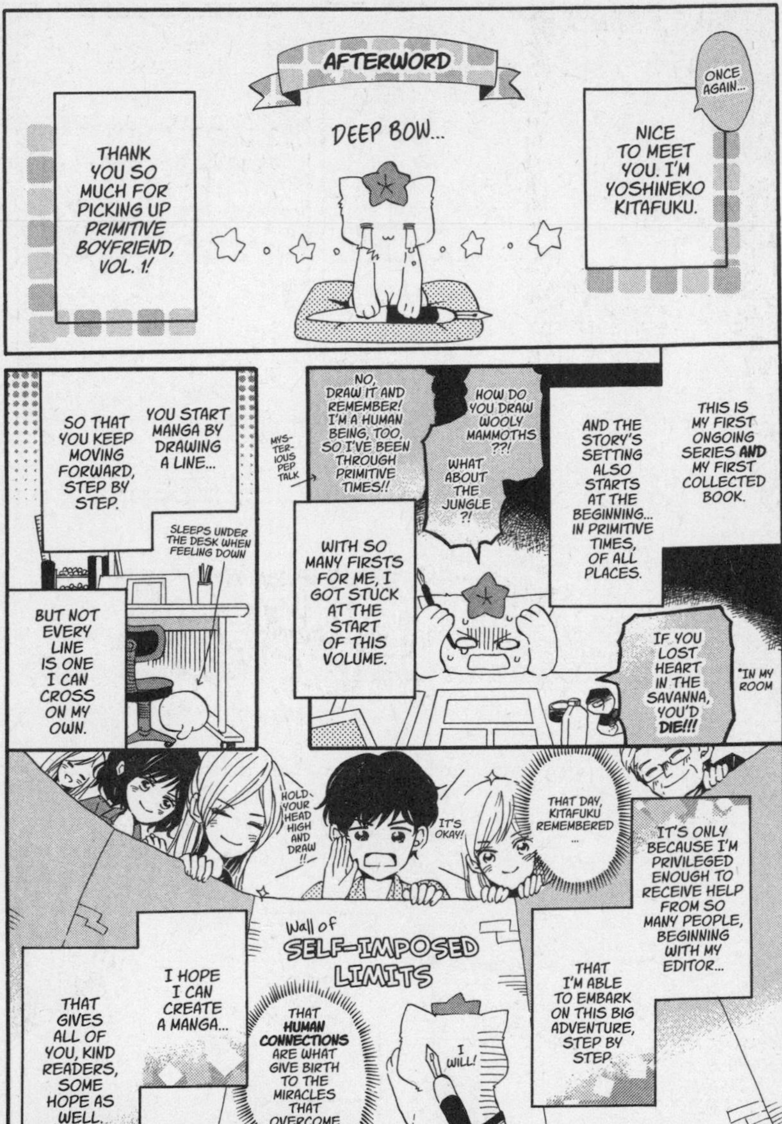
AFTERWORD
ONCE AGAIN...
NICE TO MEET YOU. I'M YOSHINEKO KITAFUKU.
DEEP BOW...
THANK YOU SO MUCH FOR PICKING UP PRIMITIVE BOYFRIEND, VOL. 1!
THIS IS MY FIRST ONGOING SERIES AND MY FIRST COLLECTED BOOK.
AND THE STORY'S SETTING ALSO STARTS AT THE BEGINNING... IN PRIMITIVE TIMES, OF ALL PLACES.
HOW DO YOU DRAW WOOLY MAMMOTHS ??!
WHAT ABOUT THE JUNGLE ?!
NO, DRAW IT AND REMEMBER! I'M A HUMAN BEING, TOO, SO I'VE BEEN THROUGH PRIMITIVE TIMES!!
MYS-TERIOUS PEP TALK
*IN MY ROOM
IF YOU LOST HEART IN THE SAVANNA, YOU'D DIE!!!
WITH SO MANY FIRSTS FOR ME, I GOT STUCK AT THE START OF THIS VOLUME.
YOU START MANGA BY DRAWING A LINE...
SO THAT YOU KEEP MOVING FORWARD, STEP BY STEP.
SLEEPS UNDER THE DESK WHEN FEELING DOWN
BUT NOT EVERY LINE IS ONE I CAN CROSS ON MY OWN.
THAT DAY, KITAFUKU REMEMBERED ...
IT'S ONLY BECAUSE I'M PRIVILEGED ENOUGH TO RECEIVE HELP FROM SO MANY PEOPLE, BEGINNING WITH MY EDITOR...
THAT I'M ABLE TO EMBARK ON THIS BIG ADVENTURE, STEP BY STEP.
IT'S OKAY!
HOLD YOUR HEAD HIGH AND DRAW !!
Wall of SELF-IMPOSED LIMITS
I WILL!
THAT HUMAN CONNECTIONS ARE WHAT GIVE BIRTH TO THE MIRACLES THAT OVERCOME WALLS...
I HOPE I CAN CREATE A MANGA...
THAT GIVES ALL OF YOU, KIND READERS, SOME HOPE AS WELL.

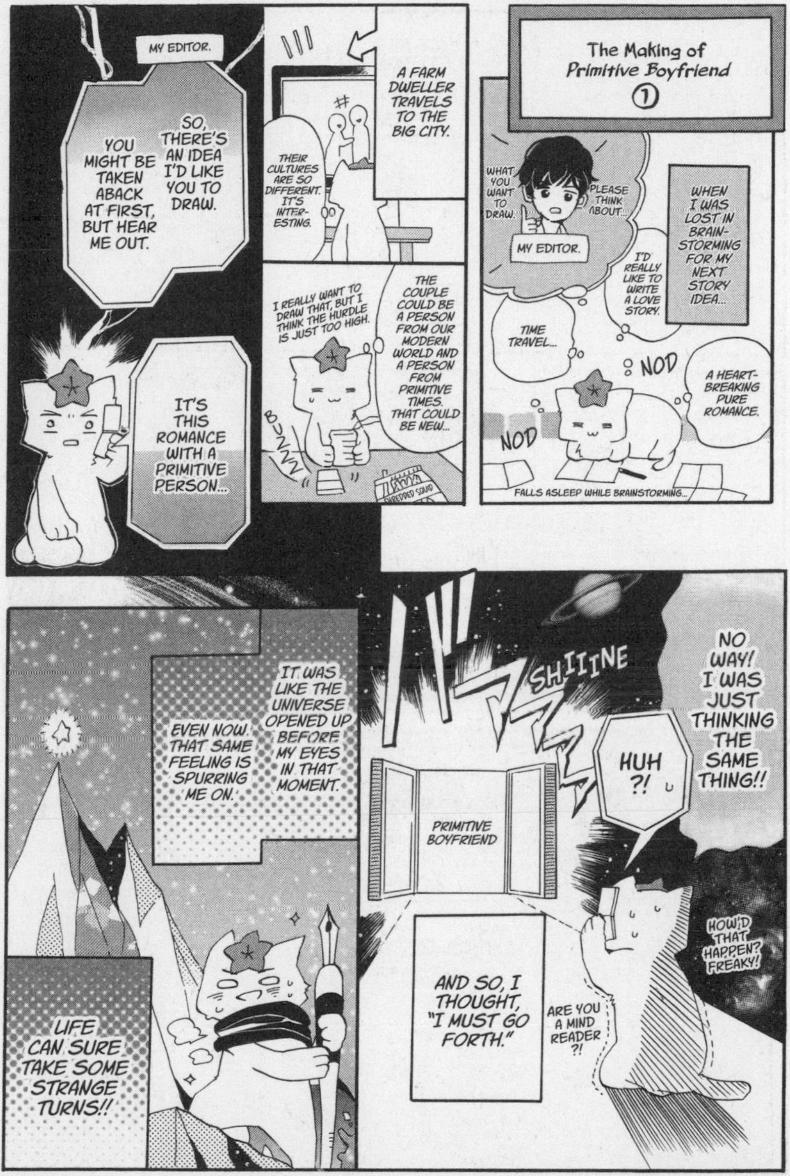
The Making of Primitive Boyfriend ①
WHEN I WAS LOST IN BRAIN-STORMING FOR MY NEXT STORY IDEA...
I'D REALLY LIKE TO WRITE A LOVE STORY.
PLEASE THINK ABOUT...
WHAT YOU WANT TO DRAW.
MY EDITOR.
A HEART-BREAKING PURE ROMANCE.
NOD
TIME TRAVEL...
NOD
FALLS ASLEEP WHILE BRAINSTORMING...
A FARM DWELLER TRAVELS TO THE BIG CITY.
THEIR CULTURES ARE SO DIFFERENT. IT'S INTER-ESTING.
THE COUPLE COULD BE A PERSON FROM OUR MODERN WORLD AND A PERSON FROM PRIMITIVE TIMES. THAT COULD BE NEW...
I REALLY WANT TO DRAW THAT, BUT I THINK THE HURDLE IS JUST TOO HIGH.
BUZZZ
SHREDDED SOUND
MY EDITOR.
SO, THERE'S AN IDEA I'D LIKE YOU TO DRAW.
YOU MIGHT BE TAKEN ABACK AT FIRST, BUT HEAR ME OUT.
IT'S THIS ROMANCE WITH A PRIMITIVE PERSON...
SHIIINE
NO WAY! I WAS JUST THINKING THE SAME THING!!
HUH?!
PRIMITIVE BOYFRIEND
HOW'D THAT HAPPEN? FREAKY!
ARE YOU A MIND READER?!
AND SO, I THOUGHT, "I MUST GO FORTH."
IT WAS LIKE THE UNIVERSE OPENED UP BEFORE MY EYES IN THAT MOMENT.
EVEN NOW, THAT SAME FEELING IS SPURRING ME ON.
LIFE CAN SURE TAKE SOME STRANGE TURNS!!

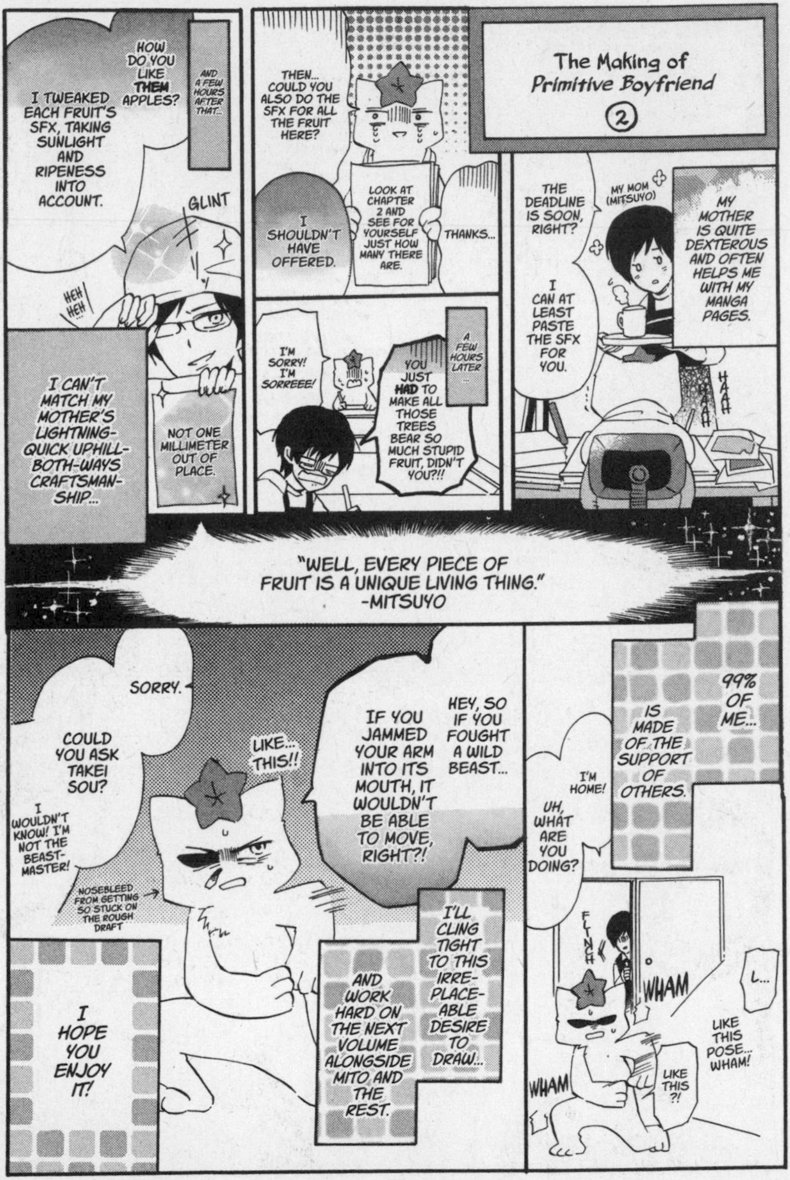
The Making of Primitive Boyfriend ②
MY MOTHER IS QUITE DEXTEROUS AND OFTEN HELPS ME WITH MY MANGA PAGES.
MY MOM (MITSUYO)
THE DEADLINE IS SOON, RIGHT?
I CAN AT LEAST PASTE THE SFX FOR YOU.
HAAH HAAH
THEN... COULD YOU ALSO DO THE SFX FOR ALL THE FRUIT HERE?
LOOK AT CHAPTER 2 AND SEE FOR YOURSELF JUST HOW MANY THERE ARE.
THANKS...
I SHOULDN'T HAVE OFFERED.
A FEW HOURS LATER...
YOU JUST HAD TO MAKE ALL THOSE TREES BEAR SO MUCH STUPID FRUIT, DIDN'T YOU?!!
I'M SORRY! I'M SORREEE!
AND A FEW HOURS AFTER THAT...
HOW DO YOU LIKE THEM APPLES?
I TWEAKED EACH FRUIT'S SFX, TAKING SUNLIGHT AND RIPENESS INTO ACCOUNT.
GLINT
HEH HEH
NOT ONE MILLIMETER OUT OF PLACE.
I CAN'T MATCH MY MOTHER'S LIGHTNING-QUICK UPHILL-BOTH-WAYS CRAFTSMANSHIP...
"WELL, EVERY PIECE OF FRUIT IS A UNIQUE LIVING THING." -MITSUYO
99% OF ME... IS MADE OF THE SUPPORT OF OTHERS.
I'M HOME!
UH, WHAT ARE YOU DOING?
FLINCH
L...
LIKE THIS POSE... WHAM!
WHAM
LIKE THIS?!
WHAM
HEY, SO IF YOU FOUGHT A WILD BEAST...
IF YOU JAMMED YOUR ARM INTO ITS MOUTH, IT WOULDN'T BE ABLE TO MOVE, RIGHT?!
LIKE... THIS!!
SORRY.
COULD YOU ASK TAKEI SOU?
I WOULDN'T KNOW! I'M NOT THE BEAST-MASTER!
NOSEBLEED FROM GETTING SO STUCK ON THE ROUGH DRAFT
I'LL CLING TIGHT TO THIS IRRE-PLACE-ABLE DESIRE TO DRAW...
AND WORK HARD ON THE NEXT VOLUME ALONGSIDE MITO AND THE REST.
I HOPE YOU ENJOY IT!

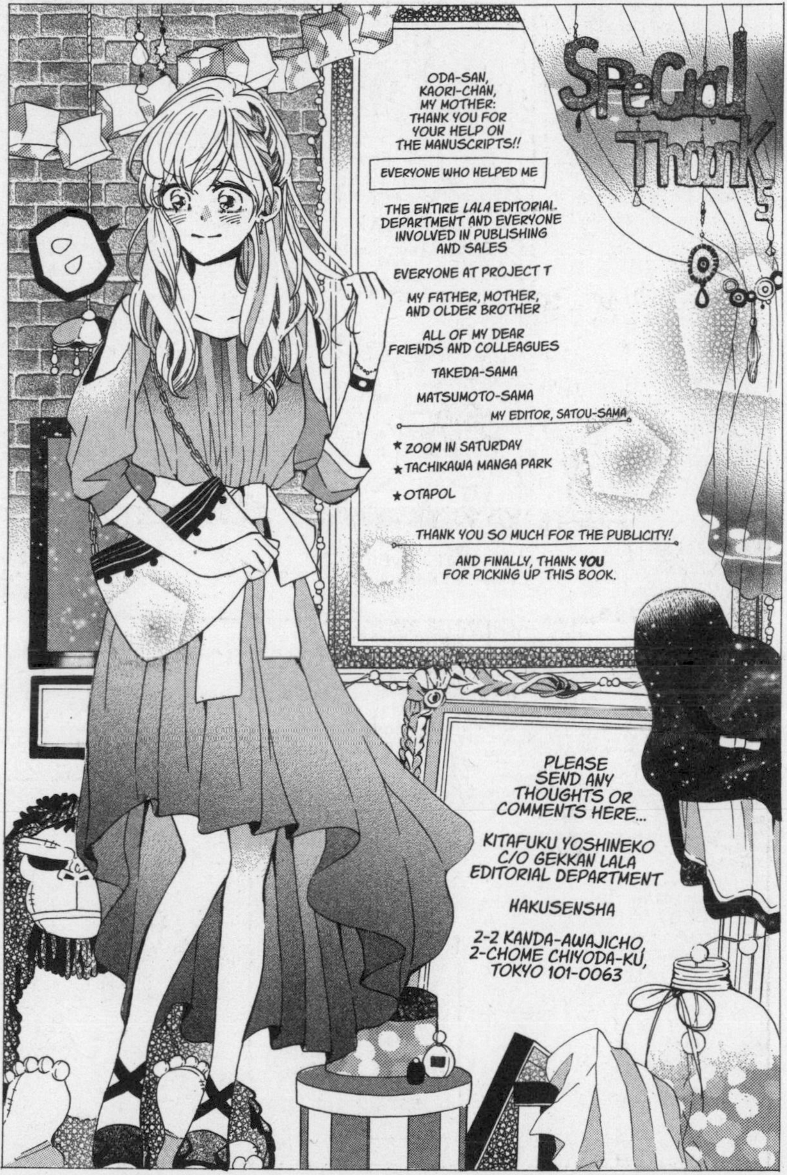

Special Thanks
ODA-SAN, KAORI-CHAN, MY MOTHER: THANK YOU FOR YOUR HELP ON THE MANUSCRIPTS!!
EVERYONE WHO HELPED ME
THE ENTIRE LALA EDITORIAL DEPARTMENT AND EVERYONE INVOLVED IN PUBLISHING AND SALES
EVERYONE AT PROJECT T
MY FATHER, MOTHER, AND OLDER BROTHER
ALL OF MY DEAR FRIENDS AND COLLEAGUES
TAKEDA-SAMA
MATSUMOTO-SAMA
MY EDITOR, SATOU-SAMA
★ ZOOM IN SATURDAY
★ TACHIKAWA MANGA PARK
★ OTAPOL
THANK YOU SO MUCH FOR THE PUBLICITY!
AND FINALLY, THANK YOU FOR PICKING UP THIS BOOK.
PLEASE SEND ANY THOUGHTS OR COMMENTS HERE...
KITAFUKU YOSHINEKO C/O GEKKAN LALA EDITORIAL DEPARTMENT
HAKUSENSHA
2-2 KANDA-AWAJICHO, 2-CHOME CHIYODA-KU, TOKYO 101-0063

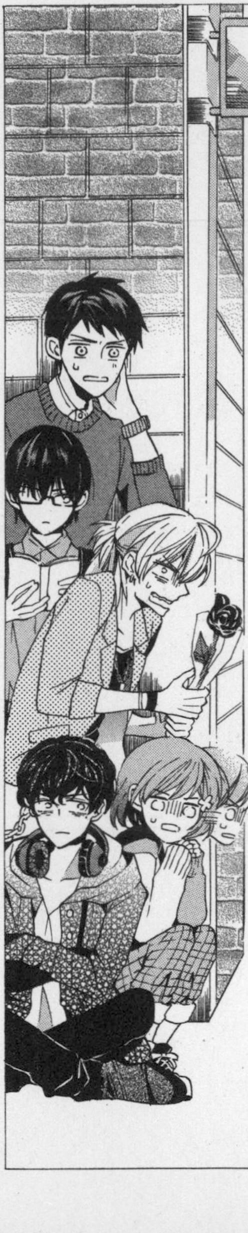

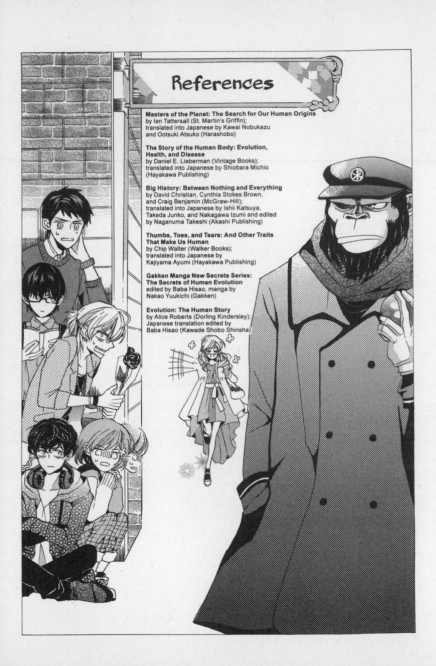

References

Masters of the Planet: The Search for Our Human Origins
by Ian Tattersall (St. Martin's Griffin);
translated into Japanese by Kawai Nobukazu
and Ootsuki Atsuko (Harashobo)

The Story of the Human Body: Evolution, Health, and Disease
by Daniel E. Lieberman (Vintage Books);
translated into Japanese by Shiobara Michio
(Hayakawa Publishing)

Big History: Between Nothing and Everything
by David Christian, Cynthia Stokes Brown,
and Craig Benjamin (McGraw-Hill);
translated into Japanese by Ishii Katsuya,
Takeda Junko, and Nakagawa Izumi and edited
by Naganuma Takeshi (Akashi Publishing)

Thumbs, Toes, and Tears: And Other Traits That Make Us Human
by Chip Walter (Walker Books);
translated into Japanese by
Kajiyama Ayumi (Hayakawa Publishing)

Gakken Manga New Secrets Series: The Secrets of Human Evolution
edited by Baba Hisao, manga by
Nakao Yuukichi (Gakken)

Evolution: The Human Story
by Alice Roberts (Dorling Kindersley);
Japanese translation edited by
Baba Hisao (Kawade Shobo Shinsha)

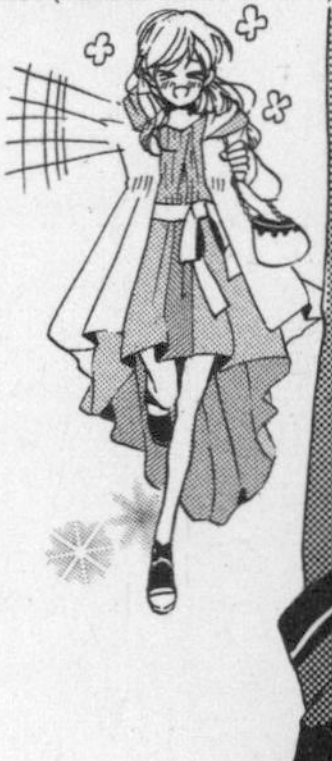

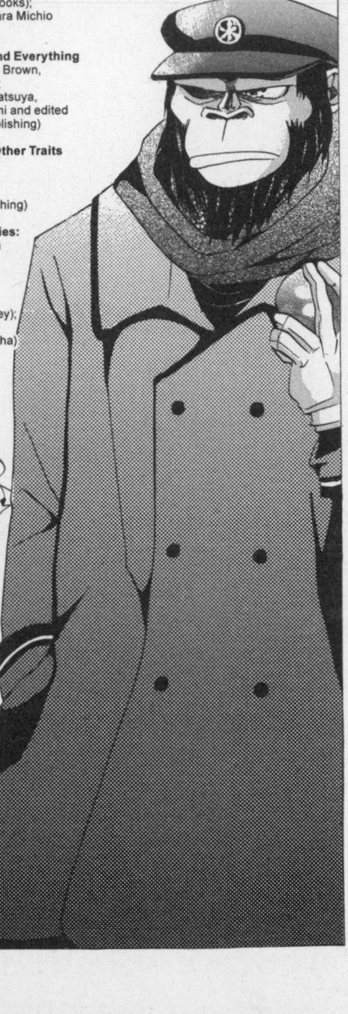

PRIMITIVE
Boyfriend

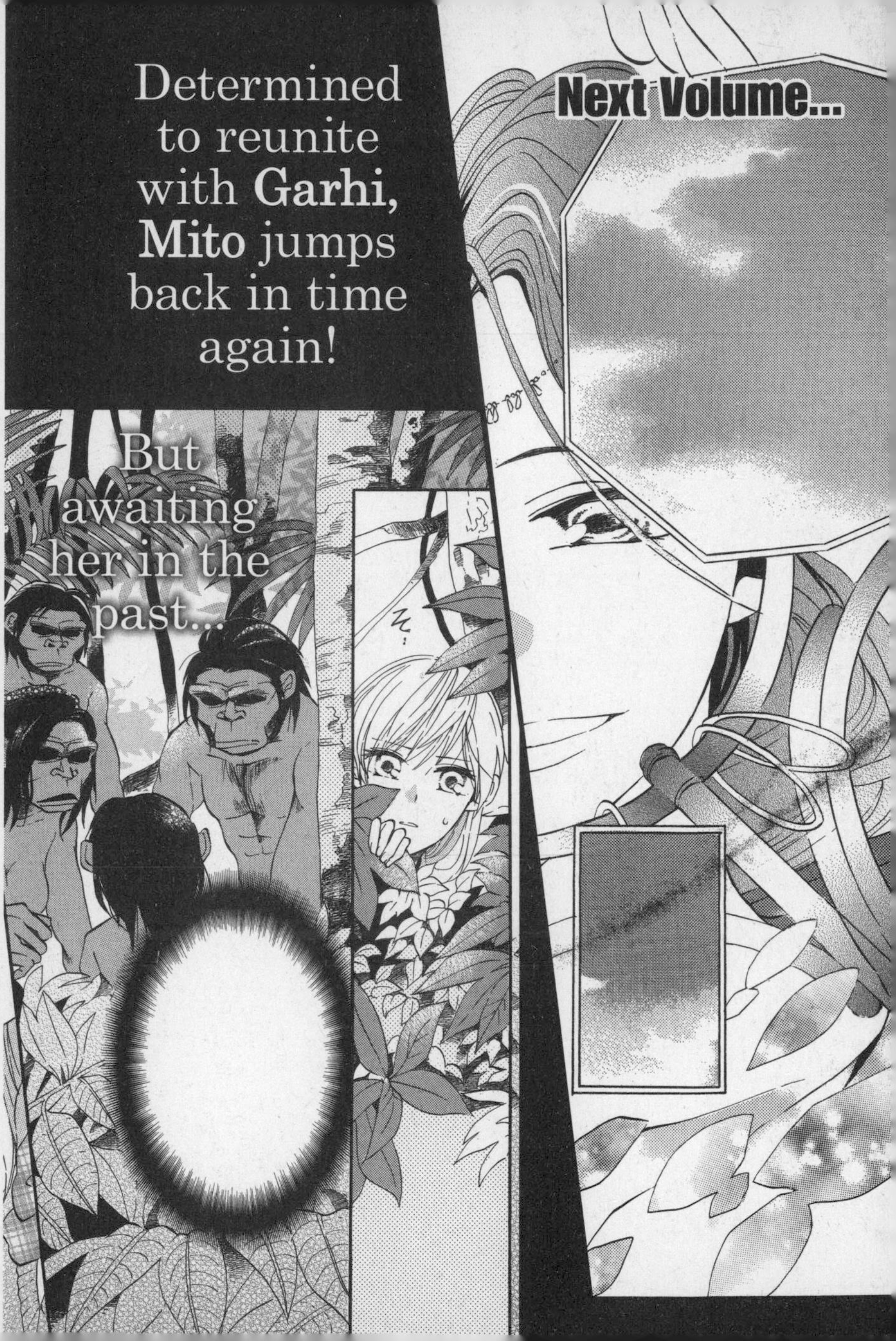
Next Volume...
Determined to reunite with Garhi, Mito jumps back in time again!
But awaiting her in the past...

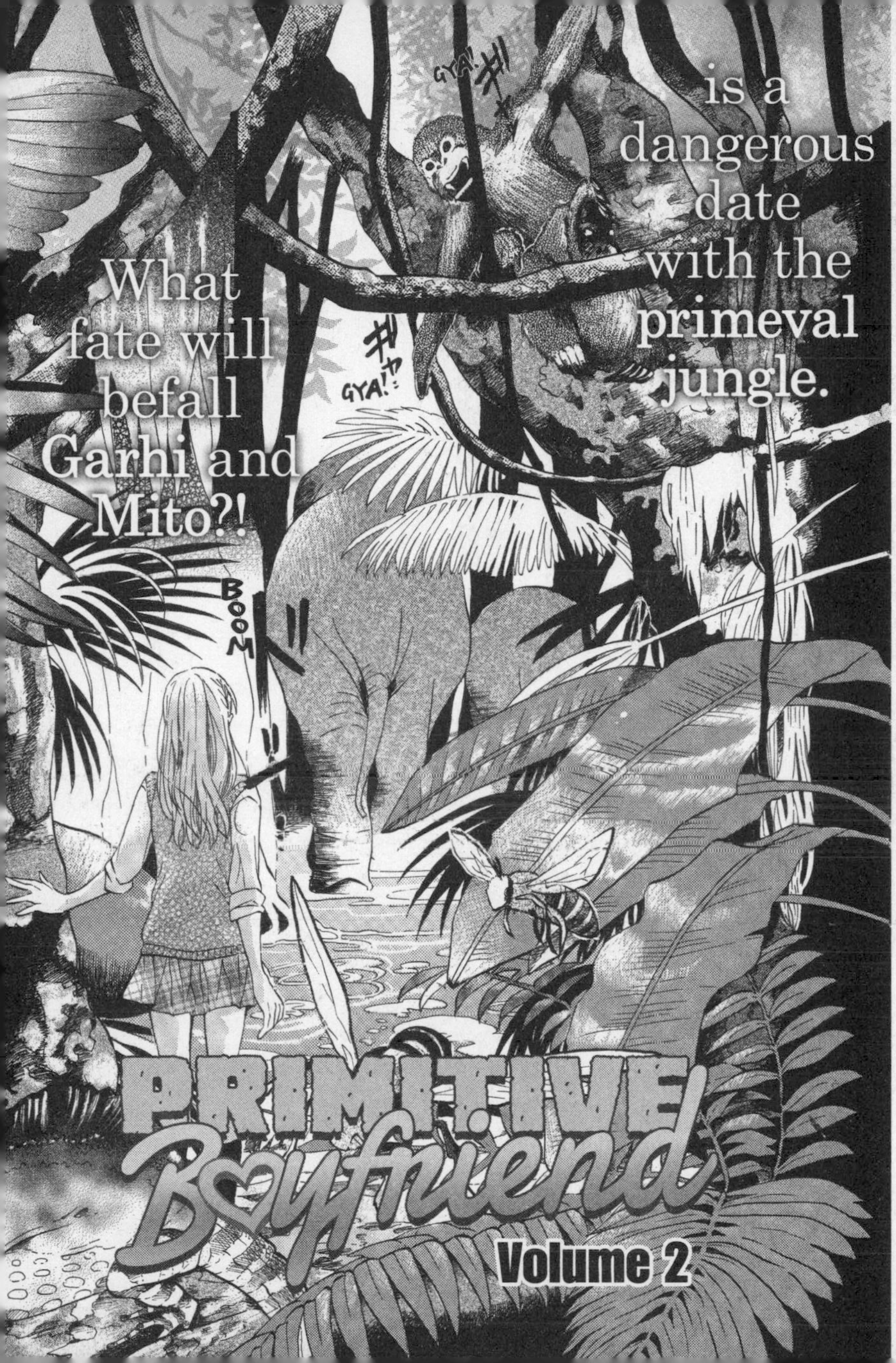

is a dangerous date with the primeval jungle.
GYA!
GYA!
What fate will befall Garhi and Mito?!
BOOM
PRIMITIVE Boyfriend
Volume 2

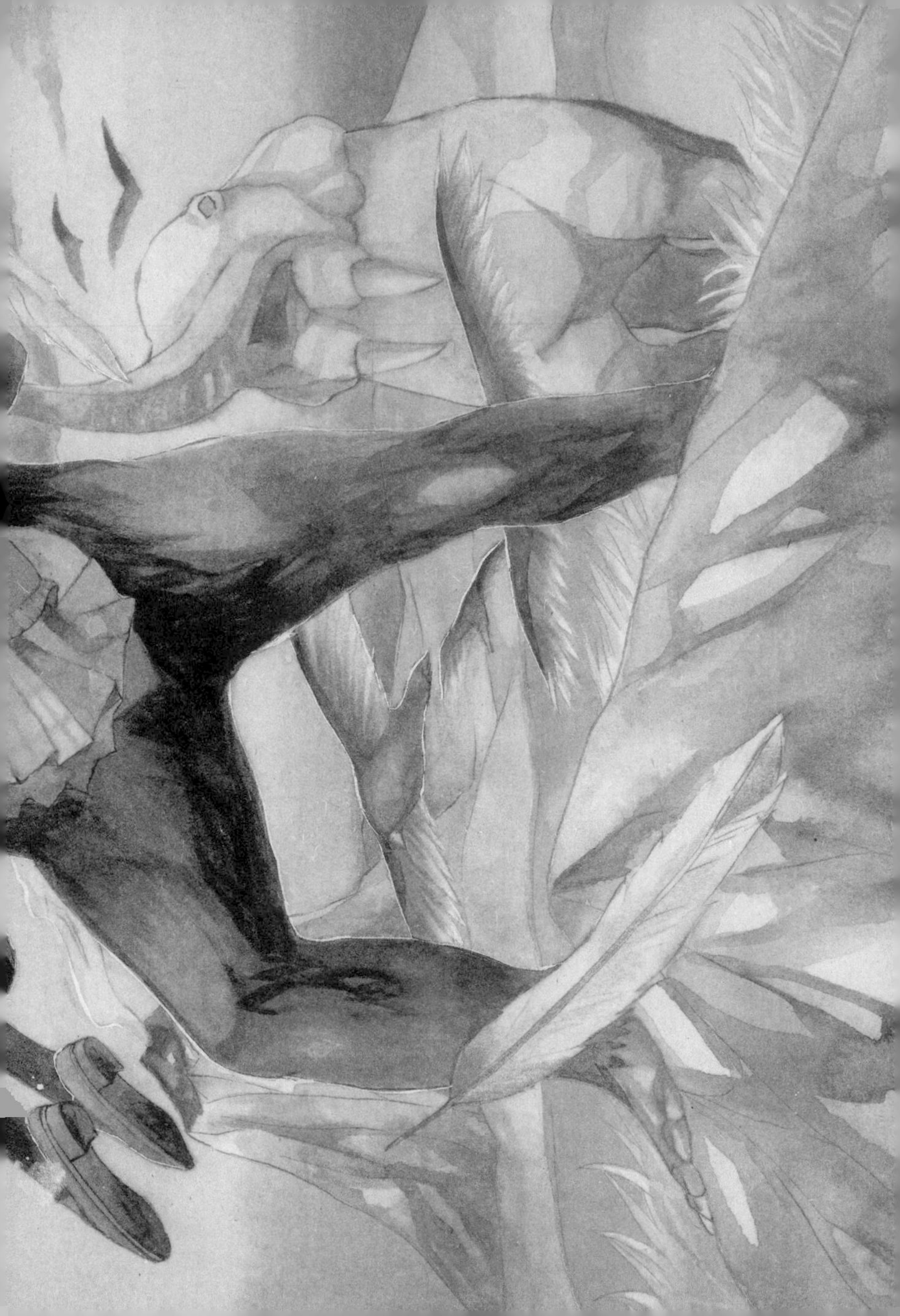

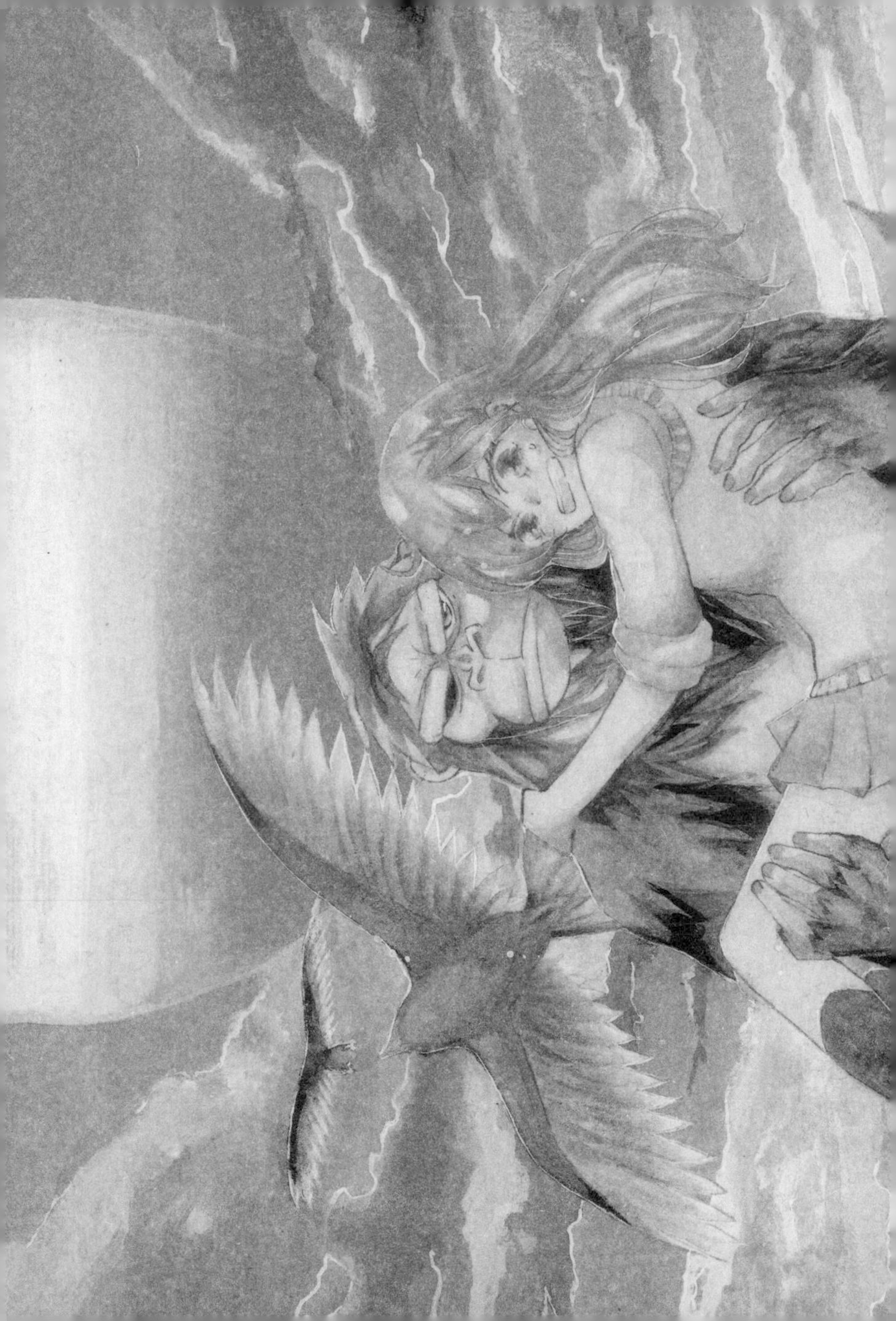

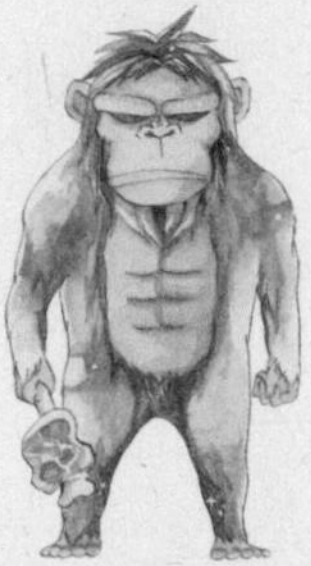

PRIMITIVE Boyfriend

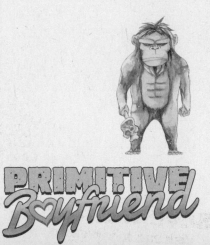

SEVEN SEAS ENTERTAINMENT PRESENTS

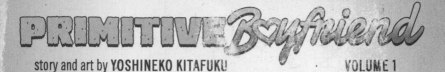

PRIMITIVE Boyfriend

story and art by YOSHINEKO KITAFUKU

VOLUME 1

TRANSLATION
Amanda Haley

ADAPTATION
David Lumsdon

LETTERING AND RETOUCH
Brandon Bovia

COVER DESIGN
Nicky Lim
George Panella (LOGO)

PROOFREADER
Kurestin Armada

EDITOR
Peter Adrian Behravesh

PREPRESS TECHNICIAN
Rhiannon Rasmussen-Silverstein

PRODUCTION MANAGER
Lissa Pattillo

MANAGING EDITOR
Julie Davis

ASSOCIATE PUBLISHER
Adam Arnold

PUBLISHER
Jason DeAngelis

GENSHIJIN KARESHI
by YOSHINEKO KITAFUKU

First published in Japan in 2017 by HAKUSENSHA, INC., Tokyo.
English language translation rights in U.S.A. arranged with HAKUSENSHA, INC., Tokyo through TOHAN CORPORATION, Tokyo.

Seven Seas press and purchase enquiries can be sent to Marketing Manager Lianne Sentar at press@gomanga.com. Information regarding the distribution and purchase of digital editions is available from Digital Manager CK Russell at digital@gomanga.com.

ISBN: 978-1-64505-298-2
Printed in Canada
First Printing: April 2020
10 9 8 7 6 5 4 3 2 1

FOLLOW US ONLINE: ***www.sevenseasentertainment.com***

READING DIRECTIONS

This book reads from ***right to left***, Japanese style. If this is your first time reading manga, you start reading from the top right panel on each page and take it from there. If you get lost, just follow the numbered diagram here. It may seem backwards at first, but you'll get the hang of it! Have fun!!

1
2
3
4
5
6
7
8
9

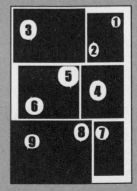